JOHN FORD
Poet in the Desert

Joseph M. Malham

ADVANCE PRAISE FOR
John Ford: Poet in the Desert

*"In **John Ford: Poet in the Desert**, the reader learns of
a 20th century film auteur who led a creative life of great
deliberation and planning. Ford's films of personal intent and
preference are analyzed with the same aplomb as the movies
or programmers that Ford made for an allowance of time and
money to direct. Not satisfied with œuvre highlights, Malham
is a completionist. He examines with synoptic intent of both
criticality and pleasure all of the extant Ford films."*

—**Dan Sutherland**, Faculty,
Film & Video Department,
Columbia College Chicago

*"This book is long overdue and hopefully will put Ford
in a proper light as a man of great faith, sensitivity and
genius—an immortal symbol of how culture can be
lifted through truth, beauty, and goodness."*

—**Fr. Don Woznicki**,
Founder & Executive Director of
New Ethos and Project Leader of
The Hollywood Project

JOHN FORD
Poet in the Desert

Joseph M. Malham

CHICAGO, ILLINOIS

Lake Street Press
4044 N. Lincoln Avenue, #402
Chicago, IL 60618
www.lakestreetpress.com
lsp@lakestreetpress.com

Grateful acknowledgement is given to Dan Ford for permission to reprint 14 photographs from The John Ford Papers in The Lilly Library. Photos provided courtesy of The Lilly Library, Indiana University, Bloomington, Indiana.

Cover photo by Mary Buczek; Cover design by DM Cunningham

Printed in the United States of America

ISBN 978-1-936181-08-7

Library of Congress Control Number 2013941824

Publisher's Cataloging-in-Publication Data from Cassidy Cataloguing
Malham, Joseph M.
John Ford : poet in the desert / Joseph M. Malham. -- Chicago, IL : Lake Street Press, c2013.
p. ; cm.
ISBN: 978-1-936181-08-7
Includes bibliographical references and index.
Summary: Joseph Malham offers an uncommon biography of the legendary Irish-American film director, John Ford. Influences on Ford's work from art, history and politics, to the man's mystical faith are woven together with insights into his famous films.--Publisher.

1. Ford, John, 1894-1973. 2. Ford, John, 1874-1973--Knowledge and learning. 3. Motion picture producers and directors--United States--Biography. 4. Irish Americans in the motion picture industry--Biography. I. Title.

PN1998.3.F65 M35 2013   2013941824

791.4302/33092--dc23   1311

For Mom and Dad
Without whom I would not have known life,
faith, art and movies

CONTENTS

Acknowledgments _____ ix

Introduction _____ xi

Foreword _____ xiii

1   Beginnings: *The Boy Who Would be Pappy* _____ 1

2   Hollywood: *"Any relation to Francis Ford?"* _____ 15

3   The Fox Years–I *"Just a job of work."* _____ 29

4   The Fox Years–II *Portrait of the Young Director as an Artist* __ 55

5   Apogee, 1939–1941 *"Bound for Lordsburg!"* _____ 91

Photos _____ 133

6   World War II *The War According to John Ford* _____ 147

7   Independence *"Been thinkin' I'd maybe push on west."* _____ 173

8   The 1950s: *"Home to Ireland to forget his troubles."* _____ 201

9   The 1960s: *"Print the legend."* _____ 265

10   The Final Years: *"Lest we forget."* _____ 305

Notes _____ 315

Bibliography _____ 323

Index _____ 325

About the Author _____ 331

ACKNOWLEDGMENTS

Unlike Blanche DuBois in *A Streetcar Named Desire*, I have had to rely not only on the kindness of strangers but dear friends as well, in the researching and writing of this study. There are, in fact, so many in both categories that I do not have the memory or space to list them.

I would, however, like to attempt to thank some of the many good people who helped me in taking *John Ford: Poet in the Desert* from an idea over drinks in a north side Chicago bistro one rainy night in 2010 to publication. First and foremost, heartfelt thanks and loving gratitude to Mary Osborne, my dear friend and head of Lake Street Press. Mary not only suggested the topic of John Ford to me but mentored, encouraged, supported, coddled and then forced me to take the reins and press on when the literary stagecoach seemed stranded in the desert or besieged by hostile forces. Dan Ford, grandson of John Ford and author of a very fine biography of "Pappy," was generous not only in his time in helping me tweak the focus and direction of my book, but graciously opened to me the archives of the John Ford Estate. To the staff of the Lilly Library at the University of Indiana (Bloomington), in which the John Ford Archives are housed, many thanks for your friendliness, helpfulness and infinite patience in shelving and retrieving box after box of Fordiana (including two of Ford's Oscars) for a fascinated and rather obsessed author. David Newman, son of Twentieth Century-Fox music legend Alfred Newman, and famed composer in his own right, graciously responded to many questions regarding his father's work as well as his role as the head of the studio's music department.

Mildred Kemp, my very own benefactor, underwrote my travels and stay in Bloomington during my research time and for this I am grateful and indebted. Mary Buczek did an extraordinary job in photographing the jacket illustration, which wonderfully captured the mood and mystery of John Ford while our graphic designer Erin Howarth did a superb job in her design for the book. Hazel Dawkins, my patient, professional and gracious editor, transformed the rough manuscript into a tight, lean narrative and with her keen eye and attention to detail, pacing and structure has literally transformed the look and substance of the finished work. Kathryn Rose assisted me in the early stages of the manuscript and helped me with correcting and editing while Chad Dillingham patiently retyped the manuscript with my myriad changes. Lake Street Press interns Jonathan Dale and Meghann Workman showed tenacity and wisdom beyond their tender years in assisting me with the marketing and publicity of this study. I would also like to thank Father Don Woznicki (Archdiocese of Los Angeles), director of *The Hollywood Project* for his support and offer to help spread the word through the entertainment industry. Similar thanks to Dan Sutherland, professor of film at Chicago's Columbia University. Walter Hill, director of *The Long Riders, The Warriors, 48hrs* and producer of *Aliens*, graciously consented to read the manuscript despite his workload of projects and travel. His graciousness and consideration to an unknown author, especially given his name and reputation in the industry, is gratefully acknowledged.

To Howell and Martha Malham, my parents, as well as my siblings, Deacon Paul Spalla, Fr. Paul Wachdorf and Fr. James Kastigar and and the staffs of, respectively, St. Gregory the Great Church and St. Mary of the Lake Church in Chicago (in whose hallowed halls and rooms I researched and wrote this study), Fr. Phil Horrigan (who advised me on salient points of Catholic theology), I offer my sincere thanks for their love, encouragement and unfailing support. To Julia and Dan Fagan, Chicagoans now but originally from Spiddal, County Galway, Ireland, I likewise extend gratitude for their insights regarding life in the tiny hamlet from which John Ford's family originated.

INTRODUCTION

It is probably best, as in a *via negative*, to say what this book is not rather than what it is. It is not an exhaustive or scholarly biography of John Ford. That good work has been ably and thoroughly achieved by authors such as Scott Eyman, Joseph McBride and Ford's own grandson, Dan Ford. Neither is it an intellectual critique of Ford's *oeuvre* in the tradition of the influential film journals *Cineaste* and André Bazin's *Cahiers du Cinéma*, as that has also been nobly done by Tag Gallagher, Andrew Sarris and the extraordinary British director and patron saint of all serious *Fordophiles*, Lindsay Anderson.

My intention in writing this book is rooted in neither academia nor the historical critical method, but in the desire simply to tell a good story about a fascinating, troubled and extraordinarily talented man who, for nearly half a century, struggled to articulate without that which was deeply felt within. Hence, the subtitle of "Poet in the Desert." I cannot illuminate the innermost recesses of the heart and mind of a poet like John Ford and frankly, I do not believe that that is completely possible.

Even if one were writing the biography of a parent, a spouse, a sibling, a lover or best friend, one knew to the core of their being, the story would invariably turn out patchy and incomplete. The unseen recesses of the human heart are riddled with endless locked rooms, hidden valleys, dead ends and secret sunny gardens known only to the solitary adventurer to whom they all belong. While it may be well nigh impossible to solve the "mystery" of the John Ford we really do not know, it is always possible and actually more interesting to arrive at a better understanding of the man from the externals of his life and work that we do know. It is this tack that I am taking in the writing of this study.

This book proposes to look at John Ford through the clearest and most readily available lens at our disposal, namely his life, his films and the recurring emotional, spiritual, cinematic and historical forces that influenced and shaped a shy, sensitive man who ultimately became the greatest cinematic chronicler of the American experience. If it seems as though this book will stray too far into people, films and events that are seemingly disconnected from the central thesis, it is the intention to weave them back into a unified tapestry of Ford's life and work. For those who do not yet know John Ford and his cinematic legacy, it is my fervent hope that this "job of work" will provide an informative and enjoyable introduction that will leave one hungry to delve deeper into his life and films. For the seasoned *Fordophile,* I hope that a nugget or two, even if it is merely a few flecks of gold dust previously passed over in the waters that have rushed before me, can be assayed and pocketed.

John Ford made films that, for half a century, both changed and defined the landscape of cinema in the twentieth century. However, he spent his life angrily rebuffing even the slightest suggestions that he was a poet, an artist or the Grand Old Man of the Western Saga. Ford saw himself simply as a working stiff who, blessed with a great eye for composition and surrounded by other talented individuals, simply did a job to pay his bills, support his family and spend as much time as he could sailing and drinking on his beloved yacht, *Araner.* Perhaps in the end he was right and there was no secret or mystery to his craft. But, then again, was there? It is that question mark I intend to examine in the pages that follow.

FOREWORD

The experience was like something halfway between an archbishop entering his cathedral for solemn vespers and the admiral of the fleet being piped aboard his flagship before the great battle.

It is nine o'clock in the morning, but the sun already is hammering the desert floor with an intensity that, in a few hours, will escalate into merciless punishment. With an irony of extremities that, if nothing else, demonstrates God's playful sense of humor, the vast expanse of this arid, windblown valley was once the floor of a prehistoric ocean teeming with carnivorous reptiles, some only slightly smaller than the towering buttes that picturesquely punctuate the otherwise flat desert floor.

However, that was tens of millions of years ago and the ocean and the monsters have long since disappeared. Only the sand, sun and sky remain. Here within the confines of Monument Valley, approximately 30,000 acres of Navajo reservation stretching from northern Arizona into southern Utah, the ever-widening arc of time, from the beginning to the present, is breathtakingly spanned. It is a place to contemplate the awesome beauty of the created world and the terrible and unforgiving effects of time, the inscrutable mystery of God's purpose and man's attempts to fathom it in the endless cycle of war and peace, growth and decay, joy and sorrow, life and death that make up the drama of existence.

However, for the tourists who flock here from all corners of the United States, but especially from across the Atlantic and Pacific, Monument Valley is simply an archetypical representation of the American West. Whether a family from Keokuk, Iowa, or a photojournalist from Hamburg, Germany, cycles of life and death be damned. For them, Monument Valley is simply the iconic locale where a stagecoach rolled its passengers toward a fateful rendezvous with Geronimo, Wyatt Earp and Doc Holliday threw down with the plug-ugly Clantons and an icy-eyed loner in a Confederate greatcoat embarked on an obsessive search for his kidnapped niece. For the weekend adventurers, safely ensconced in the air-conditioned rooms of Goulding's Lodge, Monument Valley is not so much an existential metaphor or a terrestrial mystery as it is a destination to be experienced and photographed before moving on to the Grand Canyon and Disneyland.

However, to dig below the crust of the granite and sand, to take command of its essence and then use it as a canvas upon which the vagaries of the human experience could be rendered in black, white or a chromatic fantasy in Technicolor, one would need to be made of sterner stuff. Much sterner. In fact, one would need to possess, in equal measures, the tragic moxie of a battle-scarred soldier, the holy rage of an Old Testament prophet and poetic sensitivities strong enough to withstand the primal brutality of the desert elements. Most importantly, one would also have to possess the artistic skills simply to tell a straightforward story about interesting people in a way that makes it our story...everyone's story. There, indeed, was such a man and, after finishing his breakfast of bacon and eggs at Goulding's Lodge, he would soon arrive.

<hr/>

The thirty or forty members of the film crew, who stood anxiously around the cameras, lights, generators and cables scattered around the old ocean floor, were arrayed like bluejackets on the deck of the HMS *Victory,* on the morning of Trafalgar. They all knew their duty but that their director, not England, expected them to do it. They were like a family but everyone, from the paunchy, middle-aged grips and gaffers who served with the Old Man in the navy to the stuntmen and fresh-faced young actors (God help them) serving a first apprenticeship, knew that their *paterfamilias* was a not-always-benevolent dictator.

The easy going, summer camp bonhomie of the evenings on location, replete with campfires, sing-alongs, skits and "Taps," was over. It was time to work and earn the paycheck cut and messengered by the studio back in Hollywood. Any dereliction of duty, any lack of professionalism or the slightest whiff of a *prima donna* attitude would be summarily dealt with by the Old Man and the experience would not be pleasant.

As the dusty truck pulls up, all the members of the company fall silent and stiffen into what any old sailor or soldier would immediately recognize as nothing less than attention. The Old Man alights from the truck onto the set and a short, bearded man named Danny Borzage, brother of noted film director Frank, slowly pumps out the melodious notes of *Bringing in the Sheaves* on his large accordion. After a few grumbled "Good mornings" to the assembled crew, the Old Man strides to the canvas chair next to the camera with the authoritative air of the captain striding onto his quarterdeck. And from that moment on, he is just as unchallenged and unapproachable.

The Old Man is tall, taller than one would expect from the pictures and reports of his craggy and aged appearance, but then again, he looked craggy and old even when he was young. A shapeless military jacket, bearing the stripes and bars of his naval rank of captain, envelops his torso. His pants are typically wrinkled old flannels, turned up at the cuffs, which hang limply over big weathered boots and expose a long length of leg when he sits and crosses them.

Everything about the Old Man's attire and bearing was iconic, and it made great fodder for caricaturists, artists and imitators. The studied rumpledness of his clothes was as immediately identified with him as the tuxedo was with Cary Grant, dancing pumps with Fred Astaire and martinis with Noel Coward. Everything but the eyes, that is. They were the windows of his soul but they couldn't be more fiercely guarded if three-headed Cerberus himself stood in front of his chair. His eyes, rapidly failing from cataracts and macular degeneration, held the secret to his art and poetry but whatever passions or lights burned behind them were his own possession and his own business. To drive home the point, he kept them forever shaded behind darkly smoked glasses and, to add a further measure of protection from both painful sunlight and psychoanalytical locksmiths, he added a black patch over the left eye.

Completing the look was a battered fedora, often alternated with a similarly battered baseball cap, the brims of which were permanently cocked down over those unseen, sensitive orbs. It took a Churchill to neatly sum up Russia for the world when he called that nation a riddle, wrapped in a mystery, inside an enigma. Too bad he never took a whack at the Old Man.

———————

A few minutes after nine, the "job of work," as he repeatedly called his vocation, is almost under full sail. There is no equivocation, no hand-wringing indecisiveness as to how to frame and choreograph the first camera set up. Despite the handicap of his poor eyesight, he always understood the delicate alchemical balance between geometry and artistry that transmuted an average shot into cinematic gold, and he dives to it like an eagle swooping in on his prey from high above. After a *sotto voce* conference with his cinematographer, he steps over and adjusts the brim of John Wayne's trooper slouch, Victor McLaglen's non-com kepi or, for a laugh, the spacious seat of Ward Bond's pants. Details of no apparent consequence to anyone, but to the consummate artist, they are the individual parts that when put together make for a lyrical and poetic entirety.

Stretching his lanky frame into the canvas throne, the Old Man has a steaming cup of coffee—the first of dozens for the day—thrust into his freckled hand. He says nothing as he sips his coffee, lights his pipe and begins to chew on the frayed edges of an old handkerchief, somehow managing to keep all three competing for space in his mouth with the dexterity of a four-armed statue of Kali. For a moment, there is nothing but the sound of the dry, hot wind blowing across the old ocean floor. One more sip, one more puff and one more tear of the dirty old kerchief and then, as if invoking the blessings of God from the high altar, John Ford growls, "Action!"

———————

John Ford (1894-1973) is considered the greatest artist in the history of American cinema; some would argue in the history of the medium, period. Even though his direct artistic heirs and admirers in American film include Orson Welles, Martin Scorsese, Peter Bogdanovich, Steven Spielberg, Clint Eastwood, Walter Hill, John Carpenter and, across the oceans in both directions, Jean-Luc Godard, Lindsay Anderson, Wim

Wenders, Sergei Eisenstein, Sergio Leone and Akira Kurosawa, such superlatives could still seem to be subjective matters of personal taste and opinion. No doubt even today the academic woods are still full of modern and post-modern film theorists who remember John Ford simply as the guy who directed all those John Wayne horse operas. Harder to contest, however, are the six Academy Awards, awarded him by his peers, that at one time sat on the mantle of his modest Odin Street home in Hollywood. Even if that record is surpassed, the uniqueness and poetry of his cinematic vision can never be bested, if for no other reason than the Hollywood in which he worked and flourished, like the Tara plantation that stood on the back lot of the Selznick Studios and the Xanadu of Charles Foster Kane on the old RKO lot, is long gone.

The name John Ford (or Jack in the early days) ran on the credits of feature films from 1917 until 1966 and while the last decade of his career unfortunately produced rather the same journeyman efforts of the first decade, what came in between constitutes some of the greatest work ever captured on celluloid. These include *The Iron Horse* (1924), *The Informer* (1934), *The Hurricane* (1937), *Young Mr. Lincoln* (1939), *Stagecoach* (1939), *Drums Along the Mohawk* (1939), *The Grapes of Wrath* (1940), *How Green Was My Valley* (1941), *They Were Expendable* (1945), *My Darling Clementine* (1946), the so-called Cavalry Trilogy of *Fort Apache* (1948), *She Wore a Yellow Ribbon* (1948) and *Rio Grande* (1950), *The Quiet Man* (1952), *The Searchers* (1956) and *The Man Who Shot Liberty Valance* (1962).

There were many well-meaning stillbirths such as *Tobacco Road* (1941) *Mister Roberts* (1954) and *Cheyenne Autumn* (1964), enjoyable fluff like *Mogambo* (1953) and even outright disasters such as *Mary of Scotland* (1936) and *The Fugitive* (1947), but his worst was often better than many director's best and his best fills an entire shelf of national treasures of American cinema.

Ford was the great chronicler of the American experience, an irascible, no-nonsense Yankee, who more than any other artist, made the Western hero the archetypal American, propelling him into the pantheon of such classical heroes as the Spartan warrior, the Viking, the Knight Errant and the Samurai.

Unlike the historian, who charts the rise and fall of nations by the events that mold and direct the destinies of millions, Ford was a bard who saw the human element at the center of the ongoing story: the ordinary men and women who shape their destinies by their ideals, aspirations and choices, both good and bad. Steeped in a scholarly knowledge of history, American history in particular, Ford nevertheless used history as a deep focus background, the distant vista in front of which time passed, families were sundered or reunited, lovers frolicked, loners wrestled with their darkest demons and men marched off and returned from war, both ennobled as well as deeply scarred by the experience.

While Ford primarily projected his vision through an American lens, his themes ran to deeper places where, as Saint Augustine said, the beauty of it all was ever ancient and ever new.

<hr />

Ford's ability to universalize uniquely American themes in his work, especially in his Westerns, stems from both his Irishness and his passionate love for America that was almost as devout and contradictory as his Catholic faith. This melancholy, brooding man, although American born, nevertheless remained something of a son of Eire his entire life, and as such, keenly understood the soul-searing effects of poverty, oppression and the need to counter them with unvarnished blarney, a devilish sense of humor and liberal measures of a "wee drop of the *craiture*."

As an American, Ford had the good timing to be born into what Tom Brokaw called in his eponymous book, *The Greatest Generation.* Ford, like millions of his compatriots who were born between the close of the nineteenth century and the beginning of the Great Depression, was the son of immigrants who saw America as the last, great beacon of hope, freedom and opportunity in the world. He passionately honored America and the pioneering spirit of fair play, hard work, tenacity and high optimism that made her great among the nations.

After the attack on Pearl Harbor and America's subsequent entrance into World War II, Ford put aside the comforts of family and his flourishing career, and along with endless legions of his countrymen, signed up to defend his nation's flag and democratic ideals. He served with honor and distinction as a naval officer in both the Pacific and Atlantic theaters of war and, with a staggering dose of courage and not a little bit of Irish luck, on the morning of the great engagement, even managed to capture the Battle of Midway with a hand-held camera.

For Ford, it was not maudlin flag-waving or theatrical heroics (despite his weakness for both) that motivated him in his service to his country. It was simply a matter of the gratitude and sense of debt he felt was owed to the nation that gave the son of an immigrant saloon keeper the opportunity to go as high and far as his thirst for success, prestige and security could take him. That is how Ford and his great generation thought and that simple hierarchy of values consciously formed the substance of his art and gave its contours such a timeless sense of depth and beauty.

Yet, while the values and ethos of Ford and his generation were simple and transparent, the man himself was anything but. More than any other artist produced by the epic of American cinema, Ford was an impregnable fortress of contradictions and enigmas and even lifelong friends paradoxically said that the *more* they knew him the *less* they knew him.

A man capable of great depth of feeling and unabashed sentimentality, Ford was also an incurable alcoholic, a man of towering rage who, for the slightest real or perceived insult, would banish even close friends from his set, which meant his life, for years, sometimes forever. A man of exquisitely refined literary and artistic tastes who could hold his own on a broad intellectual field, Ford lived in horror of being perceived as a sensitive man and affected the swaggering, often brutal machismo of a schoolyard bully. He was a man who celebrated the sacredness of the nuclear family and portrayed the love of parents, children and siblings as the glue that held the world together, yet his own family relationships were a Sophoclean morass of dysfunction and brokenness. A man who felt deeply the pangs of injustice and could be unstintingly warm and generous to the weak, the vulnerable and the down-and-out, Ford was also a cruel and vindictive manipulator who sought out a person's weakness in order to dominate and often humiliate them.

And that was how he treated his friends.

The intrepid journalists who entered Ford's presence with the jaunty assurance that they would finally nail down the Old Man and get the straight dope from the horse's mouth, usually exited a dazed, quivering mess. Even in his early years, tired with reporters' redundant questions about his "art," Ford became increasingly intolerant toward interviewers and responded with behavior that was a combination of erratic quirkiness, gruff playfulness and, if he really did not like you, downright orneriness.

Asked about one subject, Ford would suddenly begin to expand at length on another and completely unrelated subject. Monosyllabic responses to complex or laudatory questions would be followed by retractions or contortions of statements he grandly made to different interviewers the month before. If he was irritated or bored with a question—which was almost always—he would cup his bad ear and bark, "What?" several times and then repeat an entirely different question back to the interviewer to confirm that that was indeed the question they asked. Yes, a very enigmatic man.

Then there were fibs, tall tales, obfuscations and outright lies he continually spun about his life. He made up stories about his youth and early career, claiming to have been an Arizona cowpoke when in fact the only horse he rode into town was an iron one originating on the East Coast. He claimed to have been a comrade-in-arms with the Irish Republican Brotherhood during the Black and Tan "troubles" of the 1920s, whereas his support leaned more toward the financial and the moral rather than the militant. He even spun yarns about his very name, letting people believe, if they desired to do so, that he was born Sean Aloysius O'Fearna on Ireland's Aran Islands, when, in fact, his birth certificate (duly issued by the State of Maine) proclaims another, albeit less exotic, name and birthplace.

Whether it was because he knew the power and importance of myth in history (he did) or that he was a master of blarney who enjoyed pushing the limits of credulity among his followers (he was), Ford's psychological sleight of hand was as much a part of his persona as his grouchiness, unkempt appearance, Irish sentimentality and identification with the American West. He was a sphinx in a fedora and gray flannels and whether he placed himself at the center of an emotional labyrinth to keep people out or make himself more fascinating to them is something that can only be guessed at rather than fully resolved.

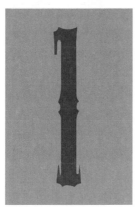

BEGINNINGS

The Boy Who Would be Pappy

In *The History of the Town and County of Galway* (1820), James Hardiman, aka Séamus Ó hArgadáin, wrote that the second-century historian, Ptolemy, gave a precise and detailed account of the settlements, rivers and tribes of western Ireland, that later historians said were false flights of poetic fancy. The great man simply employed half-truths, hunches and outright lies to give his epics more heft and dramatic punch. In this, the Greek geographer and John Ford shared much in common.[1]

John Ford's *people*, as the Irish are wont to say, were the Feeneys. They came from the town of Spiddal, some ten kilometers west of Galway, and situated on the coast of what (depending on your national origin) could either be the Irish Sea or the Atlantic Ocean. They were and continued to be Feeneys until their famous descendants adopted a new stage name in the early 1900s. The only Ford they would have known was the smelly, noisy tractors and automobiles slowly replacing their plow and carriage horses.

Ford's version of who his forebearers were and whence they came was almost as convoluted, fanciful and contradictory as the smoke screen he untiringly threw up around his own life. Proudly declaring

1

that he was the descendant of land-tied, hard-working peasants, Ford could also sniff that he was directly related to old, titled families to the manor born. Knowing the Aran Islanders to be among the most hardy, independent and fiercely Gaelic citizens of the Emerald Isle, Ford routinely and erroneously stated the island cluster as the birthplace of his mother. The reality is that the Feeneys were indeed simple, hard-working people of the mainland soil and, like millions of their compatriots, could have summed up their lives as Lincoln did of his by quoting a line from Grey's *Elegy Written in a Country Church-Yard*: "The short and simple annals of the poor."

Spiddal, even today known for its quaint shops, local crafts and proficiency in the Gaelic language, takes its name from the hospital that in medieval times used to stand in the village as a refuge for the sick, the incurable and the dying. The land upon which the Feeneys dwelt and scratched a living for generations was called Tuar Beeg. It was a satrapy of Spiddal proper that, along with a few other farms, actually comprised one quarter of the village. Like most of the denizens of the western coast of Eire, all eyes looked primarily to the sea and not only did the North Atlantic prove a steady and beneficent employer but a guarantor of fresh food for the family table. For the less adventurous, but no less hardy souls, whose vocation was to work the rich, black soil, there was (at least in the years when there was an absence of famine and blight) a regular harvest of cabbage, onions, carrots and, of course the national vegetable, the potato. Meat came from the sheep that bucolically, if not noisily, populated most of the countryside.

According to Joseph McBride, author of the magisterial biography, *Searching for John Ford*, the clan Feeney (and its numerous, tongue-twisting Gaelic variants) can be traced back to the mid-4th century. Around the time the Roman Emperor Constantine was building his Second Rome on the shores of the Bosporus, the Feeneys were flourishing, and no doubt fighting, first in the northern County of Sligo then down through Roscommon and Mayo and finally into Galway.[2] Surviving Viking invasions (later abated by the paying of the Danegeld, or tribute money, to the bearded and horn-helmeted gentlemen), 12[th-] century slaughters by the English King Henry II and yet another and more thoroughly accomplished genocide undertaken by the Lord Protector Oliver Cromwell in the 17th century, the lives and fortunes of the Feeneys waxed and waned with the vicissitudes of time.

However, what even Cromwell failed to accomplish in terms of wholesale devastation of the Irish people was completed in the mid-19th century by a blight, *phytophthora infestans*, or, as it is more commonly known, the Potato Famine. Oddly enough, the blight that was to devastate the island and send a million of its residents scurrying across the sea to the New World, actually began in the Americas and made its way back to Ireland by way of the guano used as cheap but effective fertilizer for the potato crop. The resulting famine caused the potato crop to fail partially in 1845, completely in 1846 and again in 1848. With the average peasant consuming a mind-boggling fourteen pounds per day, the death of the potato crop resulted in a combination of the Black Death, the Old Testament plagues and a touch of Dante's lower regions thrown in for good measure. Widespread starvation, attended by a host of diseased handmaidens such as malnutrition, dysentery and typhus, soon began their grim work and the death toll quickly soared to frightful heights. The traditionally hearty and robust Irish people were reduced to shriveled scarecrows and, from the combined effects of death and emigration, the population went from 8 million in 1841 to an appalling 6.5 million just a few years later.[3]

The blight, coupled with the dreaded penal laws of the 17th and 18th centuries that made it a crime for Irish Catholics to own land, vote, enter a trade or even receive an education, truly made the island inhabitants people of *"an drochshaol,"* the "bad times." Enough was enough and, like the Jews of old, the Irish of the mid-century fled from discrimination, oppression and an almost institutionalized hatred, dispersing out over the globe only to find that the same waited for them in another land under another flag. However, the New World sang its siren song across the North Atlantic and even the denizens of happy, hidden little Spiddal were not immune to its charms.

John Augustine Feeney, who would in time become the father of John Ford, was born on December 3, 1856 (given by fellow Ford biographer Scott Eyman as June 16, 1854) in the family cottage at Tuar Beeg. His parents, Patrick and Mary (nee Curran) Feeney were local residents despite Ford's claim of direct descent from the Araners. Like all the Irish, the Feeneys were not solitary genetic entities like the Hapsburgs, whose blood remained unmingled with the common masses. On the contrary, the Feeney blood intersected and crisscrossed with others like a road map of Connemara. There were the Currans, the Connellys and the O'Flahertys, the last producing the great novelist Liam O'Flaherty, whose masterpiece *The Informer* won his distant cousin his first Oscar when it was translated to the big screen.[4]

Ford's mother, Barbara Curran (but always called by the more lilting diminutive Abby), was born the same year as his father and in the same village. Oddly, it was claimed by Ford that, while their paths could have randomly crossed in Spiddal, they actually met in America.[5] Like John Augustine, Abby was a well-sculpted personality and her willfulness, protectiveness and no-nonsense approach to life was such a force that it likewise consciously insinuated itself into Ford's work. While by no means a "mama's boy" or even a "papa's boy," Ford was heroically devoted to Abby during throughout his life. Foregoing the typical and testosterone-driven tendency of Hollywood directors of his time to obsessively idealize the sizzling sexpot or tempestuous ingenue, Ford instead evolved Abby into a sort of spiritual *Earth Mother.* A combination of Gaia, Sophia and the Blessed Virgin who, as the repository of all wisdom, strength, nurturing and love, is the very ground upon which we stand and to whom we will ultimately return. Indeed, one can hopscotch through Ford's films and in Margaret Mann (*Four Sons*) to Jane Darwell (*The Grapes of Wrath*) to Sara Allgood (*How Green Was My Valley*) and assorted Mildred Natwicks and Mae Marshes see the ghost of Abby wafting behind the silvery frames flickering in the dark.

In the summer of 1872, young John Augustine, heartbroken at having to bid farewell to his family and home but swelled with a young man's passion for adventure in a brave new world, left Spiddal and hurried aboard a Cunard steamship bound for America. The Atlantic crossing, which could last anywhere from four to eight weeks, was fortunately uneventful. While Augustine's Irish luck held, thousands of his fellow citizens were not so blessed. Preying on the immigrants who were desperate for passage to the New World, steamship lines generally packed the poor into creaking, waterlogged and unseaworthy vessels for journeys that were just several notches above the "Middle Passages" of the slaves from the Ivory Coast. They came honestly by the grim term of coffin ships. The ones who were fortunate to arrive at all endured horrendous voyages in stinking steerage holes marked by seasickness, cholera and abysmal privations of food, sweet water, privacy and basic sanitation. Women and children were often the first victims.

Immigrants, first from central and northern Europe and, after 1850 from Ireland, were grist for the belching mills that began to choke the eastern seaboard in the wake of the Industrial Revolution. John Augustine was just one grain among millions. The benefactor and catalytic agent for his grand adventure was his uncle, Michael Connolly. Uncle Mike, a tough and well-seasoned bird whose life read like something out of a Robert Louis Stevenson novel, would become, for Ford, a sort of prototypical man whose fearlessness, resourcefulness and heroism represented the essence of America's pioneering spirit. Uncle Mike was more than a colorful character; he was a Technicolor epic. As Ford saw it, both personally as well as artistically, the West was not forged and formed by politicians, generals and great ideals but by the backbreaking sweat and wit of the Uncle Mikes who longed to see what was beyond the next valley. Ford did, however, see him in later years through roseate lenses that were slightly tinted with a mythical mist that obscured the contours and details of real time.

According to Ford, Uncle Mike came to North America a decade before his father. So far, so good. Then, so Ford said, Mike was slipped a Mickey Finn in Quebec and awoke a prisoner of the Blackfeet Indians in Duluth. After having secured his freedom through the largesse of a friendly French trapper, Mike then enlisted in the Union army at the outset of the American Civil War. Paid to stand substitute for a man who could afford the $200 fee (a common practice among the upper northern classes), Mike again supposedly advanced with the boys in blue upon Lee's infantry impregnably entrenched on Marye's Heights in the small Virginia hamlet of Fredericksburg. However, when the Union soldiers were mowed down like wheat in what proved to be one of the bloodiest engagements of the war, Mike quietly deserted and headed west. Signing on with the Union Pacific, which was steadily advancing across the plains to meet the Central Pacific at Promontory Point, Mike laid miles of track and thus helped bring to a glorious completion America's sense of mandated Manifest Destiny.[6]

What can be known for certain is that Uncle Mike eventually found a home and a fair measure of prosperity back east. Bypassing Boston, which was still a bastion of Yankee Brahmins with know-nothing leanings, Mike made his way up the coast to Portland, Maine, and married a local widow. Puffed up with success and enough adventures to fill five historical novels, Mike returned to Ireland. It was at that moment that John Augustine decided to follow his uncle back to the bustling seaport city in America.

When Ford's father arrived in Portland in 1872, he did not waste any time drifting about looking for a new life or mooning over the old one back in Ireland. On the contrary, he rolled up his linen sleeves, spit in his large hands and got to work in a variety of professions. He would do anything to put relatively warm food on the table in a reasonably dry flat. Young, canny and cognizant of the prestige and prosperity available to immigrants who knew how the game was played, John Augustine slowly found his way among the shops, factories and dock- front bars of Portland. He tried, as Sheriff Perley "Buck" Sweet (Ward Bond) says of his brother-in-law in Ford's 1948 Western, *3 Godfathers*, "everything but preaching." While food, clothing and shelter were relatively easy for the young man to procure, the stability and emotional fulfillment that only a wife could provide temporarily managed to elude John Augustine. However, his Irish luck still held and that fulfillment came in the person of the redoubtable Abby Curran, the fair blonde lass from Spiddal who had also immigrated to Portland in 1872.

Abby worked as a domestic in hotels and private residences and, like John, she looked to the present rather than a life left behind in Ireland. Despite the fact that she never learned to read, Abby made a good go of it in Portland, as did her bar-owning sisters. When she met John Augustine in 1875 she was immediately taken by his rugged good looks, gentle disposition and healthy appreciation for hard work and money. Several months after their courting, they were married in 1875 in Portland's St. Dominic's Catholic Church. They immediately got down to the serious business of raising a family and their efforts did not go unrewarded. Their first child, a daughter named Mary Agnes (thereafter called Maime) arrived in 1876, followed by Della, Patrick, Francis, Bridget, Barbara, Edward, Josephine, Joanna, John and the last, Daniel, in 1898. The terrible mathematics of infant mortality during that time did not escape the Feeney household, and only Maime, Patrick, Francis, Edward, Josephine and John survived birth and childhood.[7]

Despite Ford's populist penchant for trumpeting his agrarian roots and claiming he came from nothing but a long line of farmers and laborers, the truth is a bit more textured. The Feeneys and their newly Americanized cousins were hard working, industrious and concerned not only for their families but for the larger community as well. Aside from Abby's go-getter sisters, John Augustine's brother Martin pressed on to Minnesota where he worked his way up from a laborer on the Great Northern Railroad to wealth and prominence in his field. Uncle Mike's son, Joseph E. F. Connolly, earned a law degree and eventually became Superior Court Justice for Cumberland County; he pushed for immigrant reform and was a particularly passionate advocate of child welfare and public health. The future film director and favorite son of Portland would go on to achieve success and notoriety on a global scale but many of his forebearers and relations had already done so on a local one.[8]

After several peripatetic years of moving from increasingly larger lodgings, the Feeneys finally settled in 1894 on a 40-acre farm in the Portland suburb of Cape Elizabeth. It was situated on the southern shore of Casco Bay on a promontory between the Fore and the Spurwink rivers. While John Augustine added farming to his curiously speckled *curriculum vitae*, on February 1, 1894, Abby gave birth to their tenth child, John Martin, named after John himself.

<hr />

For the present, though, life proceeded relatively even-keeled for the Feeneys on the shores of Casco Bay. When Jack was around two, John Augustine gave up farming on Cape Elizabeth and moved the family back to Portland. He assumed the new mantle of publican and political boss. It was this vocation that became, for young Jack, his father's most iconic role. For Jack it was a source of great admiration and pride. It would also, in a curious way, come to exert some measure of influence on his art and adult personality.

Around this same time, one of the earliest known photos of Ford was taken in a Portland studio. Although it bears the formulaic benchmark of every child portrait in the proper Victorian age, the image still carries with it a strangely prophetic dimension. Two-year-old Jack wears the *de rigeur* blue sailor suit, knee britches and high black socks, red hair neatly combed; his large, sensitive eyes stare resolutely ahead. The stolid, unsmiling boy in the sailor suit foreshadows the dozens of portraits taken of Commander and then Rear-Admiral John Ford. Interestingly enough, the boy's sleeves bear a thick row of gold braid.

As Jack continued to grow in the hurly-burly of the Feeney household, John Augustine and Abby continued to move the family from place to place like Bedouins. From the age of three, in 1897, and for the next ten years, the Feeneys lived in no less than four houses. They finally settled more or less permanently at 23 Sheridan Street in Portland.[9]

The Munjoy Hill area of Portland where Jack grew up was a melting pot of sorts. It boasted a wide ethnic range of Blacks, Jews, Swedes, Poles and Irish mixed in with the dominant Yankee denizens. It fostered in the young man not only an egalitarian sense of inclusion and peaceful coexistence (a trait that would come to color his social and political conscience) in friendly baseball and street games but a healthy sense of boundaries and self-defense when the coexistence strayed into the more bellicose. Like the West before the civilizing influence of the law, pre-politically correct urban America was an ethnically divided place where epithets like "Mick" and "Bohunk" and worse could send baseball gloves, football helmets and fists flying in every direction.

Even if it was feigned, a boy on Munjoy Hill had at least to convey the impression of being a street-smart, two-fisted tough and capable of standing his ground on the gridiron or in a street-corner fight. For sensitive and thoughtful boys like Jack, who bore the double stigma of wearing glasses and needing them to read books about art and literature, the efforts to maintain the facade of a young plug-ugly in front of a crowd were constantly being redoubled.

Josephine O'Gorman, Jack's teacher at Emerson Grade School, was one of the first to recognize Jack's potential and steered him toward higher goals and greater application. Her good work obviously bore fruit for his 1906 report card showed him progressing in the course of a year from a mixed bag of "good," "fair" and "poor" to a steady stream of "good" and "fair."[10]

Jack enjoyed robust good health as both a boy and man (marred only later by failing eyesight and the horrendous effects of alcohol) but took a hit when he came down with a serious case of diphtheria at the age of twelve. Having dodged the disease bullet that tragically took the lives of several of his siblings, Jack took the illness hard and the long road to recovery was so onerous that the boy was kept back a year in school.

One of the most poignant scenes in *How Green Was My Valley*, played out in almost total silence, save for Alfred Newman's magnificent score, is when Huw, bedridden for months following a plunge into an icy river, begins the arduous struggle to regain the use of his legs. Being lucky, as the young pastor Mr. Gruffyd (Walter Pidgeon) says, to suffer, Huw uses his time of recuperation to expand his mind and spirit in the company of classic books. Making his way through

Treasure Island, The Pickwick Papers and others, Huw enters a new world and a new place of ideas and dreams. It was the same with young Jack as he lay in his bed recovering from diphtheria. Nursed by Abby and his older sisters, Jack threw himself into a self-structured college prep of sorts, reading Robert Louis Stevenson, James Fenimore Cooper and Mark Twain with a fury.[11]

Jack was not only blessed with the gift of time and solitude but a budding intellect. His intellect coincided nicely with his increasingly voracious and surprisingly mature literary and artistic tastes. Like a student of architecture glimpsing the cathedrals of Europe for the first time, Jack quickly absorbed the surface beauty while, at the same time, he began to grasp the structural components that held the beauty of the whole together. The power of narrative and centrality of characters who were well-crafted and possessed of larger than life qualities became increasingly clear. In Hawkeye, Long John Silver, and Huckleberry Finn, Jack would come to see how wordsmiths could not only produce heroes against the backdrop of historical events, but how their character's virtues and self-sacrifice could affect history as well. As one of the dominant leitmotifs of the mature director would attest, Jack began to see history as the individual looming large and solitary in the foreground as the events of history swept by in the distance.

Other activities necessary for Jack to conform to the rigid standards of manhood were being increasingly and more publicly performed. If there was any insult worse than "Mick" that could have been hurled at Jack it was "sissy." If he wanted to show his face around the streets and fields of Portland he needed to be able to not so much refute but kick the words back into the teeth of the speaker. The counterbalance to Jack's aptitude for art, writing and reading was football and, like his burgeoning aesthetic tastes, the gridiron machismo that comes with the turf would also manifest itself in Jack's adult and professional personality. Unlike art, however, football would show another side of another Jack Feeney, first to older brothers, friends and potential bullies and later to the world. It was an aggressiveness and a combative sense of "Give no quarter, receive no quarter" that would also define Jack on the field and on the movie set.

Jack entered Portland High School in 1910 and, while he continued to explore his love of art and writing, it would be football that would come to shape his adolescent personality. Following an ethos stretching back to the formation of the British public school system, sports were seen in Jack's day as an integral part of a young man's liberal education. Viewed as sort of a (relatively) bloodless precursor of military service, sports were needed to foster a sense of toughness, discipline, camaraderie and a dogged determination to get the job done. This would eventually make a boy into a man. If one could do that in four quarters or nine innings then one could do it for life.

Not surprisingly, Jack excelled in the sport as a fullback. He developed such a reputation for indomitable bullheadedness that he quickly acquired a nickname that stuck, at least with his former teammates, for the rest of his life: "Bull" Feeney. While Jack Feeney the student was pensive, playful and shy around girls, Bull Feeney the fullback was a medieval assault weapon of sorts. He was a human plow so fierce that he would come to earn three letters, frequent press notices and interest from local and out-of-state colleges.[12]

While Jack continued to bulldoze his way across the ten-yard line, improve his grade point average and serve early morning Mass at St. Dominic's church, the highlights of Portland also began to pique the young man's cultural and professional interest. Despite its starchy Yankee respectability, Portland was a hub of theatrical activity and citizens of the thriving seaport demanded and received a host of first class shows, lectures and the celebrated luminaries who brought them to life.

The Deering was later known as the Portland Theatre until 1910, when it was renamed The Nickel. As its name implied, The Nickel was a nickelodeon, a five-cent, jaw-dropping wonder that wowed the masses with silent and crudely filmed "flickers" that included Shakespearean dramas filmed in Central Park and Westerns shot in New Jersey.

The famed Keith-Albee Circuit, a vast empire of theaters and vaudeville houses across the country, made its presence known in Portland as well. Within its rococo, gilded interiors, complete with pipe organs, fountains and miles of red velvet everything, young Jack and his parents could have seen minor, third-billed acts like monologist Walter Kelly and hoofer Jack Donohue to legendary and iconic stars like Sarah Bernhardt and Ethel Barrymore.

With interests ranging from literature and sports to creative writing and art, it was only a matter of time before the intellectually curious and teenaged Jack began to wonder what this theater stuff was all about. While still a student at Portland High School, Jack got a job as an usher at the Jefferson Theatre, yet another Portland venue that attracted top names and shows from New York. As he did with everything else in his life, Jack threw himself, mind and body, into his work. He contributed everything he had and looked to older and more experienced people in the profession to teach and nurture him. The latter, usually a source of great comfort and satisfaction to him as a young man, proved a fateful (and nearly fatal) object lesson for the star-struck teen. Sidney Toler, a seasoned stage actor who some two decades later would find fame on screen as one of the many and decidedly non-Asian Charlie Chans, was starring in a play the night Jack was thrown on as a substitute butler.

The seemingly innocuous role required Jack simply to deliver a telegram to Toler and then exit stage left. Abandoning the script as well as all mercy for the hapless boy, Toler proceeded to grill Jack as to who sent the telegram. The ad-libbed barrage took the novice actor completely unawares and within seconds he was reduced to a quivering and stammering bowl of jelly. The temptation to play armchair psychologist is always great in a biographer, but it does appear that the public humiliation Jack experienced that night cut deeply into his psyche. The on-set behavior Ford would come to exhibit toward actors, technicians and even executives who were timid, unprepared or just plain vulnerable makes it fairly clear that he spent a lifetime repaying the world for the insult he so brutally endured as a teenager.[13]

Jack graduated from Portland High on June 18, 1914, just two months before the outbreak of the Great War on the European continent. After yearbook sentiments were inscribed and promises to stay in touch were made to friends, Jack began to cast about and decide what he wanted to do with his life. He toyed with the prospect of enrolling in the University of Maine in Orono but since no paper trail exists it is probable that it was just an idea that was never followed through. In fact, Jack's attention was being absorbed more and more by the flickers, the melodramas, comedies, Westerns and historical epics that continued to enthrall audiences at The Nickel in Monument Square.

It is therefore easy to imagine the shock and awe felt by the whole Feeney family when one fine day they were told that John and Abby's fourth born, Francis, or Frank, who had left home in rather rushed and mysterious circumstances years before, was seen on-screen as an actor in a Monument Square flicker. The parents rushed to the theater and bought a ticket. They emerged some time later, dazed, bemused, relieved and not a little awed, and confirmed that it was indeed their boy Frank on the screen. Not only was it Frank, but they soon discovered that Frank was making a name for himself as a stage and screen actor under the new, streamlined name of Francis Ford. How and why Frank came to drop the Feeney name and began to sign his contracts as Francis Ford is lost in the compost of fact and fiction. However, there are two theories that appear the most plausible. One that Jack later proposed is that Frank took the name of a stage actor he substituted for after the gentleman became too drunk to say his entrance line. Frank himself said that after searching about for a less Gaelic and more neutrally acceptable moniker, he simply pinched it from the radiator of a passing automobile.[14]

Whatever charms the lights of Orono and a university degree held for Jack were quickly eclipsed by the blazing glory of Frank as he re-entered the family fold as an increasingly famous movie star. Awed by his brother's newly acquired fame, wealth and panache, Jack now knew what he wanted to do with his life. Just a few months after collecting his high school diploma, Jack set out by train to work for brother Frank in a sleepy little hamlet of vineyards, barley fields and orange groves northwest of Los Angeles called Hollywood.

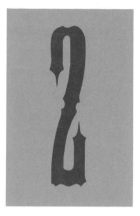

HOLLYWOOD

"Any relation to Francis Ford?"

It can be stated without hesitation that had there been no Francis Ford, the matinee idol of the early silents, that there might not have been a John Ford, the master director *non pareil*. When Jack got off the train in Los Angeles in the fall of 1914, Frank was enjoying a reputation in the industry as a daring leading man, innovative director and writer of some of the most popular serials of the silent period. However, Frank would eventually become just another victim of Hollywood's tradition of cold-blooded irony. Twenty years later, Jack would be one of the top directors in the industry while Frank would be haunted by bit roles in B pictures with an occasional role in an A one. In fact, it was due to the grudging largesse of his younger brother that Frank managed to minutely partake in most of Jack's classic and mature films. In *Stagecoach*, *Drums Along the Mohawk*, *Young Mr. Lincoln*, *My Darling Clementine* and *Fort Apache*, Frank can be seen, almost exclusively in uncredited performances, as a scruffy, chortling, inebriated old coot adding a pinch of spice and color to a scene or two. He is probably most famously remembered today as the bearded, tam-o'shantered codger in *The Quiet Man* who tells death to take a hike so he can dash off to see the long-awaited fight between Sean Thornton and Red Will Danaher.

How this seismic reversal in the turn of fortune's wheel for both brothers happened is, at least from Jack's side, a case of fierce sibling rivalry, studious discipleship and his uncanny ability to always be at the right place at the right time.

Frank exhibited from his earliest years a roguish restlessness and longed to see something marginally more exciting than the tree-lined streets and shaded porches of Munjoy Hill. He dropped out of high school at seventeen and promptly joined the army. Coincidentally, this was at the same time the United States declared war on the Spanish empire as it tried to flex its feeble muscles for the last time in the New World. When the recruiters discovered, however, that Frank was underage, he was just as promptly sent home.

The discipline that Frank could have acquired in the ranks rapidly deserted him in the boudoir. Upon returning home to Portland, he promptly got a local woman very pregnant. The hasty union, followed by the birth of a son, Phillip, limped along for several years until both mother and child deserted Frank to his amorous and professional wanderings. Not sure what to do with himself but painfully cognizant of the shame his shenanigans were bringing upon the honored name of Feeney in Portland, Frank wandered around the East Coast where he stumbled into vaudeville while padding his meager income with odd jobs. Following in a time-honored show business tradition, Frank was spotted on the streets of New York by a film company factotum and offered a job in pictures. For reasons known only to God, it was then that Frank changed his name to Ford and entered the movie business. The year was 1907.[1]

Frank's tall, dark and chiseled looks served him well. Within a few years he was more or less gainfully employed in the film business; first as an actor and then on higher rungs of the production end. In 1907, the year Frank got into films, the profits from both stage and vaudeville both were surpassed by those generated from the infant motion picture industry. The eastern titans, led by Thomas Edison, struggled desperately to take complete control of the production, distribution and income of motion pictures throughout the United States. In 1909,

Edison and the eight corporations that formed the Motion Picture Patents and General Film Companies controlled the industry by force of law. When they were joined by the two major French film corporations, Pathé and Méliès, the world stopped laughing at the "flickers" and deriding them as a crude pastime for the unwashed masses. The motion picture industry was now, as the crime boss Hyman Roth grandly declared of his union with Michael Corleone in *Godfather Part II*, "Bigger than U.S. Steel."[2]

After several years with Méliès (the American arm of the Gallic film company formed by the French magician and film pioneer Georges Méliès) in New Jersey, Frank then moved on with the company to production facilities in San Antonio, Texas. His deft balancing act between acting in front of the camera and performing myriad duties behind gave Frank a certain heft. In 1911, he joined early film pioneer Thomas H. Ince at his Bison Studios in Santa Monica, California. Ince, like Frank, was a New Englander whose knowledge of the West could have fit into a child's thimble. Nevertheless, he was in the process of developing a theorem for the western film and crafting formulae that would inform the genre for generations to come.

Ince was bedazzled by the Western for its own sake. A vain, tight-fisted dictator, Ince was the first director/producer to bring a studious authenticity and sense of rugged humanism to the Western. When Frank arrived at Ince's Bison Studios, the young actor encountered something that was a strange admixture of a natural history museum and Buffalo Bill's Wild West Show. There were Native Americans, attired in the garb of their tribes, who lived in tepees and mingled freely with authentic cowpokes in actual Western rig riding horses or wagons past livestock grazing behind wooden fences. In Ince's Westerns, the Indians did not come from Central Casting but Navajo pueblos and Sioux reservations (one of his greatest stars was an authentic chief named William Eagleshirt). His cowboys were not gathered off the farms of Glendale or the employment agencies of Los Angeles but came off working ranches and had a firsthand knowledge of horses, saloons, cattle drives and the real way to throw down on an opponent in a gunfight. Everything from the headgear and saddles to the accoutrements and weaponry was as authentic as the men who used them. Ince's investment paid off and his films crackled with a raw realism that gave every scene the dusty texture of a painting by Frederic Remington, Charlie Russell or Charles Schreyvogel.[3]

Balancing the authenticity of Ince's films was a deep respect for the indigenous people of America who, up until then, had received short cinematic shrift or were already being stereotyped as mindless and brutal savages. In films such as *War on the Plains, Blazing the Trail, The Invader, The Deserter* (starring Frank), *The Battle of the Redmen* and *The Indian Massacre* (all 1912), one can see the pictorial style that would trickle down through Frank when he began to direct. This style would ultimately be displayed in the films of John Ford.

In several of the aforementioned films, it was more than likely that Frank did double duty as actor and director. However, Ince in all his glory, was loathe to share the title card with anyone, let alone one of his lowly actors. While Frank was the acknowledged star of *The Deserter* and *The Indian Massacre*, it is also believed that he either had a hand or completely took the helm in the direction of *Custer's Last Fight*, another 1912 film that told the story of Little Big Horn. *Custer* was a well-received and much-lauded film that, aside from Ince's customary realistic texture, took the seminal approach of sympathy toward the Indian point of view. In all Ince's films, as would come to be the case with Jack's films, settlers were portrayed as bold and noble sodbusters worthy of respect but the Indians were also shown as a virtuous and oppressed race of human beings struggling in the face of uninvited aggressors in an attempt to preserve their land and way of life.[4]

In 1912, the year of Frank's numerous successes with Ince, The Universal Film Manufacturing Company pitched Frank an offer to set up a production office within their vast 235-acre complex recently opened in the San Fernando Valley. Universal, which would go on to become one of the most massive dream factories in Hollywood, was helmed from its inception until 1936 by Carl Laemmle, one of the first great and powerful movie moguls. Laemmle (pronounced *Lem*-lee) was a diminutive and white thatched ball of Old World moxie and New World gusto from Laupheim, Germany. He made film history by dodging the legal meteorites hurled by Edison and his Motion Picture Patents' goons back East. Defying the holy writ that was forbidding anyone outside the MPP fold from producing and distributing motion pictures, Laemmle combined his distribution firm with four others and, in 1912, formed what would eventually become known as Universal Studios.

Laemmle, who liked to point out that his name was German for "little lamb," also possessed the nepotistic traits of a Renaissance pope and put so many children, nieces, nephews and distant relatives on the Universal payroll that he acquired the nickname, "Uncle Carl." Despite his avuncular weakness, however, Uncle Carl managed to shape his fledgling studio into a virtual world unto itself where films of every stamp and genre could be made with increasing thrift and efficiency. Frank's apprenticeship under the brilliant but miserly Ince made him a perfect candidate for Laemmle's stable of talent. By 1913, Frank was directing films at Universal.[5]

When Jack arrived at the Los Angeles train depot in 1914, Frank was well established as an actor, director and writer with a growing reputation. By then he had taken up with his leading lady, Grace Cunard, who would likewise earn her own stripes as a writer and director. Frank and Grace, lovers and creative collaborators, were on their way to dizzying heights of success at Universal. They arrived at the depot in a style befitting their newly acquired status as members of Hollywood royalty. Frank was dressed in a Cecil B. DeMille-esque getup of jodhpurs, boots and a scarf and seated behind the wheel of a sleek touring car. It was a way of letting his baby brother know who was the brains, the boss and star of the outfit. The reconnection of the brothers proved a seminal moment in both of their lives but it also planted the seed for a fierce sibling rivalry that would never entirely burn itself out. In Jack's imagination, and in Frank's absence, Frank was a dashing, mysterious man of the world. However, in the confines of a working relationship with clearly defined roles of superior and subordinate, Frank's condescending, needling haughtiness combined with Jack's resentment and jealousy created a perfect storm of dysfunction and anger that would seethe and frequently boil over for the rest of their lives.

———————

Under Frank's not so benevolent dictatorship, Jack was assigned the role of everything from bit player (his screen debut was in Frank's *The Mysterious Rose* in 1914) to set dresser and stuntman. Whatever Frank needed, Jack earned his $35 per week by making it materialize and happen. As much as Jack grumbled and groused about his indentured servitude to his older brother, he jumped to every task he was assigned with diligence and gusto. It was the beginning of a lifelong work ethic in which he tended to eschew the path of comfort and ease and opt for that of the long, grinding process of pre-production, studio and location shoots. The pattern that was to be both the catalytic agent for his brilliance as well as his demons was already being set. Work, even at this early stage of his life and career, gave Jack an endorphin-fueled rush of energy, clarity, purposefulness and immense artistic fulfillment. It put him at the center of the action and provided him with an easy meaning and identity.

For the present, however, the twenty-year-old simply wanted to work and win the validation and respect of his older brother and peers. His resourcefulness and quick thinking produced any number of props and gadgets from the prop department. His prowess on the gridiron and his lean, taut build served him well as a stuntman. When Frank barked through his megaphone, Jack unhesitatingly jumped off bridges from moving trains, drove cars over explosive devices and, while doubling for Frank in a Civil War picture, once took a powder bomb explosion under his chin that landed him in the hospital. Frank's only words regarding his younger brother's injury were those of relief that in the printed scene it was not obvious that Frank was using a double. In what would become Jack's trademark passive-aggressive behavior, he swallowed the indignity without incident and quietly bided his time. Twenty years later, when Jack was one of Fox's top directors and making

Judge Priest with Will Rogers, there was a scene where Frank, playing his signature later role as the town drunk, sat inside a wheelbarrow. Unbeknownst to Frank, Jack had a rope tied from the wheelbarrow to a passing carriage which yanked the vehicle and sent its terrified passenger hurtling down the main street. When Frank stumbled shakily back to the camera crew, Jack stuck a quivering finger in his older brother's face and triumphantly snarled, "That was for the grenade!" as if the most heinous crime of the century had just been avenged.[6]

Even though Frank was the center of Jack's world, the sun around whom his dark little planet revolved, all cinematic roads at that time still led to the Master, D. W. Griffith. Like Ince, Griffith explored the Western film as a sort of directorial primer and had made several good and journeyman films in the genre before moving on to urban, "social dramas" that explored the weals and woes of both historical and modern America. With his legendary cameraman, Billy Bitzer, he began pushing the language of film with innovations such as the tracking shot, close-up and fade in and fade out.

Griffith bestrode Hollywood like a colossus and in 1915, the year after Jack arrived in town from Portland, was deep into his work on his Civil War epic, *The Birth of a Nation,* that would prove not only a tremendous success but a highly controversial telling of war and Reconstruction from a pro-Southern, pro-Ku Klux Klan point of view. Ford claimed to have been a Klansman in the famed scene of the hooded horde riding to the rescue of beleaguered whites and, indeed, stills from the film show one rider lifting up his hood just to see where he was going. According to Ford, his abysmal eyesight served him ill and he was knocked off his horse and lay unconscious on the ground. True to form and his tendency toward *braggadocios* and tall tales, Ford claimed that he awoke to none other than the Master himself reviving the wounded young extra with a flask of whiskey. For Ford, American film began with Griffith but the way of all flesh would insure that he would eventually be forgotten by time and the industry. As Ford told journalist Axel Madsen in 1966, "A very fine gentleman. And he certainly pulled the business on his feet [sic]. He died broke, though. We all die broke."[7]

Jack's star began to rise at Universal through a combination of his talents, tenacity and Frank's increasing carelessness with his own career. In 1916, Frank was at the top of his form in the industry, writing, directing and starring in a wildly popular serial and enjoying the artistic and creative freedom every actor longs for with an almost religious zeal. However, Frank's fast living, combined with his rising price tag, monstrous ego and affairs both with Grace Cunard and the bottle resulted in the studio's increasing hesitancy to offer him the *carte blanche* he once enjoyed. He was rapidly becoming like the character played by Tyrone Power in the 1948 noir classic *Nightmare Alley*, who, as the hobo says at the end reflecting on Power's rags-to-riches-to-rags journey, simply "reached too high."

According to Jack, his first foray into the rarefied realm of movie directing came in 1916 when he had to stand in for Frank, who was suffering from what was pejoratively known among the brethren of the bottle as "the Irish flu." Carl Laemmle was showing off the charms of Universal City to a group of executives from the East Coast and wanted to impress them with a real Western shoot-'em-up on the back lot. Eager to please Uncle Carl, Jack had groups of cowboys ride from one end of the plywood town to the other, whooping, falling off horses and blasting each other to hell with blank cartridges. Not sure exactly what to do as an encore to that rather pointless exercise, Jack then bellowed out orders to burn the entire set to the ground. When a picture became available soon after, Laemmle supposedly said in his thickly crusted English, "Give Jack Ford the job—he yells real good."[8]

Under the banner of Frank's Bison Production Company, Jack directed *The Tornado* (1917), a blarney-laden quickie with Jack doing double duty (a la Frank) as star-director with the ever reliable Grace Cunard on board as the credited writer. *The Tornado* was a singularly journeyman effort and as such garnered little to no attention. But with his next efforts, *The Trail of Hate* and *The Scrapper*, he began to receive not only notice but notices as well. Universal's in-house trade publication, *The Weekly*, printed modestly laudatory reviews of his second and third pictures, commenting (undoubtedly to Frank's growing chagrin),

"For a long time people have said, as they heard the name 'Ford' in connection with a picture: 'Ford? Any relation to Francis?' Very soon, unless all indications of the present time fail they will be saying: 'Ford? Any relation to Jack?'"[9]

One of the greatest cinematic prophecies was about to be fulfilled and all Jack needed now was a star with enough wattage to make them stand out in "the early western sky." He found exactly what he needed in the unlikely person of a middle-aged actor hailing from a patrician family back in the Empire State. Henry DeWitt Carey, born in 1878, was the son of a White Plains judge who envisioned a similarly lofty career in law for his somewhat rowdy and randy son. After an unsuccessful attempt to study law at New York University (he was expelled after an incident involving a bloomers raid on a local brothel), Henry, soon to become simply Harry, drifted about the city and eventually found a job acting with D. W. Griffith's Biograph Company. By 1915, Griffith had moved to the West Coast and Harry did as well and soon crossed the aisle over to Carl Laemmle and Universal. Like Frank, Harry was a tall, two-fisted man with rugged looks that suggested a man of mystery and action who had experienced both the light and dark corners of life. In contrast to the socially conservative Jack, who still wrote Abby and John Augustine on a regular basis, attended Mass when he could and dutifully joined the local Knights of Columbus Council, Harry exuded a warmth and affability tinged with a certain dark edge and moral ambiguity. In the parlance of western film it was a unique characterization called "The Good Bad Man," and in Harry, George O'Brien, Henry Fonda and John Wayne would come to constitute a core element in the vision of John Ford's films.[10]

Although the Edison Company had been producing Westerns since the late 1800s, the Western *qua* Western actually began with Edwin S. Porter's *The Great Train Robbery*, made in 1903. *The Great Train Robbery* was one of the first narrative-driven motion pictures that presented a beginning-middle-end story rather than a series of kinetic

tableaux, closing with the famous—and inexplicable—shot of mustachioed cowboy George Barnes pointing his Colt at the camera and
firing. It was also noted for its violent gunplay, villains and heroes and
horseback chases, all filmed in the wild badlands of New Jersey. Like
Cody's Wild West Show, *Train Robbery* and Westerns that followed
were basically a mélange of action and danger centered around groups
of human beings confronting or falling victim to the hostile forces of
nature or other groups of human beings.

The idea of the cowboy star, the individual on which the drama
focused and who increasingly possessed the power to save, right and
avenge was born in the person of Broncho Billy Anderson. Born Max
Aronson in Arkansas in 1882 to Jewish parents recently immigrated
from New York, Aronson followed the seemingly proscribed route of
every early film actor in that he drifted in and out of jobs and vaudeville before landing a job with an East Coast film production company.
Despite his doughy midsection, irregular features and inability to sit
a horse for a few minutes without tumbling off, Aronson managed to
score an extra's role in *Train Robbery*.

A sharp-eyed entrepreneur as well as an actor, Aronson joined forces
with Chicagoan George K. Spoor to form the Essanay Studios ("Ess"
for Spoor and "Ay" for Anderson) that eventually relocated to Los Angeles. Rechristened Broncho Billy Anderson, Aronson starred in and
(with Spoor) produced over 375 two-reel Westerns. With the appearance of Broncho Billy, the narrative shifted from the community in
danger or need to the individual hero who, like a *deus ex machina* with
studded chaps and a Colt Peacemaker, provides protection, resolution
and redemption. Within a few short years Anderson's roster of two
reel silents went from titles like *Western Justice* (1907) and *A Tale of the
West* (1909) to a seemingly endless stream of eponymous offerings like
Broncho Billy's Adventure, *Broncho Billy and the Schoolmistress*, *Broncho
Billy and the Bandits* and *Broncho Billy's Narrow Escape*. Thus, the Western cowboy star was born.[11]

Without doubt, the greatest Western hero of the silent era, the actor
who gave new elements of depth, contour and authenticity to the genre

was William S. Hart (1864-1946). Like Harry Carey, Hart was a New Yorker by birth but as a boy was taken to the Dakota Territory by his father. There he learned frontier survival skills and met Sioux and Blackfeet braves who had fought in the Indian Wars. With his long and handsome face, narrow piercing eyes and thin line of a mouth Hart was a perfect candidate for the big screen and after being signed by the redoubtable Thomas Ince in 1914, he started shooting films on the West Coast.

Hart wanted his films to reflect the reality of the West he knew, as opposed to the Hollywood version where art directors put Cheyenne war bonnets on Apaches and Texas hats and Mexican spurs on Montana range riders. The films that Hart made for Ince showed people, saloons and landscapes that were gritty, raw and, when freeze-framed, bore striking resemblances to the photographs of Matthew Brady and Edward S. Curtis. The exterior and visual in his Westerns, however, were novel and fascinating only insofar as they were extensions of the interior and psychological landscape over which his cowboys trod and from which they emerged. As film historians Richard Griffith and Arthur Mayer observed, sympathy for Hart's characters arose from his adherence to a basic code. While gunning someone down was a hard, cold fact of frontier life, more serious crimes such as cattle-rustling, horse-thieving and claim-jumping affected and undermined the community as a whole. These were boundaries he would never cross. He could shoot a man through the heart, chug whiskey, fall prey to either the virginal minister's daughter or the vampish tramp and traverse some inner badland wrestling demons too awful to verbalize, but he would never break faith with the community he could protect but of which he could never be a part.[12]

Newhall, California, lies around twenty miles north of Los Angeles in the Placerita Canyon and from the early days of motion pictures its destiny became inextricably linked with the Western film.

Not only did the studios succumb to the rugged charms of Placerita Canyon but their stars did as well, the most famous of them being William S. Hart, Gene Autry (who in 1953 purchased a Western set and studio in Newhall from Monogram Pictures) and Harry

Carey. While Hart built a palatial Spanish Colonial mansion in Newhall in 1924 (today a museum dedicated to his career) and Gene
Autry became a savvy real estate mogul, Carey opted for a life that
approximated that of the cowboys he was playing with such verve and
accuracy. To that end, he and his new wife, actress Olive Fuller Golden,
purchased a small house in Newhall and invited Jack to move in with
them. The house, as far from Hart's rambling palace as Newhall was
from Portland, boasted only a living room and kitchen which the two
men gallantly surrendered to Olive while they happily made do in bed
rolls outside under a canvas tarp. Like Carey, Jack gloried in the raw existence out on the rugged terrain; it was a genuine *Boy's Own* adventure
and the Newhall period soon evolved into something like an extended
adolescent camping trip for all parties.

Despite the open range atmosphere at Newhall, Jack and Carey's
primary purpose was to make pictures. They soon developed an easy,
mutually respectful friendship and, despite the inevitable hazing and
joshing the young man had to endure from the older one, it proved
infinitely more nurturing and loving than the one Jack enjoyed with
Frank. In short, Carey slowly became a beloved and much-honored
mentor rather than a needling, condescending overseer.

After one of Olive's hearty breakfasts of flapjacks and coffee, the two
men would huddle over the scenario of their next picture, tweaking and
fine-tuning despite Jack's growing genius of doing his best work on the
impromptu fly. Afterwards they would head over to Universal, sometimes in a frightening, malfunction-prone jalopy but more often than
not on horseback through the towns and over the hills of Newhall. It
was a grand adventure that, for Jack especially, always remained bathed
in a warm, golden glow. Jack was living a life he could only have dreamed
of just a few years back, unconditionally loved, respected and affirmed
by people he cared for and now collaborated with in an artistic field he
adored. Frank's shadow, in which Jack had maundered about so unhappily, was slowly being obscured by the sun of Placerita Canyon.[13]

Carey, who like Frank, had his own production unit at Universal,
convinced Laemmle to give Jack the helm on his future Westerns and

in 1917 they went to work on their first, *The Soul Herder*. Beginning
with this opus and throughout their four year, twenty-five film collaboration, Ford and Carey refined the approach to their work using a language that, while it had many influences and stood on other shoulders,
was a new and unique voice all their own. Concentrating in particular
on character, motivation and a certain moral struggle both manifested
as well as interiorized, Ford and Carey gave their films a humanity and
an accessibility that for the first time allowed an audience to identify
with the character rather than simply worship him.

Aside from his craggily handsome presence, Carey was also able to
project worlds of thoughts and emotions through his eyes and movements. It is well to remember that this was a time when silent film actors
employed a checklist of histrionic eye and body movements correspond-
ing to every known human emotion, ranging from terror and sadness to
joy and passion. Carey, however, managed to pare everything down to a
sort of emotional baseline, thus allowing the audience not only to participate in the mystery of his moment but to project their own thoughts
upon his world and form a sort of bond with him. This symbiotic relationship between actor and audience would endure in Ford's work and
in a way come to explain the power and universality inherent in his most
memorable protagonists in a way that few directors ever achieved.

The plot for *Straight Shooting* (1917) was, even for its time, well-
worn territory in the cinematic canon. The villainous land baron against
the poor but honest homesteading folk was merely a variant on the top-
hatted and mustachioed landlord vs. the virtuous, comely tenant that
formed the basis for countless stage and film melodramas. However, as
Jack's earliest surviving feature, *Straight Shooting* showcases the young
director's deft hand in breathing freshness and a certain maturity into a
fairly stock story. Cheyenne Harry (white-hatted Carey) is brought in
as a hired gun by greedy rancher Flint to force the peaceful Sims family
off their land. Seeing the family grieving over the grave of Sims' son,
murdered by Pacer (Vester Pegg), Flint's enforcer and Cheyenne Harry's
erstwhile drinking partner, Harry experiences a repentance followed by
a conversion. This leads to the inevitable showdown with Pacer.

Instead of a gunfight using the traditional six-shooters, Winchester rifles are cleverly used and aside from Pacer's unintentionally comic contortions after being shot down by Harry (to be parodied countless times on future television variety shows featuring Western skits), there are several nice touches that would eventually evolve into what would become Ford's "grace notes." These include Harry holding his hat as a decoy around the corner to attract Pacer's fire, blowing smoke out of the barrel of his rifle after gunning his opponent down and hopping gingerly into the stirrup before riding off (the last pinched by Montgomery Clift and used to great effect as his own grace note in *Red River* thirty years later).

The most memorable legacy of Cheyenne Harry, however, was a simple gesture bequeathed to his direct cinematic descendant. Harry's seemingly simple yet poignant habit of grabbing the upper arm of his dropped limb with his other hand managed to convey a sense of loneliness, of noble solitude, of a man in the wide open spaces ranging over an infinitely wider range of emotions within. The ultimate tribute to Harry Carey would be lovingly and iconically paid by John Wayne in the final scene of *The Searchers* (1956). Framed in the dark doorway of the farmhouse where he has returned his niece after a five-year search, the Duke's character, Ethan Edwards, momentarily grabs his upper arm before turning to wander off into the desert.

Carey, as the star and the public, visible face of the collaboration, saw his popularity rise along with his salary while Jack the director was treated more or less as a simple technician and received a commensurately paltry pay hike. Jack was now feeling more comfortable and sure of himself in his directorial vocation and was less and less inclined to be treated like an unwanted waif at the hands of Dickensian executives. Taking a good look at his own good but not great income and modest lifestyle and then glancing over to Harry's growing spread and luxurious lord-of-the-manor living at Newhall, Jack concluded that it was time to move on to greener pastures with the emphasis on greens. In December of 1920, Jack left Uncle Carl's sheepfold at Universal and was signed over on a loan to William Fox Pictures.[14]

THE FOX YEARS–I

"Just a job of work"

William Fox, like his fellow movie moguls Samuel Goldwyn (Schmuel Gelbfisz), Louis B. Mayer (Lazar Meir) and all the Brothers Warner (recently revealed as originally being Wonskolaser), was an eastern European Jew who left behind grinding poverty, institutionalized oppression and even pogroms in the Old World and through hard work, vision and buckets of self-confidence, forged a new life for himself in the new one. Born Vilmos Fried in a remote corner of the Austro-Hungarian Empire in 1879, the future studio titan came to America before his first birthday. Soon after, his name was changed to William Fox, William to supplant the decidedly Magyar Vilmos and Fox as an anglicization of his mother's maiden name, Fuchs.

Although Fox was undoubtedly one of the movie midwives who helped birth Hollywood's studio system, especially in his deft wiggling out from under the legal jackboot of Edison's MPP monopoly, he was something of an anomaly among his mogul brethren. While Laemmle (Universal), Louis B. Mayer (M-G-M), Adolph Zukor (Paramount), Harry and Jack Warner (Warner Brothers), Pandro Berman (RKO) and even the notorious philistine Harry Cohn (Columbia) were bottom-line businessmen obsessed with power and profits, they still were fired by a basic passion for movies and sought the prestige pictures and stars that would give their studios a certain stamp and unique look. Fox, on the other hand, was first and foremost a businessman and as such focused on mergers, acquisitions and a single-minded mania for expansion and dominance in the industry rather than quality pictures.

His ace in the hole, like the other studios, was what was known as block booking. All the major studios, particularly Fox, guaranteed themselves audiences through the chain of theaters they ran throughout the country that showed only their films, much like the breweries who also built chains of taverns that carried only their label of beer. Block booking may have been a fail-safe method of insuring a return on expensive celluloid investments but it also violated the government's anti-trust laws and Washington had no problem telling the moguls the error of their ways. In a 1948 landmark ruling, the government broke up the studio's nationwide chain of theaters and with it dissolved their one time absolute control over film distribution throughout the country. Tragically, or poetically, William Fox died in 1952 and with him the last of his once mighty empire of eponymous theaters. Now, the studios had to join millions of other entrepreneurs and salesmen risking the sale of their product on the fickle whims of the consuming public.[1]

With Fox otherwise engaged in his attempts to become the J. P. Morgan of the film industry, the day-to-day running of the studio fell to two very colorful though well-seasoned old birds, Sol Wurtzel and Winfield "Winnie" Sheehan. Sol Wurtzel (whose brother Harry would become Jack's agent and long-time friend) ran Fox's West Coast studios with a vigilant, cigar-chomping intensity that served him well in his role as bean-counter, efficiency expert and enforcer. Winnie Sheehan, contrarily, was a cherubic-faced Irishman from New York whose Damon Runyan-esque looks and manner belied his ambition and drive to do the bidding of whichever master was currently writing his check. As his early career in New York showed, this was often accomplished with little to no moral filter. While secretary to New York's police commissioner, Sheehan was caught up in a nasty scandal involving kickbacks and protection for illegal gambling rackets, which understandably necessitated a trip out West for his health. Fox, never one to exhibit tea-room manners and sniff prudishly at a fellow traveler on the road of avarice, welcomed Sheehan into his fold as private secretary and eventually as head of production at his studio.[2]

Ford was now a contender in the young director pool at Fox with an adequate salary and a growing reputation all the while his brother Frank was becoming increasingly obsolete, but the 1920s would prove a somewhat spotty decade for Jack. Without his older brother around to outdistance and no Harry Carey to pal around with as a mentor and collaborator, Jack seemed content to drift from picture to picture and happily accept with little sense of selectivity and particularity, whatever assignments the studio gave him.

However, there is a wide and substantial difference between drifting and being completely lost at sea and, like the 1930s, the 1920s proved for Ford a mixed bag of mediocre programmers and a smattering of extremely fine work. His first film for Fox, *Just Pals* (1920) starring Buck Jones, proved to be just one of those highlights. *Just Pals* is a refreshing and interesting departure from the brooding Westerns Jack and Harry had recently made at Universal (although he did return to Uncle Carl's fold on reverse loan to do a few more films with Harry). In his first film on the Fox lot there is no moral ambiguity or internal existential struggles, but a leisurely paced, easy-going knockaround so rhythmic that it looks as though it were acted, directed and edited to the beat of a metronome. Jones plays Bim, the town bum and general ne'er do well who takes on a second job—his first is doing absolutely nothing—of becoming best pal, mentor and surrogate father to a ten-year-old vagabond boy (George E. Stone).

The film is an early example of Ford's increasing self-confidence in taking his time to establish a mood of time and place and making that the hook for the audience rather than relying solely on plot development and construction. Despite packing in nearly a baker's dozen subplots and ancillary adventures, Ford trusts himself—and the audience—in letting Bim meander about his friendship with the boy and his budding romance with the school marm. In an obvious tip of the hat to the Master, D.W. Griffith, Ford does not so much give the viewer simply a story to follow but with a very real and personal stamp shows instead how human beings react to given situations—and each other—in ways that are endearing and genuine.

The first several years of the decade saw other changes in Jack's life besides his move to Fox and increasing variety in the look and subject matter of his films. Some of them were momentous and others were minor, but all were ultimately to have a great impact on the trajectory of his life and artistic vision. The first change came in the person of Mary McBryde Smith, who Jack met at a St. Patrick's Day party in 1920, thrown by Rex Ingram, an Irish-American director who was on his way to becoming one of Metro's top talents in the silent era. Mary Smith was, in effect, everything Jack was not in terms of lineage and upbringing, thereby effectively proving the old adage that in love opposites certainly do attract.

The daughter of a prominent New York stockbroker, Mary was raised in the lap of luxury and educated in elite boarding schools on the East Coast. On her mother's side Mary was descended from the English Roper family, one of whom, Wil Roper, married the daughter of St. Thomas More and thus linked the otherwise devout Presbyterian clan to one of the greatest Catholic martyrs in English history. By the time the Smiths and the Ropers planted their buckled shoes on American soil, their blood turned from simple blue to absolute indigo. Both families were southerners by geography and conviction and the Smiths paid the price for that conviction when their plantation was burned to the ground in the Civil War by the troops of General William Tecumseh Sherman during his march from Atlanta to the sea.[3]

With her long dark hair (usually worn in a bun, Spanish style) and aristocratic bearing, Mary was a genuine beauty who could have easily had a career in films herself if she had been so inclined. When America entered World War I in 1917, Mary, with her familial sense of service and patriotism, became a student nurse at the Army School of Nursing in Washington, D.C., in October 1918. Mary completed her studies in the June of 1919 and graduated from the Training School for Nurses at the New Jersey State Hospital. Jack, though hampered with poor eyesight, registered for the draft in 1917 and was classified as 1A even though his number was never called.[4]

The armistice was a season away, and the war to end all wars was winding down in the mud of Flanders when Mary went west to nurse a brother who was convalescing in California after suffering war wounds. The following year she met Jack. Mary, with her East Coast refinement and no-nonsense nursing sensibilities, certainly wasn't bowled over by the garish Hollywood scene or Jack's looks (then or in the future). She was, however, fired by his intelligence, ambition for success and most importantly, his wonderful sense of humor that tottered constantly on the edge of cutting sarcasm. It was this last that helped seal the bond of friendship and affection between the two.

Jack and Mary were married on July 3, 1920, in a civil wedding at the Los Angeles County Courthouse. For Jack, a practicing Catholic, this was an anathema but an unfortunately necessary way to begin their life together. Mary, however, was a divorcee and had endured a short, whirlwind marriage to a young soldier during the war and because of that they could not be married in the church. For the Feeneys on one side of the aisle and the Smiths on the other, this was a Capulet and Montague roadshow of sorts and neither set of parents were over the moon with joy. John Augustine and Abby were predictably incensed that Jack had entered into marriage outside the church and without benefit of the sacraments, while the Smiths were put off by Mary's marrying a Catholic and a movie person, neither of which exactly qualified him for the Social Register. The marriage ultimately bucked the Hollywood law of averages and endured for half a century and while Jack and Mary would snipe, grumble and test the limits of each other's endurance, they remained devoted to each other until death.

The newly minted Mr. & Mrs. Jack Ford (although on all legal documents, from his marriage certificate to his death certificate, he was still known by his real name of John Martin Feeney) wasted no time in terms of conjugality, and exactly nine months to the day after the honeymoon, Mary gave birth to Patrick Michael Roper Ford. In 1922, a year later,

Mary gave birth to a daughter, Barbara Nugent Ford. Ford's relationship with both his son and daughter was troubled and highly dysfunctional for his entire life. He was "Pappy" and an unquestioned and often benevolent father figure to so many actors and technicians, but sadly he was unable to connect with his children on a deep emotional level. Although they wanted for nothing materially, unconditional love and understanding would be a deficit their entire lives that took an awful toll. Patrick would work off and on for his father as an associate producer and editor but their relationship remained strained and combustive. Barbara fared no better. A genuine Irish Hollywood Princess who could never pull her life together, Barbara went through life crippled by alcoholism, emotional problems and two failed marriages while her parents shrugged helplessly and continued to cover her financially.

At the same time that Jack and Mary were beginning their family and deepening their relationship, another one was unceremoniously coming to an abrupt close. It would not be mended for over two decades. While Jack was getting more notice as a young director, Harry Carey's bright star was sinking slowly into the western horizon. When Jack departed Universal for Fox, Harry was dropped by the studio and left, like Francis Ford, to wander around the low-rent districts of the industry, including vaudeville, searching for work.[5] Ford's biographer, Scott Eyman, quotes Dan Ford, Jack's grandson and also a biographer of the director, as saying the rupture in the friend's relationship resulted from the fact that Carey's salary at the studio skyrocketed upwards while Ford's mercurially blipped along.[6] Another theory from Dan Ford, stated by Joseph McBride in his book, *Searching For John Ford*, has the relationship foundering on the rocks due to Jack's competition with his erstwhile mentor/friend and his desire to break free of corn-pone Westerns and find acceptance as a "prestige" director.[7]

What most likely caused the rift, as McBride writes in his Ford biography, was in fact a nastier and more emotionally lacerating bit of business than a case of filthy lucre or egotistic insolence. Ford, even during his young adulthood, always remained respectfully aloof around girls and focused more on his work and easy-going and (seemingly) uncomplicated relationships with his hard-drinking, horseplaying male friends. This is not to say that Jack did not play the field as a young man, because in fact the funny and fun-loving young man apparently made it to the five-yard line quite a few times. A letter from his friend Ralph Lingley, dated February 18, 1917, breathlessly reads: "All O.K. to meet the girls. You will find them a great pair. Call up the Continental Hotel… and explain you are the chap I spoke about." Another, dated the same day from the same matchmaking friend reads: "Friend Janet, this will serve to introduce you to Jack Ford. You will find him an alright chap, who appreciates good company. May you have a good time."[8]

Jack's lack of philandering in his bachelor days also raised a few eyebrows in a culture and profession where the demeaning use of women as sex objects was almost enshrined in the unwritten law of society. As he grew older, Ford developed an extraordinarily chivalrous code of behavior toward the women on his set and in general, expected the same behavior from every member of the cast and crew. While it is all too easy to attribute his prudish, puritanical abstemiousness to his Catholic faith and attending guilt, this tired theory is neatly demolished when one considers the long list of similarly catechized Irish actors, directors and writers who exhibited no such moral or spiritual qualms in their amorous pursuits.

While young Jack was in his younger years by no means an unattractive man, he did not possess the dashing good looks of his brother Frank, the rugged appeal of Harry Carey or the *bella figura* of William S. Hart. Also, unlike other legendary directors of his time such as Victor Fleming, John Huston, William Wellman and Raoul Walsh, Jack did not possess the chops or the reputation for the Hemingway-esque life of adventure and machismo that made their lives as fascinating as the studio-fabricated mystique of the stars. Fleming (*The Wizard of Oz, Gone With the Wind*) was a two-fisted tough guy who cavorted with the top male stars like Clark Gable and Gary Cooper on motorcycles and hunting trips. Huston was an accomplished boxer who prospected for gold and served in the Mexican cavalry and "Wild Bill" Wellman flew with the *Lafayette Escadrille* in World War I. While Humphrey Bogart,

Gary Cooper and Errol Flynn, great actors all, could play at finding the treasure of the Sierra Madre, engage in dogfights with the Red Baron and lead the charge of the Light Brigade, these guys actually did it. Jack would eventually come to be famed for the uncorked fraternity atmosphere of his booze cruises and poker games, but he was to the end of his days basically an introspective, intellectual loner who seemed most content brooding in solitude over a good book.

According to Joseph McBride, just prior to the time he met Mary, Jack was the victim of a scurrilous and puerile whispering campaign questioning his sexuality, spread by two gossipy stalwarts of the Ford Stock Company, J. Farrell McDonald and Joe Harris. Rumors, which Carey apparently did little to quash or repudiate, abounded that Jack's habit of keeping company with handsome actors and going off with them on extended vacations attested to his latent homosexuality.

Ford was a man who lived by ideals that both motivated and inspired him but could also bedevil and frustrate him. When it came to national myths and heroes whose virtues manifest the identity of an entire community, Ford soared with the eagles. When he personalized the heroes he created, however, Ford could become a bit bogged down in an emotional quagmire. Ford never saw himself as a handsome or particularly heroic man. He therefore tended to live vicariously through the heroes he created and project his persona on larger-than-life types like Carey and eventually George O'Brien, Victor McLaglen, Henry Fonda and John Wayne. The rumors about Ford's sexuality, especially when directed toward such a sensitive and inwardly vulnerable man who since his childhood had continually to prove his red-blooded manhood, cut deep wounds that eventually would only be salved by alcohol, overcompensation and a thickening façade of aggression. Despite Olive Carey's best attempts to tell the two gossipy actors to grow up and stop their nonsense, the damage had been permanently done. Harry's tacit approval of their behavior and refusal to defend the young director's name and reputation placed him on Jack's list of banishment. It would be the first of many such lists Jack would draw up over the course of his life.[9]

When he was eleven, Jack was taken back to Galway by his parents but that trip was veiled in the roseate hues of time. All that remained were memories of green fields, wee, charming villagers and tales of leprechauns and banshees. When Jack returned nearly two decades later, in the year 1921, the wee villagers and leprechauns were obscured by the dark and ominous clouds of civil war, terror and devastation not seen in the Emerald Isle since the potato famine some eighty- five years before.

The *Sinn Fein* (We Ourselves) Party was founded in 1905 as a means by which the Irish could form a legislative body speaking for the Irish people rather than a mouthpiece of their British overlords. Impatient with the dilatory process of political squabbling and compromise, several underground organizations like the Irish Volunteers and the Irish Republican Brotherhood (IRB) were formed with the intention of taking the country back by force and blood. On Easter Monday of 1916, members of the Volunteers and the Brotherhood rose up in the Easter Uprising, a bloody, heroic yet ultimately ill-fated revolt. Centered around Dublin's General Post Office on Sackville Street, the uprising nobly held on for a week before being brutally crushed by British regulars under the command of Generals W. H. M. Lowe and John Maxwell. A heartlessly swift trial and execution of the leaders, including the beloved warrior poet Patrick Pearse, the steel-jawed Socialist James Connolly and the tragic Sir Roger Casement, followed soon after. Instead of quelling revolt, the magnificently failed Easter Uprising was the match that set off the renewed conflagration of Irish nationalism and by the decade's end, the island had erupted into all-out civil war.

When Jack sailed for Europe in November, 1921, he did so almost as though he was a doughboy sailing off to do battle with the hun in the late, Great War. Before embarking on the S.S. *Baltic* he stopped off in Portland to see Abby and Daddo Feeney for a short homecoming and to no doubt huddle with his father about family to contact and places to see. The elder Feeney had remained stalwart in his support of the Irish rebels and was understandably proud of his famous son for placing himself at risk in entering a fairly dangerous war zone. What was less admirable, but more curious, was the fact that Jack had casually left his new wife and son and excitedly set off on a sentimental journey to a very dangerous part of the world. Although Mary was proffered a pro-forma invitation, the idea of the trip was impractical and, as she did when Jack went off on male-bonding booze cruises, location shoots and even a second world war, she accepted his absence with a shoulder-shrugging resignation that she came to realize was the price she paid for being Mrs. Jack Ford. Jack did keep Mary abreast of the journey through a series of letters about the boat trip, his traveling companions and, of course, his drinking.[10]

After reaching London, Jack sailed for Dublin on a mail packet. The western counties, including the Feeneys own Galway, were hit particularly hard and were the scene of brutal reprisals at the hands of the notorious Black and Tans. Formed basically as an auxiliary force to assist the constabulary in policing the cities and villages, the Black and Tans soon devolved into a roving terror squad so mindlessly brutal that it took generations for the memory of their depredations to be erased from the Irish psyche. Comprised of unemployed, aimless and even emotionally unstable British veterans of the Great War, they acquired their name from the hodge-podge of khaki tunics and dark blue police trousers cobbled together for their uniforms. Their reputation was acquired from a systematic policy of looting, burning villages and beating and killing both IRB members and innocent civilians throughout the Irish countryside.

Jack's letters home to Mary, which up till this point had a breezy, chatty feel to them complete with baby talk and childishly playful misspellings about how much he missed his "fambly," suddenly took on a serious tone as he ventured deep into battle-scarred Galway and Spiddal, his parents' hometown. "Spiddal is all shot to pieces," he wrote to Mary. "Most of the houses have been burned down by the Black and Tans and all the young men had [sic] been hiding in the hills."[11] Galway was in the heart of Republican turmoil and it was inevitable that many of Ford's relations were either passive victims or active combatants in the war. In fact, his cousin Martin Feeney (son of his father's brother) was one of the young men hiding in the hills that he wrote home about. Martin, an IRA commando on the lam from the British, had sought refuge in the hills of Connemara, where his American cousin found him. Ford apparently brought him food, money and not a little encouragement, acts the young man remembered gratefully to the end of his days.

Martin, for his part, said that Jack paid for his foray into the hills and the rebel cause by getting "roughed up" several times by the Black and Tans before being put on a ship for America and told never to return. Ford's involvement in the Irish troubles probably extended no further than this elliptical footnote and "roughed up" can be interpreted many ways, from verbal abuse to a real and bloody pasting. However, the fact that a Yankee Irishman ventured into the heart of a dangerous war zone during a civil war nevertheless evidenced real and undoubted bravery and the event indelibly marked Ford's soul for the rest of his life.[12]

Perhaps the greatest influence Ireland had on Ford, though, was artistic. The period before, during and after the civil war saw what was known as the Irish Literary Revival. Outstanding figures like W. B. Yeats, Lady Augusta Gregory, Sean O'Casey and Liam O'Flaherty (Ford's distant cousin), used their poems, books and plays the same way the Sinn Fein and the IRB were using speeches and guns. All of them were committed to the cause of Irish freedom to the extent that O'Casey and O'Flaherty were members of the IRB, O'Casey was a radical socialist and Lady Gregory was a *force majeure* in the founding of the nationalist Abbey Street Theatre in Dublin.

Ford began more and more to identify with the cause of Ireland and nationalism and indeed all things Irish, from his flannels and briar pipe to his radical politics and somewhat successful attempt to master the Gaelic language, and it did much to solidify the emerging myth and legend of John Ford. Up till now Jack had always considered himself Irish and American. What the cause did was to replace the *and* with a hyphenation that forever re-cast himself in one symbiotic persona as an *Irish-American*. Slowly, Ford's identity as a journeyman director and solid craftsman was being augmented with the façade of rebel, the aura of mystery and the soul of a poet.

⸻⸻⸻

Ford's return from Ireland may have initiated a second Gaelic awakening of sorts in his soul but it did not precipitate an immediate damburst of artistically noteworthy films. Even though he was comfortably ensconced in the Fox organization with steady work and was numbered among a stable of bright and talented young directors, the only thing that increased during the early to mid-1920s was his salary and reputation for quick, good work.

In Jack's mind, the habit of drifting from picture to picture without regard to its particular merit or how it would advance or hinder his career was actually an intentional operating procedure he diligently pursued his entire life. In a 1965 interview with French journalists Jean Narboni and André Labarthe, Ford explained his professional modus operandi. "Some men will make a good picture then keep on trying. They won't work for a year and a half; they're trying to beat the last one. I just keep on going, making pictures, good, bad, indifferent. I just like to work around the studios. I like the people I work with. I'm absolutely without ambition. I have no ambition. I like pictures. I like to make pictures."[13]

There were, however, a few semi-precious stones among the paste jewelry he produced during the 1920s that added luster to his otherwise journeyman period at Fox. *The Village Blacksmith* (1923) was an ambitious outing into the realm of the prestige picture, being based upon the classic work by Henry Wadsworth Longfellow. Ford had tried his hand at a classic several years earlier with his screen adaptation of Bret Harte's uniquely American evergreen, *The Outcasts of Poker Flat* (1919 and presumed lost) but it turned out to be a vehicle dominated by the mega-wattage of its star, Harry Carey. In 1923, Ford also filmed *Cameo Kirby*, an antebellum costume piece starring a young John Gilbert, who was on his way to stratospheric stardom as one of M-G-M's top male stars of the 1920s and one of the highest paid actors of the silent era. *Cameo Kirby* was also notable for the fact that a new name appeared on the credits of Ford's films, one commensurate with his growing reputation as a serious and respected filmmaker. As "Jack Ford" sounded too casual and plebian for a man slowly evolving from craftsman to *auteur*, all of his films would henceforth announce to the world, "Directed by John Ford."

The Iron Horse (1924) was Ford's and Fox's screen version of the building of the Transcontinental Railroad and stood as one of the studio's most ambitious and expensive undertaking up to that point. The film was ostensibly a response to James Cruze's *The Covered Wagon*, Paramount's grandly filmed tale of the pioneer trek westward that was shot and released the previous year. Boasting a $750,000 budget, buffalo stampedes, Indian attacks and snowbound track-laying locations throughout several states, *The Iron Horse* not only cemented Ford's reputation as a reliable artisan but proved that Westerns could not only go wide but deep as well.

The film was meant to be an expansive and handsome epic, but the backstory of the film was just as fascinating as the tale itself. While Sol Wurtzel kept an eagle's eye watch over the film's progress and lush budget, the cast and crew slugged through weeks of filming conditions almost as raw and rugged as those endured by the real rail laborers over fifty-five years earlier. The location shooting was done in New Mexico but primarily in Nevada, where heavy snow and glacial temperatures insured that everyone moved fast and with little margin of error. The base camp was in train cars and circus tents heated by pot-bellied stoves and sustenance came from army-style commissaries augmented by copious amounts of liquid courage. Indians were played by authentic natives like Chief John Big Tree and Chief Eagle Wing and laborers of every ethnic stamp were imported to rub elbows with what was believed to be genuine ladies of easy virtue. Thus, the touches of verisimilitude throughout the film were raw and legion.

The plot, loose and shaky, is basically centered upon the journey of Davy Brandon (George O'Brien) from antebellum Springfield,

Illinois, to the promised land beyond the Missouri River. En route, the boy Davy's father is killed by Indians prompted by a mysterious, fingerless man who later appears in the railroad camps as a land-speculating, black-hatted nemesis of all the simple, hard-working laborers. Aside from the theme of American history recast in the mold of Homeric epic and common man integrity, *The Iron Horse* employs Ford's other recurring motif of Abraham Lincoln. Played to lanky, homely perfection by the eerily similar Judge Charles Edward Bull (a Reno magistrate), Ford's Lincoln is not apotheosized as the great emancipator or savior of the Union, but as an avuncular and sagacious earthen vessel. He is first seen in Springfield as a beardless, fur-hatted lawyer playing Cupid to the boy Davy and his sweetheart Miriam Marsh. Later in 1862, as Lincoln signs the Pacific Railroad Act that will begin the monumental rail-laying endeavor across the prairie, Ford first shows Lincoln ambling through the White House charmingly blowing his nose with a handkerchief tugged from his back pocket. As he would in later films like *Prisoner of Shark Island* (1936), *How the West Was Won* (1962) and even as a simple ghostly reflection in a daguerreotype in *Cheyenne Autumn* (1964), Ford presents Lincoln not as the center and focus of history, but rather as a homespun Greek chorus and *paterfamilias* who appears intermittently to impart his benediction on his fellow common men as they continue his work of democracy-building.

Ford's casting of *The Iron Horse* was typical of the studio protocols of the day. Aside from the novel use of Judge Bull as Lincoln, the film showcases the journeyman talents of contract players like the virginal Madge Bellamy as the love interest and J. Farrell McDonald as the comic relief Irishman. McDonald, a burly bald actor with legendarily bushy eyebrows which he put to great quizzical effect, was the notorious gossipmonger who had made scurrilous accusations about the young director's private life. His comic turn as the Civil War veteran turned track layer was Ford's slowly evolving interpretation of Shakespeare's Wise Fool and, in actors from Francis Ford and Stepin Fetchit to Barry Fitzgerald and Hank Worden, would come to represent resurrected versions of the Bard's Pistol, Nurse and Grumio.

The stand-out performer however is George O'Brien who plays the lead role of the adult Davy Brandon. Born to upper-crust San Francisco parents in 1899 (his father would become the city's chief of police), O'Brien was, by his teens, an expert horseman and boxer whose physical prowess landed him stunt and extra work in Hollywood in the early 1920s. A magnificently sculpted Adonis, remembered as one of the most genial men in Hollywood, O'Brien was also a career military man of extraordinary courage who served his country in both world wars as well as the Korean and Vietnam conflicts. In every engagement he was decorated for bravery under fire.

O'Brien was, like Harry Carey before him, another of Ford's beau ideal of American masculinity and in *The Iron Horse* he is not so much photographed as a protagonist as he is rendered in tableaux showing him as a David or home-grown Greek god. His Davy Brandon is heroic, unassuming, virtuous, physically and morally virulent and like Harry Carey before him and Henry Fonda and John Wayne after, leads by example and quiet dignity rather than bravado or power. Ford's iconic presentation of O'Brien in *The Iron Horse* and subsequent films was, in fact, so influential that the brilliant German director F. W. Murnau chose O'Brien as the lead in his seminal expressionistic classic, *Sunrise,* three years later.

O'Brien and Ford, both Irishman with a thirst for spirits and hijinks, bonded off the set as well and soon the two were close friends and drinking partners. In 1931, their friendship culminated and then disintegrated in a fateful adventure on the high seas. In one of his many legendary adventures (with the long-suffering Mary once again left at home to watch the children and tend the garden), Ford cajoled O'Brien into joining him on a four-month-long voyage to the Philippines that was straight from the pages of Joseph Conrad. After a violent Pacific crossing, the two Irish Lord Jims boozed, dined and brawled (O'Brien participated in several boxing tourneys with local pros) for several weeks with dignitaries, sultans and drunken salts in seedy waterfront dives.

As was his wont when not working, Ford immediately shed his fastidious on-set sobriety and went on a bender of gargantuan proportions. The more disciplined and less demon-ridden O'Brien apparently had enough of Jack's self-defilement and pressed on to the other islands while his traveling companion attempted to sober up back in Manila. It was a mortal sin that O'Brien committed to his everlasting regret. Unfailingly kind and doggedly loyal to his friends when they were the same to him, Ford could also turn the other side of his Janus face and become Medusa in the blink of an eye. In Ford's bleary eyes, O'Brien's abandonment of him in Manila was the ultimate betrayal of friendship and for that O'Brien would pay the ultimate penalty. In his typical passive-aggressive fashion, Ford shrugged off the incident weeks later when they reunited with back-slapping bonhomie and good natured ribbing, but the damage had been done. Henceforth, O'Brien was banished from the inner circle of Ford's stock company and did not work for him for the next seventeen years. Like the disobedient Israelites in the Old Testament, O'Brien was forced to wander through Western serials and B movie roles until, properly chastened and shriven, he was allowed back into the fold in Ford's *Fort Apache* in 1948.[14]

To the delight of William Fox, Sol Wurtzel and Winnie Sheehan, the raw footage of *The Iron Horse* was sent back to the studio from Nevada and New Mexico where, cut and scored, it was deemed a very exciting and marketable movie. Against a negative cost of $275,000, *Iron Horse* not only proved to be, along with the silent version of *Ben-Hur* and *The Big Parade*, one of the most successful epics of the decade, but also landed Fox film a Broadway premiere for the very first time.[15]

In a material sense, *The Iron Horse* ended Ford's trail of tears through the levels of apprentice and journeyman and placed him squarely in the ranks of the Hollywood master craftsman. He was now an A-list director whose work was lauded both domestically and around the world. Although Ford cared little for the money and perks that prestige in the industry brought him, Mary found that the rewards for his physical and emotional absences, along with his moods and drinking marathons, were paid in dividends like money, expensive clothes, club memberships and the immense respect she received in simply being Mrs. John Ford.

While she put up with the vicissitudes of her husband's personality with forbearing exasperation, Mary was still part of a team and there were minor and monumental faults on both sides. Mary had long given up on being "one of the boys" like Olive Carey and found that fur coats, designer clothes and even a Rolls-Royce (Jack had bought her one in 1933 with the Depression raging all around them) could assuage her hurts but could not mystically bond her to a husband she adored but did not truly understand.

They may have differed in so many ways but one way that found Jack and Mary lockstep in unison was alcohol. Like Jack, Mary liked her liquor. Every Sunday afternoon during Prohibition years, their house on Odin Street became the scene of regular violations of the Volstead Act. A disparate cast of characters, ranging from cowboy star Tom Mix and stuntmen from Jack's pictures to Mary's society friends, would mingle and imbibe copious amounts of homemade hooch hidden in secret compartments throughout the house.[16]

As the emotional and relational terra firma in Jack's real life became shakier, his success gave him the power, the resources and the need to construct the formidable and impregnable fortress slowly becoming known as the "John Ford Myth." Ford began to put in place the traditions and behavior that would come to constitute the Ford legacy, and they would begin to forever blur that interesting line between the reality of his life and the vision of his art. He began to have high teas, English style, on his movie sets during afternoon shooting breaks. Complete with Earl Grey tea and Jacob's biscuits, these teas were carried out with a hieratic, almost liturgical formalism that placed Ford at the head of the table as a combination of both paterfamilias and Miss Manners. Shop talk about movies was forbidden, as were off color jokes or any breach of courtesy to the women present, to the point where fines were levied against any of those who breached the rules. In another sense, these rituals went deep into the heart of his Irish Catholic soul and represented the sacredness of the table and the almost Eucharistic dimension of the people gathered around it. This sacramental element was not lost on Ford, and from this point on meals, poetically choreographed scenes of family seated around a patriarch or parent, begin to figure prominently in his work. From *Four Sons* and *Stagecoach* to *How Green Was My Valley* and *The Searchers*, the table as altar becomes a locus of unity, healing and revelation.

One of the perks of fame and power that Ford did take full advantage of was the coveted director's prerogative to surround himself with crew and actors who were used with such recurring regularity that they became known to film history as the "John Ford Stock Company." If one looks at the actors who formed this august group, they would find a series of "types," standard stock characters representing various faces of humanity, with roots in silent films and vaudeville as well as Elizabethan drama and even the drama of antiquity. Aside from the Hero (Harry Carey, George O'Brien, Henry Fonda, John Wayne), there is the Heroine (Maureen O'Hara, Anna Lee, Vera Miles, Shirley Temple), genial, blustery Blowhard (J. Farrell McDonald, Victor McLaglen, Ward Bond), the Sage (Will Rogers, Russell Simpson, Arthur Shields), the Heavy (John Carradine, Vester Pegg), the Fool as Chorus (Barry Fitzgerald, Stepin Fetchit, Hank Worden), the Innocent Youth (Harry Carey Jr., Ben Johnson, Patrick Wayne, Jeffrey Hunter) and, of course, the Mother (Jane Darwell, Mildred Natwick).

However, there were thorns among these sacred rosebushes and they would draw much blood over the years. Ford's newly minted prominence within the industry gave him a cachet that he used wisely and generously but often times as a weapon. Ford was a fragile vessel who lived his whole life with a crusty, hard-bitten façade that covered up a man desperately in need of love, admiration and affirmation. He found it increasingly difficult to be nourished in these areas in his family and private life but he was able to insure it in his professional life with a cleverly constructed variant on the carrot-and-stick routine.

Australian actor Frank Baker, a bit player in Ford's films who was never afraid of locking horns with the Old Man, told a story that perfectly illustrates Ford's Manichean duality and his unfathomable ability to be both perfectly bad and perfectly good at the same time. According to Baker, an old actor who worked with Ford at Universal shuffled into the director's office during the Depression, destitute and desperately in search of money to care for his sick wife. In front of several horrified onlookers, Ford verbally decimated the old man, first hurling insults and then physically hurling him through the front door with threats of worse treatment if he ever came begging again. Moments later, Baker spied Ford's business manager Fred Totman rushing down the street where he handed the man a check, signed by Ford, to cover his wife's surgery. Ford also flew a specialist down from San Francisco to perform the operation and later bought them a house and covered their living expenses for life. Everything was done secretly and *sotto voce*, lest anyone discover Ford's sentimental and loving side and deem it unmanly weakness. A complex man indeed.[17]

Ford, true to his pattern of treading water after making a big splash, followed his biggest hit to date with a series of insipid works that are like curios given to Grandma on her birthday; nice and cute but immediately tucked away on the shelf of a dusty cabinet. *Lightnin'* (1925) is a low-brow comedy about an old couple, not unlike Ma and Pa Kettle, trying to sell their hayseed hotel with less than hilarious results. *Kentucky Pride* (1925), filmed on location in the eponymous state, tells the tale of a horse (who also serves as the film's narrator) on its way to racing fame and success. *The Fighting Heart* (1925) has George O'Brien back again in a turgid boxing melodrama centering on two of Ford's recurring motifs: liquor and proving one's manhood through duty, honor and physical prowess. *The Shamrock Handicap* (1926), another horse opera, comes off as *Kentucky Pride* simply filmed from another angle with not much to distinguish the two. All these films did well at the box office but they were hardly the work of a top-notch director coming off one of the biggest hits of the decade. On the contrary, they show Ford at his worst, which is to say, Ford at his most comfortable. Once again he had slipped into the passenger seat and dozed his way through a series of larks simply to get out of the house in the morning and take home a paycheck.

Toward the end of the decade, which coincided with his full decade at Fox, Ford awoke from his cinematic slumber and began selecting and executing his films with a renewed sense of vigor and virtuosity. *3 Bad Men* (1926), Ford's last Western of the decade, and indeed the last for thirteen years until *Stagecoach*, is one of those vigorous high watermarks. Like most of his Westerns, the plot is deceptively and almost intentionally simple in order to allow the vast sea of subterranean emotion and turmoil to bubble up to the top. Three lovable scoundrels (Tom Santschi, Frank Campeau and the ubiquitous J. Farrell McDonald) scallywagging their nefarious way around a burgeoning frontier camp, find redemption in defending the outraged virtue of one of their sisters. Like its distant cousin, remade by Ford in 1948 as *3 Godfathers*, *3 Bad Men* appears on the surface to mythologize criminality and portray, in a breezy, lighthearted manner, men who are essentially lawbreakers. It is, in fact, another recasting of a medieval mystery play in which the hurly-burly of humanity are reduced to archetypes and set to rights by the choices thrust upon them by fate and circumstance. Again, the plot is old world set in the vast western spaces of the new one and resonates more with Shakespeare than Bret Harte. The Boy (George O'Brien) and the Girl (Madge Bellamy) seek to be united but are thwarted by the machinations of the evil sheriff, played with an almost Tom Mix dandiness by Lou Tellegan.

3 Bad Men was filmed in the mountainous glories of Jackson Hole, Wyoming, and spared the arctic purgatory endured by the cast and crew of *The Iron Horse*, the production proceeded apace and pleasantly enough. The set piece in *3 Bad Men*, and one that continues to dazzle and awe even with the capabilities of today's computer-generated imagery, is the Dakota land rush, filmed in Victorville back in California's San Bernardino County. A great paroxysm of men, beasts and machinery (including an old high wheel bicycle), are unleashed across the screen at a breakneck pace as the settlers scurry for land in the gold-rich Black Hills. Ford explained to director Peter Bogdanovich, who as a young man sat at Ford's feet and fortunately gleaned firsthand accounts of his career for posterity, how the epic scene was staged. "We did a hell of a land rush; it was on level ground and they whipped the horses up—hundreds of wagons, you could pick them up cheap—going at full tilt; it was really fast. We did the whole sequence in two days."[18]

Probably the most breathtaking scene in the Dakota land rush is that showing a baby girl sitting directly in the path of the oncoming tsunami of horses and wagons. She is scooped up by disembodied hands literally moments ahead of the stampede. Done without trick photography or rear projection, it is an awesome bit of film business that, if done today, would no doubt land all parties concerned in jail for endangering a child's life.

Although in many respects *3 Bad Men* is a more thoughtful and textured film than *Iron Horse* and it did do well with the paying public and exhibitors, it failed to clear the bar with the same height of his previous epic. Regardless, after its premiere a Western Union telegram to Ford from Winnie Sheehan and Sol Wurtzel, dated September 10, 1926, declared: "CONGRATULATIONS STOP LONG MAY THE IRISH SURVIVE STOP THE THREE BAD MEN AT MODESTO." Ford publicly continued to hate premieres as much as he hated producers but privately remained sensitive to the slings and arrows of critics and the public. In that respect, this must have read like a proclamation from the Roman senate to a victorious general just home from the front.[19]

The success of *3 Bad Men*, aside from its monetary and prestige rewards, gave Ford carte blanche to continue nurturing his peculiar quirks and eccentricities, making a seamless garment of the private Jack Ford and the legendary John Ford. His actors noticed an increase of his curious habit of chewing on the corners of handkerchiefs while directing a scene. Along with his dark glasses, fedora and general dishevelment, the decimating of innocent handkerchiefs became one of Ford's most recognizable and puzzling traits. Whether it was nervous energy or an oral fixation (he was now smoking cheroots and pipes everywhere but in his sleep and in the shower), the supply of Irish linen kerchiefs Mary gave him each morning were generally shredded into lint by the time he returned from the studio in the evening.

Perhaps Ford's most notable habit that developed out of this period, but actually had been germinating since his apprenticeship with the thrifty and fast-working Frank, was his unique method of shooting set ups. The basic mechanics of shooting scenes for a film, then as well as now, were fairly standard and familiar to any young director as the rules of the road are to a sixteen-year-old aspiring driver. First, the director shoots the "master," a wide-angle shot containing all the actors delivering their dialogue with each other. Next, they go in for medium, over the shoulder and then finally the close-up shots. Inserts and "pick-up" shots, close-ups of objects, hands, or scenes where the actors are not recognized, can be done after. From there it is up to the editor to decide which shots are cut and assembled into a workable scene. The more film and angles, the better chance the editor has of developing a compelling and artistic scene.

Ford's lauded reputation for shooting quickly and exposing the minimum amount of film was actually his way of taking the ownership of his films out of the hands of the editors and almighty producers, albeit in a sly though perfectly aboveboard way. According to Scott Eyman, a cameraman Ford worked with at this time named Charles G. Clarke, noticed Ford's unorthodox method and wondered how his expeditious jumble of footage could be properly assembled into a workable film. Clarke then realized that Ford's dearth of shots limited the options of the editor to only the few that he shot. Ford was, in essence, editing the film in his camera and as he went along shot scenes in one or two takes according to a schema carefully already worked out in his mind. It was a highly intelligent formula that was not only economical but, when refined in the crucible of experience, allowed him to coax—or bully—performances from his actors that reached the screen sparkling with spontaneity, naturalness and an eternal freshness. Unlike directors such as Willy Wyler, who even on gargantuan productions like *Ben-Hur* (1959), was notorious for shooting ten, twenty and even thirty takes of a scene until he got what he wanted, Ford generally shot one or two takes of any given scene. In delivering less coverage to the editor he was learning more than how to save film, time and money to keep Wurtzel and Sheehan happy. He was learning to nail a scene, bristling with a frisson of vitality and genuine emotion, free from the artifice brought about by rote recitation and exhaustive repetition.[20]

Ford's rekindled sense of artistic purpose continued to burn brighter as the decade waned. In 1928, he directed *Mother Machree*, a decidedly more serious undertaking than the cornpone time wasters of the past year and his first wholehearted venture into his Irish Nationalist consciousness. Set at the turn of the century, *Mother Machree* deals with the theme of a family divided by a love for the Irish soil and the harsh realities necessitating emigration to the New World. Ford reached deep into his own past and identity as a Feeney to sing this ballad of a family sundered by time and distance: a love song that would become increasingly familiar territory to him. In terms of technique and vision, *Mother Machree* represents a seismic rupture in the manner in which Ford heretofore used his camera. Gone are the painterly, expansive compositions of his epics and the graceful, natural blocking of his Harry Carey Westerns, in which gesture, expression and even the landscape expressed character as much as the scenario and the acting.

Under the influence of German director F. W. Murnau, whose 1927 expressionist drama *Sunrise* (starring Ford's brawny discovery and buddy George O'Brien) played a pivotal role in cinematic history, Ford began to experiment with lighting and set design and his films during this period took on a novel and more profoundly cerebral look.

Ford followed *Mother Machree* with another successful milestone along his continued transformation from mere director to *auteur*. *Four Sons* (1928) tells the tale of a Bavarian mother (Margaret Mann) whose eponymous brood gets caught up in the cataclysm of World War I. Three are killed in the mud of Flanders while a fourth emigrates to America where he settles with a wife and child and eventually brings his beloved mother to join them. The final hurdle in *Mother's* trail of tears through war, death and separation is her near-miss of the mandatory test in which she has to recite the English alphabet. Thus the working title of *Mother Bernle Learns her Letters*. In *Four Sons*, Ford presses deep into Murnau territory, contrasting (a la *Sunrise*) the sun-dappled, glistening early scenes of halcyon days in the Bavarian village with the grim, Caravaggio-esque chiaroscuro of the battlefield and war scenes. Lighting, sets and camera angles all change with the mood of the scene and the inner emotions of the character.

Other Ford motifs, mostly Catholic in nature, are firmly entrenched in *Four Sons*, including the sacramental nature of the table, the seamless garment woven between the worlds of the living and the dead (most notably the scene in which Mother Bernle sits alone at the table imagining her dead brood once again laughingly seated with her) and the inevitable rupture of the family unit.

Four Sons is notable for another encounter Ford had on the set; inconsequential to observers at the time but ultimately fortuitous and fateful. A young assistant prop man named Marion Morrison, who had the thankless task of blowing leaves through Mother Bernle's door and then sweeping them up again for another take, absentmindedly walked on to the set during a take and began his exertions. Realizing that he was on camera, the red-faced young man rushed off the set, broom and all, firmly convinced that his career in films was finished even before it began. Ford, famously intolerant of pomposity but a sucker for genuine innocence, merely walked over, gave the mortified kid a gentle boot on the rump, and sent him off with his broom.[21]

Morrison, a sophomore at the University of Southern California with aspirations toward law and a former right tackle for Howard Jones's Thundering Herd football team, was a handsome 6'4" Scotch-Irish lad whose football career was terminated by a shoulder injury sustained while body surfing. Like many of his teammates and Sigma Chi fraternity brothers, Morrison picked up summer cash on the Fox lot lugging props and furniture and generally acting as a gofer in the days before unions regulated the do's and don'ts of every laborer in the industry.

Young Morrison, who hailed from Winterset, Iowa, was the issue of a stormy union between an aloof, icy and domineering mother and a good-hearted but ne'er do well pharmacist father. The marriage would end in divorce when Marion was still a teen. When the father's health began to fail, the family moved to the desert town of Glendale outside of Los Angeles and took up farming in the hopes that the arid and warm climate would prove salubrious to him and the whole clan. One of Marion's consolations was an Airedale dog named Duke, and the two of them were constant companions to the point where the guys at the local Glendale firehouse used to call the boy "Little Duke" as the two walked by. The name Duke, or any name for that matter, was infinitely preferable to Marion and without the prefix the nickname stuck for life.

Unlike Ford, Morrison was the soul of gentleness and amiability and to the end of his days remained a fun-loving, good-natured egg who was forever just "one of the guys." Ford, who had always instilled a sense of fear, awe and trembling respect in all his subordinates, had never experienced such a scarlet case of puppy-dog hero worship and surrogate fatherhood that Morrison now directed toward him. He immediately took the lad under his wing and began throwing extra prop work and bit parts his way, including eventual stunt work; a niche populated only by a select few on whom his favor completely rested.

In 1929, Ford recommended Morrison to fellow Fox director Raoul Walsh for the lead in his upcoming Western epic called *The Big Trail,* to be shot in an experimental wide screen 70mm format. The name Marion Morrison did not seem to dovetail with the lad and, along with Winnie Sheehan, Walsh sought out a new name for their star. Walsh, an aficionado of American history, had recently finished a biography of the Revolutionary War general, "Mad" Anthony Wayne. "Tony Wayne" sounded just as bad as Marion Morrison to the director and, simplifying the name to a more common and acceptable single syllable, it was announced to the industry and to history that the star of *The Big Trail* was a young actor with the newly minted name of John Wayne.

Due to a combination of its length, the expense of outfitting theaters with 70mm projectors and screens and the full onslaught of the Great Depression, *The Big Trail* quickly meandered off the path into ignominy and oceans of red ink. With his one hope at stardom seemingly dashed, Duke Wayne disappeared, for the time being, into a decade of obscurity and journeyman work in B Western serials at the Poverty Row studios in the nether regions of the industry.

THE FOX YEARS—II

A Portrait of the Young Director as an Artist

The influence that German director F. W. Murnau had on Ford and his art, unlike what Mark Twain said about the reports of his own death, have not been greatly exaggerated. John Ford was a man who constantly engaged in a maddening game of personality sleight-of-hand with co-workers, interviewers, friends and probably even with himself. Ford could move from brutal tyranny to weepy sentimentalism with the speed of light. In the same vein, Ford could also be one's best friend and blood brother on Saturday night and on Sunday decide not to speak to that individual for several years for no apparent reason.

One of Ford's most celebrated jack-in-the-box routines, not knowing which persona would pop out and when, was that of "I am an artist-I am not an artist." He would become distant, unfocused and occasionally hostile when asked about the artistic components of his theory, almost as if being an artist somehow emasculated him and complicated the simplicity of his vision. In the mid 1960s, while being interviewed by French journalist Eric Leguebe, Ford was asked if cinema can truly be called the Seventh Art. Ford, typically, responded "What I like in filming is the active life, the excitement of the humming of the cameras, and the passion of the actors in front of them, the landscapes on top of that, the work, work, work…it takes a huge physical effort to remain lucid and not fall into the trap of aestheticism and, above all, intellectualism."[1]

For Ford, filmmaking was, and remained in his eyes, primarily a visceral and not a cerebral endeavor. It came from the heart, nowhere near the vicinity of the head. Yet when the great Russian director Sergei Eisenstein (*Battleship Potemkin, Ivan the Terrible*) was asked if he could magically wipe the directing credits off any American film and replace them with his own name, without hesitation he responded "It would be *Young Mr. Lincoln*, directed by John Ford." It could only be imagined how Ford, with his studied indifference and feigned irritation, would rather have swallowed broken glass than admit how honored and moved he was by such an Olympian encomium.[2]

Happily for Ford, the late 1920s saw an influx into Hollywood of directors from central and northern Europe. Some passed through with a sniffy disdain for the platinum-plated industry but others remained and brought their own continental touch to American film. With their Old World aesthetics and aristocratic, patrician bearing, these cinematic *grandees* arrived as iconic idols at whose feet brash young Yankee directors could sit and learn. This time saw the import of such luminaries as Victor Seastrom and Mauritz Stiller (along with his protégé, a young actress named Greta Gustafsson whom he renamed Greta Garbo) who arrived from Sweden, Erich Von Stroheim and Josef Von Sternberg (with *his* protégé, Marlene Dietrich) from Austria and Ernst Lubitsch and F. W. Murnau from Germany. Interestingly, of all the newly arrived auteurs, it was Murnau who would exert the greatest influence over Ford during these years.

F. W. Murnau (1888-1931) hardly seems to be the varsity quarterback, two-fisted Harry Carey type that Ford admired with the same verve in which young Duke Wayne admired him. Born Friedrich Wilhelm Plumpe in Westphalia, Murnau was the personification of what Americans expected from post-World War I European *aesthetes*: regal aloofness, icy brilliance and a slight whiff of decadence. Standing nearly seven feet tall and openly homosexual (still something of a rarity even in the anything goes, pre-Hays Office Hollywood), Murnau arrived in Los Angeles in 1926 as a bona fide genius and the greatest exponent of expressionist film.

Expressionism as a language of film was actually one manifestation of a movement that influenced every art form from literature, painting and dance to music, poetry and film. Just one of the many "isms" that floated around the sociocultural alphabet soup of the late 19th and early 20th centuries, Expressionism sought to recast reality through the subjective lens of one's own feelings and experience of the world. Instead of reality shaping emotions and moods, one's emotions and moods give shape to reality and is expressed through an artistic medium.

In Hollywood's mad rush to import European directors to give the industry a cosmopolitan cachet, Murnau quickly succumbed to the mogul's siren song and signed with Fox Pictures in 1926. His first American film, *Sunrise* (1927) was not a financial success but those who had eyes to see knew that something strange and wonderful had been introduced into the language of American cinema. *Sunrise* told the deceptively simple story of a Man (played by Ford's buddy George O'Brien) falling for a mysterious Woman from the City (Margaret Livingston) who convinces him to murder his wife (Fox's top female star Janet Gaynor) in order to carry on their illicit affair. The psychological states of the couple are visually manifested in the events they experience during an outing to the city to rekindle their love.

Ford was stunned by what he saw and experienced in *Sunrise* and Murnau's influence in his own work was immediate and seismic. Ford grandly and sincerely announced after seeing *Sunrise* that he considered it the greatest picture yet made and that he doubted it would be bested within the next ten years. Little did he know critics would be saying the same about his films in the same amount of time.[3]

The greatest compliment Ford could have received during this heady and transformative period in his life would have been for his idol to return the compliment. He received it, oddly enough, in the middle of the Atlantic as he was en route to Europe for a vacation. A telegram from Murnau, dated February 20, 1927, told "Dear Jack" that he had seen *Mother Machree* the day before and proffered his congratulations on a "beautiful picture." He closed with his hopes that they could cross paths in Berlin.[4]

Murnau was not the only one on the Fox lot who was impressed with Ford's newest round of films. In May of 1927 Winnie Sheehan cabled Ford from an exhibitor's convention, "MOTHER MACHREE SCREENED AND PROCLAIMED A KNOCKOUT MANAGERS VERY ENTHUSIASTIC VOTED YOUR BEST WORK THEY EXPECT A FINE LOVE STORY AND GREAT DRAMA OUT OF HANGMANS HOUSE." They got what they expected.[5]

Hangman's House (1928) is another dark, atmospheric drama about an Irish soldier who returns to his home in County Wicklow to avenge a local's wronging of his sister that led to her suicide. The tale of lust, revenge, noble self-sacrifice and the triumph of love, set atop the powder keg of Irish politics, was again familiar turf for Ford but definitely more European than his rote, over-lit and widely played farcical films of the previous two years. With its grim castles, foggy nights and candles glowing through mullioned windows, *Hangman's House* not only followed dutifully in the wake of the German expressionists but appears to be the stylistic elder brother of Universal's horror films of the 1930s and the work of Tod Browning (*Dracula*) and James Whale (the director of *Frankenstein* and himself a European import and devotee of the expressionists). It is also notable for the first on-screen appearance of a twenty-one year-old Duke Wayne, overplaying to the back seats as an overenthusiastic spectator at a horse race who in his excitement busts down a picket fence.

The star of *Hangman's House*, Victor McLaglen, was a massive mountain of a man who was destined to become one of the most beloved and instantly recognizable members of the Ford Stock Company. Born in 1886 in Tunbridge Wells, England, McLaglen found being the son of an Anglican bishop a bit too starchy for his wandering blood and at fourteen ran away to join the British Army's Life Guards. Like the young Frank Ford during the Spanish-American War, McLaglen was sent home when his superiors discovered the lad was actually a wee laddie. From there, McLaglen set off on a series of adventures and exploits that seemed impossible for one man to live in one life.

Still in his teens, McLaglen ran off to Canada and became a boxer, wrestler and circus performer, going from an "I'll wrestle any man in the house" amateur to a boxing professional. In the early 1920s he began acting in British silent films.

When McLaglen moved to the States, his burly build and granite noggin tailor-made him for roles as a two-fisted, no-nonsense tough guy. Or, in the contemporary parlance of casting directors, a "galoot." His first film for Ford, *The Fighting Heart* (1925), saw McLaglen playing second fiddle to star George O'Brien. Like O'Brien, McLaglen's commanding presence and fine build, combined with his astounding adventures throughout the world in both war and peace, made him Ford's kind of guy. Three years later, McLaglen was elevated from plugugly to the role of the strong, silent Soldier of the Queen; a sort of Harry Carey in khaki and puttees. With the coming of sound, McLaglen's barrack-room baritone made him the perfect raw material for Ford to fashion into one of the most brilliant and expansive characters in cinematic history. In Ford's hands, the British and Church of England McLaglen was transformed into the quintessential Catholic Irishman: donnybrooking while invoking the Virgin and the saints, swilling enough whiskey to float County Cork and waxing lyrical about his exploits in the Old Country.

Unlike his personal relationships, which could be byzantine and cruelly convoluted, Ford had a purpose for bullying an actor during actual production. Ford's *modus operandi*, now that he was fully in command of his films and the giver rather than the receiver, conflated genuine impatience and irritability with a clever psychological ploy that sought out an actor's weaknesses and turned them into strengths. Ford pushed McLaglen's innately sweet and gentle disposition to the breaking point with taunts, humiliations and the occasional practical joke. The result, however, of releasing oceans of pent-up frustration and rage was a mother lode of pure cinematic gold. McLaglen's role as a brawny, volcanic sergeant major with the heart of a kitten and a weakness for children and dogs was so masterfully played that it worked magnificently, even in non-Ford films such as George Stevens' action-comedy classic, *Gunga Din* (1939).

Like all Ford's victims who toughed out the abuse long enough, McLaglen understood that the cruelty and brickbats were used to bring out a personal best and actually masked deep affection and genuine respect. In fact, McLaglen would always refer to the director as "Jack darling," and Ford always found parts in his films for the actor long after the other studios lost interest. The aging actor would also be accorded the singular and unprecedented honor of being allowed to snooze in his chair on the set in between takes.[6]

———————

"It's a freak!" exclaims the indifferent and skeptical silent film director about Warner Brothers' first talking picture, *The Jazz Singer,* in the 1952 movie *Singin' In The Rain.* However, the astounding success of the 1927 Al Jolson vehicle, with its Vitaphone sound-to-disc system, in effect heralded the end of the silent era. With the public clamoring for more all-talking (soon to include all-singing and all-dancing) movies, the major studios began the long, arduous and monumentally expensive process of building massive sound stages and acquiring both sound equipment and the stars who could speak into them without sounding like Mickey Mouse. The transition from silent to talkies was swift and merciless and the blitzkrieg warfare waged against the ruling Hollywood cavalcade of stars resulted in a long and dreadful casualty list. For every Greta Garbo, Ronald Colman and Lionel Barrymore who successfully made the transition, there were fifty John Gilberts, Marie Prevosts and Vilma Bankys whose florid declamations, Brooklyn screeches or unintelligible Carpathian accents simply didn't match the mystery of their silvery silent images.

Fox was obliged to jump on the sound wagon and with its army of directors marched onto the sound stages and began mastering the revolutionary new medium. Jack Ford fell into line with the rest and in 1928, using Fox's own sound system called Movietone, made his first sound feature called *Napoleon's Barber.* The film is a pleasant, lark-filled short about a barber (Frank Reicher) who tells a client (Otto Matiesen) what he would do to Napoleon if only he got him in his chair with a razor at his neck. Little does he know that the client is the Little Corporal himself. As always, Ford filmed *Napoleon's Barber* in his own way and own pace, throwing conventional standards to the four winds and ignoring what technicians said he could or could not do. He unknowingly added a footnote to film history when, despite the protestation of his soundman, he filmed an outdoor scene of Napoleon's carriage trundling over a bridge. The shot came out perfectly and Ford is credited with being the first director to employ sound outside a sound stage. However, as Tag Gallagher pointed out in his Ford biography, it was the first time exterior sound was used in a dramatic film. Fox Movietone News had already successfully recorded exterior sound at sports events a year earlier.[7]

Hollywood, like nations, prefers revolutions one at a time, and having adjusted to the seismic rupture caused by the advent of sound reeled from yet another blow with more grim universal repercussions. The stock market crash in October 1929 may have begun on Wall Street but by the time erstwhile millionaires began jumping from windows and bank presidents fell into free soup and bread lines, the effects of the Great Depression were felt in every American home and business. Having just gone to the exorbitant expense of building sound stages the size of zeppelin hangars, the studios now had to tighten their belts, consolidate talent and only release product that was guaranteed a profitable return. As film historian Joe Adamson pointed out, the first knee jerk reaction of the studio executives was to come in with a big broom and fire most of their top directors. However, when they realized that the public needed movies more and more as an antidote to the soul-numbing effects of the economic meltdown, they turned around and rehired them again.[8]

The Black Watch was based on the book *King of the Khyber Rifles*, written in 1916 by British soldier-adventurer Talbot Mundy. The title was changed to that of the famed Scottish regiment but the story basically remains the same. A captain of the Watch, Donald King (McLaglen) is pulled from the trenches of World War I Europe and sent to India to deal with troublesome tribesmen fomenting rebellion to the crown along the Northwest frontier. Although the movie is stripped of the theosophic and mystical elements favored by Mundy, it does retain the services of Myrna Loy as the requisitely exotic love goddess who seduces McLaglen and Mitchell Lewis as the straight-from-Central Casting rebel heavy, Mohammed Khan.

Fox had originally slated *Black Watch* as a silent but scuttled the plans when the sound craze became too great to ignore. The result is a fine looking but extraordinarily self-conscious film with actors nervously pacing and modulating their voices like community playhouse amateurs on opening night. Had it been filmed as a silent, *The Black Watch* may have been a more regal and self-confident film. Like *Four Sons*, Ford's attention to the spit-and-polish traditions of the military is evident down to the smallest detail of every subaltern's uniform and tartan trouser. One does not have to imagine the skirl of the bagpipes; they can actually be heard. Therein lies the problem. Had it been shot as a silent, Ford's economy of emotion and refusal to telegraph every thought and idea would have made for a more pervasive—and persuasive—air of mood and mystery. As it is, the good efforts of all concerned is cast to the Punjabi winds by the awkward attempts to master the newfangled sound medium. The whole movie is hampered by too many pauses, too much sound-awareness, too obvious positioning of actors within range of microphones so that they can deliver stilted and tongue-heavy dialogue. Given the uneven results of Ford's first all-talking film, it would appear that sound was not his métier and forte. However, like Michelangelo and fresco painting, he would soon make it his own.

Ford followed *The Black Watch* with two films that evidenced his growing passion for the sea, the navy and all things nautical. The first was *Salute* (1929), another oft-told tale of the fresh-faced cadet who enters Annapolis and gets the commission, the respect and the girl by the time the curtain drops. Aside from the strength of being filmed on location and released as an all-talking film, *Salute* is notable as yet another cinematic manifestation of Ford's unrealized boyhood dream of entering the U.S. Naval Academy. It was also during this time that Ford gave the first speaking role to young Duke Wayne along with a friend who would come to form the third in the triumvirate of their lifelong friendship.

Wardell Bond was a Nebraska-born, 6'2", 195 lb. lineman from the University of Southern California (USC) who, along with Duke and most of the thundering herd, was finding summer jobs doing prop and extra work at Fox. While rooming with Ford at Annapolis, Bond became good friends with the director and soon found steady work that swelled into a reputation as one of the most dependable and beloved character actors in movies (and later television) until his death in 1960. While Ward Bond found a secure niche as the grumpy marshal, crusty non-com, cop and sidekick in Ford's films as well as some of the biggest films of Hollywood's Golden Age (including *It Happened One Night, Gone With the Wind, The Maltese Falcon* and *Sergeant York*) he tended to see himself as a thespian of great stature, depth and range. This was much too perfect a scenario for Ford. He and Wayne spent countless hours trying to devise ways to let the air out of the charmingly pompous Bond. The resulting hazing and practical jokes Ford and Duke pulled on Bond, both on-set and during their infamous booze cruises to Mexico and Hawaii, became the stuff of legend and were told again and again over many a poker game and campfire for years to come. Ford's perverse delight in humiliating others could at times be brutal but at other times downright adolescent but admittedly funny. One such case was Bond's ample posterior, which Ford went to great pains to film at its most frame-filling angle. In *The Searchers* (1956) Ford offers several vistas of Bond's behind in his wonderful turn as the earthy Rev. Capt. Samuel Clayton. It becomes something of a running joke at the end, culminating in an unforgettable scene of Bond being attended to with dropped trousers after the big battle in which he is wounded by the saber of a dimwitted young lieutenant.

In 1931, about the same time Ford had his falling out with George O'Brien after the Philippine cruise debacle, he then severed diplomatic ties with young Duke Wayne. The reason for the banishment is not clear (even John Wayne in later years remained baffled by it) but apparently it had something to do with Wayne's accepting the starring role in the ill-fated *The Big Trail*. Even though Ford had recommended Wayne to director Raoul Walsh for the lead role, he felt outflanked and betrayed by the young man who heretofore had looked at Ford as his hero, mentor and surrogate father. Like his humor, there was a peevish, school-girlish quality to Ford in his intimate relationships and when he felt left out or replaced as the center of attention his revenge was swift and brutal. Following his usual pattern of behavior, the phone went silent, looks and greetings went unreturned and he did not speak with Duke for several long and, for the younger man, painfully bewildering years.

A year after the made-by-the-manual *Salute*, Ford went down to the sea again with *Men Without Women* (1930), a submarine adventure filmed on Catalina Island off the California coast. Like his previous naval film, Ford's 1930 opus is undistinguished in itself but plays a key role when inserted into a larger mosaic of the director's life. While it would be another nine years before Ford would find his voice again as a Western director, during the intervening years, the sea would be Ford's chosen setting, the place where he was most comfortable as an artist and a man. Between 1929 and 1939 Ford would make five films dealing exclusively with the sea: *Salute, Men Without Women, The Seas Beneath, Hurricane* and *Submarine Patrol*. Four of these would focus primarily on the navy and the traditions, rituals and challenges that shaped its officers and swab jockeys in both war and peace.

1931 was also a seminal year for Ford in terms of more temporal and mortal associations. In his personal and professional life, Ford liked many people, barely tolerated even more and enjoyed taking the mickey out of almost everyone, especially the pompous and egotistical (i.e. Ward Bond). Among the hosts of actors he knew and worked with, there were very few he genuinely admired, one being a young stage actor he met in New York in 1930. Although they would make just a few movies together, they would maintain a lifelong friendship and in many ways come to mirror each other both in their craft and in their lives. Spencer Bonaventure Tracy was performing in *The Last Mile*, a grim prison drama for which he was receiving great acclaim on Broadway. After a performance, Ford met the thirty-year-old actor backstage and, after an all-night drinking bout at the Lamb's Club, he talked Tracy into coming to Hollywood to take the lead role in *Up The River*, a prison comedy he was just about to start casting and shooting.[9]

The public, shaken out of economic complacency by the Depression and reduced to begging crusts from the government, was now ready for an angry, drifting Everyman who could reflect their rage and despair coupled with an underlying integrity that forced him to do the right thing. Thus the advent of a new brand of antihero that emerged in the 1930s and would include Tracy, Paul Muni, Humphrey Bogart and James Cagney. Bogart, Tracy's young co-star in *Up The River*, at the time was still playing juvenile lovers and was several years from his defining persona as a cynical drifter and tough guy that would define his reign at Warner Brothers in the 1940s.

Ford and Tracy would come to form part of the large and legendary "Irish Mafia" in Hollywood that would include actors Pat O'Brien, Cagney, Frank McHugh, James Dunn, Errol Flynn (although he was born in Tasmania), Bing Crosby and directors John Huston and Leo McCarey. Aside from their Irishness and Catholicism, however, the strongest bonding tie between the actor and director was their alcoholism. Both men were demon-ridden, dark-centered souls who suffered from a damnable Irish curse. Basically, not that they drank a lot but what they did could send them hurling over the edge of the abyss. Ford could get nasty when in his cups and was not above throwing an insult, or even a punch, at a friend who got in his crosshairs. He was basically a sloppy, sentimental drunk who, when buzzed on wine or beer, could be funny, playful and convivial before moving on to a weepy, self-pitying state of feeling lonely and unloved. When he moved to whiskey, Ford would completely unravel and become an incoherent, drooling and often incontinent train wreck of a human being. He did, however, have the good sense to unravel in the privacy of his room or den or on his boat in the company of close and solicitous friends.[10]

Despite the old, catchall explanation called Catholic guilt, Ford's faith played a pivotal role in both moderating and helping him come to grips with his self-destructive alcoholism. Tracy, the product of a cold, loveless household and stern military school education, always saw himself as a failed Catholic whose litany of sins and failings could never allow him to clear the high moral bar set for him by his church. Ford, on the other hand, probably due to the warm nurturing of his parents and siblings, took great solace in his faith and instead of judgment and condemnation always saw in Catholicism the more embraceable dogmas of conversion and forgiveness. If Tracy saw God as a cold, distant headsman with a black mask, Ford saw Him as an Irishman with a flowing white mustache who looked like his Daddo. Many times, following a particularly brutal bender, Ford would take the pledge in the presence of his parish priest never to touch the stuff again. The fact that all parties knew the pledge would be violated and nullified by the time the ink dried gave a wink-and-nod touch to the otherwise solemn proceedings.[11]

Ford would suffer the slings and arrows of the many mediocre films he made and even several bona fide bombs, but he made one film that comes honestly under the heading of "junk." *The Brat* (1931) is an absolutely pointless endeavor that both critics and biographers alike conclude is the nadir of Ford's film career. The eponymous heroine (Sally O'Neil) is taken into upper crust New York society and an attempt is made to transform her into a marriageable lady. O'Neil, whose star sizzled briefly at M-G-M and fizzled even quicker with the arrival of talkies, plays the lead with a grating annoyance that makes clear why Ford never developed a reputation for directing love goddesses, sexpots or gamins. There is no interest or effort on the part of anyone in front of or behind the camera, especially the director, and the whole eighty-one minute mess passes like a bad case of indigestion.

More interesting was Ford's collaboration with Samuel Goldwyn in the screen adaptation of Sinclair Lewis' Pulitzer Prize winning novel, *Arrowsmith*. Goldwyn, originally a haberdasher from Poland, had come out west with his brother-in-law, Jesse Lasky, and Cecil

B. DeMille and, in helping to form what would eventually become Paramount Pictures, in effect helped to also create the Hollywood Studio System. Brilliant, savvy, thorny and monumentally impatient with directors when the clock was running on his dime, Goldwyn was an attractive prospect for any director but was neither wooed nor won with any measure of bliss.

Arrowsmith is the tale about a young, quintessentially mid-America doctor who abandons his small town practice and goes off to the jungle searching for the cures that will bring him eternal fame and prestige. In his obsessive climb to the pinnacle of medical glory, he loses his wife and a sense of his primary duty to suffering humanity in his own back yard. To pull it off, Ford needed an actor who resonated the look, feel and sound of small-town mid-America and the actor chosen was about as small-town America as the Prince of Wales. Ronald Colman (1891-1958) was a British import who, having survived the transition from silent films, had developed a reputation for being handsome, dashing, classy and possessing one of the most splendid speaking voices in the history of film. Here, however, he is totally miscast and obviously was given the lead on the basis of his star power on the Goldwyn lot and around town. Despite the stellar roster of talent in front (Colman, Helen Hayes as his wife) and behind the camera, including screenwriter Sidney Howard, cinematographer Ray June, composer Alfred Newman and art director Richard Day (who would go on to build Ford's glorious Welsh mining village in *How Green Was My Valley*) the resulting film is good but lacks a consistent mood and texture. Broadly played, comic relief figures (a dicey leitmotif that would lend either sparkle or annoyance to Ford's films throughout his career) are inserted incongruously into serious, seminal moments. Another problem is the texture, in that evocative, expressionist shots filmed in deep shadow are followed by brightly lit, unimaginative set ups that look as though they were lifted from an entirely different film. Regardless, *Arrowsmith* was a financial success and was well received by both the public and critics. For Ford, the film represented a personal and professional train wreck and one of the few times during Ford's glory years that alcohol came between him and his job. The story of a man so obsessed with his work that it leads to the neglect of his wife and all those around him was, perhaps, too close to the bone and too Conradian a journey into a heart of darkness for Ford to handle. Whatever the reason, Ford again lost interest halfway through the film, abandoned his post and went off on a bender. It was one thing to do so while shooting a formula picture for Fox but to do so while working for a powerful, exacting, bean counter of a martinet like Sam Goldwyn was another. Ford was fired by the Goldwyn Corporation for breach of contract and when Fox was hit with a $4,100 bill to repay the loan-out fee, he was fired by Winnie Sheehan from the Fox Corporation as well.[12]

Ford was chastened and humbled by the humiliating termination from two major film studios at one time, especially his home lot, but he was still a hot and desirable commodity around town and he went off, cap in hand, knocking on doors. In 1932, he briefly went back to Uncle Carl's fold at Universal Studios and did *Air Mail*, a gritty, fast-paced ode to the flyboys who braved the tumult in the skies during the early days of airborne mail transport. The film is a standout primarily for the creative association Ford forged with its writer, Lt. Cmdr. Frank "Spig" Wead, a genuine war hero who, together with James Doolittle and General Billy Mitchell, helped advance the theory and execution of aviation in modern warfare. Paralyzed in a freak domestic accident, Wead turned to screenplay and book writing while continuing to offer his boundless talents and energies to the U.S. Navy. Aside from *Air Mail*, Wead would write the screenplays for *Test Pilot* (for which he would be nominated for an Academy Award) and *They Were Expendable*, Ford's first Hollywood film after returning home from active duty in World War II. Ford's penchant for real heroes and hard-drinking he men (being a crackerjack poker player didn't hurt) once again insured that he and Spig would become fast friends. He would eventually immortalize the aviator-writer in his overlooked and underappreciated 1957 biopic *The Wings of Eagles*, that starred John Wayne as Spig and Maureen O'Hara as his wife.

In 1933, a penitent and contrite Ford returned to Fox, on the condition that he accept a $10,000 per picture pay cut, to make one of his most astounding and unusual films. *Pilgrimage* tells the story of a bitter, hateful and controlling Arkansas mother named Hannah Jessop (Henrietta Crossman), who consigns her only son to military service and death to keep him from marrying and leaving the orbit of her icy and loveless dominance. Later, as a Gold Star Mother, Hannah travels to France with similarly bereaved mothers (a wide sampling of ethnic and religious types to reinforce the universality of suffering without discrimination) to lay flowers on a cenotaph raised in the honor of their dead sons. After preventing the suicide of a young soldier in whom she sees the shadow of her dead son, and experiencing the joie de vivre of a village of simple peasants, Hannah slowly recovers her humanity and comes to see the enormity of her crimes both against her son and her own soul. What makes *Pilgrimage* so arresting is that up till and after it, Ford had never violated his own code of always sanctifying Eternal Motherhood and here presents a maternal figure who is quite simply a vile monster. Hannah Jessop as played by the amazing Henrietta Crossman is without sentiment and does not change her erring ways through a formulaic conversion. Like a character from a Flannery O'Connor story, Hannah is transformed through grace, which as the great author proves, can come through the dirtiest and most unexpected channels. Crossman's character is ossified in hate, frozen in an isolated hell and her journey in rejoining the human race is measured, believable and wondrous to behold. Once again, Ford's Catholic soul, dovetailing the history of salvation with the drama of the ages, is patently bared.

Will Rogers (1879-1935) was one of the most adored, respected and quoted men of Ford's time and enjoyed a national celebrity that is, like currency of ancient times, difficult for contemporary Americans to find a parallel. Before Will Rogers there was Mark Twain, after him the closest shadow of a successor would most likely be Garrison Keillor. Rogers, a quarter Cherokee and genuine ranch hand from Oklahoma found early fame in vaudeville and as a joke-tossing, trick roper in the Ziegfeld Follies around the turn of the century. His wry, velvety and cynical on-stage humor transferred well to both radio and the silent movies and by the advent of sound, Rogers had emerged as America's greatest living humorist and political satirists.

Rogers' homespun humor and cracker-barrel philosophy was tailor made to Ford's visual American poetics and in 1933 the Maine Dr. Boswell finally met his Oklahoma Samuel Johnson. *Doctor Bull* was the first of three films Ford made with Rogers during one of the high-water periods of both of their lives. It was a relationship both professional and personal that would last until Rogers' death in 1935 in an Alaskan airplane crash along with aviator Wiley Post.

In *Doctor Bull, Judge Priest* (1934) and *Steamboat Round the Bend* (1935), Ford and Rogers created the quintessential American man of authority who slyly yet compassionately reveals the best and worst in himself and others. The character created by the actor and director is, in effect, a not so distant mirror of the man who as America's very own Moses reigns forever as the prophet and lawgiver of the Republic: Abraham Lincoln. Ford always used Lincoln as a ghostly image or historical bridge but in these three films, Dr. George Bull, Judge Billy Priest and Dr. John Pearly concretize not so much the physical Lincoln as his mystical virtues that Ford saw every American possessing through their birthright. Like Lincoln, Rogers' characters are wise, compassionate, intolerant of injustice but always dripping with a sad sense of isolation from the community; one eye on the distant past and the other on a possibly but not probably brighter future.

In *Judge Priest*, one of Fox's top grossing films of 1934, Ford tackles the problem of racism, which at the time was infecting the nation like a virus and exploding throughout the South in a horrendous lynching epidemic. Ford was very tetchy on the subject of how he presented Blacks in his films and would angrily rebut charges that he simply toed the prevalent line of stereotypical images. Oddly, the two brilliant actors who personified the main stereotypes of the age, the bug-eyed, shuffled-footed dimwit and the jovial, subservient domestic, figure prominently in *Judge Priest*: Stepin Fetchit and Hattie McDaniel.

Both Fetchit and McDaniel suffered horrendous and humiliating discriminations imposed on them by outright segregationist laws in the South and more subtle ones in the film industry. Both endured the protests of the NAACP for what was seen as perpetuating mythical stereotypes and not calling on studios to expand and normalize their portrayals of Blacks on screen. They were, however, consummate professionals and intelligent, multifaceted actors who, in their own way, broke down barriers and paved the way for Sidney Poitier, Harry Belafonte and Dorothy Dandridge in the next decades. Fetchit was the first Black actor to receive screen credit and become a millionaire and McDaniel would be the first Black actor to win an Academy Award (for the role of Mammy in *Gone With the Wind.*)

In an interview with French writer/director Bertrand Tavernier in 1966, Ford declared that he never harbored a racist sentiment nor did he pander to southern segregationist laws simply to sell tickets. "I am a Northerner," he said. "I hate segregation and I gave jobs to hundreds of Negroes at the same salary the whites were paid. Me, a racist? My best friends are black."[13]

The mid 1930s saw other changes in Ford's life: losses, gains and watersheds that would in some way or another affect the wending course of his life and art. As he inches his way toward middle age, it was inevitable that he would come to part with loved ones. Abby, Ford's beloved mother and protean symbol of eternal maternity who would factor into so many of his films in so many guises, died in Maine in 1933. Daddo survived a mere three years before dying suddenly in 1936. A photograph of Ford, taken several years before Abby's death on one of his frequent and dutiful visits home to Maine, neatly sums up their relationship. More painterly than photographic, the perfectly composed shot shows Ford, pipe in hand, kneeling at Abby's feet while the old white-haired woman in black satin dress and white lace shawl, adjusts a rose in his lapel. If it was a painting from the previous century, it could very well have been called, "Leaving for the New World" or "Off to War," for the silent, intense bond between the two patently speaks both farewell and a love stronger than the fragile, shifting ground of temporal existence.

On the gain side, Ford formed yet another relationship with yet another Promethean Hollywood he man to whom he seemed to gravitate with an almost magnetic force. He would also come to figure prominently in the future as Ford's production partner in his independent days. Like George O'Brien, Vic McLaglen and Spig Wead, Merian Cooper (1893-1973) was a colorful, dashing figure whose life adventures were formed primarily in the crucible of war. The Florida-born Cooper was an ace pilot in World War I, surviving plane crashes and internment in a German POW camp. After the Great War, Cooper flew again, this time for Poland in the famed Kosciusko Brigade in its war against Soviet aggression, a cause which the ultra-conservative Cooper remained committed to his entire life. Shot down, captured and interned again, Cooper escaped a death sentence and, after regaining friendly turf, wrote his memoirs and was decorated for bravery by Marshal Piłsudski of Poland. Cooper returned to the States where he helped form Pan-American Airlines before moving on to Hollywood, where he took over as head of production for RKO Studios in 1933. Fresh at the helm of the studio, Cooper collaborated with Ernest B. Schoedsack on his first and most enduring classic, *King Kong* (1933) and then began casting about for more beefy, two-fisted action-melodramas that suited his masculine tastes.

While Cooper was head of production, Ford made two films at RKO, one an interesting desert war drama and the other his first truly artistic and critical blockbuster. The first, *The Lost Patrol* (1934) was an all-male endeavor combining Ford's earlier naval nail-biters (*Men Without Women, The Seas Beneath*) with the sure-fire concept of a disparate group thrown together for survival and soul-bearing.

The Lost Patrol concerns eleven British soldiers lost in the Mesopotamian desert who are taken out one by one by invisible Arab snipers with the inevitable wrap up of the last-man-standing-before–the-relief-column-arrives. Victor McLaglen, in the lead role of the sergeant, is very comfortable in his pith helmet and khakis, as is the able supporting cast that included Reginald Denny, Wallace Ford and Alan Hale. The only participants who seem out of place are actually two artists who were two of the industry's most reliable and seasoned campaign-ers. The first is Boris Karloff who, as the soldier gone native, rants and grimaces in a completely over the top performance in which the otherwise fine actor comes off more as a demented street person than a prophetic harbinger of doom. The other is Max Steiner, the brilliant and prolific composer who, as Warner Brothers' music czar for decades, helped define the texture and mood of soundtracks during Hollywood's golden age (*Gone With the Wind, Casablanca, Sergeant York, Treasure of the Sierra Madre* and Ford's *The Searchers*). What Karloff does visually in *The Lost Patrol,* Steiner does aurally and his bizarre, mournful choral pieces that attempt to approximate lost, howling souls, surely stand as some of the strangest scores from one of the industry's musical giants.

Liam O'Flaherty's 1925 novel, *The Informer,* was optioned by Ford in 1933 and was bicycled around the studios before getting the green light from Cooper at RKO. According to Ford, Joseph P. Kennedy, millionaire, future Ambassador to the Court of St. James and father of the future president, had a controlling interest in RKO and together with the top brass wanted Ford to do a Western. When Ford demurred and instead suggested a story about the Irish rebellion (which he prom-ised to bring in at bargain rate of $200,000) Kennedy signed off on the project and then left the picture business to become F.D.R.'s first chairman of the Securities and Exchange Commission. Although it had been filmed before as an English production in 1929, it was Ford who inspired his Gaelic breath into the project and turned it into one of the most celebrated and admired "art films" of the decade. For Ford, the tale of the IRA slime bag Gypo Nolan—who sells out his comrade to the British in exchange for twenty pounds and a passage to America with his streetwalker girlfriend—went to the heart of his still burning sense of Irish nationalism. Since his 1921 trip to Ireland during the Civil War Ford, remained an inveterate rebel at heart, reading deeply all the Irish Revivalists and trying to find his voice and identity in the noble cause of bleeding Ireland.[14]

Artistically, his studious apprenticeship at the altar of Murnau and expressionism took Ford intellectually to higher realms of understanding but up till this point found no solid and practical application in his work. There are splashes here and there in *Four Sons* and the Will Rogers' films but in *The Informer*, rife with political intrigue, guilt, biblical allegories, Catholic symbolism, murder and redemption all played out against a misty Dublin background, the man and the art finally met.

O'Flaherty was a distant cousin of the Feeneys from the west country of Ireland but only became acquainted with Ford when he came to Hollywood to find screenwriting work in 1932. Ford's criterion for instant male bonding had always been fairly simple and could be reduced to three categories: the military, machismo and alcohol. O'Flaherty, having served with the Irish Guards on the Western Front in World War I, knocked around Dublin as a Socialist swell during the Troubles and with a reputation for enjoying his whiskey, filled all three categories and found himself neatly in the saddle as a Ford *compañero*.

Ford's other wingman on *The Informer*, and the generally unseen creative force behind the camera, was the screenwriter Dudley Nichols. Nichols, an urbane, pipe-smoking intellectual and former frat boy from the Mid-west, fancied himself an Olympian man of letters temporarily enduring Hollywood a la Hemingway, Faulkner and Fitzgerald until he found the time to return to "serious" writing in his oak-paneled library. Nichols first worked with Ford when he scripted *Men Without Women* in 1931 and would be the defining wordsmith on Ford's most honored and accomplished films of the 1930s and 1940s including *Judge Priest, Steamboat Round the Bend, The Informer, The Hurricane, Stagecoach* and *The Long Voyage Home*. Nichols' liberal bent also influenced Ford as much as O'Flaherty and despite their intense working relationship and off set camaraderie, the two men did maintain a sort of emotional wariness about the other. Ford, forever disdainful of snobbish *poseurs*, was always suspicious of Nichols' haughty and cerebral affectations, while Nichols refused to buy Ford's transparent attempts to put on the persona of the crusty, anti-intellectual workingman.[15]

Nichols avoided linear exposition in his scripts as though they contained the plague and instead infused his work with a dearth of cryptic dialogue redolent of allegory, symbolism and an oblique mysticism that fit the expressionist creed like a glove. What endeared *The Informer* to the critics was that even though expressionism had been insinuated into American film for a decade, never before had it been so tightly condensed in overflowing measures and so artfully accomplished in every scene. Victor McLaglen's Gypo Nolan (the performance garnered him an Academy Award for Best Actor) is the quintessential Hairy Ape, a cut-rate Judas. The foggy, dark-encrusted Dublin he maunders about is a reflection of the claustrophobic, dank and twilit darkness in his soul. Everywhere Gypo turns in his attempt to flee like Jonah across the water, he runs headlong into some scriptural character reminding him of the inescapable God and His unrelenting hound at his heels. From the blind man, the streetwalker, the blood money (thirty pieces of silver becomes twenty pounds) and the suffering *stabat mater* at the foot of the Cross, *The Informer* unleashes the full fury of expressionism and Catholic imagery that collide head on like two oceans.

There are problems with *The Informer*, and they lie in its vaunted novelty and the way the critics tripped over each other to raise hosannas in its honor. Novelty is by no means transcendence, and it tends to wear off very quickly as opposed to the subtle universality Ford would achieve in his future works. The tight, airless and dark mood of *The Informer*, combined with a complete absence of the humor that elevated even the most mundane of Ford's work, ultimately chokes and pummels the film into a stilted, awkward loftiness and out of the category of his enduring classics. In terms of popular success, *The Informer* snatched cinematic victory from the jaws of financial death. Ford said in a 1936 interview, "As for *The Informer*, Hollywood didn't even know we made it. The newspaper boys around the country pounded away on it and started the public going to see it. They're the ones who made it a financial success."[16]

The word-of-mouth campaign (although, contrary to Ford's embellishments, more than newsboys were responsible) worked and not only did Ford see himself elevated to the pantheon of great American film directors but he also took home his first Oscar for Best Director. If that were not enough, he won the New York Film Critics Award for Best

Director (often perceived in the industry as more prestigious than an Oscar) as well as awards from Belgium, Italy, Holland, Japan and induction as an *Officier* into the l'Academie Française. In a little over two decades, Jack Feeney of Portland had gone from being a non-entity gofer to an artist considered by many to be one of the greatest living directors on any continent.[17]

Ford's unchallenged ranking as one of Hollywood's finest paid dividends that went far beyond gold Art Deco statues and parchment citations from the French Academy. Ford's crowning personal achievement, something that would remain his most prized material possession for over three decades, was the acquisition of his yacht *Araner*. Ford purchased the 110-foot ketch for $30,000 in 1934 and named her in honor of the Irish islands he still convinced himself were his mother's birthplace. Ford was no gentleman sailor whose yacht was merely for show and remained perpetually tethered to the pier. Ford took his new acquisition seriously and, at an expense that fast surpassed his initial cash outlay, refitted *Araner*, literally, from stem to stern. From a new mast, hull, an overhaul of the diesel engines and a refurbishing of the bedrooms, dining room and fireplaces, Ford slowly turned her into a sleek, shiny nautical dream.

Jack and Mary's modest but charming house on Odin Street was, aside from Jack's den with its pipes, bar, saddles, rifles, poker table and odoriferous masculinity, Mary's realm. It was the place where they ate, slept, hung their hats and reared Patrick and Barbara; a sort of corporate entity where Jack held the mortgage but remained a quarter owner. *Araner* was, and remained for thirty years, not so much a yacht as a parallel universe into which Jack became absorbed heart and soul almost every non-working hour of his life. On his ship's teak decks, Ford finally and totally reigned supreme as master and commander; one part Lord Nelson, one part Long John Silver and one part Captain Ahab.[18]

The *Araner* served as a release mechanism, nonpareil, from all the scalding steam generated by the pressures of Ford's profession. The ship became something of a calendar by which one could mark the progress of one of Jack's films. Pre-production, the laborious, exacting process of adapting stories, meticulously writing, re-writing and editing them, would generally take place in the cabins and on deck with Ford collaborating with the likes of Dudley Nichols, Philip Dunne, Liam O'Flaherty and Frank Nugent. Production schedule was generally breakneck and too crowded to allow for getaways but the end of filming always meant that Ford would leave post-production to the studio and weigh anchor as soon as possible.

There were the genteel cruises to the Hawaiian Islands with Mary, complete with blue blazers, white linen trousers and sunset dinners served in the dining room by a full-time staff. Pat, Barbara and their friends would sail the *Araner* while on vacation and, in time, grandchildren Tim and Dan (Pat's sons) would noisily scramble around the masts or splash in the water. However, when Mary and the kids were put ashore and the linen and fine silver stored away, the *Araner* served its true purpose and became the wildest floating bar, poker game and boys' only clubhouse on the Pacific.

Ford's own contribution to the canon of Hollywood's boozy bad boys was the seagoing club he grandly (and to anyone with the sense God gave geese) ironically called the Young Men's Purity, Total Abstinence and Yachting Association. Since it served merely as a front and excuse for the copious consumption of grain alcohol, the association existed as a formal and dues-paying organization only in the minds behind the bleary eyes of its member roster, which would include Frank Morgan, Preston Foster, Fox producer Gene Markey, Dudley Nichols, John Wayne, Henry Fonda and Ward Bond.

With the *Araner* came the unfettered freedom to take the locker room camaraderie to the high seas and act like college students during rush week. Eventually, the cynical formalities of house rules, dues and uniforms would slacken and the *Araner* excursions soon devolved into cruises down to the waters of Baja, Cabo San Luca and Mazatlan. They fished for marlin, played poker, ribbed Ward Bond and caroused in coastal towns with a drunken abandon that could have severed diplomatic ties with Mexico.

Existing film footage gives a small glimpse at what it must have been like on board the *Araner* during these halcyon days. A shirtless, smiling John Wayne, sun cream on his nose, fishes off the back of the ketch. Ashore in Mexico, a mariachi band of young boys whose instruments are bigger than they, serenade Ford and Wayne as they suck back beers at a seaside bar. Wayne, hamming it up for the camera, welcomes Bond aboard with a salute and a celebratory drink while Ford, in his skipper cap, polo shirt and pipe, watches with a benevolent smirk as though he were a scoutmaster supervising a gaggle of naughty but beloved boys.

<hr />

Ford's passion for the sea also extended past the adventurous boys' play of overgrown and bibulous Sea Scouts. In 1934, the same year that he acquired the *Araner*, Ford was commissioned a lieutenant commander in the United States Naval Reserve. In a sense, Ford's induction into the ranks of a hallowed and historic institution like the U.S. Navy would in many ways stand, even before his active involvement in the World War II, as a high-water mark of his sense of pride and self-worth. As a man and American legend, Ford invariably tends to be associated with, first, the Western film and, second, the sea. They were two mystical threads of epic and mythical magnitude that intertwined in his life and in a sense stood as the binding ties that not only explained his life but connected the surface with a reality deep in the unseen core of the man.

Even in the wake of his mature Western films of the 1940s and 1950s, Ford would casually disavow any particular affinity for the genre, always declaring his love for story and character over a particular geographic locale and historical period. Even as late as the 1960s, Ford indifferently tossed off his opinion in a filmed interview with the French journalist Andre Labarthe that *The Searchers* was, "Just a Western," when asked about his favorite films. He named the decidedly non-Western *Young Mr. Lincoln* and *The Sun Shines Bright* as his favorites. Fortunately for posterity, the gob-smacked Labarthe incredulously shouts back to Ford, "A good Western!"[19]

When it came to the sea, however, Ford unabashedly and fiercely clung to his naval persona and expanded it into not so much a profession or calling but an integral part of his very being. Along with his unchallenged rule on the deck of the *Araner*, he began peppering his already high sodium language with even saltier naval slang and actually sought out (in his roundabout fashion) every honor and trapping that went with his newly minted commission.

Like skippering his yacht, Ford took his naval commission extremely seriously and with the fervor of a young seminarian just ordained to the priesthood. For someone who disdained affected ways and arrogant posturing, Ford threw himself wholeheartedly into his newly acquired status as an officer and a gentleman. He acquired every uniform allowed his rank by navy regulations; nattily tailored blues and whites for dress and mess as well as khakis for duty. He exchanged official reports as well as breezy, chatty letters with his naval superiors with the ease of bankers lounging about the club bar after a game of golf. Ford was not only dazzled by the company of his blue-blooded band of brothers from Annapolis but he also brought his celebrity status to bear on them with equal results. Officers were invited to the studio to watch filming, meet stars and studio heads and generally experience the full Hollywood treatment. For Ford, who despite his irascibility could be a very generous man, was probably genuine in this give and take, but then again, it certainly did not hurt his reputation among his superiors.

In July of 1938, for instance, he presented the officers' mess at the Los Angeles Naval and Marine Corps Reserve Armory an oil painting of the U.S.S. *Constellation* by artist Stanley Coolson. The gift was duly acknowledged (and no doubt noted in Ford's file) in an official letter from the 11th Naval District Headquarters. Indeed, it was an honorifically busy summer for Jack. In June he received an Honorary Degree of Doctor of Fine Arts from the University of Maine, the school he claimed to have attended for a semester but whose hallowed portals he never in fact darkened. The following month he was asked by the mayor of Los Angeles to be on the welcoming committee for the arrival of President Franklin Roosevelt at the Southern Pacific railroad depot.[20]

For Ford, however, it was not all dress blues and officers' mess etiquette, and his work for the navy had a depth and *gravitas* that dovetailed with a more serious world situation fomenting further west across the Pacific. The expansionist policies of Imperial Japan in the 1930s was rapid, serious and poised on a collision course with the European powers who had their own colonial interests in the Far East. Already involved in a horrific and genocidal war in China, Japan then targeted the petroleum-rich fields of the Dutch East Indies and the natural resources found in the myriad British possessions throughout the Pacific. Faced with an embargo and the attending economic and political fallout should they lose the oil fueling their battleships, tanks and planes, the Imperial High Command had no choice but to plan for an all-out war against the Western powers siphoning off the resources they themselves desperately needed.

While to most Americans the war mongering of the Empire of the Sun was about as relevant and real as the events on the dark side of the moon, to Ford and his superiors in the U.S. Navy it was a very real threat and closer than the average American knew. Beginning in the late 1930s, Ford submitted numerous reports to naval intelligence while on his supposedly carefree booze cruises to Mexico. While Fonda, Wayne and Bond were hellin' up the coastal bars, Ford was observing the recurring presence of Japanese "tourists" and "fishermen," individually or in groups, who photographed and made copious notes on the waters and terrain of the lower Baja region. With their aristocratic bearing and tailored suits it became increasingly clear to Ford that these gentlemen were in fact agents of the Imperial Staff reconnoitering for a possible invasion of North America.

In a memo dated December 1939, Ford reported to Captain Elias Zacharias some "impressions" related to his observations of the Japanese visitors in the Mexican ports. "Cannot understand where these men could buy their liberty clothes. They were better dressed than the average American office clerk…. It is my belief that the crews and officers of this shrimp fleet belong to the Imperial Navy or reserve." In the same memo he makes a more thorough (and ominous) assessment of the Japanese "fishermen" and their intent. "It is plausible that these men know every Bay, Cove and Inlet in the Gulf of California, a Bay which is so full of islands, and so close to our Arizona borderline they constitute a real menace. Although I am not a trained Intelligence Officer, still my profession is to observe and make distinctions. I will stake my professional reputation that these young men are not professional fishermen."[21]

These impressions, coming exactly two years before America's entrance into the war, are not the wild speculations of an overexcited stoolie eager for his superior's respect. On the contrary, they are clear, concise observations devoid of fluff, conjecture and superfluous information. This is patently affirmed by the letter of commendation Ford received from the Commandant of the 11th Naval District in January of 1940: "The Commandant wishes to commend you for initiative in securing the valuable information contained in your very interesting Intelligence Report of 30 December, 1939 on Lower California and the Gulf of California. Your efforts to obtain this information, voluntarily and at your own expense, are considered very commendable."[22]

It appeared that Ford had abandoned the Western genre for the better part of the decade and opted for the mainstream idiom of romance, melodrama and historical adventures. He did, however, retain enough language of the Western to understand that there was a new sheriff in town, and that man would prove to be both Ford's most contentious collaborator as well as the flint that would produce the sparks of his mature genius. Darryl Francis Zanuck (1902-1979) was a rarity among the Hollywood moguls in every respect of his life and career. Almost all the studio heads (Mayer, Goldwyn, the Warners, Laemmle, Lasky, Cohn) were Ashkenazi Jews who cut their teeth in the nickelodeon business on the streets of Brooklyn, Boston and the eastern seaboard. Zanuck, on the other hand, was a Gentile, a Swiss farm boy from Wahoo, Nebraska, who went west with his family and broke into the film business as an extra before he was a teenager and never left it. After serving in World War I (lying about his age in order to do so), Zanuck had a succession of writing stints with Universal and comedy king Mack Sennett before moving up the ladder to Warner Brothers, where he became head of production in 1931. Aside from being the brains behind Rin-Tin-Tin, the mega dog star who saved countless babies and damsels as well as the studio long into the Depression years, Zanuck was also the driving force behind Warner's evolving reputation for gritty social drama. Under his supervision, Warner Brothers parlayed the headlines of Depression-era America dealing with organized crime and the grinding effects of urban unrest into such films as *Public Enemy* and *I Was a Fugitive From a Chain Gang*. In the process, he turned actors like James Cagney and Paul Muni into antihero icons.

When Warners let Zanuck know he would always be a factotum of the studio and would never be a big chief, Zanuck left to form his own independent company, Twentieth Century Pictures. Zanuck's partners in the new company were Joseph Schenck (brother of Nicholas Schenck, president of Loews, Inc., the M-G-M parent company) and William Goetz, son-in-law of M-G-M studio head Louis B. Mayer. This strange and almost incestuous group of Hollywood bedfellows resulted in their buying out the Fox Film Corporation when it became clear that the debt-ridden studio was hit hard by the Depression and sinking fast. After the 1935 merger of the two companies, the studio would be known as Twentieth Century-Fox.

Alfred Newman's drumroll and trumpet fanfare announcing the studio's films could have, for all intents and purposes, been announcing Zanuck himself as the new studio chief. He was a diminutive force of nature, a walking Krakatoa with curly hair, mustache and a set of irregular and gapped teeth between which was permanently clenched a massive stogie. Like King Philip II of Spain, Zanuck ruled his empire from his office (and the conference room, screening room and editing room with his trusted editor Barbara McLean) from which flowed tens of thousands of memos bearing the letterhead: "Memo From Darryl F. Zanuck." Everything, from lighting and costuming to slow pacing, fast pacing or no pacing at all, was dissected, and when finished the results generally proved Zanuck correct. Given that the studio head was an irascible, dictatorial martinet who expected to always have his way, it is fair

to ask what happened when he became the boss of John Ford, an irascible, dictatorial martinet who expected to always have his way. It was,
in fact, like the head-on collision when the Pacific and Atlantic Oceans
meet at Cape Horn. What is undeniable is that, where up to this time
Jack had made good films with several achieving the financial and critical
success to be called great, under Zanuck he now made masterpieces that
are permanently enshrined in the canon of American art and culture.

Ford's first film at Fortress Zanuck was *Steamboat Round the Bend*
(1935), the last of the three films he made with the studio's top star,
Will Rogers. His next film for Zanuck was the interesting Civil War
period piece *Prisoner of Shark Island* (1936), the story of Dr. Samuel
Mudd who is sent to prison for tending to the broken leg of Lincoln's
assassin, John Wilkes Booth, only to have his sentence commuted due
to his heroic acts during a yellow fever outbreak. As scripted by Nunnally Johnson (who would script several more films for Ford, including
The Grapes of Wrath), *Shark Island* steers the drama toward Mudd's
innocence, although scholarship continues to prove his guilt due to
previous meetings with Booth as well as a long association with the vast
network of Confederate agents who operated in his native Maryland.

Mudd, played with mustachioed and wavy-haired verve by Warner
Baxter, is shown as a simple country sawbones, devoted to his practice
and his wife (played by the luminous Gloria Stuart, known to future
generations of moviegoers as the elderly Rose Dawson in James Cam-
eron's *Titanic*) who becomes an unwitting participant in the greatest
crime in American history. Caught in the frenzied national hysteria
following Lincoln's murder, Mudd is railroaded by a military tribunal
and sent to Fort Jefferson, an island in the Dry Tortugas in the shark-
infested waters seventy miles off the Florida Keys. It is America's own
Devil's Island, a moated and turreted hell where there is no hope and
from where there is no escape.

In many ways, the film not only is a stylized image of the world but
a realistic mirror of what was happening in 1936 America. The hanging of the Lincoln conspirators, shown by Ford to be an icy, vengeful
miscarriage of justice rather than due process of law, could be Ford's

visual sense of repugnance in regards to the lynching of innocent black men at the time still rampant in many southern states.

Lincoln's appearances in the film are brief, poetic and redolent of a Fordian reverence that stops dangerously short of deification. Lincoln, played by Fox's stock Great Emancipator Frank McGlyn, Sr. (he played the president to stentorian perfection the year before in the Shirley Temple vehicle, *The Littlest Rebel*) is leagues from Judge Bull's folksy, homespun Abe in *The Iron Horse* twelve years earlier. Here, Ford shows a Lincoln aged and ravaged by war, melancholy and ethereal yet still savvy enough to ask a victorious parade of Union musicians to play *Dixie* as a symbol of unity and healing between the newly re-United States. He is first seen emerging from the curtains of the White House balcony to address the crowd reveling in the streets following Lee's surrender to Grant. A model of translucent asceticism, Lincoln is draped in a shawl resembling a Jewish *tallit* that gives him the air of Moses on Mt. Sinai or Jesus transfigured on Mt. Tabor. Lincoln is last seen slumped in his chair at Ford's Theater, a lace curtain slowly pulls across the scene. As it blurs and dissolves, it literally closes the curtain on the greatest triumphant tragedy in the canon of American mythology.

<hr />

After *Shark Island*, Ford returned to RKO for *Mary of Scotland* (1936) starring a young Katharine Hepburn as the ill-fated Catholic queen who challenged the might of the Protestant Elizabeth I and paid for her intrigues with her head. The very expensive production, adapted by Dudley Nichols from Maxwell Anderson's play, would result in one of Ford's most disappointing endeavors but also one of his most intimate and personal relationships.

When Ford forced himself to speak or adopt a style and language other than his own highly developed and natural one, he generally hit below the mark or went entirely off the board. One watches *Mary of Scotland* with the feeling Ford was struggling to pull on a boot three or four sizes too small for his foot. It is private, remote and so closed in on itself that it feels as if Ford and Hepburn were creating something private and for their hearts alone. And therein, once again, lies the problem.

If *Mary of Scotland* feels like a love song Ford was crooning to the radiant young Kate Hepburn, it is because soon after beginning production they began a relationship that lasted for several years. While in the end there is speculation and no hard facts from all quarters whether the relationship was sexual or intensely platonic, what is known is that Kate, like Ford, was a tough, no-nonsense New England Yankee who sized up Ford's strengths and weaknesses and refused to be buffaloed by his tyrannical blow-hardiness and thorny façade. Hepburn called his bluff at every turn and, with his emotional defenses breached by such a strong willed character, Ford soon fell deeply in love with her. Jack was in his early forties, and while he remained devoted to Mary, her Social Register airs and country club ways, coupled with his own mercurial moods, made an emotional drift and physical rift inevitable. Kate, already manifesting her legendary intractability and pants-wearing reputation for taking on the male establishment, sailed, golfed, played tennis and generally approximated the outdoor virtues Ford up to this point found only in his closest male companions.

Like Spencer Tracy, who Kate would meet in 1941 and begin a discreet but passionate love affair with until Tracy's death in 1967, Ford was a moody, troubled and brilliant alcoholic Irishman. Both were also Catholics for whom divorce was an absolute impossibility, and it was only after Tracy's death that Hepburn would finally meet his patient, long-suffering wife Louise. Kate, on the other hand, was the quintessential "modern woman," the Bryn Mawr graduate and lifelong atheist liberal who championed the cause of women's rights, birth control and abortion. Ford, who despite his avowed leftist politics and sympathies for radical political causes, basically remained a morally conservative man for whom being boxed into the conformities of work, wife and family was simply one of the consequences that he accepted as part of his Irish, Catholic and American heritage.

According to Scott Eyman, John Wayne told his first wife, Josie, that were not Ford a practicing Catholic he would have divorced Mary in a heartbeat and married Hepburn. While there is no reason to doubt this statement, the real question is whether or not the relationship would have been tinted in the same roseate and passionate hues after marriage. The reality with so many men who have had extramarital affairs in middle age is that the passion is of the moment and not of the long run. For two driven, volcanic creative forces like Jack and Kate, one of the two would have had to surrender their careers and become the passive, stay-at-home stabilizer or the two would have simply collided and exploded like supernovas. Even while she pursued her relationship with Tracy, Hepburn continued to intensely re-define her image and career both on stage and in film, maintaining a separate residence and leaving Louise to attend to the day-to- day duties such as washing his clothes, cooking his meals and running the charities to which she was so devoted. In the end, Jack needed to go home to a wife who, despite an emotional distance, kept the house, paid the bills and provided him with the environmental stability that acted as a counterweight to the onerous business of movie making.[23]

After several years of idyllic companionship and voluminous letter-exchanging, Jack and Kate decided to go their separate ways. Kate did, however, leave her mark on Ford in ways that eventually informed his future and highly productive work. For many years, Ford's only respite and release from the stress of his work and challenges of his domestic life was drinking and sailing with his friends. Both were reactive rather than proactive, and the drinking binges were neither physically nor emotionally healthy and ultimately had a corrosive effect on his life. His bumptious boys' club on the briny deep did feed a deep need for companionship but his companions did little to elevate him professionally or hold him to a continually higher standard of excellence in his work. On the *Araner* he was always the master and commander who brooked no insolence and, like his poker nights and on-set high teas, shop talk was strictly verboten.

Hepburn's relationship with Jack, whatever its nature, in many ways limbered him up emotionally and broke the cycles of both domestic conformity and adolescent socializing that up to this point marked the cycles of his life. With Kate, Jack (whom she always referred to as Sean), loosened his tie, shed his carefully constructed image as an indifferent, working class stiff and delved for a short time into what approximated the world of the free-thinking and free-loving bohemian artist of the nineteenth century. While Kate teased Jack, romped with him, sobered him up and mothered him in turns, she also challenged him as an artist and helped him fully embrace his artistic identity instead of constantly and shamefacedly distancing himself from it.

Despite their mutual yearnings for each other, Hepburn sagely understood that, ultimately, their happiness together would have quelled the turmoil and demons that were actually the catalytic agents for his brilliance. She summed up that up in a letter to mutual friends dated 1938, on the eve of Ford's emergence as the acknowledged poet of American cinema: "Had he been happy, he never would have been the artist he is."[24]

In 1936, Ford followed *Mary of Scotland* with another film at RKO, *The Plough and the Stars,* a drama based loosely on the Sean O'Casey play about a young Irish couple caught up in the Easter Rebellion of 1916. What should have been a triumph deluxe for Ford, especially since it dealt with a subject he knew and felt so passionately to his core, somehow slipped through his fingers and drifted away, forgotten and unnoticed, in the wind.

Preston Foster (a charter member of Ford's yachting-drinking club) and Barbara Stanwyck play Jack and Nora Clitheroe, a young couple whose marriage is threatened by Jack's determination to stand with his I.R.B. comrades in the ill-fated uprising against the British in Dublin during Easter week. Although both manage passable brogues (and Stanwyck's is infinitely better than the annoying, Lucky Charms Leprechaun one she assaulted audiences with three years later in DeMille's *Union Pacific*) it quickly devolves into an interminable exercise of him brooding and her clinging and crying to no end or identifiable purpose. Like *The Informer*, there are expressionist and symbolic touches aplenty, including the street balladeer with the lilting tenor brogue and the shafts of light piercing the darkness on misty Dublin streets. However, like *Mary of Scotland*, the canvas here is too broad and the claustrophobia and tension that made the earlier film so compelling get lost in the wide open spaces and compost of events.

Ford wanted to import the entire Abbey Theatre ensemble to fill out the major and supporting roles. RKO brass refused but conceded to bringing over a few players, including Arthur Shields and his older brother William. Arthur, who played the role of Patrick Pearse, was a skinny, birdlike man who actually fought at the Post Office during the Uprising, and with his pinched, gently ascetic visage was superbly type-cast in the following years as a doctor or minister. In subsequent Ford films, he would memorably add his talents several times, including turns as Mr. Parry in *How Green Was My Valley*, Doctor O'Laughlin in *She Wore a Yellow Ribbon* and the Reverend Mr. Playfair in *The Quiet Man*.

His older brother, William, likewise a Protestant Nationalist player from the Abbey, was an elfin, broth of a boy who, as Fluther Good, shamelessly stole every scene he appeared in with exaggerated, almost Kabuki-like expressions and gestures. It was something of which he became the undisputed master and, soon rechristened with the name Barry Fitzgerald, he went on to win an Oscar for his unforgettable performance as Father Fitzgibbons in *Going My Way* (1944); for this he made history by being the first and the last actor to be nominated in both the Best Actor and Best Supporting Actor categories. He also did turns with his brother in *How Green Was My Valley* (as Cyfartha) and *The Quiet Man* (as Michaeleen og Flynn) and is cherished as one of the most beloved and successful character actors in film history.

In 1937 Ford returned to Fox and Zanuck to make *Wee Willie Winkie*, starring a nine-year-old curly-haired girl who not only carried on her tiny shoulders the studio but, in many ways, the movie industry and the American people as well as they struggled out of the Depres-sion and into the light of prosperity. Shirley Temple was, quite literally, the most popular movie star in the world and as such Zanuck chose vehicles for her that emphasized themes that made her vulnerability and triumph over adversity more beloved to people who were pretty much in the same boat. Thus, in films like *Curly Top*, *The Little Colo-nel*, *Captain January*, *The Littlest Rebel* and *Poor Little Rich Girl*, Temple was cast as either an orphan, little girl lost or daughter of a single and estranged parent acting as the catalytic agent for reunion.

Wee Willie Winkie is nominally based on a Rudyard Kipling tale but here the boy, Percival, is transformed by screenwriters Julien Josephson and Ernest Pascal into the little girl, Priscilla, traveling with her widowed mother to a British garrison on India's Northwest frontier commanded by her gruff paternal grandfather. At first, Ford balked at Zanuck for saddling him with the precocious moppet and for the bulk of the production (exteriors were filmed on elaborate sets at the Iverson Movie Ranch in Chatsworth, California) treated Temple with an aloofness and icy professionalism the universally adored starlet had never encountered before. Temple, however, was even at the tender age of nine a very savvy pro and, as she would do in the movies to countless judges, grandfathers, jaded playboys and even presidents, she turned on the charm to almost incinerating levels of intensity. She called Jack "Ford V-8" and showed her mettle in learning the manual of arms for the parade scenes and fearlessly (if not unwisely) performing her own stuntwork when she dashes out of the way seconds before a stampede of horses and riders thunder by. Ford's *modus operandi* of detached and impersonal direction, conscious or unconscious, worked beautifully and like Priscilla, Temple herself ended up earning the respect of well-seasoned old birds on a tough, dusty location shoot far from the high fructose, song-and-dance studio shoots she had done up till that point. Of all her celebrated Fox films, Temple would claim *Winkie* as her favorite, and not only would Ford use her again eleven years later in *Fort Apache* but he would also stand godfather to her very first child.[25]

Ford's second film in 1937 was *The Hurricane*, done on a loan-out to Samuel Goldwyn for whom he made *Arrowsmith* several years earlier. The film tells the tale of two beautiful Polynesian lovers, Dorothy Lamour (sporting the sarong that would become her trademark in the Hope and Crosby "Road" pictures) and Jon Hall (the Tahitian bred nephew of the *Mutiny on the Bounty* trilogy co-author James Norman Hall) separated by the machinations of an evil colonial governor but reunited after a cataclysmic hurricane that devastates their island paradise.

On the surface, *The Hurricane* appears to be a continuation of the themes of injustice and penal brutality first examined in *The Prisoner of Shark Island* but actually in many respects pays homage to Murnau's 1931 film, *Tabu*, co-made with famed documentarian Robert Flaherty. Both films deal with the corruption of primal innocents by the so-called civilizing influence of western culture. However, the lovers of *Tabu* are destroyed for their refusal to appease the pagan gods of blood and sacrifice. This reflects a pagan world view and decidedly animist take on the nature of the universe. In *The Hurricane*, the native lovers are redeemed and washed clean in the tempest, clinging to the tree of life as though it were the old rugged cross while the colonial evildoers are destroyed in what amounts to a Polynesian version of Noah and the flood.

Despite the overtly religious symbolism of purifying and purging tempest (the last refuge for the islanders is the church, pastored by an old priest played by the redoubtable C. Aubrey Smith), Ford engages in little artistic shilly-shallying or attempts to cover his aesthetical tracks. On the contrary, *The Hurricane*, like *Wee Willie Winkie*, is simply an enjoyable and eminently watchable film because it shows Ford at his most unpretentiously professional. He is confidently helming a solid picture with a tightly constructed narrative acted by seasoned pros (Thomas Mitchell, Mary Astor, Raymond Massey and the ubiquitously villainous John Carradine) culminating in a special-effects set piece that, along with the recreation of the 1906 earthquake in *San Francisco* the year before, still stands as one of the decade's most breathtaking cinematic achievements.

Ford next sleepwalked through *Four Men and A Prayer* and *Submarine Patrol*, both made in 1938 and both starring Fox's current heart-throb Richard Greene; the former featured David Niven, a young actor and member of Hollywood's British ex-pat colony. There is nothing notable or distinguishing about either of these films, except that *Four Men and A Prayer* resembled the flip side of *The Black Watch* and *Submarine Patrol* allowed Ford to pay yet another tribute to the bluejackets of his beloved navy.

The decade was coming rapidly to a close in a very inauspicious way. It was almost as if Ford was barreling through the year as quickly as possible with the vague notion that the next year was going to herald the greatest run of sequential masterpieces in the history of cinema.

APOGEE: 1939-1941

"Bound for Lordsburg!"

Despite the protestations of a handful of revisionist critics (who tend toward the innovations of the New Wave imports of the early '60s), it has been called the greatest year in the history of motion pictures. The year 1939 saw the release of, among others, *The Wizard of Oz, Gone With the Wind, Mr. Smith Goes to Washington, Wuthering Heights, Jesse James, Ninotchka, The Women, Juarez, The Hunchback of Notre Dame, Gunga Din, Of Mice and Men, Beau Geste* and *Goodbye, Mr. Chips.* The Depression was coming to a rapid close, the studio system was at its pinnacle of polish and power and Hollywood was turning out classic films the same way Detroit was turning out cars, Pittsburgh was turning out steel and, in a few short years Boeing would be turning out military aircraft. Conspicuously absent from this Olympian gathering of celluloid gods and goddesses, however, was the lonesome Cowboy.

By 1939, the Western film, like the nation itself ten years earlier, had fallen on hard times and was living a meager and obscure existence in the shadows. The genre had reached its maturity in the 1910s and 1920s and in the hands of novel and visionary artists like Ford, Thomas Ince and even Francis Ford had not only proved a broad canvas of cinematic expression but had also become the internationally recognized calling card of American mythology. With the full onslaught of the Jazz Age with its requisite "It Girls" and "Swedish Sphinxes," followed by the coming of sound and the craving for snappy dialogue and all-talking, all-singing and all-dancing musical extravaganzas, the generation born in the year when *The Great Train Robbery* was released had grown up and moved on. The coming of the Great Depression did not help matters and with the bread basket of the nation a dustbowl and bread lines and Hoovervilles everywhere else, not only had moviegoers' tastes become more sophisticated but the idea of Manifest Destiny and frontier nobility had become passé and irrelevant.

By the 1930s, the need for quick, inexpensive pictures to fill the second bill for Depression era audiences had reduced the mighty Western film to the ignominy of cheap serials produced by tenement studios like Monogram and Mascot. The Homeric humanism of Harry Carey and William S. Hart was soon replaced by the embroidered shirts and glitzy rodeo horsemanship of Tom Mix, Bob Steele and Gene Autry and no one but kids and desperate theater managers took the western seriously any more.

In 1937, Ford read Ernest Haycox's "Stage to Lordsburg" in *Collier's*, a weekly magazine and, liking the basic premise of the story, optioned the film rights for $2,500. The story of Malpais Bill and a disparate assemblage of frontier types journeying by stage from Tonto to Lordsburg, New Mexico, through hostile Apache territory struck Ford as an ill-developed story with strong characters that in the hands of Dudley Nichols could be transformed into a substantial vehicle. After shopping it around to various producers, who picked up the story outline as though it was contaminated with smallpox, he got an interested nibble from independent producer Walter Wanger. Wanger, a natty, handsome and Cornell-educated Hollywood lifer whose producing credits extended from Rudolph Valentino's 1921 mega-hit *The Sheikh* to Elizabeth Taylor's 1962 mega-ulcer *Cleopatra*, put up half the estimated production cost for the film (reduced to the simpler yet meatier title of *Stagecoach*) and secured a release through United Artists.[1]

Wanger agreed to give Ford a relatively free hand on the production but he was adamant about the casting. He envisioned the film as a perfect vehicle for Gary Cooper and Marlene Dietrich. Ford was never impressed with the clout of a producer, let alone the heft of such cinematic supernovas like Cooper and Dietrich, and he held his ground against Wanger's dictums. He had casting plans of his own.

Since the failure of *The Big Trail*, Duke Wayne had been slugging his way through what was perceived as a purgatory of cheap Westerns and dismally interminable serials at the Monogram and Mascot studios. Although *The Hurricane Express*, *The Three Mesquiteers* and *Riders of Destiny* are largely forgettable, the experience of making them was a proving ground and a crucible that prepared him for the trial by fire he would soon receive from Ford, who sculpted Wayne into an actor as well as a star.

Like the early world of silent film, Wayne's experience of making cheap Westerns was a world of little star treatment, long hours on location and what would be known in contemporary parlance as multitasking. In the Spartan world of Poverty Row Studios, Duke did not have the luxury given the A-list stars at Metro, Paramount and Warners who would show up at the studio, stand on their marks and recite their lines. Coming through the ranks as a young gofer at Fox, young Duke Wayne became not only educated in but fascinated by almost every facet of film-making, from stunt work and props to camera angles, costuming and dialogue. In the evenings he took acting lessons from actor Paul Fix (an eminently reliable and instantly recognizable character actor best known for his roles on television as Sheriff Micah Torrance in *The Rifleman* and on screen as the judge in *To Kill A Mockingbird*), who transformed Duke's flat and non-descript Mid-western accent into a rich, measured and sonorous drawl. Unlike Spencer Tracy, Humphrey Bogart and Clark Gable, who often saw movies as a rather silly way for a grown man to make a living, Wayne not only took his profession very seriously but also had great pride in his vocation as an actor.

At Monogram, Wayne became friends with Enos Canutt, a champion rodeo rider turned stuntman from Yakima, Washington. Canutt was slowly taking the world of movie stunts from a dangerous pastime of underemployed buckaroos into a carefully executed and almost scientific art. It was from Canutt that Wayne learned the ropes of horse riding, shootouts and movie fights. While no one was paying attention to the two young men on location of a B Western shoot at Monogram's studio ranch, Canutt and Wayne were perfecting the language of the movie fight, developing proper camera angles and changing them from mindless and indecorous melees into choreographed, visual ballets of grace and power. Although Wayne remained indifferent to horses and saw them as little more than a tool of his trade (as opposed to Gene Autry and Roy Rogers, who seemed to love their horses more than the cowgirls they always saved from fates worse than death), he learned from Canutt the fine art of sitting a horse, galloping and mounting and dismounting with grace and style. Between Fix and Canutt (who, rechristened Yakima Canutt, would go on to be considered the father of movie stuntwork and direct, among others, the chariot race in *Ben-Hur* and battle scenes in *El Cid, Spartacus* and *The Fall of the Roman Empire*) Wayne also learned to carry his 6'4" frame in a light, almost musical walk that would become one of his later and numerous trademarks.

Most importantly, Wayne was refining the elusive art of acting for the camera and connecting with the audience in a powerful and intimate way, a highly intelligent yet difficult art mastered by few actors then and even now. Unlike many male and female Hollywood stars and even the great comedians with their vast vaudeville and music hall background, Wayne did not have the benefit of stage experience where he could learn to inhabit a character in a single, non-stop performance and draw from the energy of a live audience. Wayne's acting technique, often and unfairly dismissed by serious film theorists as too broad and mannered, was actually crafted for the camera and the heroically expansive language of the Western film. Even in his early Westerns he was slowly mastering the art of filling a scene with his presence and, although hampered with mediocre plots and dialogue, drawing the eye to his handsome and quietly majestic person. Ford would indeed become Duke's Michelangelo and shape him into the legendary persona that lay in his future, but in all fairness it is well to remember that Ford's task was made infinitely easier since the block of marble he worked on already contained the David within.

Since their reconciliation following Ford's peevish banishment of the young actor several years earlier, Ford maintained a friendship with Wayne that even brought him into the fold of the sacred and bibulous brotherhood of the *Araner* excursions. While preparing to cast the lead role of *Stagecoach* in 1938 (the young protagonist's name had been changed from the unpronounceable Malpais Bill to the simpler and sturdier Ringo Kid), Ford invited Wayne on board his yacht for a seagoing story conference. Ford, with his typically brutal way of torturing those closest to him at their most vulnerable moments, asked Wayne's thoughts about a bevy of actors capable of playing the plum role of the Ringo Kid. He even asked Wayne about Lloyd Nolan, a dependable B actor known for his hardboiled detective and urban tough roles, who enjoyed a career in film and television well into the 1970s. Duke, not seeing through the ruse and believing he would return to dry land as a third rate star of depressingly interminable cheap Westerns, said that Nolan would be fine. In unprintable language as salty as the air whipping their faces, Ford summarily cut Wayne off and told him that he was going to play the Ringo Kid.

The plot of *Stagecoach* is fairly thin and linear and at the time was inevitably compared to M-G-M's all-star blockbuster *Grand Hotel* (1932), with the well-heeled plot of the strange group of people thrown together in dangerous, tense and dramatically exaggerated situations that reveal their strengths and weaknesses. In plot and character development, however, Ford and screenwriter Dudley Nichols crafted the story more as homage to Bret Harte's *The Outcasts of Poker Flat*, the evergreen classic of American literature that Ford had filmed with Harry Carey in 1919. The stage from Tonto, Arizona, to Lordsburg, New Mexico, is thrown off its regularly irregular schedule by the arrival of two bits of disturbing intelligence. The first is that Geronimo has jumped the reservation and, having cut the telegraph connecting the frontier towns to the outside world, is returning to his Apache lands (through which the stage must pass) and slaughtering every white homesteader and rancher in his path. The other is that the young Ringo Kid, a genial yet duty-bound young cowpoke, has busted out of the penitentiary with the intention of getting to Lordsburg and avenging the death of his brother at the hands of Luke Plummer.

On the surface, the nine characters who form the core of the plot of *Stagecoach* appear to be pulled off the dusty shelf of Ford's stock types from his silent Westerns; Shakespearean prototypes ranging from the buffoonish to the heroic once again standing in for the vast panoply of humanity. Buck (Andy Devine) the tubby, childlike driver who never stops talking nonsense yet can never seem to get a word in edgewise with anyone, is joined on the driver's box by Curly (George Bancroft), the bullnecked yet fair-minded marshal who rides shotgun in the hopes of intercepting the Kid before he can throw down in Lordsburg with Luke Plummer (Tom Tyler).

The passengers inside the coach, a decidedly motley assemblage, guarantee an interesting ride through the now-hostile and Apache infested desert. Lucy Mallory (Louise Platt), is an uptight, prissy, clam of a woman (also very pregnant) en route to see her captain husband just dispatched with his command into the desert to find Geronimo. Hatfield (John Carradine), an elegant gambler with a mysterious background and decidedly Confederate sympathies, climbs aboard at the last minute as a gallant knight errant determined to protect the person and honor of Mrs. Mallory. Samuel Peacock (played by the wonderful and aptly named Donald Meek), a bald, diminutive whiskey drummer afraid of his own quivering shadow, becomes a source of casual confusion to everyone he meets. He is called every variation of Peacock except Peacock, including "Haycock," probably Ford and Nichols' playful homage to the original author of the story, Ernest Haycox. He is mistakenly pegged as being from Kansas City, Missouri, instead of Kansas City, Kansas, and his prim fastidiousness in soberly guarding his precious satchel of whiskey samples and habit of calling all men "brother" leads his fellow travelers to assume that he is a clergyman. Ellsworth Gatewood (Berton Churchill), a pompous, frock-coated blowhard of a banker who rails at every perceived slight against his august person, unexpectedly hails the coach outside of town with nothing but a small valise. What the viewer sees, but not the fellow passengers, is that the bag contains stacks of money this respected pillar of society has purloined from the safe of his bank. And those are the upright and righteous folk.

The more unwelcome and reluctant occupants are Doc Josiah Boone

(the superb Thomas Mitchell who would win an Oscar for his performance but, alas, is better known to cinematic posterity for playing Scarlett
O'Hara's father in *Gone With the Wind* the same year), a cynical, humane
and Shakespeare-quoting alcoholic who for non-payment of his rent is
sent packing with his shingle into the coach. Aside from Doc Boone, the
other outcast of Tonto is Dallas (the luminous Claire Trevor, future queen
of film noir classics who would win an Oscar for her performance in
Key Largo), the quintessential whore with the heart of gold expelled from
the town by a group of prune-faced old harridans styling themselves the
Ladies of the Law and Order League. Despite his nasty habits of chain
smoking stinking stogies and drinking himself into a befuddled stupor,
Doc is, like Dallas and her horrid profession as a soiled and fallen woman,
an unalloyed symbol of honest, genuine and compassionate humanity.
Both find themselves at odds with intolerance and hypocrisy (manifested
by not only the townspeople but their fellow passengers in the stage) mas-
querading as civilization and slowly encroaching on the primal integrity
of their disappearing West. He and Dallas, as Doc says when they march
to the stage as though they were in a tumbril on the way to the guillotine,
"are victims of a foul disease known as social prejudice."

The overland stage leaves Tonto and heads past the fence and into
the vastness of Monument Valley, neatly serving as a visual delineation
between the artificial confines of what is perceived to be civilization
and the primal expanse of the eternally abiding desert. In the high
chaparral country, a warning shot fired in the distance introduces the
passengers and the viewers to the Ringo Kid (John Wayne) holding
the saddle of his lame horse and hoping to hop a ride into Lordsburg
to settle with the plug-ugly Plummer brothers who recently murdered
his brother. Curly immediately arrests the Kid as an escaped convict
but soon confesses to Buck that he did so less with a desire to grab
the reward money than to protect the boy from the drilling he would
certainly receive in a throw-down with the Plummers.

The most rapidly developing relationship, however, is between Dallas
and Ringo, although it is mostly conveyed through silent but passionate

glances across the stage interior and over candlelight as Dallas holds Mrs. Mallory's newborn child. Ringo is polite and deferential to the prostitute, holding her chair and sitting with her when everyone moves away during their stopover meal. Ringo, not sensing their repugnance at having to sit at table with a prostitute, automatically assumes that he is the reason and muses, "Looks like I got the plague, don't it?" Like two publicans adrift in a stage full of pharisees, both Dallas and Ringo are so absorbed with the rotten mess they have made of their lives that they cannot see faults or failings in anyone else. After more delays at coach stops pillaged by Geronimo, the band is attacked on a vast salt flat by the Apaches. Hatsfield is killed and Peacock is wounded just as the cavalry arrives in the most stirring (if not implausible) eleventh hour rescue in film history.

In Lordsburg, the group parts ways but Curly allows Ringo the time to shoot it out with the Plummers before possibly returning him to prison. Three bullets are left in Ringo's hat. He uses them to fell all three then is met by a tearful Dallas who thought for sure he himself was killed. Doc and Curly put the two in a buckboard, ostensibly to ride for a spell together before Ringo is carted back to Yuma. Instead, on a cue they throw rocks at the horses and allow the lovers to escape across the border to the safety and obscurity of Ringo's ranch, thus, as Doc facetiously says, sparing them the "blessings of civilization."

<hr>

From the outset, Ford strategically groups the nine passengers in three categories, producing blocks of alliances and antagonisms that gives *Stagecoach* its dramatic *frisson*. There are the judgmental and self-righteous (Mrs. Mallory, Hatfield, Gatewood), the non-judgmental and righteous (Curly, Buck, Peacock) and the outcasts (Ringo, Doc Boone, Dallas). The alliances do not shift nor does one group totally move into the moral posture of the other. For a short time, fear of attack and events such as Mrs. Mallory giving birth gives them common cause and at least on the surface they share a tenuous *entente cordiale*. However, no one in any camp is either completely corrupted or converted by the other and by the time they arrive in Lordsburg, each one reverts to who they were, both good and bad, before they alight from the stage in Tonto. Dallas goes off to the brothels, Doc to the saloon, Gatewood to jail and Ringo off to his destiny face to face with the Plummers. *Stagecoach*, for all its thematic clichés and stock Western characters, is not a morality play, fable or classical Greek drama, and aside from surviving the Apache attack and Ringo triumphing over the Plummers, nothing really is affirmed or resolved in the characters. The film simply *is* and the double climax is evidence of Ford moving away from the structured confines of the script to a more organic and non-linear reality in his work.

Despite the fascinating texture of characters Ford weaves into the fabric of *Stagecoach*, allowing them to shamelessly ham it up and play to the gallery, the two most majestic stars of the film are John Wayne and Monument Valley. Both would be destined to become perpetually and inextricably linked to the iconography of the Western film, yet paradoxically both are intentionally underused so as to maximize the impact of their onscreen time. Wayne's first shot, rightfully celebrated as one of the most famous in American film, has been seen as an almost biblical announcement that not only has a new star arisen but has eclipsed all the others in the western sky. After a signal shot is heard in the distance and the stage comes to a halt, Bert Glennon's camera rapidly tracks in on the Ringo Kid, briefly blurring out of focus before stopping full frame on his youthful face (even though at the time Wayne was a still young but by no means boyish thirty-two). His pose, twirling a Winchester with one hand and holding the saddle of his lame horse in the other, is sculptural, classical and reminiscent of a heroic Greek warrior stepped off a plinth or down from a temple frieze. The background, a nondescript rear projection, focuses all the attention on Wayne and in the screen-filling close-up draws him out of the obvious artifice of the studio confines and into the eternal reality of our imagination. Not so much has a star been born as a neologism in the sacred canon of American mythology.

It became apparent to Wayne early in the production that although he was technically the star of the film (second billed only to Claire Trevor) he seemed to be standing around most of the time holding up scenery while observing seasoned pros who were busily chewing it up. It slowly dawned on Duke that the Coach was intentionally crafting out of the clay of the Poverty Row cowboy a silent and strong persona, tinged with an air of solitude and mystery and devoid of the frontier palaver that marked his mediocre serials at Monogram. While one listens to the witty repartee of the bibulous Doc Boone, the nonsensical ramblings of Buck or the nervous twitterings of Peacock, the eye is ineluctably drawn, in silence, to Wayne's Ringo Kid and invited into his deceptively simple and infinite world of thoughts, emotions and stolen glances. While the studio hacks and publicity department could shake the San Fernando dust out of the ears of any cowboy and make him into a star, Ford was helping to give Wayne something infinitely more important, magical and portentous for his career: presence.

———————

Ford's treatment of his new star was, for the most part, indicative of the way he would treat Duke for the rest of their professional lives. It was, in a few words, a needling, badgering and humiliating pummeling bordering on a brutality straight from the darkest pages of Dickens. Into the 1950s and 1960s, when Wayne was a major star soaring on his own horsepower, the actor always remained childlike and deferential around Ford and always strove to please him as though Ford were his father or high school coach. On *Stagecoach*, which Duke knew was a make-or-break opportunity, he was especially studious and attentive to every one of Ford's dictates as though they were orders from the general barked during the heat of battle. For each of his efforts, great and small, he would be verbally decimated like a fresh-faced recruit in the hands of a Marine drill instructor.

The reasons, like Ford himself, were complex and operated on many conscious and subconscious levels. By this time, Ford and Duke were more than drinking pals, they were bonded on a deep level in their personal and professional lives. In many ways Ford, the successful, redoubtable and awesome patriarch stood *in loco parentis* for Duke, whose own father, Clyde, was a loving, good-hearted failure in everything. Conversely, Ford's relationship with his son, Patrick, always shaky at best, continued to worsen and eventually deteriorate over the years. For a man like Ford, who desperately needed to be needed, many young protégés like Henry

Fonda, Harry Carey, Jr. and Ben Johnson would be filial stand-ins of sorts but none would become so much like a son to him as John Wayne.

Ford always tried publicly to cover his private emotional tracks and, to dispel any notions of favoritism and mask the great affection he had for the young man, he would destroy Wayne on the set with an almost Carthaginian efficiency. *Stagecoach* was an ensemble piece, and to coddle his drinking and sailing buddy was to invite mutiny amongst a company of seasoned pros with the monumentally sensitive egos to prove it. Another reason is that Ford saw great potential in Wayne and he knew from experience that the only way to take the Monogram out of the B cowboy and craft him into a professional, mature and thinking actor was to break him into a million pieces and put him back together again. Yet another, and simpler, reason is that with Ford's perverse love of cruelty, especially when directed toward guys like Duke and Ward Bond, whom he publicly demeaned as big dopes, he knew they would stand there and take it without talking back.

Wayne knew, as did everyone else in the Ford Stock Company, that when Pappy did not scream and curse and began to treat one civilly, that was really the time to start worrying. It was a bit of smoke-and-mirrors bluster but not everyone was stunned into a state of shock by his emotional parlor tricks. Thomas Mitchell, like his Doc Boone character, was too canny a cat to fall for any of Ford's well-rehearsed spontaneous combustions. When Ford had a go at him on the set one day for some infraction or another, Mitchell politely let Ford finish his tirade and then simply responded "Just remember: I saw *Mary of Scotland.*" With this casual reference to his recent and very expensive turkey, a humbled Ford mumbled something under his breath and walked away. He did, however, maintain a respectful posture toward Mr. Mitchell for the remainder of the shoot.[2]

The Navajo name for Monument Valley is, surprisingly, the equally touristy sounding "Valley of the Rocks," but to both the native peoples and Ford, the place resonated with a mystical depth and spiritual beauty that only they seemed to grasp. While he would make the Valley famous, to the point where other directors refused to shoot there out of fear of copyright infringement, he was neither the first filmmaker nor white to make any sort of enterprising endeavor there. In the early 1920s, none other than Zane Grey took Paramount executives on a swing through Monument Valley and it served as one of the locales for their Western, *The Vanishing American,* starring Richard Dix. Harry Goulding, a tall, weather-beaten cowboy, who could have been created by the pen of Jack London, moved to the valley about the same time with his wife, Lorena. At first they lived in tents, then Harry built a trading post and began doing business with the Navajo people. Mastering the almost unfathomable intricacies of the native dialect, Harry and Lorena "Mike" Goulding ingratiated themselves with the tribe not only with their trading post and luxury goods but with a fairness and respect continually denied them by all other white people.

When hard times and drought hit the local region in the mid-1930s, Harry had the idea of pitching Monument Valley as a movie location and lit out for Hollywood with a satchel of photographs. In reality, no one knows exactly who is responsible for Ford's discovery of Monument Valley but, despite the surfeit of apocrypha, Harry apparently did make landfall at several of the studios, including the production offices of Mr. Wanger. He was unable to meet Walter Wanger but was introduced to Ford, who mused thoughtfully over the photographs. His silence, more than his words, were the surest indications of his emotions and he was immediately sold.[3]

Ford was known for his love of location and the more remote the better, but even the icy Nevada desert he used for *The Iron Horse* was primitive yet still accessible by train and car. Monument Valley, nearly two hundred miles from the nearest railhead, could not have been more remote if it were on the dark side of Saturn. And with names given to the gargantuan rock formations like The Mittens, the Totem Pole, Three Sisters and The King on his Throne, the Valley took on an even more primal, mythological and epic hue. In Monument Valley, Ford found the visual grid upon which he could frame his stories about history, community, honor, love and death backed by towering sentinels acting as reminders of our fragile and transitory nature. It is, as it were, a sort of a pure American twist on the medieval concept *of Media vita in morte sumus*: "In the midst of life we are in death." In Monument Valley, Ford's soul breathed and expanded and it became for him not just a location but his private ocean that he alone came to master and intimately know much as Magellan mastered and intimately knew the Pacific.

The climactic stagecoach chase, a wild and breakneck dash across a vast expanse of salt flats with Apaches in hot pursuit, is probably what the film is best remembered for today. As in many subsequent Ford classics, it is only one of several climaxes. The chase was filmed at Muroc Dry Lake near Victorville, outside Los Angeles, later famous for the Right Stuff fly-boy outpost that became Edwards Air Force Base. On Wayne's recommendation, Yakima Canutt was brought in to supervise the shooting of the sequence, including the choreography of all the famous and very dangerous stuntwork.

Yet as exciting and iconic as the chase is, it is, at least historically, somewhat superfluous. A future Ford screenwriter, Frank Nugent, told Ford after he saw the film that if the Apaches really wanted to stop the stage all they had to do was to shoot one of the horses. Ford pondered this shaft of searing logic for a moment and then told him he was right but then that would have been the end of the story.[4]

———

The critic's reaction to *Stagecoach* nearly dovetailed with the public's. Even in a year stacked with enduring classics like so many poker chips, both sectors knew that they had seen a new type of Western. The premiere in February 1939 was enthusiastic and, according to Wayne, the audience stood and cheered during the chase scene. The most amazing part of it all was that the kudos and encomiums were being poured out on a Western, which up to that time had been considered the realm of kiddy matinees and, to paraphrase the parlance of the day, pix for hix living in the stix. Not only kudos went out but awards and nominations as well. Aside from Thomas Mitchell's win for Best Supporting Actor and Richard Hageman, et al, for music scoring, Ford picked up the New York Film Critics Circle Award for Best Director.

The film also received Oscar nominations for Best Picture, Direction, Cinematography and Otho "Lovie" Lovering's crisp editing. However, the best tribute came from none other than the film's producer, Walter Wanger. He never regretted or second-guessed his decision to literally give Ford the reins of the coach from beginning to end. It was the true measure of the man that even after the film was a critical, although not a runaway financial, success, Wanger stepped out of the spotlight and directed it toward Ford. In Hollywood, then as now, finger pointing in the face of a critical or financial failure is as sure as the sun setting over the Pacific Ocean. However, such self-effacing humility and gracious deference to a subordinate in the face of a *success* does not deserve respect as much as it does canonization. Writing to Lynn Farnol in the United Artists office in New York the day after the premiere, Wanger, ever a class act, said "I read the story—but only after Ford had purchased it and brought it to me. Again, it was Ford who worked with Dudley Nichols in creating a fine script; and John Wayne as the Ringo Kid was also Ford's idea. While I am proud to be the producer of 'STAGECOACH,' will you do everything in your power to see that the picture is known as John Ford's achievement."[5]

Abraham Lincoln (1809-1865) was another emotional legacy bequeathed to Ford by his big brother Frank. Ford's love of the sixteenth president was deep and abiding and over his career he insinuated Lincoln into his films in various stages of his life through the slightly misty lens of myth and idealism but never divinization. He was seen as a hick lawyer turned lanky president (*The Iron Horse*), benevolent martyr to the cause of the Union (*Prisoner of Shark Island*), brooding congressman contemplating the coming cataclysm of civil war (*How the West Was Won*), and even a ghostly reflection looking down from a framed daguerreotype (*Cheyenne Autumn*).

And yet, in 1938 when Zanuck gave Ford the director's job for his upcoming biopic *Young Mr. Lincoln*, it was not the great, brooding savior of the Republic who was the subject but a shy, awkward backwoods lawyer with just the faintest hints of future greatness clinging to his frock coat and stovepipe hat. Ford, like his brother Frank, was steeped in Lincoln history and lore and read deeply on the life of the nation's sixteenth president. Ford's vision of Lincoln, as manifested in all his cinematic presentations but most in *Young Mr. Lincoln*, was not so much romantically rosy as it was profoundly mystical. Both Lincoln and Ford were self-made men from humble backgrounds and their rise to fame and great heights was what America is all about. America is not simply a geographic location on a world map, but a lived experience rooted in the concept of man's innate condition of freedom and infinite potential.

Zanuck's choice for Lincoln was a young, dark-haired Fox contract player named Henry Fonda who, after several years of slugging it out on stage and film, scored a hit as Bette Davis's love interest in Warner Brothers' 1938 antebellum drama, *Jezebel*. The Dutch-Italian Fonda was, like Zanuck, Nebraska-born but, finding acting an exciting antidote to his laconic shyness, left and worked his way through summer stock and eventually some minor successes on Broadway. Fonda moved to Hollywood in 1935 with his lifelong friend and occasional roommate, James Stewart, and the two young actors got studio contracts and second-banana juvenile roles in several good and several forgettable films.

The young actor's combination of innocent integrity and brooding complication struck Ford deeply and he knew that in Fonda he had his Lincoln. Fonda, however, was not so sure and tried to back out of the project with both Zanuck and Ford. Smelling weakness in the young actor like a shark smelling blood in water, Ford smacked his lips and gleefully went on the offensive with the best weapon he had in his well-stocked emotional arsenal: humiliation. Ford called the young actor into his office and let loose a tirade on him, asking Fonda if he thought he was going to play the Great Emancipator. Hell no, Ford said, he was going to play a (blank) (blank) jack-legged lawyer from Springfield. Fearing for his career, and probably for his life, Fonda gave in and was soon doing makeup and costume tests.[6]

The ball was now in play. In a memo dated December 3, 1938, Zanuck wrote Ford: "I am anxious to have you see the test that Fonda made. He looks exactly like Lincoln and he really was immense. I want to start shooting the picture on February 20th, if that is possible."[7] Zanuck tapped Lamar Trotti for the screenplay, based not only on his competence as a wordsmith (he would win an Oscar for writing Zanuck's beloved but ponderous presidential biopic *Wilson* in 1944) but also, as he told Ford in another memo, Trotti was "practically an authority on Lincoln."[8] If so, it would be a strange fascination for Trotti, who was born in Atlanta just some thirty years after Sherman burnt it to cinders and who graduated from the University of Georgia during a time when Old Mr. Lincoln did not exactly top the regional popularity polls.

Young Mr. Lincoln is different, and that difference separates the good films Ford made prior to 1939 and the classics he created after. The film moves at a leisurely, meditative pace unified by a painterly glaze of feeling, emotion and moments that are felt rather than exposited by the script (although Trotti's fine work for the film earned him an Academy Award nomination). The plot of *Young Mr. Lincoln*, like Ford's subsequent films, can be explained in a few sentences but the patina of mood and depth of feeling in the film is what gives it a heart to beat and lungs to expand. At first, Zanuck did not grasp what Ford was doing, and he expressed his concerns in March 22, 1939, memo. "Do you feel that at times the tempo is apt to be a trifle slow? I don't mean we should speed up Fonda, as it is the slowness and deliberate character that you have given him that makes his performance swell, but I have had a feeling that at times we seem to be a little draggy as far as mood is concerned."[9] Fortunately for Ford and posterity, Zanuck's concerns remained simply concerns and not action items.

Lincoln, a failed New Salem shopkeeper, goes to Springfield to read law after losing the first love of his life, Ann Rutledge (although historians are unsure as to the early love life of the notoriously homely and painfully shy young Lincoln). As a young lawyer, he becomes a beloved pillar of the bustling prairie town with his wit, his homespun legal wisdom and his moral and physical strength. He is called upon to defend two brothers accused of killing a man in a brawl and pledges to their mother (Alice Brady, as yet another indomitable and unifying

Fordian symbol of eternal maternity) not to save one at the expense of the other. The climactic courtroom scene, in which Lincoln pleads the innocence of the young men, is based upon Lincoln's real-life and celebrated defense of Duff Armstrong in 1858. As Lincoln did in real life, so the films shows the quick-witted lawyer using the *Farmers' Almanac* to prove that the witness could not have seen the boys kill a man by the light of the moon. The film closes with Lincoln seeing the mother and her free and exonerated boys off, receiving their love, their gratitude and the few pennies they can afford to pay him.

Early in the film, Lincoln visits the grave of Ann Rutledge, and employing one of Ford's most enduring motifs of the unbreakable and enduring bond between the living and the dead, he speaks to her about his aspiration for law and his desire to go somewhere in life. Lincoln uses a stick to decide, letting his future decide on the direction in which it falls. When it falls toward Ann and the study of law, Abe smiles and says, "I wonder if I could've tipped it your way just a little."

Thus, when Lincoln becomes a lawyer it is not so much a way to advance his career from the backwoods mud of New Salem to the respectability of Springfield but a vocation. Lincoln's contemplation of the law as a divine gift, a living reality and not a dead letter, stands Lincoln in good stead throughout the film. The highlight of the trial is not in the courtroom but at the jail where Lincoln singlehandedly stops an enraged mob from hanging his two clients. Although he uses humor and calm, reasoned logic to defuse the mob, it is a plea for justice that eventually helps Lincoln win the crowd over. The highly charged and emotional scene is given more heft by the fact Fonda played it from experience and dark, painful memories. As a boy in Nebraska, Fonda was taken to a window by his father to watch a Black man being lynched. The memory of that horrific event seared the actor's conscience for life and eventually helped shape his radical commitment to social justice in his adult life.[10]

Ford ends the film with a lyrical coda that symbolically closes out one chapter of Lincoln's life while hinting at the greatness that lies ahead. After getting the two young men acquitted of murder, Lincoln makes his farewells and sees the family off in their wagon. When his buckskinned sidekick (symbolizing the wild backwoods and prairies of Illinois) asks if Lincoln is coming back (to what he formerly was), the young lawyer enigmatically replies, "No, I think I'll go on a piece... maybe to the top of that hill." In the Old and New Testaments, the mountain or hill symbolized the lofty heights where Man encounters God and, like Moses, is transformed (or like Jesus, transfigured) and receives a mandate to carry out a sacred mission. As Ford shows Lincoln in a long shot walking slowly up the hill, the *Battle Hymn of the Republic* building slowly to a crescendo, the young man is actually ascending to a higher place where he will encounter not only the divine, but himself and his sacred calling to law and the justice that will result in men being set free. A single, low rumble of thunder, followed by a burst of lightning foreshadowes the cannons, guns and tumult of future civil war by which that mission will be accomplished.

Hot on the heels of *Young Mr. Lincoln* and its attending success (Lamar Trotti received an Academy Award nomination for his screenplay and in 2003 the film was entered into the Film Registry as a national treasure), Zanuck assigned Ford to the historical epic *Drums Along the Mohawk*, which he planned to shoot in the still relatively novel Technicolor process. The film tells the tale of the hearty colonial pioneers during the American Revolution as they carve a community out of the wilderness of New York's Mohawk Valley. The script once again fell to Lamar Trotti who, along with Sonya Levien and uncredited help from William Faulkner, adapted it from Walter Edmond's novel.

1939 was not only a cinematically fertile year but an alchemical one as well, and it transmuted two traditionally poisonous film genres, the Revolutionary War and the Civil War, into box office gold. Although *Gone With the Wind* fared much better financially with the Civil War at the box office, *Drums Along the Mohawk* was and remains an exciting and attractive film that at least proved that, if done right, Americans would actually pay to see their stars in hoop skirts, pigtailed wigs and buckled shoes. It was also notable in that it would be the first film Ford would shoot in three-color Technicolor format. It was an expensive process that required an enormous amount of lighting, a recalibration and coordination of cinematography, production and costume design, and the omnipresence of Technicolor Corporation's Natalie Kalmus hovering over productions like Hamlet's ghost.

Henry Fonda, launched by the success of the Lincoln film into the ranks of Hollywood stardom, was tapped by Zanuck for the lead role of Gil Martin, the young homesteader who takes his spoiled, nervous bride (Claudette Colbert) from the comforts of her Albany home into the dense woods of Upstate New York to begin a new life. They and fellow settlers fight the elements, geography and hostile Indians stirred into holy war by Tory agents of the British army.

Like *Young Mr. Lincoln, Drums Along the Mohawk* unfolds at a leisurely, unhurried pace simply resting in the integrity of its mood, the robustness of its characters and the richness of its images. On the surface, nothing seems to happen except pretty tableaux and romantic horseplay in between elaborate action pieces. It has been said that drama is nothing more than real life with the dull bits left out. What Ford was innovating in his personal style was the inclusion of what many would take to be dull, uneventful moments that actually make up the mystical seasons of our being; marriage, planting, childbirth, harvesting, war and death. Within the loose confines of its plot structure, *Drums Along the Mohawk* is a visual and decidedly American exegesis on the Book of Ecclesiastes, with its times to live, times to die, times to make war, peace, and so on. Early scenes show the jittery, almost childlike Lana trying to adapt to frontier life and going into full-throttle screaming meltdown at the first appearance of the Indian chief, Blue Back (Chief John Big Tree). Just when Lana thinks she and her scalp are done for, Gil calms her by saying he is not only a good friend but a Christian, to which Blue Back responds with the heartiest "Hallelujah!" this side of heaven (a routine the Chief would repeat with even greater panache and humor as the war-weary tribal leader in *She Wore a Yellow Ribbon*).

Slowly, Lana grows into a strong, mature wife, neighbor and mother and ends up helping to defend the fort against the British and Indians. She wears a soldier's tunic and cartridge belt and fires her Brown Bess musket like a colonial Calamity Jane. Ford never had time for ingénues or cheesecake sexpots in his film and he wastes no time transforming Lana from a porcelain doll into the redoubtable Maureen O'Hara-Jane Darwell-Mildred Natwick types who were more to his liking. Another well-sculpted character is the Widow McKlennar, the salty-tongued, steel-spined but warmhearted homesteader who takes Gil and Lana into her home as hired help after their farm is burned during an Indian Raid. The role was played to comedic perfection by Edna May Oliver, who can be deemed inimitable for no other reason than the horse-faced "biddiness" that made her one of Hollywood's great character actresses. Oliver specialized in playing matronly, school-marmish, grande dames and is best remembered for her Dickensian turns in M-G-M's versions of *David Copperfield* and *A Tale of Two Cities*. She received a well-deserved Academy Award nomination for her role as the widow and had she lived past 1942 she surely would have been included in the battle-scarred ranks of the Ford Stock Company.

The lyrical pace of the film is best manifested during the scenes showing the community of Deerfield celebrating the harvest festival, complete with dancing, music, likker and carved jack-o-lanterns. The settlement is at peace, the war seems far away to the South and Gil and Lana deeply love their life together and their newborn son. Gil sneaks away to the house to gaze at his sleeping son, not knowing that Lana has likewise left to gaze silently on the both of them. Sitting on the staircase bathed in the warm glow of moonlight and utter content, Lana prays, "Please God. Please let it go on like this forever." With the clouds of war gathering on the other sides of both the Atlantic and the Pacific and the likelihood of a global conflagration in which many families will be shattered and many sons will die and we know along with Lana that, alas, the prayer will not be answered.

Stylistically, Ford clearly reveled in the sumptuous chromatic possibilities of the three-color Technicolor process, and Utah's Wasatch Range proved a fairly impressive substitute for upstate New York. The chiaroscuro lighting indoors and the saturated palette of greens, reds, blues and earth tones of the exteriors were expertly shot by Bert Glennon and Ray Renahan (the latter also doing double duty that year as

one of the cinematographers for *Gone With the Wind*). The Ford Stock
Company nearly populated his Mohawk Valley, including Ward Bond,
Arthur Shields (as Reverend Rozenkrantz), Russell Simpson (Dr.
Petry), his brother Frank (now reduced to playing the obligatory drunken codger with a handful of lines). John Carradine was by this time a regular
heavy in Ford's films, despite the fact both were hard-headed Irishmen
who were convinced that they had forgotten more about the art of film
than the other ever knew. Here, as Caldwell, the pro-British Tory, Carradine's innate ability to look sinister is neatly abetted by an eye patch
and cloak that gives him the look of an N. C. Wyeth illustration.

The ending, in which colonists triumph over the British and Indians
and the surrender at Yorktown is announced by a relief column, swells
mere populism to an inclusive patriotic symphony of countless notes.
When the homesteaders see the new red, white and blue American flag
paraded in, Dr. Petry says, "So that's the thing we've been fighting for?"
As the flag and Alfred Newman's stirring rendition of "America" rise to
the heavens, a common blacksmith and his wife gaze upward, the Black
servants' eyes fill with tears and Blue Back the Indian raises his hand in
salute. To today's audiences, this could come across as a groan-inducing
and high-fructose bit of sap. It could also be rendered dangerously ironic
given the fact that while Ford was filming this scene, entire families were
living in poverty across the nation, Black Americans were being lynched
and denied basic civil rights and Native Americans were barely existing
as third-class citizens throughout the West and Southwest.

Gil's curtain line to Lana, however, disproves any suspicion that
Ford was merely foisting hokum or attempting to gild the tarnished
lily of the Republic. Ford never made any secret of where his sympathies lay in regards to social conscience, politics and justice for the
oppressed. In one short, symbolically rich scene Ford once again shows
his heartfelt aspirations toward the Peaceable Kingdom, the best of all
possible worlds where all people will dwell together in peace, harmony
and equality. America, with all her gifts and blessings is not a finished
utopia but a work in progress, and the victory over the British was not
an end but a beginning. The nation Ford loved and the cherished, like

Lincoln, as humanity's last great hope, was still fraught with problems and unresolved issues like injustice and inequality. If what Jefferson called "We the people" can conquer the mightiest army on the face of the earth to secure our liberty, they can, and hopefully one day would, certainly conquer themselves. "Well, I reckon we better be getting back to work," Gil tells Lana, and the audience, still gazing up at the flag, "there's gonna be a heap to do from now on."

From the time of its publication in 1939, *The Grapes of Wrath* has not ceased to be a glorious, powerful and celebrated burr under the American hide. John Steinbeck's magnum opus about an Oklahoma family's Depression era trek from the Dust Bowl to what they hope will be a life of work, bread and dignity in California remains in many ways the proto-American novel of the twentieth century. Steinbeck, an avowed left-leaning radical who, as a young man, picked fruit with migrant workers in California, crafted his novel as a celebration of the human spirit and American soul while laying a frontal, pro-union siege on the corporations and institutions that sought to extinguish it. Like *Gone With the Wind*, *The Grapes of Wrath* was an overnight literary smash that screamed for a rapid translation to the big screen. The major problem facing the studio who picked up the property was that, with labor on one side, capitalists and corporate titans on the other and a patriotic populace in between, the film would be a potential time bomb in which pretty much everyone would take a hit. Even though America was just crawling out from under the devastating effects of the greatest financial crisis in its history and labor unions tore into the formerly untouchable bastions of capitalism, the ticket-buying folks in Peoria still preferred Astaire and Rogers to Samuel Gompers and John L. Lewis. Any producer who tried to film the book would be precariously poised on a high wire with no net and shark tanks below. Enter the arch-conservative capitalist Darryl F. Zanuck.

Whatever sins can be laid on the doorstep of Zanuck's office at Twentieth Century-Fox, being an illiterate philistine is not among them. From his apprenticeship at Warner Brothers through his supremely autocratic reign at Fox, Zanuck always possessed a keen nose for great literature and great writers and on his watch some of the most serious and controversial books of his time became celebrated Fox pictures. Securing the rights from Steinbeck in 1939 for $100,000, Zanuck began assembling his team of actors, technicians, writers and, of course, the director.

Zanuck promised from the outset of production that the screen adaptation of *Wrath* would be absolutely faithful to the book but he and everyone else knew that would simply be impossible. Not only the length of the book militated against that possibility but also the radical political rumblings that murmured like a *basso profundo* underneath every page. The book was basically a pro-union, anti-capitalist polemic that in attacking big business, banks, the police and anyone who was not a member of the oppressed working class, was seen by many as a clarion call for revolution springing from the heartland of the republic. Politics aside, there were also parts of Steinbeck's book that would never have received the seal of approval from the Hays Office. America in 1939 was not ready for scenes such as the stillborn baby of Rosasharn (the teenage and pregnant Joad daughter) floating down the river or breastfeeding an old, dying man with milk intended for her dead child in the same year that *The Wizard of Oz* and *Goodbye, Mr. Chips* hit the silver screen.

The task of translating Steinbeck's massive work into a filmable script went to Nunnally Johnson, one of the most respected scribes in the industry who would meet and later marry his third wife, actress Dorris Bowden (who played Rosasharn) during the production of the film. Johnson was something of a rarity in Hollywood, in that he successfully won the trifecta crown of writer, producer and director in a career that spanned four decades. Johnson enjoyed an extremely prolific and varied career in all three capacities, with films to his credit such as *Jesse James*, *The Keys of the Kingdom*, *The Mudlark*, *The Man in the Gray Flannel Suit* and *The Dirty Dozen*. Johnson had also worked with Ford before, writing the script for *The Prisoner of Shark Island*, so his knowledge of Ford's style and rhythm as well as his own journalistic background gave him the chops needed to tackle Steinbeck's lean, taut and dangerous prose.

Zanuck's first choice for director, oddly enough, was not Ford. From notes scribbled on the front of Johnson's script draft, it can be gathered that Zanuck was leaning toward Clarence Brown, the stalwart M-G-M maestro responsible for nearly all Greta Garbo's greatest films at the studio and a host of other classics. However, Zanuck soon began to woo his top director on the lot and Ford, fully cognizant of the *gravitas* of the project, rapturously responded to the love song. Deep into the production of *Drums Along the Mohawk*, Ford sent Zanuck a telegram dated July 17, 1939. "If I were assured a month off, I would leap at the chance of doing "Wrath"—as I have several things to do in the East. Could you leave it this way: wait until I return from location, by then you will have seen the stuff and will know if we are on the right track, then let us make a decision."[11]

While Zanuck bandied about names for the major roles in the film, including the centrifugal role of Ma Joad (he eventually and wisely settled on Jane Darwell, who gave an astonishingly rich performance), both he and Ford were certain about using Henry Fonda in the lead as Tom Joad. His laconic, introspective reserve had given his Abe Lincoln a brooding mystery and his Gil Martin a noble, quiet strength. His Tom Joad would be a dangerous, wound-up ex-con willing and able to do anything to serve his family and, later, an even larger segment of humanity.

In telling the story of the Joads' migration from their foreclosed and burnt-out farms in Oklahoma to the fruit-rich Salinas Valley in California, Zanuck promised also that the film would be strictly non-political. Zanuck's pronouncement was a *de jure* bone thrown to the nervous board of directors in New York but the *de facto* reality was that making a film about the economic meltdown of Depression-era America and not mentioning politics would have been like making a film about the New York Yankees and not mentioning baseball. Zanuck knew this well and while he protected his production with a certain amount of hush-hush and tight security, Ford had the tetchier task of making the film a powerfully moving, and not merely a politically angry, drama. With Nunnally Johnson's keen sense of story construction and editing, Ford basically kept the sense of economic and personal desolation intact while re-shifting the focus on the Joad family's struggle to reach California in order to give it an emotional, rather than a political, core.

The film was stunningly shot by the legendary cinematographer Gregg Toland, a brilliant painter of light and shadow whose masterful work with Ford on *Wrath* led to another association even more celebrated. Orson Welles, a twenty-five-year-old enfant terrible recently arrived from the New York stage, was preparing to shoot his first film over at RKO and was desperately in need of mentors to guide him through the byzantine labyrinths of Hollywood movie-making. Welles reportedly saw *Stagecoach* dozens of time in order to understand the art of composition and his admiration of Ford and his collaboration with Toland on *Wrath* and *The Long Voyage Home* the following year led him to use the cinematographer on *Citizen Kane.*

Like Steinbeck's prose, Toland's black and white camera work is harsh, uncompromising and deftly composed with expressionistic bravado that emulated the famous photojournalistic work of Dorothea Lange, whose images of the Okies and their plight seared the American psyche. The actors wear no makeup, five o'clock shadows grow into scruffy beards and costumes look like they were dragged through a cornfield behind a backhoe. The first quarter of the film, which opens with Tom fresh out of prison and making his way back to his family farm, is all thin stretches of land dominated by vast expanses of sky. These early shots are reminiscent of the Dutch landscapes of Van Ruisdael and his emphasis on man's isolation and insignificance in the cosmic order. It is as if humanity has been forgotten, and it is forgotten people Tom returns to find. There is Casey (John Carradine in a performance of extraordinary novelty and controlled goofiness), the itinerant preacher who has lost his faith not only due to the hard times but his weakness for drink and the sinful women whom he leads deeper into sin. His former neighbor, Muley (John Qualen), once a prosperous farmer is now a displaced squatter living alone in the deserted Joad house, laying his head wherever he can, dodging police and wondering if he is slowly going mad. The next day Tom is reunited with his family, including Ma, Pa (Russell Simpson), Grandpa (Charley Grapewin, fresh from his memorable turn as Uncle Henry in *The Wizard of Oz*), his uncle and siblings. Everyone he comes home to is defeated, beaten down into the dust like their withered crops. Men who were once solid sodbusters and indomitable manifestations of the American spirit are now useless, impotent vagrants on their own land, haunting the fringes of life like, as Muley says of himself, "graveyard ghosts."

The glue holding the tenuous circle of brittle humanity together is Ma. Unlike Ford's previous and future maternal figures, Ma Joad is no Gibraltar-like bastion of strength and fortitude. Like the men, Ma is shattered by the destructive forces of time and socioeconomic realities that are far beyond her grasp. Ma is haunted, but not in the same way as the men. Her ghosts are the howling banshees of hunger, displacement and where her brood will find their next job and meal. Her men may have sprung from the earth but Ma, like O-Lan in *The Good Earth* and Scarlett O'Hara in *Gone With the Wind, is* the earth upon which everyone around her lives and moves and has their being. There are poignant moments of sentiment in which Ma gives way to remembrance and loss, such as the incredible scene where she is going through her personal letters and memorabilia and tossing most of it into a small stove fire. She pockets a small pair of earrings, but not before holding them up to her ears and looking at herself in a cracked mirror; the seemingly insignificant trinkets brings a universe of emotions and memories to her aged and careworn face.

The only Elysian field of tranquility the Joads find in their hellish odyssey is the refugee camp run by the Department of Agriculture. For the first time in weeks, under the gentle wing of the New Deal, the family finds a safe haven with clean cabins, running water, and a sanctuary where sheriffs and their goons cannot arrest or even touch anyone without due process of law. In fact, the old gentleman running the USDA camp (Ford is prudent enough to zoom in on the sign and name of the department lest anyone not get the point) is so benevolent, so avuncular and solicitous that one expects him to greet the Joads in a white beard, rosy cheeks and a red velvet and fur suit.

It is in this harbor of peace and dignity that Tom has the epiphany that leads to his finding his voice and vocation in life. Before Casey meets his death at the hands of anti-union thugs stalking the fringes of the camp, the ex-preacher who had lost his faith in prayer and formal religion finds it anew in a labor-oriented universal religion of man. If the martyred proletariat is the Word, then Casey and all who profess the worker's creed of work, bread and dignity are the apostles called to take the message of salvation throughout the world.

Tom's transformation from moody ex-con and passive victim of the times into a prophet and champion of the workingman is no less political but decidedly more spiritual. Ford's Catholic worldview by definition entailed a belief in the transforming nature of grace. In his hands, Tom's conversion and radical call to a higher path is not a mere reaction to Casey's death but a proactive embrace of a vocation. A mere political conversion would have robbed the ending of its universality and power and thus what Tom experiences is not so much a commitment to worker's rights as it is a Pentecost of sorts.

When the sheriff starts combing the camp after the big dance (another Fordian motif symbolizing the bond of community) and looking to arrest Tom for his part in the fight that got Casey killed, Tom goes on the lam. Waking Ma, they sit by the side of the empty dance platform and commence one of the most enduringly beautiful scenes, not only in the film but in film history. There is no score behind the scene to ratchet up the emotion, no overwrought feelings and Gregg Toland's simple and diffused lighting strips the moment down to an integrity as simple and unaffected as the characters. Tom does not simply say goodbye to Ma, he struggles to convey his epiphany in a soliloquy as well known to cineastes as Lincoln's Gettysburg Address is to a grade-schooler. "Wherever there's a fight so hungry people can eat, I'll be there. Wherever there's a cop beatin' up a guy, I'll be there. I'll be there in the way guys yell when they're mad. I'll be there in the way kids laugh when they're hungry and they know supper's ready. And when the people are eating the stuff they raised, livin' in the houses they build, I'll be there too." Like Casey, Tom's soul has merged from his little one to be a part of greater, universal one "that belongs to everyone." Unlike Casey, however, Tom is not a mere agitator, he is the New Man, filled with the gifts of the Consoler such as wisdom, courage, understanding, right judgment, wonder and awe. And like the Consoler, he will be everywhere for all peoples. He sets off into the dark, sure of the path he must take, a missionary taking the word of abundance, joy and equality to the poor, suffering and marginalized of the world.

⸺•⸺

When Ford shot the scene between Ma and Tom, according to Henry Fonda he did so with a minimum of rehearsal since he felt both Darwell and Fonda were well into the hearts of their characters to be able to do it in one take. After some brief direction on the set, the two actors wisely chose to underplay their emotions for what was undoubtedly a highly emotional scene, holding them in check rather than give into the tempting histrionics and gushing that would have ruined the moment. The result is that the actors do not speak their lines as much as inhabit the emotions behind them, giving the moment spontaneity and depth that is as powerful as it is movingly beautiful. When the scene was finished, Ford, as was his wont when particularly pleased, and even touched, by an actor's performance, quietly said, "Cut," and walked away. Fonda thought he may have even been crying.[12]

After editing and a massive media blitz, accompanied by a series of illustrations by artist Thomas Hart Benton, *Wrath* opened in early 1940 to almost national acclaim and hosannas. The critics, including the jaded gladiators of the pen behind the arts desks at the *New York Times* and *The New Yorker*, were effusive in their praise for the style, substance and meaning of the film. Even the First Lady, Eleanor Roosevelt, gave the film a primly activist nod in her daily newspaper column. Ford's peers in the Academy shared the opinion of the press and the White House, and the following year he won his second Oscar for Best Director while Jane Darwell took home the award for Best Supporting Actress.[13]

⸺•⸺

As the new decade moved into its second year, Ford showed no signs of abating in his transformation from A list director to a total and complete *artiste* of international repute. He was, as it were, ready to leave the shadowy shores of expressionism and press out into the deeper and more treacherous waters of Existentialism. His craft on his next journey, with an appropriately nautical theme, would be provided by America's premier existentialist playwright.

Eugene O'Neill (1888-1953) is rightly considered America's greatest playwright of the twentieth century and his canon, like Ford's films, include an almost unbroken and unsurpassed line of classics that explored the darker sides and twilit corners of the American psyche. These include *A Long Day's Journey Into Night, The Iceman Cometh, Anna Christie, Desire Under the Elms, Strange Interlude* and *Ah, Wilderness.* In many respects, the Irish Catholic native of the East Coast, Gene O'Neill, was a shadowy and literary *doppelganger* of the Irish Catholic native of the East Coast, John Ford. Like Ford, O'Neill was a moody, brooding genius who was plagued by melancholia and a lifelong, soul-lacerating alcoholism, both of which would insinuate themselves into the DNA of his work. Both men flirted with radical politics early in their lives; Ford with the I.R.B. and the cause of Irish nationalism while O'Neill joined the IWW and chummed around with Greenwich Village bohemian artists and radical writers like John Reed, Max Eastman, Louise Bryant and Emma Goldman. Mostly, however, O'Neill and Ford were bonded by their common love of the sea. O'Neill had served with the merchant marine service as a young man and, like Ford, embraced the sea not only physically but spiritually as well, seeing in its infinite expanse a metaphor for the weals and woes of life as well as a mirror of eternity.

Walter Wanger, the producer who had given Ford such rewarding latitude during the production of *Stagecoach,* was sure that cinematic lightning strikes twice in the same place and in 1940 signed a two-picture contract with Ford's and Merian Cooper's Argosy Pictures.[14]

Ford was intrigued with the idea of filming O'Neill's sea works and sequestered Dudley Nichols doing double duty to conflate four O'Neill plays, *Moon of the Caribbees, Bound for East Cardiff* (O'Neill's first play), *In the Zone* and *The Long Voyage Home* into one seaboard saga. Eventually, it came to bear the title of the last play, *The Long Voyage Home.*

The newly conflated and restructured quartet tells the story of the men of the merchant ship S.S. *Glencairn* in the tense and anxiety-ridden opening days of World War II. The film opens in a hot, airless Caribbean port where the restless and sex-starved sailors await the arrival of seaside tarts, spirited aboard by the pugnacious, bellicose but eminently fair and just-minded Irishman "Drisk" Driscoll (Thomas Mitchell). The crew also includes the blustery Yank (Ward Bond), the weasel-like steward Cocky (Barry Fitzgerald), the young Swede Ole Olson (John Wayne), the thoughtful, pipe-smoking Donkeyman (Arthur Shields), the simple, music loving Norwegian Axel (John Qualen) and the mysterious but obviously well-born Englishman Smitty (Ian Hunter). Drisk is the unofficial leader of the group of sailors who, despite the hearty and salty nature of their profession, all appear as lost, brittle and deeply fractured men who are corroded by alcohol and exhausted by the pursuit of some nameless existential hound that snaps at their heels. Like the Joad men from *The Grapes of Wrath*, the men of the *Glencairn* are emotionally and spiritually adrift and haunt even their own beings like ghosts of a graveyard put out to sea.

On their way back across the Atlantic, Yank is injured during a fierce storm and soon dies from his wounds. He enters the cold embrace of death with a horror and fear of the dark and the unknown, a terror that symbolizes the general drift of the *Glencairn* and all the men who sail on her. Despite Drisk's attempts at being a leader, there are no heroes on this long voyage home, just victims and survivors. The captain and officers are much like the law enforcement officials in *The Grapes of Wrath*; they do not protect or serve but merely pop in out of nowhere to bully and dictate policy before disappearing again. The crew of the *Glencairn* do not go to sea out of love for adventure and solitude on the vast expanse of ocean. They sail because there is no home for them on land and the only home they will eventually find will be the one that Yank found. And in the same way will they enter that final door of fear with the terror and futility that comes of never finding the meaning of one's life. Drisk sums it up for the whole crew when, after a dockside constable orders them to move indoors and extinguish the lights before a blackout, he cries out, "Everywhere people stumbling in the dark.... Is there to be no more light in the world?" Suffice it to say the film is no carefree cruise on the *Araner* but it is definitely, along with *The Searchers*, one of Ford's most darkly daring endeavors.

Unlike *The Grapes of Wrath*, *The Long Voyage Home* has a grim sense of oppression and hopelessness that is not tempered by uplifting "we the people" endings or signs, weak though they may be, that family and community will somehow endure. Even though Ford is deep into the dark expressionism of *The Informer*, there are no themes of crucifixion, madonnas, sin and forgiveness that peppered the earlier film like a Catholic catechism class. The sailors of the *Glencairn* are no Gypo Nolans, attempting to flee from God across the water like Jonah only to find redemption at the end of the journey. On the contrary, the seamen here are more akin to Ancient Mariners, Wandering Jews of sorts, condemned to drift, forever homeless, while telling their tale of woe to future generations.

There may be no heroes on board but, thankfully, there is innocence. Ole, the young Swede who wants to return to his mother's farm, represents the last hope of the crew and they are intent on getting him home. Ole in some respects is the only spiritual symbol among the broken men, but calling him a Christ figure is both too easy and too far out of the park in terms of how O'Neill and Ford envisioned him. However, the whole Catholic concept of The Body is manifested in Ole, and like the church, if he accomplishes his own salvation the other members, closely tied to him in the bond of love, will somehow participate in the graces. Ole's salvation, in the end, is theirs as well.

Like Ford and O'Neill, the crew are men used up and wasted by alcohol, either as a stopgap against past memories (like Smitty, who turns out to be British officer washed out from the ranks because of his weakness for the bottle) or a buffer against the interminable gray awfulness of the present. Back in England, alcohol almost leads to calamity and the undoing of their noble plans. While his friends are distracted in the back room of a dive pub, Ole falls prey to a tart (played by Mildred Natwick in the first of many roles she played as an esteemed member of the Ford Company) who slips him a mickey in order that he can be shanghaied aboard the ship *Amindra* by press gangs. Drisk catches on to the scheme and they all fight their way on board the dark vessel and rescue the doped up Ole. In the ensuing scuffle, Drisk is knocked unconscious and hauled below to take Ole's place. As the crew stumbles back on board the *Glencairn* several days later to begin their climb to Calvary once again, an airborne newspaper blown by the wind is picked up to reveal the headlines that the *Amindra* was torpedoed by a German U-boat with the loss of all hands. Drisk, the cynical, whiskey-soaked hard nose, it turns out, gave his life so that his brother could live. Drisk, like Ole and Yank, is free while the men of the *Glencairn* continue their interminable voyage.

Ford was not the only genius on the film, and he gladly (and literally) shared the credit with the astounding cameraman Gregg Toland. Toland's brilliance in shooting *Voyage* lies not so much in camera movement or lack of it as it does in his superb use of lighting and composition. Aside from his signature use of deep focus (composing a wide field shot with close, middle and distant people or images all in focus), Toland also employs harsh linear compositions throughout the film with both light and objects. Beaming shafts of light pierce the misty and foggy nights, taut ropes stretch in geometric patterns and even shipboard gratings convey a sense of prison bars as if the men of the *Glencairn* are trapped forever on their existential ship. Ford's immense respect for Toland was boundless, and it is obvious that, from the cameraman's technique to Ford's sharing of the title card with him, Toland's work on *Voyage* inspired Orson Welles to use him the following year with even more magnificent results on *Citizen Kane*.

The Long Voyage Home opened in November of 1940 to nearly unanimous critical acclaim. Bosley Crowther of the *New York Times*, the elder statesman of movie reviews who held great sway from the 1930s through the 1950s, said, "John Ford has fashioned a modern Odyssey...it is harsh and relentless and only briefly compassionate in its revelation of man's pathetic shortcomings."[15] The film picked up Academy Award nominations for Best Picture, Toland's cinematography, Dudley Nichols' screenplay, editing and music score and Ford won the prestigious New York Film Critics Circle Award for Best Director. The ticket-buying public, however, battening down the hatches in anticipation of a rousing sea yarn, abetted by movie posters showing beefy sailors leering over the railing at buxom native girls, found the film much too grim, dark and arty for their tastes. Its initial run only earned back $600,000 of its $680,000 cost but the sting of perceived failure was salved by a congratulatory note from Eugene O'Neill, who presciently saw it as the masterpiece of American cinema it has become. Ford received a note, dated July 29th, 1940, from Carlota O'Neill, the playwright's wife, who wrote, "Gene and I love the job you did. The casting was marvelous and the photography was very fine. We were deeply moved and proud that you had directed it."[16]

The Promethean lightning bolt that Walter Wanger had hoped would be hurled from the heavens missed, at least commercially, a second time in what would prove to be Ford's only stumble in his triumphal three-year run. The power and the glory of *The Grapes of Wrath* apparently still tingled in the spines of Zanuck and Ford, and when Erskine Caldwell's celebrated novel *Tobacco Road* (which was transformed into a long-running hit on Broadway) was acquired by Fox, they thought they had another working-man blockbuster at their fingertips. The studios had scrambled over each other in an attempt to secure the rights to the novel, although the raciness of certain portions of the plot, like the union politics and leftist screeds of *Wrath*, had to be cleaned up for 1941 American moviegoers. Casting proved problematic from the start as well, and names like Henry Hull and Walter Brennan were bandied about for the role of Jeeter, the poor Georgia cotton farmer tossed off his sharecropping farm during the Depression. Eventually, Charley Grapewin, so memorable as Grandpa Joad, took the lead with a young Gene Tierney (soon to become one of Fox's top stars of the 1940s), with Ward Bond and Dana Andrews in support.

Ford can be forgiven his sloppiness, his tired and unfunny habit of inserting broad humor at inappropriate moments in his narratives and even his outright failures. In *Tobacco Road*, however, Ford is uncharacteristically a bit dishonest. Time and again, Ford (perhaps to justify his boredom with a project and its resulting failure) would say that he simply liked to make movies and tell simple stories with no attempt to top his last success. Here Ford obviously was coasting on the steam generated by *The Grapes of Wrath* and simply hoped to knock it out of the park without having to perfect his batting technique. The Joads' journey ultimately led to the sun-dappled valleys of peaches and hope in California. *Tobacco Road*, like Ada and Jeeter's journey to the poorhouse, simply leads nowhere. Fortunately, Ford's next project buried the memory of this stillborn child in ways that even he could not have imagined.

How Green Was My Valley, considered by many film historians and critics (along with the director himself) to be Ford's masterpiece, was oddly enough almost the greatest film never directed by John Ford. Richard Llewellyn's 1939 novel, *How Green Was My Valley*, told in 651 pages the story of family turmoil and labor upheaval in south Wales in the early 1900s. Although the story centers around the shifting personal and labor alliances of the Morgan family, presided over by a genial dictator of a father, Gwilym, the narrative is told through the memories of the youngest boy, Huw (pronounced Hugh). Llewellyn claimed to have based the book upon his own childhood experiences but, being London-born and having spent precious little time in Wales, this can be seen as so much Celtic braggadocio.

Zanuck envisioned the big screen version of *Valley* as a three hour Technicolor roadshow; a sweeping historical epic of family, love and conflict that would be Fox's answer to David O. Selznick's *Gone With the Wind*. The plan to shoot on location in Wales, however, was stymied by a small problem called World War II. Germany's invasion of Poland in September of 1939 plunged Europe into a continental war, and in 1940 the nightly blitzing of London transformed the island kingdom into a veritable fortress. The thought of moving film units from the still non-belligerent United States across the Atlantic and setting up production in the beleaguered island, even in the lull before the blitzing of London, was simply out of the question.

Another fly in the Welsh buttermilk was the subject of oppressed laborers, strikes and unions, which raised its beefy, clenched fist on almost every page of Llewellyn's book. Once again the Fox board of directors in New York flipped through the story outline with jittery nerves, afraid that Zanuck was going to lob yet another political time bomb into the theaters of America. Matters were not helped when Ernest Pascal (who had co-authored Ford's *Wee Willie Winkie* in 1937) delivered a script that focused on the political rather than the human side of the story. Zanuck threw out Pascal's script and hired Philip Dunne, one of Fox's top screenwriters from the 1930s through the 1960s with excellent films to his credit such as *The Last of the Mohicans* (1936), *Stanley and Livingstone* (1939), *The Ghost and Mrs. Muir* (1947), *The Robe* (1953) and *The Agony and the Ecstasy* (1965). Although he was a tough, pro-union liberal who went on to do battle with the House Un-American Activities Committee (HUAC) during the 1950s blacklist, Dunne wrote with great emotion and sentiment and could give a sense of historical sweep without losing the intimacy of personal drama. Dunne's new script enacted a seismic shift in focus and balanced the plight of the pro-union miners with the withering effects of time and turmoil, a la *The Grapes of Wrath*, on the poor but proudly noble Morgan family. Dunne also, at Zanuck's insistence, kept the narrative a flashback through the eyes of Huw, who though he tells the story as an adult packing his things and leaving his valley for the last time, remains a boy throughout the film. When the epic story was pared down to a more practical running time of two hours, Zanuck also resisted the temptation to insert his top star, Tyrone Power, into the second half as the adult Huw.[17]

While Dunne labored over the script in the fall of 1940, Zanuck borrowed William Wyler from Samuel Goldwyn to direct the picture. Like Ford and Zanuck, Wyler and Goldwyn irritated, outraged but ultimately challenged the other into more daring visions and better work. Unlike Ford, Wyler labored over his scripts with medical precision and had a reputation for shooting some thirty takes for an individual scene. Legend even had him driving Greer Garson through nearly forty some takes for one scene of *Mrs. Miniver* and Charlton Heston through a similar amount on *Ben-Hur*. This *modus operandi* on all his films drove even those normally placid and easy-going actors into frothing madness. The lean budget and tight schedule led the Fox brass to conclude that they could not afford the exacting and expensive perfectionism Wyler was afforded by Goldwyn's deep pockets and by the end of 1940 Wyler was out and Ford was in.

When Ford came aboard the project as 1941 began, Zanuck, Wyler and Dunne had almost all the key elements in place, including the casting, which Willie Wyler had begun to supervise. The key role of Huw Morgan was given to a twelve-year-old English import, Roddy McDowall. He had made a few films in England and after being sent over to the States at the outbreak of World War II was one of hundreds of boys who responded to the Fox casting call. Wyler liked what he saw and had Zanuck sign him and Ford ended up getting an astoundingly deep and highly intelligent performance from the boy.

Irish actress Sara Allgood was cast as Beth, the matriarch of the Morgan family and, as Huw says, "It's heart." The venerable Donald Crisp memorably filled the part of the iron-willed yet benign Gwilym who presides over the dissolution of his family and the old ways of the valley. The noble Canadian stalwart Walter Pidgeon, who could not play a cad or a lout if his life or career depended on it, was signed on as Mr. Gruffyd, the progressive new minister who, as both a man of God and social justice, supports the idea of a union as long as it does not embrace violence or beget more injustice. English actress Anna Lee, an elegant and lofty beauty who Ford adored to a point just short of canonization, took the role of Bronwyn, and although she marries the oldest Morgan (Patric Knowles) she becomes the object of young Huw's boyish passion.

Rounding out the major players was the twenty-year-old actress Maureen O'Hara, who played Angharad, the only female member of the Morgan clan who loves Mr. Gruffyd yet locks herself into a miserable and loveless marriage with the wealthy son of the mine owner. Born Maureen FitzSimmons in Dublin, O'Hara received her training at the Abbey Theatre but had her major film breakthroughs, both with Charles Laughton, in 1939. The first was the screen version of Daphne du Maurier's *Jamaica Inn* and then to greater acclaim as Esmeralda in RKO's much-beloved *The Hunchback of Notre Dame*. Although it took Technicolor film to awe the world with her flaming red hair that glowed like an Arizona sunset, even in black and white, O'Hara conveyed a rare and original blend of strength, fire, sexuality, gentleness and vulnerability. Her Angharad is, unlike Mr. Gruffyd and his single-minded devotion to his ministry, complex and moves from an adoring young girl to a mature married woman unhappy with her life, saddened by her choices and disconnected from the family and valley that nurtured and strengthened her.

O'Hara, who developed a close and lifelong friendship with Duke Wayne, went on to make five films with Ford and like her male co-star became the actor most closely identified with the director. Unlike the timidly deferential Wayne, who could never imagine talking back to Ford, O'Hara had a combustive relationship with the director on almost every picture they made together. Oddly, for a man who liked his women tough and indomitable in the Kate Hepburn mold, Ford found O'Hara's intractability infuriating and his lifelong relationship with the actress was a curious combination of combativeness and affection.

The valley itself features prominently in the film and although Ford always seconded fabricated sets to the natural poetry of actual locations like Monument Valley, he presided over one of the greatest and most famous single sets in movie history. The town, complete with a colliery tower, chapel, shops and three-dimensional houses was a masterpiece of set design built by art director Richard Day and associate Nathan Juran. It was made at the Fox studio ranch in the hills of Malibu (later the location for the field hospital in the studio's long running hit TV series, M*A*S*H) and was used again in 1943 as a Norwegian town in the war film *The Moon is Down*. Arthur Miller, one of the studio's most proficient black-and-white cinematographers (he won an Oscar for *Valley*, along with the studio's future hits *The Song of Bernadette* and *Anna and the King of Siam*) shot the film and, like Gregg Toland, enjoyed an excellent working relationship with Ford during production. Miller used the sets to their fullest and expertly balanced the sweep and wideness of the outdoor shots with a silvery intimacy for the interiors as well as a dirty, gritty wetness for the mining scenes.

Artie Miller, like Ford, was a stern-faced, pipe-chomping old pro who always wore a battered fedora and did masterful work with no fanfare or nonsense. Although they made fewer than half a dozen films together, the cameraman and director had an instinctively symbiotic relationship and were able to understand each other with a minimum of verbiage. They were basically like two crotchety uncles on a fishing trip; all work, little chatter and achieving the best results by brooking no interference from meddling civilians. From beginning to end, the entire film is composed of scenes of grace, power and beauty but, like great music, poetry and art they do not feel forced or cloyingly sentimental. Like the visual elements of good liturgy such as color, movement and images, the compositions of *How Green Was My Valley* do not distract or dominate but support and drive the narrative forward.

Two shots from the same scene perfectly illustrate both Ford's emotions and Miller's Mephistophelian prowess in manifesting them visually. Following Angharad's marriage to Iestyn, the wealthy but pompous and cold fish son of the mine owner, her long lace veil soars straight up into the heavens like a rocket as she enters the carriage outside the chapel. Urban, and even suburban, myth had this glorious and obviously phallic image the result of Ford's timing and perennial Irish luck. Blarney, Maureen O'Hara would aver, and reveal that the effect was achieved by several wind machines strategically placed by Miller and Ford until they got the magic moment they sought. The other shot from the same scene is when Mr. Gruffyd leaves the church after performing the wedding service and watches the woman he loves ride off with another, and vastly inferior, man as her new husband. Instead of cutting in for a close-up, as any other director would have instinctively done (and any actor would have relished) to get the look of pain and desolation on Gruffyd's face, Ford kept it as a single shot of the actor in the distance. Not only did the shot emphasize Gruffyd's isolation and loneliness but it also served Ford's vaunted pragmatism in giving the editing department as few shots as possible and thus allowing the film to be cut his way. When Miller asked Ford if he wanted a close-up of Walter Pidgeon watching the couple ride away, Ford growled back an unequivocal, "Hell no." If the studio had the shot, he said, they'd only use it.[18]

How Green Was My Valley is often called a memory play. It is in fact Ford's greatest, and in that is exactly what, on the surface, it is. Ford has also been criticized for the bucolic and roseate hues through which he shows poor and oppressed miners singing and celebrating their way through their days. This cannot be more of a misreading of the work than if people mistook it for a Western. The film is Ford's most personal work, not just in theme but in the autobiographic nature of young Huw as the doted-on youngest child of a large working class family. Even though Ford filmed the script pretty much as Dunne wrote it, within the framework are the flourishes and grace notes that reveal much of his own childhood memories of Maine. Donald Crisp and Sara Allgood bear more than a passing resemblance to Daddo and Abby, from his benign dictatorship to her strong-willed tongue lashings and protection of her brood. Like Huw, Ford endured several months in bed while recuperating from diphtheria and took the opportunity to immerse himself, at the insistence of family and teachers, in the great works of literature. And finally like Huw, young Jack had to watch older brothers and sisters disappear before he himself left the fold forever. Hence, the preponderance and persistence of memory in the film in a way he never really employed before or after.

In all Ford's mature works firmly rooted in memory and myth, most notably *Fort Apache, She Wore a Yellow Ribbon, The Quiet Man* and *The Man Who Shot Liberty Valance*, he does not foist lies or frauds but shows us reality as well as the mythological lens through which the protagonist chooses to see it. He does not, in fact, show one at the expense of the other.

Huw's valley at the beginning is indeed a place of desolation and poverty, populated by yet more graveyard ghosts, covered in grime and polluted by the slag of the played out coal mines. Ford is quite honest in showing us the awful truth but instead of a flashback, where the narrator endeavors to accurately recount a series of events, he allows Huw simply to remember the people and things that were but are no more. For Huw, memory is equal to reality and it is the power of memory that makes everything gone live in an eternal present. Memory is the spiritual alchemy that makes the past and all it contains more present than the present.

"Memory," says the voice-over of the adult Huw (Irving Pichel) as he packs his things in his mother's shawl and prepares to leave the valley for the last time. "Strange that the mind will forget so much of what only this moment has passed and yet hold clear and bright the memory of what happened years ago. The memory of men and women long since dead. And yet who shall say what is real and what is not? Can I believe my friends are gone when their voices are still a glory in my ears? No, and I shall stand to say no and no again!" Despite what Huw says, memory play is much too confining, much too parochial a definition for what he, through Ford, is saying. Memory is merely the catalytic agent here, but what Ford achieves is the reality of the past in the present, the actual presence of the dead among the living in a real and tangible way. Although the communication between the living and the dead was a recurrent theme in most of Ford's better and even great films, in *How Green Was My Valley* it forms the core heart and soul of the entire film in a way so poetic, so complete and so real a manner that it honestly comes by its designation of a classic. It is also, without doubt, Ford's most integrally Catholic film.

In the voluminous discussion of the works of John Ford, not only in books but in interviews and documentaries, it is not long before the words "Irish" and "Catholic" enter the conversation. His Irishness and how it formed and informed his work has been examined more times than one can shake a shillelagh at it. His Catholicism, when discussed at all, usually drops the Ford scholar in murkier depths and leaves them hinting here and generalizing there while quickly paddling through to clearer water. From interviews and research it has often been declared that Ford was a good, while not devout Catholic, who baptized his children, befriended priests and observed pro-forma attendance at mass while maintaining a hardy Irish skepticism about it all and remaining particularly wary of the clergy and hierarchy. Scott Eyman, author of the Ford biography, *Print the Legend*, touches on Ford's Catholicism throughout the entire book but concludes that in the end Ford's faith was that of the immigrant. As Eyman says, Ford's Catholicism was an adjunct of Old World genetics; unquestioned, obligatory but not resulting from a conscious choice based upon core beliefs. In the end, Eyman says, Catholicism chose him.[19]

The most comforting Catholic doctrine exposited in *Valley*, and the one that becomes the blood of its heart, is that which is called the Communion of the Saints. Quite simply, it is the belief that all are members of one body, one living organism and the actions of one, good or bad, have a profound and lasting effect on the others. More than just some mystical mutual aid society, the Communion of the Saints is an eternal tether that binds the living and the dead in a lifeline that breaks down the doors of death and connects the two worlds and all those dwelling there. The dead are always with us, Huw says, not as shades or ghosts in a dark mirror, but as real and present to us now as they were to us then. *"Vita mutatur, non tollitur,"* the liturgy for the old Latin funeral mass proclaimed: "Life has changed, it has not been taken away." Without this decidedly Fordian and Catholic understanding of life and death, *How Green Was My Valley* loses its patina of greatness and becomes just another good, sentimental film from the golden age of the Hollywood studio system.

The first fifteen minutes of *Valley* is one of the most extraordinarily moving quarter hours in the history of film history, mostly because it contains all the aforementioned Catholic themes packed, in full measure, into the space of a few minutes. Ford shows the living bond of the family/community/body, the table and ritual. Most importantly, there is the unity between the living and the dead. Huw does not so much conjure up the spirits of his family and friends as allow the viewer to enter into the very real fellowship of love they all still enjoy. And if we believe them to be actually gone forever, Huw emphatically responds no, no and stands to say no again. When, in the prologue, Angharad calls out to Huw across the valley as he walks with their father, it is as if she is calling to him from across the bridged abyss of eternity. At the end of the film, as he cradles the body of his dead father who was killed in a mine cave-in, Huw once again reveals the mystery of the film's heart. "Men like my father cannot die," the adult narrator intones. "They are with me still, real in memory as they were in flesh, loving and beloved forever. How green was my valley then."

As the film began, so it ends with a pastiche of images, some previously seen and then new shots showing the family, separated by death and time, reunited once again in an eternally green valley. The last shot, played in front of the Welsh singers' majestically swelling "Myfanwy," shows Huw again a boy walking with his father on one of the valley roads, his brothers coming to meet them from one direction and Angharad waving to them atop a hill from the other. Like the final shot of *Young Mr. Lincoln*, they do not walk away into the distance as they crest the hill but toward us, joining their reality with ours and inviting us, as Ford's favorite hymn went, to gather at the river.

—————

How Green Was My Valley opened on October 26, 1941, to more national acclaim and huzzahs than even Zanuck had hoped for or anticipated. The film was nominated for a staggering ten Academy Awards with Oscars going to Zanuck for Best Picture, Ford for Best Director, Donald Crisp for Best Supporting Actor and Arthur Miller for Cinematography. Richard Griffith (no doubt slightly prejudiced due to his own Welsh surname) wrote in his review for the *Los Angeles Times* on November 11, 1941, "As for John Ford, '*How Green Was My Valley*' is a crowning achievement, the most intensely real of all his fine pictures. It is so because he was given the freedom to experiment with camera and sound, and for this, critics credit Darryl F. Zanuck."[20]

The sense of hope and enduring community in the face of change and threats from dangerous, outside forces was lapped up by American audiences like water in the proverbial desert. Europe was entering its second year of world war and it seemed like just a matter of time, despite the strength of isolationist politicians and general sentiment, before America was forced to enter the fray. By the time the film was in general release in early 1942, America was at war with the Empire of Japan and most of the cast and crew, including Donald Crisp, art director Nathan Juran and Zanuck himself, were in uniform. For Lt. Cmdr. John Ford, USNR (United States Naval Reserve), however, the war had already begun months before the first Zero torpedo tore into the sides of the U.S.S. *Arizona* at Pearl Harbor.

PHOTOS

Grateful acknowledgement is given to Dan Ford for permission to reprint 14 photographs from The John Ford Papers in The Lilly Library. Photos provided courtesy of The Lilly Library, Indiana University, Bloomington, Indiana.

The poet recapturing his Irish soul. Ford in a white jacket (reflected in the window on the lower r) directs Preston Foster in his 1936 adaptation of Sean O'Casey's play, *The Plough and the Stars*. The film, a story of young lovers caught up in the turmoil of Dublin's 1916 Easter Uprising, was expected to be a grim, expressionist film in the spirit of Ford's *The Informer* two years earlier. Alas, the result was a lackluster, half-hearted offering quickly forgotten.

The poet as warrior. Lt. Commander John Ford, USNR (seated center with pipe and dark glasses and holding the camera) poses with fellow soldiers in the Pacific around the time he filmed the Battle of Midway (1942). The actual footage he shot during the heat of the battle, later edited into an Academy Award-winning documentary, was an extraordinary historic record that helped give meaning to the conflict for Americans back home.

3 Godfathers (1948). John Wayne (l), Harry Carey, Jr. (c), and Pedro Armendariz (r) are three desperadoes trapped in the Arizona desert who find a newborn baby and redemption on Christmas Eve. The film not only showed Ford at his most unabashedly sentimental and Catholic but also showcased the humanistic concept of "The Good Bad Man" he began exploring with actor Harry Carey, Sr. thirty years earlier.

History as ritual. Captain Nathan Brittles (John Wayne, 2nd from r) leads his troopers on one last cavalry charge before retiring in *She Wore a Yellow Ribbon* (1949). The sumptuous Technicolor production was the second of Ford's celebrated Cavalry Trilogy, in which he explored the themes of courage, honor and tradition with an almost hieratic and liturgical formalism.

The Wagon Master (1950). This gentle, lyrical Western (one of Ford's personal favorites) told the tale of a westward-bound Mormon party guided by two cowpokes through land rife with hostile and harmless characters. Ford's recurring leitmotif of dynamic humanity moving past static sentinels of time and history may appear to dominate; the film is most notable as a beloved example of pure storytelling by a supremely confident artist.

Michelangelo's David. John Wayne, Ford's *beau ideal* of American masculinity, leads the charge in a heroically staged pose in *Rio Grande* (1950) the last and arguably weakest of the Cavalry Trilogy. Although Ford mercilessly berated Wayne for his failure to serve in World War II, he nevertheless always framed Wayne in larger-than-life roles and gave him the substrate upon which to build his superhero persona.

"Home to Ireland to forget his troubles." Sean Thornton (John Wayne) courts the fiery Mary Kate Danaher (Maureen O'Hara) under the watchful eye of the impish Michaeleen Flynn (Barry Fitzgerald) in *The Quiet Man* (1952). The film was one of Ford's most personal and long-cherished projects and ended up as a family affair filmed on location in County Mayo, Ireland. The film was an international hit and won Ford his sixth and last Oscar.

The calm before the storm. William Powell (l), the easygoing movie legend, coaxed out of retirement to play Doc in the 1955 screen adaptation of the Broadway hit *Mister Roberts*, speaks with Ford aboard ship on location in the Pacific. What started out as another family atmosphere on a dream project soon turned into a horrendous hurricane when Ford and star Henry Fonda clashed over the translation of the script from stage to screen. The debacle led to the dissolution of their nearly twenty-year friendship.

The desert as heart of darkness. Ethan Edwards (John Wayne, in hat), is welcomed home by his brother Aaron (Walter Coy) in the opening scene of *The Searchers* (1956), considered by many to be Ford's masterpiece. Shot in his favorite location of Monument Valley, *The Searchers* was Ford's violent, brooding meditation on racism, revenge and redemption that gave Wayne one of his most terrifyingly powerful roles.

Ethan Edwards (John Wayne) hovers over his niece, Debbie (Natalie Wood) in the climax of *The Searchers*. Ethan's years-long odyssey first to rescue Debbie and then to kill her when she becomes the Indianized wife of his Comanche nemesis took both Ford and Wayne to depths they never reached and rarely spoke of ever again.

Ford on location in Ireland with Abbey Theatre actors during the production of his independent film, *The Rising of the Moon* (1957). The outwardly gruff and bullying but inwardly sensitive and fragile Ford always felt most loved and secure when surrounded by the familiar faces of actors, stuntmen and technicians. This surrogate family atmosphere on Ford's films became famously known as The John Ford Stock Company.

Print the legend. Tom Doniphon (John Wayne) and his girl, Hallie (Vera Miles), ponder the arrival of tenderfoot lawyer Ransom Stoddard (James Stewart) in *The Man Who Shot Liberty Valance* (1962). Ford's brilliantly stark and minimalist anti-Western, often seen as his pulling the curtain of reality back on a West he helped to mythologize, is actually a poignant, honest tribute to the values he held most dear.

The Communion of the Saints. "Old friend, what would you do?" Secretary of the Interior Carl Schurz (Edward G. Robinson) asks the ghostly image of Abraham Lincoln during the Cheyenne crisis in *Cheyenne Autumn* (1964). The real and unbreakable bond between the living and the dead, one of Ford's most deeply held and mystical Catholic beliefs, is a recurring theme in almost all his work. The film, a very long and expensive epic undertaken by an aged and ailing Ford, fared abysmally at the box office.

Strike the set. Ford (r) with his producer Bernard Smith and star Anne Bancroft enjoys a light moment on the otherwise unhappy set of *7 Women* (1966). Although the film had interesting elements and garnered later praise among European *cineastes*, *7 Women* was the work of a man who was tired, bored and out of touch with contemporary audiences. It proved to be Ford's last feature film.

WORLD WAR II

The War According to John Ford

Shortly after President Franklin D. Roosevelt declared war on the Empire of Japan on December 8, 1941, nearly 900,000 men volunteered to augment the standing army of almost a quarter million soldiers. For Ford, who had been filing reconnaissance reports for the Navy since the late 1930s, the war had already begun and his services were already being rendered to the cause.

In 1939, as the probability of war became a global reality, Ford began recruiting a wide array of Hollywood's top-notch cameramen and technicians into a crack team to be placed at the disposal of the military. Unlike the lean, fit farm boys, soda jerks and varsity football stars who marched or flew into the front lines, Ford's unit was comprised of highly talented but singularly long in the tooth patriots who, as Mary Ford said, were too old and too rich but still jumped when Commander Ford barked. By the time of America's formal entry into the war, his unit would include Ford cameramen such as Lt. Gregg Toland, Lt. Joseph August, future Oscar winner Lt. Arthur Arling and Ensign Ray Kellogg, who would go on to head Fox's special effects unit in the 1950s and co-direct John Wayne's 1968 love sonnet to the Vietnam conflict, *The Green Berets*. Like Ford, his unit was middle-aged and slightly paunchy old Hollywood country clubbers but they knew their stuff and were ready to do their bit.[1]

147

The catalytic agent and prime mover in the forming of Ford's photographic unit was Colonel (later Major General) William Joseph Donovan, known to history and legend as "Wild Bill" Donovan, with whom Ford had become close friends before the war. Donovan was one of the most decorated soldiers in American history and as a colonel in World War I led the celebrated Fighting 69th Regiment of Irish soldiers to glory; he won the Congressional Medal of Honor for his conspicuous and meritorious bravery. Donovan, like George O'Brien and his Argosy business partner Merian C. Cooper, was yet another battle-tried man of unquestioned bravery and unassuming heroic proportions whom Ford admired and was proud to befriend. Like all his notable military friends, Donovan was deeply patriotic but shared with Ford the special and mystical bond of Irish Catholicism and being the progeny of immigrants from the old country. They did, however, diverge at a critical junction of the relational road. Donovan, despite his Irish heritage and moniker of "Wild" (there are many theories as to how he acquired it) was an abstemious and lifelong teetaler who vigorously enforced Prohibition in his native state of New York.

After World War I, Donovan rose to prominence as a Republican politician and successful Wall Street attorney, and although he served as U.S. Attorney for western New York, failed in his bid to become Lieutenant Governor and then Governor of New York. Despite his party and his wealth, both of which put him in direct opposition with Franklin D. Roosevelt (F.D.R.) and his New Deal, Donovan became an intimate of F.D.R. as the latter rose through the ranks from governor of New York to president of the United States. In the decades between the two world wars, Donovan acquired a deft skill for gathering and processing intelligence and backed with his diplomatic prowess and extensive world travel, convinced Roosevelt of the need for a centralized office for international intelligence within the government. To guarantee its success and efficiency, Donovan said that it had to go beyond the domestic boundaries of the Federal Bureau of Investigation (FBI) and over the heads of the military branches with their own intelligence gathering operations. With F.D.R.'s benediction, Donovan created for himself the position of Coordinator of Information (COI) in 1941 and cemented his reputation as America's first and greatest spymaster. Ford's unit was absorbed into the Office of the COI, which in 1942 became known as the Office for Strategic Services (OSS). Eventually and permanently, it morphed into the Central Intelligence Agency (CIA). Despite the great power and autonomy that earned him the ire of J. Edgar Hoover, General Douglas MacArthur and Roosevelt's successor, Harry S. Truman (who cashiered Donovan after the war), Donovan created a rogue, outside-the-box dis-organization with a shadowy and even dubious reputation. Eventually, Wild Bill employed such disparate notables as baseball player Moe Berg, actor Sterling Hayden, future treasury secretary C. Douglas Dillon, mobster Lucky Luciano and none other than television's "French Chef" Julia Child in his secret war on the Axis Powers.

Ford, with his love of panoply and tradition but disdain of institutional bureaucracy, found a kindred spirit in his friend Donovan and what was known before 1941 as the Field Photographic Division of the COI became known officially after the outbreak of hostilities as the Field Photographic Branch (FPB) of the OSS. Donovan was like Ford in that while he worked within a structure with delineated boundaries and a hierarchical chain of command, he was basically an independent operator who liked to move and do as he pleased with little to no opposition from jealous enemies. The chain of command of the FPB was quite simple: the unit answered to Ford, Ford answered to Donovan and Donovan answered only to F.D.R. It was all very convenient and allowed Ford to act with great cachet and the widest possible latitude. Like the Flyboy squadrons of World War I, the unit was an elite, A-list team and was run by Commander Ford the same way he ran his movie set: with hard work, professionalism, loyalty and absolute obedience to his unquestioned authority.

Directly after the attack on Pearl Harbor, Ford was ordered by Admiral Chester Nimitz to report to the port director of the Third Naval District in New York, "On or around December 10, 1941," and from there to obtain transport to Reykjavik, Iceland, for temporary duty with the COI. On December 20, Ford received orders from the Bureau of Navigation to proceed to the decidedly warmer climes of Miami, Florida, and from there to proceed to the Panama Canal Zone. The war was less than a month old and already Ford was hopscotching bases in the northern and southern parts of the hemisphere. A few days after Christmas, Ford was in Washington, D.C.[2]

In the nation's capital, Ford found himself hard against the jetty of wartime housing shortages (delightfully spoofed in George Stevens' 1943 comedy, *The More the Merrier*) and was lucky to obtain first a small hotel room and later a small apartment. While not on duty Ford, as was his wont, usually laid abed smoking and devouring books through the night and snatching catnaps through the day. In war as in peace, Ford never cut the cloth of his personality to suit the fashion of those around him, and basically retained his abrupt, occasionally rude, but always forthright manner with superiors and subordinates alike. He couldn't give a damn about navy regulations *qua* regulations and focused primarily on his men and his responsibility to the job at hand, which was winning the war.

While Ford continued to put his unit together and wait for his real marching orders, Mary anxiously settled into the routine of life without her husband on Odin Street. Their son, Pat, was also in uniform with the navy which did little to strengthen the tenuous emotional bond between them, at least until the birth of Timothy in 1944, Pat's first child and Ford's first grandchild, which filled him and Mary with great pride and joy. Like tens of thousands of other couples separated by the conflict, the two deeply felt the pangs of distance and their letters to each other took on the sentimental and passionate tone that only the climate of war and possible death could foster. At first, Mary was understandably jittery and lonesome, jumping at every crack of thunder and backfiring car as though the Japanese were invading Long Beach. Jack did his best to assuage Mary but eventually had to lower the boom and make her realize that, with a war on, they were just another military couple and simply had to adapt. In late 1941, Ford wrote "It was swell hearing from you last night—but Ma—you can't call up long distance just when you're blue and lonesome—It's just too damned expensive—we've really got to adjust."[3]

Mary finally discovered that the best antidote to her fear and loneliness was work, and like thousands of other Hollywood wives she threw herself heart and body into volunteer work on behalf of the war effort. Her particular vocational outlet was the legendary Hollywood Canteen, an old skating rink on Cahuenga Boulevard that became a beloved and badly needed home away from home for thousands of young soldiers on their way overseas. The Canteen (which was so enmeshed in wartime lore that a movie was made about it) was the brainchild of Bette Davis and other top stars and it was primarily the stars who became the hosts, entertainment and chief bottle washers in the kitchen. Between 1942 and 1945, the nearly three million servicemen who entered the Canteen's doors (many never to return home, let alone to the club) had the good chance of being served cake by Errol Flynn and Marlene Dietrich, dancing the jitterbug with Betty Grable while Spencer Tracy and Gary Cooper washed dishes in the back. Mary eventually became the vice-president of the Canteen and the exhausting, nonstop work on behalf of lonely, scared young soldiers helped transform her timidity and isolation into a life of purpose, mission and fulfillment.[4]

More problematic and less efficacious during the nearly four years of war was Ford's relationship with Duke Wayne. Much has been written, theorized and postulated as to why the forty-seven-year-old Ford, who was nearly blind in one eye, served both in front and behind the lines while the robust thirty-four-year-old Wayne stayed home and fought the Battle of San Fernando Valley. World War II proved the last unifying political and historical event in Hollywood and after Pearl Harbor nearly everyone in the industry—certainly the studios—spoke, worked acted and even died for the triumph of democracy over fascism and totalitarianism. A-list stars like Clark Gable, James Stewart, Henry Fonda, Tyrone Power, Douglas Fairbanks, Jr., Robert Montgomery, Mickey Rooney and even the Indian "Elephant Boy" Sabu (who became an American citizen so that he could serve his adopted country) put aside flourishing and lucrative careers to enlist in various branches of the military. Many, especially Gable and Stewart, flew dangerous bombing missions over Axis territory and received numerous decorations and commendations. Aside from Ford, other directors and even studio heads enlisted and served with honor and distinction in Europe and Asia. Willy Wyler flew bombing missions over enemy territory with a B-17 crew (later immortalized in the documentary and feature film *Memphis Belle*), John Huston and even Fox's Darryl F. Zanuck served with the Army Signal Corps; George Stevens was not only one of the first U.S. soldiers to arrive in but he also documented the horrors of newly liberated concentration camps in Germany. Sabu, due to his diminutive size, served as a ball turret and tail-gunner in B-24 "Liberators." On the home front, stars like Humphrey Bogart (who served in the navy in World War I), Judy Garland, Fred Astaire, Bob Hope and Bing Crosby, Marlene Dietrich and Carole Lombard endured long and grueling tours to sell war bonds and entertain soldiers home and abroad in USO shows.

While many top male stars such as Gary Cooper, Spencer Tracy, James Cagney and Fred MacMurray (one of the highest paid actors of the 1940s) did not serve, the judgment of history seems to fall hardest on John Wayne. This was most probably due to his post-war, unflinching machismo, hawkishness and anti-Communist obsession both on-screen and off, which many saw as overcompensations for his failure to serve during the war. It was not for want of courage or trying, and with four children and several impeding injuries from his football and stunting days, he was entitled to deferments. But despite a vigorous campaign of letter writing and declarations of intent to enlist, Duke simply could not bring himself to, literally, pull the trigger.

Instead, he continued to make cheap and profitable films for the cheap and profit-loving Herbert J. Yates of Republic Studios, who was more than willing to continue to file deferments for his top star. He got drunk and went hunting with Ward Bond (who was 4F because of epilepsy), bravely toured southeast Asia with the USO and madly pursued a volatile yet dubious Mexican "actress" named Esperanza "Chata" Bauer, who would become his second wife.

Both Mary and Ford made no secret of their disappointment (he, his disgust) with Duke's carefree and apparently indifferent behavior during such a serious time of national crisis. Ford wrote to Mary in October of 1941, two months before the outbreak of war, "To hell with the [Ward] Bonds and the [John] Waynes—they don't count—the blow will hit them hard next year—let's hope they can take it like we have."[5] In January of 1942, with the war in full motion, he wrote Duke a bit more playfully though the sardonic dig in the ribs was obvious. "I hear you are doing a hell of a job at air-wardening. How does Uncle Ward look with a tin hat and a pair of binoculars?"[6]

The thought of letting down Coach, his country and himself weighed heavily on Duke during the war and after and, regardless of his level of seriousness, he sent letter after letter stating his readiness to serve. Part of the puzzle perhaps can be found in a letter from Wayne, addressed to "Pappy" in May 1942, in the Ford archives at the University of Indiana. "Have you any suggestions on how I should get in? Can I get assigned to your outfit and if I could would you want me? I just hate to ask favors but for Christ sake you can suggest, can't you? No kidding, Coach, who'll I see? [Naval Attache A. J.] Bolton?"[7]

Could it be that Duke, with his special and unique emotional bond with Ford, felt that of all people he should be at Coach's right hand in the unit and share in the glory? Could it be that he was holding out for an invitation that never came, or, worse, would come after he already enlisted as a dogface grunt or swab jockey? Could it be that Ford, with his perverse love of sensing an individual's weaknesses and wants, and either exploiting that which they most feared or denying them what they most desired, purposely kept Duke out of his unit out of sheer viciousness? The answer can only be guessed at but the failure to serve gave Wayne a lifelong sense of remorse and gave Ford a sharp set of carving knives to use on his star when he began to take his status as a superhero and ultimate warrior too seriously.

Even while Ford worked to prepare his unit for active duty, news from home continued to remind him that he was still a director as well as a serving officer in the field. Denied his steady and healthy Hollywood income and now living on their savings and meager navy pay, Ford tried to make sure Mary and daughter Barbara remained financially secure as

well as manage the ongoing business of Argosy Pictures, the independent production company he had set up in the previous decade with
Merian C. Cooper. In January of 1942, his agent Harry Wurtzel let
Ford know that Argosy's option on C. S. Forester's book *The African
Queen* was due to expire soon. This was probably for the best since
when John Huston made the film a decade later with Bogart and Kate
Hepburn it is unlikely that Ford would have made it more of a classic
than it became. Ford continued to square away his civilian business
with the matter of his beloved yacht. He offered, and the offer was
accepted, to hand the *Araner* over to the United States government
for the duration of the "national emergency" and to let the U.S. Navy
use it at its discretion. It was not only a generous and patriotic move
but a wise and practical one as well. Keeping the *Araner* shipshape in
dry dock or afloat with maintenance and full crew would have cost
Ford an extraordinary amount of money he simply did not have any
more. With the yacht in the hands of the Navy, not only would they
be responsible for her upkeep but as a formally commissioned craft
she would have the inestimable honor of flying the Naval Reserve flag
when returned to her owner upon cessation of hostilities.[8]

Finally, Ford received word in early 1942 that he was nominated for
both an Academy Award as well as the, in many ways more prestigious,
New York Film Critics Award for his direction of *How Green Was My
Valley*. He would indeed win the award in 1942 but was serving in
the Pacific when his name was called at the ceremonies. If Ford was
honored, he either did not show it or was too preoccupied with his
work to give the news more than a passing fuss. In any event, there was
something more massive brewing in the Pacific that would mark not
only Ford and his career but the very tide of the war itself.

The initial national shock of the Pearl Harbor attack had hardly
worn off as the Japanese naval and ground forces began steamrolling
over allied strongholds with terrifying rapidity throughout southeast
Asia and the across the breadth of the Pacific. One by one, the Dutch
East Indies, Singapore and the Philippines fell like dominos before the

seemingly unstoppable Japanese juggernaut. It was the intention of the Japanese Imperial Staff to wipe out the American fleet in one decisive battle and with it their resolve and resources to continue the war in the Pacific. From the American side, it was time to get stubborn and push back or face certain defeat and possibly complete annihilation.

Despite great infighting, rivalries and jealousy among the Imperial Staff (and it was no different among their Allied counterparts), Admiral Isoruku Yamamoto, the fun-loving, bridge-playing and geisha-courting brains behind the attack on Pearl Harbor, persuaded, threatened and cajoled the other members of the Imperial Staff until they accepted his complex battle plan. Yamamoto held that the destruction of the U.S. aircraft carrier fleet was critical to Japanese victory, and when accomplished would effectively take the U.S. out of the war in the East and give Japan unquestioned hegemony over the Pacific theater. The admiral chose the staging area for the execution for his plan and, when successful, would not only once again threaten the U.S. fleet at Pearl Harbor but give the Japanese a launching point for bombing raids on the American West Coast. In theory, Yamamoto's victory plan was not only feasible but with superior force brought to bear on an inferior fleet with great speed and surprise, almost inevitable. The admiral's plan, however, was hampered by several structural flaws, some of which he did not even know, that eventually reversed the fortunes of war in favor of the Americans.

Six months after Pearl Harbor, America was not the same unprepared and complacent nation it was before December 7. Outrage and a thirst for vengeance had galvanized the nation into a strong and cohesive whole; the industrial, economic and labor resources throughout the nation were pulled together to create the greatest and most efficient war machine in history. After 1942, America produced men and war material in vast and seemingly endless numbers while Japanese output of the same increasingly diminished. Next, there was General Jimmy Doolittle's bombing raid over Tokyo in April 1942. While of no real military or strategic significance in itself, the "Thirty Seconds Over Tokyo" dealt a great psychological blow to the Japanese and gave a badly needed morale boost to the Americans. In one historic raid, Doolittle and his crew took the war to Japan's front door and smashed the Empire's long-cherished belief in isolated impregnability.

Last and most important, American cryptanalysts had broken, unbeknownst to Yamamoto, the Imperial Navy's code (known as JN-25) and through Japanese responses to cleverly fabricated American messages, deduced exactly where and approximately when Yamamoto intended to strike. Although outnumbered and with the fate of the nation literally hanging in the balance, Admiral Chester Nimitz and his fleet were ready and waiting at a small atoll literally dead center between North America and Asia called Midway Island. It was now time for payback.

The rumblings naval intelligence picked up through wire transmissions convinced them that the big show was about to happen. On May 9, Ford received orders to ship out to Honolulu and three days later received a transmission from Donovan that said, "In connection with the photographic work upon which you are now engaged, under the direction of this office, at the request of the Navy Department, you are hereby authorized to exercise full responsibility relative to the carrying out of the projects assigned to you."[9]

Ford arrived at Midway with a young associate, whom the older man was intent on keeping as far out of harm's way as possible. The battle was spread over a 300-mile range (and not merely on and around the island as many assume) so there was virtually nowhere anyone could hide from the furious onslaught of machine guns and shells from the Japanese Zeroes and warships that began pounding the region on the morning of June 4. Ford, who was bunking in the powerhouse, was rocked into action with the impact of the first wave of the attack. Operating on pure adrenaline and disregarding the fact that his outpost was one of the enemy's first and most vital targets, he rushed outside with his 16mm Eyemo camera with several spare Kodachrome cartridges in his pocket and started filming the attack. The earth was literally exploding around him with a relentless fury and the impact of the explosions was so intense that the frames of the developed footage actually jump as though they were popping out of a red-hot toaster. Ford was still filming when a piece of shrapnel tore into his upper arm, and only then did he stop and stumble off the infirmary.[10]

At the infirmary, Ford was treated with merthiolate and sulfanil-amide and, after he was given a tetanus shot, he returned to action with his medical chart stating that while fit for duty he needed to return for further treatments.[11]

———

Hardly had Ford's swollen and bandaged arm begun to heal when word went out about his actions on Midway and congratulatory tele-graphs began to fly in off the wire. Fellow director George Stevens wrote, "DEAR JACK WE WERE THRILLED AT ACCOUNT OF MIDWAY ACTION AND CONGRATULATE YOU ON THE SPLENDID PART YOU PLAYED IN IT." Walt Disney wrote several weeks after the battle, "The trades are full of your doings at Midway and if you keep up this pace, you're going to be the hero of the indus-try." A naval memo marked "SECRET" was sent to Colonel Donovan on June 15 and read in part, "I think and believe Jack will be given the Navy Cross as a result of his conduct in the Midway action. He was sta-tioned at an observation post with one enlisted man. The observation post was on top of the power house which is a hot place to be during an air raid where the first objective is the power house." However, of all the telegraphs and memos sent and received after the battle was over, the most important was the blessedly laconic one Mary received on June 8. It simply read, "OK LOVE = JOHN FORD."[12]

———

The Battle of Midway, the footage that was edited into a documen-tary and released in theaters across the country, is in many respects the most astounding film Ford ever made. This is not due solely to the images shot of the battle itself as it raged around him but what he was able to convey, both historically and emotionally, within the confines of its eighteen extraordinary minutes. There is an organic quality to the work, an unforced lyricism that not only shows history as it is being made but the cycles of life, love, war and death that transcends a nation's destiny and the awesome sweep of worldwide national conflict.

As a director in the studio or on location, Ford was the master of achieving what he wanted by basically enforcing his control over the artificial or natural environment in which his films were created. He tweaked the script, added touches and flourishes of his own device and either waited for the light or created it until he got the right mood and emotional ambience. Here, Ford is obviously not able to control anything: the weather, the looks and movements of soldiers before or during the battle or their burial after. Especially, he had precious little say in when and where the Japanese would come streaking from the skies hurling bombs and spitting machine gun fire. What Ford does is observe in an objective manner and allow the naturalness of the images to carry the documentary forward on the emotional power of pure, unvarnished reality.

There are the birds, the feathered "residents" of the island whom Tojo has promised to "liberate," who quizzically if not stupidly peck along the beach and stare at the camera. More poignant are scenes of young lieutenants in front of a blazing tropical sunset, listening to an enlisted man (dubbed by Danny Borzage) squeeze out the sentimental notes of "Red River Valley." It is the calm before the storm, a few minutes of precious peace sweetened with memories of a home that is far away. The attack itself is an impressionistic mélange of images so intense and shockingly awesome that one forgets the skies are actually raining death and destruction. The frames jump with the impact of every explosion and scenes are filled with fire, debris and Marines and sailors in doughboy helmets running and firing back at the enemy. An oil tank is hit and a massive cloud of ink-black smoke shoots into the sky as though it were coming out of an exhaust duct from hell itself.

Perhaps the most striking shot, one that ranks with the Marines raising the flag on Iwo Jima's Mt. Suribachi, is the image of the soldiers hoisting the flag on the pole while the battle still rages. The angelic voices of Alfred Newman's alto choir raise "The Star Spangled Banner" on the soundtrack as Old Glory soars into the sky in a tilted frame, the bright and cloudless blue sky darkened with the black smoke of war. Then, narrator Irving Pichel sums up the whole essence of the set piece, and quietly intones "Yes, this really happened."

Ford knew he had something spectacular in his little 16mm camera and under a veil of great secrecy and without his superior's knowledge (and in violation of naval and OSS regulations) he sent the film back to Hollywood and entrusted it to the care of Robert Parris, his young associate and fellow FPB officer. Parrish was a skilled editor who worked with Ford on several of his earlier films and, having become one of Ford's most trusted technical assistants as well as a close personal friend, would go on to become a highly respected editor, director and author in his own right.

Soon it was like old times at the studio as Ford asked or ordered members of the stock company to lend their talents to the stateside completion of the film. To supply the voices of the narrator, soldiers and the folks back home, Ford first enlisted Donald Crisp who, despite his age and Oscar for *How Green Was My Valley*, was in uniform with the Army Reserve and soon to rise to the rank of colonel. Jane Darwell and Henry Fonda (who, like Ford, would enlist and serve in the navy with honor and distinction) were reunited in a continuation of their *Grapes of Wrath* relationship as the Every Mother and Every Soldier who exchange breezy chatter about fighter planes as well as the girl left behind.

The interspersed scenes of a soldier's pa working on the Ironton Railroad, his ma knitting in the parlor and his perky, bobby-soxed sister (Darwell: "She's about as pretty as they come!" Fonda: "I'll say so!") could come across as corny and stilted but, oddly, they do not. The fact that no one is an actor and that these folk are as real as the soldiers back on Midway, gives a touch of heartbreaking verisimilitude to the proceedings that preclude groans or chuckles. It is not a simple bit of "why we fight" propaganda but every scene shows real people in real time, juxtaposing the sacred nothingness of everyday life on the home front with the terrifying reality of war and death in all its naked awfulness. As a coda to the film, Ford shows the actual burial of the honored dead. A priest vests in the field and puts on a black stole and then a silent procession of the color guard marches past the rows of coffins and white crosses.

Still in pain from his wound, Ford hurried back to Hollywood to assist Parrish in assembling the footage in the studio. When it was cut and scored, he jumped on a plane with a print and headed to Washington where he premiered the finished film at no less a venue than 1600 Pennsylvania Avenue. According to Parrish, President Roosevelt and the First Lady talked throughout the entire film until they came to a shot that Ford wisely told Parrish to edit in at the last minute showing Lt. Col. James Roosevelt—serving with the Marines on Midway—saluting at the burial service. At the sight of their son everything stopped; Eleanor began to cry and F.D.R. said to Ford that he wanted every mother in America to see the movie. Thanks to F.D.R.'s unequivocal benediction—thus skirting any potential naval or intelligence restrictions—many mothers as well as fathers, brothers and sisters saw the film as well. It was premiered a second time at Radio City Music Hall and the phenomenally positive reception that followed not only brought Ford great acclaim from the military and general public but, the following year, his fourth Academy Award.[13]

All the cachet, clout and veneration from both the military and civilian sectors that Ford had built up with *The Battle of Midway* was nearly squandered the following year with *December 7ʰ*, a documentary he helped make. The film would prove as perilous and potentially catastrophic to Ford as the eponymous date had proved for the U.S. Navy, two years earlier.

At the command of Navy Secretary Frank Knox, Donovan ordered Ford and his unit to create a documentary, with full military cooperation, chronicling the events that led up to the debacle at Pearl Harbor. The crew faced few restrictions, any questions could be asked, and Ford went to Honolulu in the spring of 1942 before Midway to begin hashing out ideas with his unit. In Hawaii, Ford, Gregg Toland and Sam Engel (who would go on to produce Ford's first post-war Western, *My Darling Clementine*), got the ball rolling while Ford pushed on to his rendezvous with destiny in June. What Toland and Engel created was a stage-bound and scripted polemic, an 85-minute, finger-pointing at America herself presented as a classical Greek or medieval dialogue, with ideas and concepts debating as personified human beings.

Uncle Sam (Walter Huston, the actor and father of director John Huston) and Mr. "C," or Conscience (Harry Davenport, who played the billy-goat bearded Doctor Meade in *Gone With the Wind*), banter on December 6, 1941, about the state of the Territory of Hawaii. Or, as Uncle Sam calls it, "T.H…Territory of Heaven." They go on to discuss the supposedly patriotic and peace-loving Japanese residents on the island and just how patriotic and peace-loving they actually are. Uncle Sam argues that the Japanese Americans are part of the melting pot that makes America great; they run shops and civic organizations, their children join the Boy and Girl Scouts, say the Pledge of Allegiance and sing patriotic songs. Yes, says Mr. C, but their true allegiances run deeper and they actually follow the dictates of their Shinto religion that calls for honoring ancestors and the motherland while demanding absolute obedience to the authority of their real leaders in Japan.

The genial give-and-take that alludes to America's naïveté and the military's unpreparedness, suddenly gives way to shots of the morning of Sunday, December 7. Seamen play a lazy game of catch, a white-thatched priest in a fiddleback chasuble gives a sermon at an outdoor mass and fighter planes are lined up in neat, symmetric rows at Hickam Field. Suddenly, the sky fills with Japanese Zeroes that descend on the unsuspecting paradise. What follows is not the *cinema verite* of *The Battle of Midway* but a composite of exploding hangars and diving bombers using miniatures, matte paintings and rear projections made in the studio and back lot. The film then cuts to a series of stills showing soldiers killed in the attack; they and their hometowns are identified by the same narrator again and again (Irving Pichel, who narrated *How Green Was My Valley* as the adult Huw). After every soldier's picture appears, the film cuts to shots of his parents: a white suburban couple, a Black woman hanging clothes on a line and a noble Navajo husband and wife from New Mexico. Like *The Battle of Midway*, the shots of real boys who gave their life and the real folk back home who mourn them, *December 7th* delivers a raw and emotional knockout beyond the images of war and destruction.

The reception of *December 7th* among the top brass of the uncut, 85-minute format ranged from glacial to officially hostile. Ford and company, uttering a collective "Uh-oh," realized that they had seriously overstepped their boundaries and waited for the fallout. It was not slow in coming. The navy found the format much too incriminating and inflammatory and saw it as a bitter, "J'Accuse" hurled at the venerable institution that had suffered the most on December 7. Realizing that something needed to be done, and fast, to get his, Toland's and Engel's head off the block, Ford and Parrish quickly rushed into the editing bay. They whittled the film down to an acceptable half-hour, leaving on the floor the offending scenes with Uncle Sam and Mr. C. They emerged with a much more clear and linear telling of the events as they began on the morning of the attack. Ford's editing of the film snatched victory from the jaws of career death and possible official recriminations. Now the film stood as a complementary bookend to *The Battle of Midway*. Although made after the Midway film, *December 7th* showed a champion felled and KO'd in the first round while the earlier film showed a giant awakening and roaring back in victorious defiance.

Despite more public acclaim that brought Ford yet another Oscar, the damage had been done. The long and generous leash Donovan had given Ford and the FPB proved embarrassing and problematic and they were quickly reined in. Following the fallout over the film, Roosevelt ordered that henceforth all films created by Ford's unit be subject to official scrutiny and, if need be, censorship. It was just like being back at Fox under the nicotine stained thumb of Darryl F. Zanuck.[14]

<hr>

Ford always disavowed any notion that he was personally brave and that he carried out any heroic feats beyond the call of his duty. In a 1968 interview with British journalist Philip Jenkinson, Ford was asked about the "incredible story" of his filming the Battle of Midway. Ford irritably replied that there was nothing extraordinary about his actions and that he was simply doing what the navy was paying him to do. "What else could you do?" Ford said with a shrug. Like hundreds of thousands of returning soldiers of his generation, Ford was deeply affected and personally changed by the war but, like so many, he protected himself with buffers that by necessity minimalized the amazing things he did and the horrible things he saw.[15]

Despite experiencing the trauma visited upon every soldier serving in the field, Ford was extremely proud of his military work and the fact he was able to serve his country in a righteous cause as well as prove his courage in the fury of fierce battles. While Ford hated the wages of war, which were death, he honored the camaraderie and fellowship of the band of brothers who had to fight it. In the safe and ordered, all-male world of the military (much like his movie locations and *Araner* cruises) Ford flourished and moved with ease and with certitude. The responsibility for his men, high level duties and sense of import with the mission at hand sat well with Ford and he drank less, ate better and recovered something of the lean build that middle age, alcohol and chocolate had indecorously taken away. He wrote to Mary from Claridge's Hotel in London on September 15, 1942, "We are working hard digging in—things moving satisfactorily—weight 172 lbs—appetite swell—feeling great."[16]

Ford's contentment with himself not only sweetened his disposition toward those he loved but also toward those with whom he traditionally had a thorny relationship. His older brother Frank, his fraternal bête noire, attempted to enlist in the military, despite the fact he was (almost) old enough to have fought in the Spanish-American War forty-four years before and World War I. In April 1943, Ford wrote an uncharacteristically warm and emotional letter to his brother upon getting the news. "I was truly delighted and proud of you when I heard that you had joined up with the Army. Good luck fella! God bless you and hope to see you one of these days."[17]

Like every war fought by every soldier in history, the Second World War was a maddening imbalance of excruciating boredom and mundane routine punctuated by heart-pumping periods of action and horror. In

November of 1942, in between his work on the Midway and December 7th films, Ford flew from London to Algiers to prep his crew for documenting the invasion of North Africa. At Bône he met up with his former Fox boss, Colonel Darryl F. Zanuck, who was serving (with an ego the size of the Sahara Desert) with the Army Signal Corps. According to Ford, they had but one precious cigar between them, which they treated more reverentially than the proverbial water in the desert. When they scrambled for safety after a German air attack, Ford's first question was not about Zanuck's safety but if the cigar survived unscathed. Later, while filming a dogfight overhead, Ford captured a downed Luftwaffe pilot and turned him over to a local Free French unit. However, when he saw legal interrogation devolve into illegal torture, Ford recaptured the hapless fellow and placed him in safer hands.[18]

In 1943, Ford was once again ensconced in Washington, D.C., saluting superiors, meeting with Donovan, filing endless reams of paperwork and downing copious amounts of liquid restoratives with his crew during his off hours. Donovan was eager to begin an OSS operation in China and in early 1943 took Ford on a flight from India (where he waxed lyrical at the sight of the Taj Mahal), over the Himalayas, "flying the Hump," into China despite the wary hesitation of General Chiang Kai-shek to have any American intelligence crew befoul his sacred turf. Ford visited Tibet, where he was photographed stretched out in a jeep and looking like he was resting in a Mexican coastal village while fishing with Duke and Hank Fonda. On the return trip Ford nearly circumnavigated the globe and after the first of the year in 1944 was back in Washington. He was loath to admit it, but he was having the time of his life.[19]

In 1944 the eyes of the Supreme Allied Command focused primarily on Fortress Europe and the invasion that would wrest the continent from Axis hands and bring about the end of the war. In order to exploit their victory over Rommel in North Africa, the British and the Americans planned the invasion of Sicily and then Italy. Their thinking was that a push northward would not only take Italy out of the war but the necessity of transferring Italian and German soldiers from Russia would take the pressure off Stalin's beleaguered Red Army in the east. The Italian Campaign began in September of 1943 and by 1944 the inevitable plans for D-Day and the invasion of France began to gather steam.

Despite his part in planning the mind-boggling logistics of the greatest armada in military history, Ford continued to stay connected with goings on in the film industry to which, barring any acts of God that would take him valiantly to his eternal rest, he would one day be returning. During the war years, Hollywood lent its efforts to the cause by producing films with strong patriotic, humorous and spiritual themes to inject a note of uplifting hopefulness into the war weary nation. Ford received news from Harry Wurtzel of Fox's plans to begin production on *The Song of Bernadette*, based on Franz Werfel's best-selling novel about the apparitions of the Blessed Virgin experienced by Bernadette Soubirous in 1858 in the south of France. Wurtzel said he was trying to get Ford's daughter, Barbara, an interview with the director Henry King in hopes of securing for her the plum role of Bernadette. Ultimately, the role went to Jennifer Jones, who gave a luminous performance and for her efforts won not only the Best Actress Academy Award but a niche as a top female Hollywood star. The film went on to become an international blockbuster and one of Fox's top grossing films of the decade.[20]

As early as 1943, Ford began kicking around ideas for a war film that would serve as a realistic and serious tribute to the men and women with whom he had served. His friend and fellow naval officer Frank "Spig" Wead, who though paralyzed was once again serving in uniform, pitched Ford on scripting and shooting *They Were Expendable*. William L. White's book chronicled the exploits of their mutual friend, Lt. John Bulkeley. A Congressional Medal of Honor winner, who pioneered the use of PT boats early in both the Pacific and European war, Bulkeley would actually serve with Ford during the D-Day invasion.

On March 9, 1943, Wead wrote to Captain L. P. Lovette, director of the Naval Office for Public Relations, about releasing Ford from active duty in order to shoot the picture. "We all feel Jack is the one man in the world to direct this picture. It isn't just another picture to us—we're trying to make it the best Navy picture ever made, one that will thrill and inspire the country and be a lasting tribute to the service all of us have so much feeling for."[21]

There was a fly in the ointment, however, and it actually had little to do with naval red tape and bureaucracy and more to do with filthy lucre. On the same day that Wead wrote to Captain Lovette, he also penned a note to Ford warning him of the possible fallout that could ensue from getting both navy pay as well as a big fat paycheck from the studio. Not only would that set an expensive precedent that other studios would be obliged to honor but it could initiate congressional investigations by some nosy politicians gunning for Hollywood pros in uniform trying to cash in on the conflict. For the present, Ford and Wead continued the discussion with M-G-M while Ford turned his eye back to France and the coming invasion.[22]

As the Allies planned for the invasion, now set for the coast of Normandy and not across the channel at Calais, Ford and his unit once again were preparing to go ashore with the first wave. To insure that the documentation was coordinated and cinematically symbiotic, Ford was put in charge of an international contingent of military photographers representing almost every nation that was sending troops ashore.[23]

Using the maps drawn by his close associate Mark Armistead, Ford determined the best locations for cameras on landing points, including the Normandy beaches known to history as Sword, Juno, Omaha and Utah. Ford had Armistead place cameras on the landing crafts to film the action as the soldiers saw it while hitting the beaches. The fact that they would also be capturing men dying in front of their eyes was part of the emotional fallout they would have to deal with later. Ford's duties, however, did not simply entail setting cameras in motion and then retreating safely to the bowels of a destroyer anchored offshore. Ground crews were necessary to insure that the operations went according to plan, and not only Ford and Armistead but young FPB cameramen Junius Stout (son of Ford's Hollywood cameraman, Archie Stout) and Brick Marquard went in with the first wave of the invasion. Amazingly, while all survived the initial invasion, young Stout was killed several months later when his DC-3 was shot down over the Guernsey Islands.[24]

Johnny Bulkeley, Ford's and Wead's friend, commanded PT boats during the invasion and actually took Ford on recon missions around Bayeux, home of the famed medieval tapestry. Ford told Peter Bogdanovich during an interview that even though Bayeux was loaded with Hitler's crack SS troops, Bulkeley would sail his boats up an unguarded creek on one engine and either deposit or pick up agents gathering intelligence behind the lines.[25]

While the outcome of the war was by no means certain, as the fall of 1944 moved into the winter of 1945, it was increasingly clear that time was running out on the clock of Hitler's thousand year Reich. His generals would turn and make several more stands like the Battle of the Bulge but with the British and Americans moving inland from Normandy and the Red Army sweeping over the Germans in the east, there was no place Hitler could hide from the juggernaut closing in on him from all sides. Ford's part in the invasion was finished, however, and by the end of the summer of 1944 he was stateside where, at the personal request of Navy Secretary James Forrestal, Ford was released from active duty to begin production on *They Were Expendable*.[26]

By the winter of 1945 Ford had been in the Naval Reserve for ten years and in the war since December of 1941. During that time, he saw action both in the Pacific and in Europe and was wounded in battle. His responsibility to film the war as it happened as well as care for the hundreds of men under his command (including several who died in the line of duty), travel in transport planes all over the world and the the emotional damage sustained by a soldier during war took a toll on the warrior, the man and the director. After the Germans surrendered in April 1945, America emerged victorious and the strongest nation on the face of the earth, but Ford and his fellow directors who had served could no longer see war and peace through the same lens simply because they were not the same men. Nor was America the same place. With Ford especially, there would always be a spirit of patriotic pride and always, always honor for the traditions and courage of the nation's fighting men. However, his work would now be tinted with new notes of melancholy and sadness, looking back instead of forward with more and more memories of loved ones, traditions and communities that were quickly fading. When Ford began making feature films again in 1945, they would be the works of an older poet; thoughtful yet somewhat solitary reflections of a bard whose art would be glazed hereon with the patina of a beautiful yet bitter wisdom.

Production of *They Were Expendable*, given the green light by both the navy and M-G-M, began in Florida in the winter of 1945, several months before the actual surrender of Germany to the Allies in Europe. As far as Ford was concerned, he was not simply a director again shooting on location with movie stars, character actors and union technicians. He was Captain John Ford, USNR, and as such he ran his production almost like a military operation supervised by an actively serving officer.

The film begins, literally, at the beginning with Lt. John "Brick" Brickley (Robert Montgomery standing in for the real Johnny Bulekely) and his PT boat officers and crew put on alert in the Philippines after the attack on Pearl Harbor. Brick, like his men and crew, wants to fight and see their boats as a secret yet untried weapon in winning the war. His superiors, however, are wary of the PTs effectiveness and relegate them to inter-island courier duty with an occasional sortie against Japanese destroyer.

As the admiral (Charles Trowbridge) tells Brick in the rubble of Cavite after the Japanese have bombed it to pieces: "Listen, son, you and I are professionals. If the manager says 'sacrifice,' we lay down a bunt and let somebody else hit the home runs. Our job is to lay down that sacrifice. That's what we were trained for, and that's what we'll do, understand?"

Brick, the consummate navy lifer, does indeed understand and is ready to sacrifice everything, even the ego and ambition that he clearly doesn't have in the first place, in order to achieve the objective. Less easy to placate is Brickley's impatient and short-fused young second-in-command, Lt. Rusty Ryan (John Wayne). He is itching for a fight but, like Georges Santayana's definition of a fanatic, he seems to redouble his efforts when he has forgotten his aim. After being wounded in a skirmish, Rusty is sent to hospital on Corregidor where he meets and quickly falls in love with his nurse, Lt. Sandy Davyss (Donna Reed). As the romance blossoms, Brick and Rusty continue to sell the idea of their boats as an integral component of the expanding war; a crack hit-and-run squad to harass and harry the increasingly victorious enemy until the navy has recovered its ability to launch fleets of carriers and battleships into the Pacific Theater.

The film follows in the structural and emotional footsteps of the previous four or five films that marked Ford's brilliant and mature evolution in storytelling. The plot is extraordinarily loose (basically, take the war to the Japanese navy) and the pace is leisurely and, for a war film, gently paced. Like all of Ford's best work, *Expendable* is a series of unhurried scenes linked together by highly emotional grace notes (those unmotivated gestures that drove screenwriter Philip Dunne mad) that truly reveal an artist firmly yet understatedly in control of his art.

Some scenes are indelible: the group at the table for the dinner Brick throws for Sandy and Rusty in his hut; the graciousness of the officers bowing to Sandy one at a time (like the brothers meeting Bronwyn in *How Green Was My Valley*) is particularly moving. In the latter, we see Sandy shake her hair down and put on a thin string of pearls to recapture—if only for a moment—her youthful grace and femininity. The non-coms, led by "Boats" Mulcahey (Ward Bond) serenading the young couple outside the hut is a charming touch Bond would repeat the following year as Burt the Cop in Frank Capra's *It's A Wonderful Life*. There is also the wordless, nerve-wringing surgery in the hospital on Corregidor under Japanese fire, shot in deep shadow and employing close-ups of Sandy and the ragged, bearded wounded to convey the exhaustion, fear and horror of the moment; the scene of the two young ensigns running off before the big battle into the jungle, to kneel silently and say a prayer by the graves of their fallen comrades and friends. Pops (the ever faithful Russell Simpson), the boatyard owner who refuses to give up all that he worked for in the face of the approaching Japanese and sits with rifle across his knees and jug of applejack at his side to await his fate. The accordion rendering of *Red River Valley* that accompanies the shot is an obvious yet poignant tribute to Simpson's role as Pa Joad in *The Grapes of Wrath*. Perhaps the most powerful note in this or any Ford film is one that is hardly ever mentioned. In the final scene, Brick and Rusty have boarded the last transport off the island and, in returning to Washington to build up the now esteemed PT program, leave their crew behind to certain capture and probable death. They have lost everything, their crews, their boats and, it appears, even the battle and now retreat in defeat. Brick, his face bearded and forlorn, stares grimly into space while Rusty, who now grasps what the terrible wages of war are, simply and silently drapes his arm over Brick's shoulder in a final and permanent bond of love, support and shared grief.

⸻ ❖ ⸻

The mortar that holds the film's center solidly in place is Robert Montgomery's aptly named "Brick." In creating a tribute to his friend upon whom the character is based, Ford also created one of the most unusual and mystically intriguing characters in the history of war films. Brick moves with grace, ease and calm in every situation, even battle. Unlike Rusty, who is ambitious for career advancement and looks to a future relationship with Sandy, Brick does not speak of a past, of a wife, family, home or, for that matter, any needs or desires other than protecting his men and taking the fight to the enemy. In fact, one gets the feeling that when the war is over and victory is achieved, Brick will simply disappear as though he never existed. In a sense, Brick is not so much a character of flesh and blood as he is a symbol, a calm, caring but brave and determined manifestation of America's fighting spirit and resolve to see the war to a victorious conclusion.

Montgomery (whose daughter Elizabeth became known to the western world as Samantha Stevens, TV's lovable blonde suburban housewife and witch in *Bewitched*) fits the role to perfection because in many ways he was Brick. The scion of a patrician New York family, Montgomery went on to a successful stage and film career where he developed the reputation for being one of the classiest (and best dressed) leading men in Hollywood. After Pearl Harbor, Montgomery enlisted in the Navy and actually served on PT boats in the Solomon Islands and on a destroyer during the invasion of Normandy. In fact, the entire production of *Expendable* appeared to be an extension of the Navy's operations because the credits would read "Directed by John Ford, Captain, U.S.N.R., "Screenplay by Frank Wead, Comdr. U.S.N. (Ret.)", "Starring Robert Montgomery, Comdr., U.S.N.R." and "Cinematography by Joseph H. August, Lt. Comdr., U.S.N.R."

Alas, into this sea of initials, gold braid and war experience stepped the civilian Duke Wayne. He was never so self-conscious about his failure to serve as he was when he showed up in Florida and played soldier among a cast and crew of real warriors and wounded veterans. He remained tense and understandably as edgy as a guppy in a shark tank, and the Great White with the sharpest teeth was none other than good old Coach himself. Ford gleefully made no secret of his respect for his fellow officers and enlisted men on the set and his disdain for Wayne and his play-acting the impatient JG itching for action. In one scene, where Wayne and Montgomery salute the admiral after he watches their PT maneuvers, Ford yelled, "Cut!" and, in front of the entire cast and crew, told Wayne to try the salute again. This time, he shouted at Duke, "At least pretend to look as though you had served in the military." Duke, rightfully outraged and humiliated, stormed off the set. Montgomery, who had proved under fire that he was not afraid of the Japanese or the Germans, did what few mortals ever attempted to do and went over to Captain Ford, on his own set, to set him straight in no uncertain terms. Gripping the arm rests of his director's chair, Montgomery leaned over Ford and in an icy stage whisper heard in Miami, said "Don't you ever speak like that to anyone again." Ford, who could be mean and cruel to get what he wanted from an actor, had never been so heartlessly and publicly vicious to Duke who had always shown Ford nothing but boundless love and respect. Like all bullies when confronted with a clearly moral superior who stands up to them, Ford retreated, became defensive and wanted to know what he did wrong. Montgomery, however, was in no mood to continue the discussion and soon Ford was in tears and off to apologize to Wayne.

The incident gave Ford a renewed respect for his leading man, who had felt unsure of himself and his acting abilities after four years of active military duty. Back in the Hollywood studio, when Ford fell from a scaffold and broke his leg, he did the most magnanimously unthinkable thing imaginable and asked Montgomery to direct the remaining shots of his picture for him.[27]

The public reaction to *They Were Expendable* was mixed. The battle scenes with the PT boats were crisp, exciting and for their time quite realistic, while Arnold Gillespie's masterful use of miniatures made it often difficult to distinguish them from the full-scale PTs. The mood of the nation, however, was jubilant, celebratory and looking forward to the peace and prosperity that would follow V.E. and V.J. days. America was flush with victory and not eager to see a film showing exhausted men reeling back from the first defeats of a war the country wanted to put behind them. America was looking forward because, despite the victory, looking back was still too sad and depressing. Critics, even to this day, are also respectful yet unwilling to place the film on the shelf alongside *Stagecoach*, *Young Mr. Lincoln* and *The Grapes of Wrath*. Tag Gallagher declared the film lacking in the strongest Fordian qualities of invention and texture and felt that the length of the film militated against it.[28]

Indeed, it may appear to be too long, with just too many scenes of Brick and Rusty walking up and down the docks, too many goodbyes, too many farewell speeches and just too heavy a pall of gloom draped over its scenes.

They Were Expendable, however, was not made by Ford as mere entertainment. It was a tribute to the men and women, unnamed and unrecognized by a country now moving on to peace and prosperity, who dug in their heels to strike back at the enemy in dark early days of the war when all seemed lost. It was not so much a movie made by Director John Ford as it was a debt, repaid by Captain John Ford, USNR, to those who, as the quote from MacArthur proclaims after the opening credits, lay "forever stilled among the jungles and in the deep waters of the Pacific."

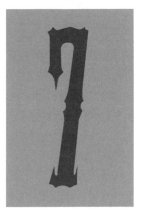

INDEPENDENCE

"Been thinkin' I'd maybe push on west."

Ford, like all the warriors coming home from Europe and the Pacific, had to find a way to start over and get to know his wife, his children and grandchildren and somehow find his way once again as a civilian in his profession and his community. With a chest full of medals and a mantle full of Oscars, Ford knew that, while it would be relatively easy for him to pick up and move on, the road would be a bit rockier for others with whom he had served. Directly after the war Ford began to put out feelers in the hopes of finding a respite, a retreat, a Shangri-La where he and his boys could rest and heal in the warm bond of community. Ford literally shamed Louis B. Mayer of M-G-M into paying him $400,000 (the highest salary paid to a director up to that point) for *They Were Expendable*. The caveat was that the paycheck would be the seed money needed to purchase a home for veterans of the Field Photographic Branch. Ford did not want a simple American Legion Hall with a bar and a dartboard that closed at midnight. What he envisioned, and what he got, was the Field Photo Farm, a vast ranch in Reseda, nestled in the San Fernando Valley, complete with swimming pool, stables, a bar called the Starboard Club and a mansion to house men whose marriages were either on the rocks or who simply had no other place to go. Paraplegics from hospitals in the area were welcomed as well. Like the *Araner* cruises, the Field Photo Farm became the stuff of legend and while it was a given that Andy Devine would play Santa at Christmas, the residents never knew when John Wayne, Henry Fonda or Jimmy Stewart would show up to hand out presents, sing off-key during skits or just sit, drink and listen.

More important for the men of the Field Photo Farm and for Ford himself with his love of tradition and ritual, was the solemn ceremony held every Memorial Day. All the men would gather, in full dress, in the non-denominational chapel as the names of the thirteen members of their unit who had died in the war were solemnly read aloud. Outside, there would be a procession of bagpipers and a lone bugler would play "Taps," then came the singing of "The Battle Hymn of the Republic." It was a moving and memorable bit of patriotic theater stage managed by Ford to insure that neither his soldiers nor the cause they fought and died for would ever be forgotten.[1]

Aside from the Field Photo Farm and his interest in veterans' affairs, Ford was evincing a desire to exercise greater control over his professional life as well. Many of the top male stars were content to return to the studio fold as contract players but established directors, like Ford, seeking artistic freedom and simply matured by their war experience, found the idea increasingly unpalatable. The path from the slavery of the studio to the promised land of creative liberty was called independent production. Like the Israelites in the desert, they would find the path long, torturous and thorny but independent production combined with the slow demise of the studio system in the post-war years would eventually change the way Hollywood films were made. The pioneers of post-war independence soon learned that while they did secure creative control over the scripting, casting and (most importantly) editing of their films, the price was an expensive and byzantine labyrinth of legalese entailing venture capital, copyright laws, shareholders, dividends and contracts as long as the scripts. In fact, accountants and lawyers became just as important as actors and writers and even highly successful independent films often returned partners little money by the time everyone was paid off.

The first independent outfit of note was Liberty Films, formed in

1945 by directors Frank Capra, William Wyler and George Stevens. Their logo, the ringing Liberty Bell, did not so much celebrate democracy and the American Way as it sounded the tocsin of freedom from Warners, Paramount, M-G-M, Universal and the other giants. When their first film, a small and rather rosy item called *It's A Wonderful Life* proved a modest success but unable to recoup its investment (little did they know what the future bode for the film), the partners put the company up for sale and moved on to other successful projects. Capra, the *force majeure* behind the exodus from the studios, later said that his move: (A), changed the course of Hollywood history; (B), made three ex-servicemen very wealthy; and (C), nearly proved fatal to his career. Like all pioneers, the trio had to endure the slings and arrows of production and distribution but there was no turning back, and their breakthrough paved the way for more successful independent giants like producers Walter Mirisch, Howard Koch, Stanley Kramer and actors Burt Lancaster, Kirk Douglas, Marlon Brando and John Wayne in the next decade.[2]

Ford likewise was eager to go independent and with his Argosy business partner Merian C. Cooper, longed to join the ranks of those making films outside the ironclad studio system. While Cooper and his one-man brain trust set about the mechanics of turning Argosy into a viable independent outfit Ford returned to Fox for a film he still owed Zanuck. It would prove to be a return to emotionally, as well as geographically, familiar territory.

Wyatt Berry Earp (1848-1929) was reputed to be a lousy shot with a six-shooter but, oddly enough, given his particularly dangerous profession, was never wounded in a gunfight. The Illinois-born Earp headed west with his brothers Virgil, Morgan and James (as well as a succession of common-law wives) to find their fortunes in the boomtowns springing up like prairie grass along the western and southwestern frontiers. When he wasn't investing in mines, dodging lawsuits and increasing his wealth at the faro table, Earp took up the profession of lawman and as a deputy marshal in Wichita and then Dodge City developed a reputation for integrity and a steely-eyed, cool-headed courage in a confrontation.

In Texas, Earp met and befriended a tubercular, Georgia-born dentist named John Henry "Doc" Holliday, who was known for gambling and hot-headed gunplay more than he was for fillings and extractions.

Drawn to the opportunities provided by the silver mines of Arizona, Earp and his brothers set up business in the desert town of Tombstone in 1879 and Wyatt was soon appointed sheriff of the county. Along with Doc Holliday, the Earps attempted to break the power of a loosely organized but extremely dangerous gang of thugs, horse thieves, cattle rustlers and stagecoach robbers known as the Cowboys. On October 26, 1881, Wyatt, Virgil, Morgan and a temporarily deputized Doc Holliday attempted to disarm Cowboys Ike and Billy Clanton, Tom and Frank McLaury and one Billy Claiborne in a dusty lot abutting the O.K. Corral on the edge of town. A shootout ensued between the lawmen and the Cowboys, and when it was over the McLaurys and Billy Clanton were dead and everyone else, except the seemingly iron-plated Wyatt, was wounded. The most famous gunfight in the history of the American West had lasted less than one minute.

The gunfight at the O.K. Corral, like Wyatt himself, would have been a minor footnote in western lore had it not been for a highly sensationalized 1931 biography by Stuart Lake called *Frontier Marshal*. The mythologizing of Earp's exploits as a marshal, and especially the shootout at the O.K. Corral, led to an apotheosis much the same way Ned Buntline's penny dreadful bio lionized Buffalo Bill Cody the century before. In 1939, veteran director Allan Dwan (who would direct John Wayne in *The Sands of Iwo Jima* in 1949) made a film version of *Frontier Marshal* starring the ever stalwart Randolph Scott, whose on-screen persona was so noble, virtuous and upstanding that he could have been a blood relation of Walter Pidgeon.

Ford claimed that he knew Earp from the days when the old lawman was living in California, hawking his story to the studios in the 1920s and spinning wild and woolly yarns about his adventures that became wilder and woollier with every telling. While Ford and Harry Carey did meet Earp, his claim to have had long and intimate conversations about the details of the gunfight is more of a testament to the fact that if anyone knew how to sell a boatload of clams more than Earp, it was Ford. He could talk authenticity and accuracy until he was blue in the face but what Ford strove for in his telling of the Earp story in *My Darling Clementine* (1946) was texture, mood, pacing and a memorable meditation on men, peace, violence and community majestically framed against the desert he knew and loved so well.

My Darling Clementine was scripted by Winston Miller and Samuel Engel (Ford's FPB associate who also produced the film) and photographed by Joseph McDonald, who would go on to do fine work on Fox pictures like *Titanic* and *Broken Lance* as well as its Cinemascope extravaganzas *How to Marry a Millionaire* and *Will Success Spoil Rock Hunter?* For his actors, well, Ford has his own central casting and from the stock company (which he claimed never existed) came the usual cast of characters to populate his Tombstone. Henry Fonda, recently mustered out of the navy, climbed back into the saddle as Wyatt Earp, the cattle drover and retired lawman who takes up the profession of enforcer after his brother James is killed by the barbaric Clanton clan. Ford regulars Ward Bond and Tim Holt played Earp's brothers and other stalwarts like Russell Simpson, Jane Darwell, Grant Withers and Mae Marsh showed due diligence as some of Tombstone's good and bad residents.

Some new faces in the ensemble included Victor Mature as Doc Holliday, the quiet but deadly dentist with a quick draw. The Kentucky-born Mature, originally of Italian descent (his real name was Maturi), was an affable and uncomplicated guy who served in the coast guard and who, despite his limited acting abilities, became a matinee idol in the late 1940s and early 1950s, playing hunky film noir heavies and beefy biblical heroes. Much of Mature's appeal stemmed from the fact that neither he nor the studios took his acting abilities too seriously. It was a mutual understanding of his limitations that led him not only to fame but to famously protest to a Hollywood country club that refused him membership because of his profession that he was *not* an actor... and had the films to prove it.

Despite Zanuck's enthusiasm for Mature, Ford knew that his Doc Holliday was best used sparingly. Instead of large chunks of the dialogue that he knew Mature could not handle, Ford instead directed him much like he did John Wayne in *Stagecoach*; making him observe, react and emote with a surfeit of silent glances and a dearth of words. It was a wise move indeed and one that served Mature well as his understated performance conveying the pains, loss and longing of a mysterious gunfighter proved the finest of his career.

Other new faces included Fox's sizzling, raven-haired beauty Linda Darnell in the role of Holliday's short-fused, spitfire of a girlfriend, Chihuaha. Curiously and for reasons clear to Zanuck and God alone, the beautiful Darnell, who was known for her sex appeal to the nth degree, was cast by the studio head as the Virgin Mary in *The Song of Bernadette* several years before! Cathy Downs, a high-fructose Fox contract player, safely and harmlessly played the role of Earp's love interest, Clementine, in a way that was beige and bland enough not to distract from the more chromatically rich male characters.

A Ford production would not be complete without the designated whipping boy, the lightning rod to take the Promethean bolts hurled by the temperamental director. This time around, and in the absence of Duke Wayne, it was Walter Brennan who was playing Old Man Clanton, the brutal patriarch of the brood who go up against the Earps and Holliday. Brennan was a three-time Oscar winner and as a top character actor carved out a unique niche for himself as a sidekick, preacher, deputy sheriff or gramps both in film and television for nearly half a century. When Brennan took his teeth out he could be a cackling, lovable old codger, but when he put them back in he proved that he could bite, and hard. Ford did not so much needle Brennan as verbally stab him to death, giving him hell at every turn and pummeling him nonstop on every aspect of his performance. Ford, ever the manipulative, Machiavellian psychologist, knew what he was doing and Brennan's vicious and borderline psychopathic performance could only have come from the pent-up rage and frustration the actor felt toward the director. In fact, when Clanton beats his sons out the door with a bullwhip after his first encounter with Wyatt, Brennan probably added the requisite verisimilitude to the scene by envisioning none other than Captain Ford as the recipient of the blows.

The standout performance and anchor of the film, however, is Fonda as Wyatt Earp. It had been six years since he acted for Ford and the intervening years and war experience gave him a finer, older and slightly harder edge around his persona. Here, he is no longer the young Mr. Lincoln or the stalwart Gil Martin, nor does he possess the raw anger of the ex-con Tom Joad who is always itching for a fight. His Earp is a balanced man of controlled passion who is capable of anger and even violence but, having experienced the consequences firsthand, prefers to find other solutions in a spirit of economy of effort. Unlike Stuart Lake's frontier marshal, Fonda's Earp is not a marble man of heroic courage and selfless, unimpeachable integrity. He is a practical man with one eye on the business at hand and the other on business opportunities in the future. The Clantons represent the old, violent West fighting back against the inevitable tide of law, order and progress symbolized by the Earps. What Wyatt does is for himself, his loved ones and his investments and if his actions make for a safer, prosperous and more law-abiding community all the better.

It is the first hints of a direction in which Ford would move in a few more years; reflecting upon the heavy burden of power and the responsibility (or lack of it) that people and even governments must exercise in maintaining it in justice and equity. For the present, Ford is content to give full rein to his impressionistic palette, allowing Earp to simply be and let his movements, gestures and persona expand and contract with an organic rhythm and unhurried spontaneity. The grace notes in the film include the long, solemn and almost liturgical walk to the church dance and the fête itself where, like he did in *Young Mr. Lincoln*, Earp dances with Clementine in the worst way. Possibly the most famous grace note in Fonda's collaboration with Ford (definitely the most famous in the film) is the ad-libbed, unmotivated but amazingly resonant scene of Earp sitting on the porch of the saloon. Leaning back in a chair, he spreads his arms and dances a little gavotte on the post in front of him, tapping one foot and then the other in a seemingly pointless but ultimately memorable moment. In later years, Fonda would claim that more people asked him about that scene than any other that he shot for Ford.

The gunfight at the O.K. Corral in *Clementine*, unlike the noisy blast-fest of John Sturges' eponymous 1957 film, or the bloody mow-down in George Cosmatos's well done and highly entertaining 1993 film, *Tombstone*, is an eerily quiet and choreographed ballet of death. And like a ballet, words are replaced by symbolic gestures, graceful movements and desperately telling silent glances. Despite several glaring inaccuracies (Holliday died peacefully in a Colorado sanitarium several years after the affair and Old Man Clanton was gunned down months before it) the shootout is an exquisitely composed and executed symphony of power and raw beauty. Men approach each other down silent and empty streets and are soon lost in the tangles of fence posts and great clouds of dust raised by the passing stagecoach. Wyatt and his team carefully draw beads and take down the opposition into the dust or into horse troughs. The Clantons, outgunned and outsmarted, wildly blast into the dust clouds or through herds of frightened horses. Ford, however, could not resist having Doc go down in a blaze of lead, dust and tubercular coughs, his white handkerchief fluttering in the wind like a flag of surrender as he gives up his spirit.

Ford's Tombstone was built in a corner of Monument Valley at the then respectable cost of $250,000. Despite its rustic authenticity, the town shows signs of the encroaching civilization that, like Wyatt and his commitment to law and order, will spell the end of the Clantons and their violent and lawless Old West. There is the Bon-Ton Tonsorial barbershop, the church and the Sunday dances as well as the traveling Shakespearian troupe, starring the delightfully foppish tragedian Granville Thorndyke (Allan Mowbray) whose *Hamlet* soliloquy is enigmatically finished by Doc Holliday. To emphasize the personal over the geographical, Ford underuses both the sets and his beloved Monument Valley. Unlike *Stagecoach*, where the Mittens and Needles of the Valley overshadow and dwarf the humanity surrounding them, here they are distant sentinels, themselves dwarfed by the heroically framed men of Tombstone. Ford again employs a Dutch landscape tack showing vast expanses of sky and stretches of land with massive characters suddenly emerging into the frame as if to proclaim man's equality, if not ultimate dominance over, the eternal desert. *My Darling Clementine* is one of Ford's most humanistic Westerns, intentional and entirely sure of itself and its characters in every scene and mood.

My Darling Clementine was a great success at the box office and again even Bosley Crowther of the *New York Times* heaped encomiums on the film despite the highbrow East's innate disdain of the Western. Much of the film's commercial and post-production success was due to Darryl F. Zanuck and the scissor-and-glue treatment he gave the film back at the Fox studios. Zanuck was always obsessive about sneak previews and the reaction cards filled out by patrons afterwards. The studio chief found Ford's cut way too long and, more than that, lacking any romantic closure between Earp and Clementine before he rides off at the end. Months after they wrapped location shooting, Fonda and Cathy Downs were put back in costume in front of a rear projection to exchange the chaste kiss the audiences wrote that they were expecting. On their last studio collaboration as master and man, Zanuck and Ford proved to be an unerringly spot-on combination of artistic vision and production moxie.

───────

At first glance, Graham Greene appears to be a perfect matching with John Ford due not only to his Catholicism but the fact that his books are among the most cinematic in twentieth-century literature. Greene (1904-1991) was an Oxford graduate and atheist who dabbled in psychoanalysis and left-wing politics before converting to Catholicism and embarking on a dazzlingly successful career as a journalist, essayist and novelist. Greene was part of a fascinating revival of Catholic literature in early twentieth-century England that included G. K. Chesterton, Evelyn Waugh, Ronald Knox, Hillaire Belloc and J. R. R. Tolkien. The revival would also include, later in the century, the likes of poet Edith Sitwell and mystic Caryll Houselander.

Unlike Ford's mystical, emotional and ritualistic Irish Catholicism, Greene's faith was more of a cerebral nature and his greatest books, *Brighton Rock, The Heart of the Matter, The End of the Affair, The Third Man* and *The Fallen Idol* tend to deal with alcoholic colonial administrators, two-bit hoods, adulterous lovers and dubious secret agents whose roads to redemption are as messy and murky as their roads to perdition. In Greene, there appears to be precious little difference between the two paths and salvation is not only born of God's unmerited grace but also sheer luck and eleventh-hour moral choices as well. Thus evolved Greene's reputation for being one of the greatest chroniclers of faith's thorny and problematic road in the nuclear age.

Greene's literary masterpiece, *The Power and the Glory* (1940), appeared to be the ideal vehicle, not only for Ford but for a post-war world scarred to its core by Auschwitz, Hiroshima and the rise of Godless Communism throughout the world. In Ford's eyes, the world did not need another Western; it needed a sermon and a good talking-to and he was going to give it to them. The story, set during the anti-clerical persecution in Mexico spearheaded by President Plutarco Calles in the 1920s and 1930s, was based on Greene's earlier essay, *The Lawless Roads*, that chronicled his firsthand experience of the brutal war on the Mexican church and the peasantry's indomitable faith. The protagonist is an unnamed priest, an alcoholic weakling who has fathered a child and, seemingly bereft of God, hope and the graces of his priestly ministry, attempts to flee the country in mufti. He is doggedly pursued by a harsh but basically just lieutenant whose one desire is to rid the country of priests and what he sees as the corruption, domination and superstition they bring with them. The priest nearly makes a good run but, when a peasant (a Judas figure whom the priest knows will betray him to the authorities) tells him about a dying man in need of confession, the priest returns to administer the sacrament. Even though he has stepped into a trap and is executed, his actions not only redeem him but open the door to other priests following his example to return to minister to the persecuted populace. The book ends as an icon, a living manifestation of the third-century Christian apologist Tertullian's famous maxim: "Sanguis martyrum semen Christianorum," "The blood of the martyrs is the seed of the Church."

The casting of *The Fugitive* was creative if not a bit unusual, and putting an uncomfortable Henry Fonda (complete with shiny black hair and tan makeup) in the role of the priest has to be one of the most curious bits of south-of-the-border presentations until Charlton Heston played the Mexican-American Lt. Vargas in Orson Welles's *A Touch of Evil*. More natural and comfortable in their cinematic skins are Pedro Armendariz as the lieutenant hunting the priest and the still-radiant silent and talkies actress Dolores Del Rio as the Indian woman who conspires with the gringo (Ward Bond) in helping the fugitive to escape. Armendariz, the "Clark Gable of Mexico," was a popular actor in his native country before coming to Hollywood where, along with Ricardo Montalban, Gilbert Roland and Cesar Romero, he formed the core of a group of dependable Hispanic actors repeatedly cast as all-purpose exotics and suave Latin Lovers. Ford and Duke Wayne became good friends with the young actor and Ford would eventually feature Armendariz in three of his films. Irish-American actor J. Carroll Naish, who in his long career as a character actor played everything but an Irishman (he was dubbed by Hollywood wags as a one-man United Nations), sneered and snaked his way through the role of the traitorous peasant.

The main problem with *The Fugitive* does not lie in Fonda's unbelievable portrayal of a Mexican, interminably symbolic cruciform compositions or in the turgid philosophizing and pietistic sermonizing about good versus evil. The problem is Dudley Nichols's script that shifts the moral focus from the priest's monumental sins of commission (alcoholism, fornication) to one of omission (silence in the face of oppressive evil). The power of Greene's novel rests in the magnitude of the priest's sins that are matched by the glory of his contrition and Christ-like self-offering at the end. In defense of Ford and Nichols, the prevailing moral watchdogs of Hollywood during this time, the Breen Office and the Catholic Legion of Decency, would never have allowed the novel to be translated intact to the screen. Had he done so, he probably would have faced the same opprobrium and censure that Green experienced from the Catholic hierarchy in England for tackling such a taboo subject. The moral flaws of Greene's priest are the meat and flavoring of the story, and when Ford and Nichols removed them what they cooked up was a thin, tepid and insipid soup.

The one saving grace of *The Fugitive*, even when it is viewed today, is the stunning camerawork of cinematographer Gabriel Figuerora. A Mexican-born cameraman, Figuerora is considered even today the greatest produced by that country. He studied painting and still photography in Mexico before coming to Hollywood to study cinematography with Gregg Toland. Figuerora's artistic training is evident in every scene, and the sun-baked exteriors and smoky, chiaroscuro interiors with their stark contrasts of light and shadow, evoke memories of Rivera murals and the war paintings of Goya. Despite the overwhelming prettiness of Figuerora's work, the static and overly symbolic nature of the individual scenes kills any potential dynamic or hope for an organic, rhythmic whole. One feels that in *The Fugitive*, Ford is so desperate for an "art" picture and so eager to press deep into Eisenstein and Murnau territory that he moves completely out of Ford territory. Directors, even brilliant ones like Ford, can be forgiven the sin of telegraphing feelings, emotions and ideas but in *The Fugitive* it is almost as if Ford is hitting the viewer over the head with a telegraph pole. It was a mistake he would not make again, and the resulting failure of the film at the box office insured that while he would make more bad films, never again would he stray so far into the realm of intentional and self-conscious art.

The Fugitive grossed around $800,000, a paltry sum especially after profit- and-loss columns were totaled. Ford and Cooper were left around $1 million in debt. Ford knew that Argosy could not stand another failure like their first independent opus, and as he did when it was the fourth quarter, the clock was ticking and the opposition held the field: he looked west and threw a Hail Mary Pass. Argosy desperately needed a hit to recoup their losses and Ford decided to return to the more commercially viable Western; this could be done cheaply, quickly and guarantee more of a profit than a dicey "art" project. Out of this desperation evolved a trio of Westerns, made over the course of two years, that became some of his most successful and celebrated films. They have popularly, and erroneously, become known as "The Cavalry Trilogy." Technically, they are separate entities, each with its own plot line, mood and even locations. On a deeper level, the Trilogy evolved into Ford's meditation on tradition, power, duty, honor and values that he began to see as retrograde in American society.

Massacre was a fictionalized retelling of the slaughter of General George A. Custer and his 7th Cavalry on the Little Bighorn in 1876 and appeared as one of a series of Westerns that ran in the late 1940s in the *Saturday Evening Post*. The stories were born in the fertile but strange mind of a writer named James Warner Bellah. A New Yorker, Bellah (1899-1976) served with the 117th Squadron of the Royal Flying Corps in World War I. Between the wars, he became a journalist but his love of military history, particularly the Indian Wars, led him to write pulp history fiction populated by heroes who were larger than life and villains with flowery, almost Dickensian names. During World War II, Bellah served in southeast Asia with Lord Louis Mountbatten, General Orde Wingate's Chindits in Burma and the American General Stillwell. His bravery and wartime experience found its way into his writing, which was a curious mélange of the high-flown and noble prose of James Fenimore Cooper and the sweat-and-smoke violence and machismo of Raymond Chandler.

Unfortunately, Bellah was also a racist reactionary who, as Scott Eyman stated after interviewing Bellah's son, was an equal opportunity hater who lumped Native Americans into the same category with Blacks, Jews, Irishmen (including Ford) and indeed any non Anglo-Saxon race that he deemed *untermenschen*. Oddly, for a man of his democratic and inclusive social bent, Ford admired the colorful grit of Bellah's stories and his celebration of military pageantry and traditions. However, since Bellah's chauvinistic writing was more suited for the antebellum South or the British Raj, Ford brought in a script doctor to soften the blows and, ironically, Bellah's stories were transformed into Ford's first serious portrayals of Native Americans in a sympathetic light.[3]

Ford's script doctor was Frank S. Nugent, a liberal, Irish-Jewish New Yorker who had served as a film critic for the *New York Times*. Nugent was brought out to Fox by Darryl Zanuck to work as a script editor, a brilliant move that insured the often critical and highly visible Nugent would always be inside the tent spitting out rather than outside spitting in. Nugent had met Ford at the studio but when the director went independent, he remembered the writer's talents for crafting superb scripts with well-drawn characters and a core dramatic tension. After Nugent came aboard, it was determined that the title *Massacre* had too grim and blood a connotation, and after a long and exhaustive search for alternates, it was decided to rename the picture *Fort Apache*.

Colonel Owen Thursday (Henry Fonda), the new commander at Fort Apache in the southwest desert, is a man ossified in a cold, aloof isolation that renders him impotent both as a commanding officer as well as a human being. A veteran of the U.S. Civil war and an observer of Bismarck's Prussian wars, Thursday is incapable of emotions beyond a lofty, superior anger and communicates by barking orders at everyone, from his daughter, Philadelphia (a now grown-up and married Shirley Temple) and Mickey O'Rourke, the young lieutenant who falls in love with her (John Agar) to his crusty, grizzled non-coms (Victor McLaglen, Ward Bond, Pedro Armendariz) and especially his second in command, Captain Kirby York (John Wayne).

Unlike the stiff and icy Thursday, York is an easygoing, conscientious officer, comfortable in his own skin and concerned for the welfare of his men, officers and non-coms alike. More critical is York's respect for the Apache and their leader, Cochise. To York, the Apache are a brave and honorable people who have been stirred into hostility by the dubious dealings of the government agent, Silas Meacham (Grant Withers). To Thursday, Indians are nothing more than mindless, breach-clouted savages who need to be made obedient to his (and thus the government's) will or simply be exterminated. Despite the rational and humane efforts of York to parley and avoid war, Thursday picks and gets a fight with Cochise, who he believes cannot withstand the moral, intellectual and military might of the United States Army. Like Custer, he sets off on a punitive expedition and, foolishly falling into Cochise's trap, is massacred with his entire company. Only York and his troop survive.

York takes command of the regiment but not before giving an interview to correspondents from the East, who gush over the bravery of Thursday and his final charge, even mentioning the painting of the heroic event on display in Washington. Although he knows Thursday to have been a fanatical fool who killed himself and his men, York says the painting is "Correct in every detail." Of Thursday himself, he says, "No man died more gallantly" or brought greater glory to his regiment. We have seen the truth and know what York knows; it is a lie. Or is it?

Despite the touches of barrack-room bonhomie, the poignant ritual of the non-com dance to the Irish regimental tunes, or the broad and boisterous humor of the third- and fourth-billed players, *Fort Apache* is not primarily an exciting or even fun film. On the contrary, when the thin Fordian sense of history and tradition is scratched off the film, what is revealed is a dark and angry film about a world that explodes into madness and slaughter, not to mention the wholesale betrayal of the Native Americans by racist representatives of the government. Fonda's Thursday is a man consumed with a hatred and megalomania that goes far beyond mere bitterness at being demoted and sent to a forgotten outpost like Fort Apache. In the absence of any visible superiors, Fonda *is* the U.S. Government and his power that runs rampant and his impatient intolerance of any person or people unwilling to bend to his absolute authority is quite possibly Ford's statement about the direction of his country in 1948.

The House Un-American Activities Committee (HUAC), the government's watchdog on Communist infiltration of all strata of American society, had become a standing (permanent) committee in 1945. By 1948, its tentacles had extended into Hollywood and by the time *Fort Apache* was released, the blacklist was in full force. Lines were drawn, names were named and if one was not on one side, they were on the other. When Wayne's York tells Thursday that his foolhardy actions in seeking to destroy the Apache are illegal, unjust and plain stupid, the colonel dismisses him as a coward. It is 1876 but, in effect, Thursday is calling York a Communist. Thursday is a bold, chilling and daringly demented representation of a traditionally beloved and respected vocation: the career officer in the armed forces. More daringly, it is ten years before Alec Guinness's Colonel Nicholson in *The Bridge on the River Kwai*, fifteen years before Sterling

Hayden's General Jack D. Ripper in *Dr. Strangelove* and thirty years before Marlon Brando's Colonel Kurtz in *Apocalypse Now*.

The one symbol of sanity and rational judgment is Wayne's loose, limber and eminently balanced Kirby York. His easy camaraderie with the men and comfort in command is matched by his just and honorable dealings with the Apache. It is a big land with room for many people of differing backgrounds, York believes, and it is not only possible but best that everyone finds a way to coexist. At the end, when York confirms the correspondent's myth-making with regard to Thursday's charge, he does not lie, obfuscate or cover up. York, like the newspapermen in Ford's equally dark and ambiguous *The Man Who Shot Liberty Valance* fifteen years later, knows and acknowledges the harsh and unpleasant reality. In fact, we know it as well and no one is kept in the dark. However, York is aware of the importance of myth in the collective consciousness of a nation and gives preeminence to the raw and unvarnished courage that often lies beneath seemingly stupid actions. Thursday, like the HUAC, is a temporary and unfortunate blot on the American body politic. However, it is the unnamed and unsung troopers, "living on a diet of beans and hay," who will fight over cards and rotgut whiskey but share the last drop in their canteen, that symbolize the real and noble America that will endure forever.

The tetchy and tense tone underlying the film reflects the ill-humored and short-tempered atmosphere that prevailed on the set during the production. The screws were on Ford to produce a box office hit to get Argosy out of a sea of red ink, and the location shoot saw him in a particularly foul mood. The punching bag this time was John Agar, who played the young Lieutenant O'Rourke. His marriage to Shirley Temple, which would last only a few years, led Hollywood wiseguys to dismiss him as "Mr. Temple," and Ford took advantage of calling him that at every opportunity. No matter what he did, regardless of whether the cameras were rolling or not, Agar endured a firestorm of Olympian proportions, to the point where he contemplated packing up and leaving the production. John Wayne and Henry Fonda, scarred and seasoned veterans of Ford's abusive behavior, told Agar that it was simply a baptism of fire and a rush-week hazing he had to endure and convinced him to stay and tough it out. Conversely, Ford's old friend and leading man, George O'Brien, whom Ford had summarily dismissed from his life after the abandonment episode in Manila seventeen years before, was welcomed back into the Ford company when he was given the role of Captain Collingwood. In his typical manner Ford picked up with his friend as though nothing happened and even though his banishment was over neither he nor Ford discussed the details of the rift ever again.[4]

Less congenial was the director's relationship with his cameraman, Archie Stout, a Hollywood veteran who had a reputation of combativeness and on-set nastiness to equal even Ford's. Stout's son, Junius, served with Ford in the FPB and was killed in action shortly before the end of the war. Ford usually enjoyed an excellent relationship with his cameramen and, having such a masterful eye for composition himself, generally trusted them to give him what he wanted in a scene. On *Fort Apache*, Ford and Stout continually clashed but out of the crucible of their contentiousness came some of the most innovative and splendid black and white film ever exposed on a Ford film.

Stout had the idea of using infrared film, invented for use during the war, to shoot the desert exteriors. The result of using the film is a silvery-rich texture that makes the sky and clouds like bursts of mercury in the atmosphere. Instead of the usual shades of flat gray, the sky, rocks, sand and the figures are rendered in silky, creamy tones that give them a marble-like and sculpted quality as though they stepped off the frieze of a Greek or Roman temple.

Fort Apache rode to Argosy's rescue when it was cut, scored and released in March of 1948. It scored a bull's eye with both the public and the critics, not only posting (much to Ford's and Cooper's relief) a profit of nearly half a million dollars but securing for the old nemeses Best Director and Best Cinematographer Awards from the Locarno (Switzerland) International Film Festival. Ford's reputation in Europe, always very strong, had proven to emerge from the war years neither dimmed nor abated.[5]

At this point in Ford's career, namely the years directly following World War II, the director's films would show an increasing tendency to look back with a remembrance of times lost. Not only lost loved ones but more and more a sense of community, traditions, values and all the noble virtues that gave life honor and a spiritual purpose. Now safely ensconced in the womb of independent production and surrounded by a stock company of friends, family and intimates who respected, needed and, in their fashion, loved him, Ford was seen by some as slipping into a comfortably sentimental and insular world. In a way, it is true that the daring artistic innovator who made *The Informer*, *The Grapes of Wrath* and *The Long Voyage Home* was turning his camera, and the clock, back to a rosy, make-believe past rather than the present or the issues that would affect the nation's future. Interestingly, the films made during the same postwar period by other directors like *Gentleman's Agreement*, *Home of the Brave*, *No Way Out* and *Pinky* that dealt with "serious" issues such as racism and anti-Semitism, today have a quaint and rather passé feeling to them. It may appear that Ford was moving back toward a splendid cinematic isolation, a sentimental land surfeited with memory plays viewed through roseate lenses. What is often missed is that while other top directors were becoming Photorealists, holding mirrors up to the problems of the postwar world, Ford was becoming more and more an abstract expressionist who would see the same world through the dark glass of not only memory and emotion but myth.

Despite the beauty and power of his first postwar films (including parts of the insufferably pious *The Fugitive*) there was a gravitas to them, a sort of uncompromising hard edge that appeared to be a continuation of the humanism of *The Grapes of Wrath* and the existentialism of *The Long Voyage Home*. In six of the films Ford made over the next five years, a sort of cinematic symbiosis would link them together in a unique relationship. Not one of innovation but of pure and simple storytelling. In Ford's apogee—1939-1941—one gets a sense of an artistic titan struggling within the regimented confines of the studio system for his voice to be heard and his artistic vision to be expressed. A decade earlier, Ford was in his mid-forties, in his physical prime and eager to prove himself as a director of worth and stature in the industry. A young man, as it were, in the proverbial hurry. A decade, several Oscars, a string of hits and a world war later, Ford was free to make the films he wanted in the way he wanted. Although he would occasionally address "issues" such as race and politics, he now told stories as an older artist would; trusting in the strength of his characters, confident in his pace and rhythm and mystically integrating the earth into the fabric of his narratives. If 1939-1941 represented the period of Ford's greatness, 1948-1953 would be the years of his supremely lyrical maturity.

This mood was reflected in Argosy's next film, which was decidedly ratcheted up a notch or two in terms of look and emotional dynamic. *3 Godfathers* (1948) was based on a 1913 novelette by Peter B. Kyne and was actually one of many reincarnations, both before and after Ford's film, of the perennially popular story. The first film version came in 1916, followed by Ford's first whack at it in 1919 (starring Harry Carey) called *Marked Men*. Two more versions followed, including young Willy Wyler's take on the evergreen, *Hell's Heroes* (1930), and then one called, not surprisingly, *Three Godfathers*, directed by Richard Boleslawski for M-G-M a few years later. Apparently, the movie-going public could not get enough of the story, regardless of whatever title was used, and Ford's 1948 version remains the best known and most beloved of the group. Quite frankly, the story of outlaws finding a baby, and redemption, while lost in the southwest desert on Christmas Eve, was old-hat hokum even in 1948 but in Ford's hands it became his charming, unabashedly sentimental and deeply felt Christmas present to the world.

The story, adapted by Frank Nugent (now Ford's most trusted scriptwriter who would pen his best films in the late 1940s and into the 1950s) tells the tale of three drifting bank robbers, Bob Hightower (John Wayne), Pedro "Pete" Rocafuerte (Pedro Armendariz) and young William "The Abilene Kid" Kearney (Harry Carey, Jr.) who hit a bank in the small, southwest town of Welcome, Arizona. They flee into the desert without water and short one horse, pursued by the easygoing yet savvy sheriff, Perley "Buck" Sweet (Ward Bond). As the outlaws press deeper into the desert, Buck begins playing a mental game of chess with Bob, cutting them off at every watering hole he knows they will try to hit. At a dry watering hole, they encounter a pregnant woman in a wagon, abandoned by her tenderfoot husband who foolishly destroyed the well while trying to get the water to flow. Pete helps the woman give birth to a son, then she dies but not before making the three the baby's godfathers and making them promise to get the baby to safety and raise him right.

The idea of three men finding a child and mother in the desert on Christmas Eve draws immediate and obvious parallels with the Magi finding the Christ Child in the manger. On a deeper level, the journey of the three good bad men is an ancient, Old Testament journey using the desert as a metaphor for a more profound sense of loss and discovery. The three outlaws flee into the desert like prophets fleeing from the hand of God (the law). Their hearts are softened by the encounter with the woman and the care of her child. It is the desert, however, the endless stretch of sand, rock and sky that breaks them down, pummels them into the dust and nearly destroys them. In fact, two do not walk out of it. In both the Old and New Testaments, the desert is the place where men and women (Abraham, Moses, Elijah, John the Baptist and Christ) are called by God to a lonely, penitential and terrifying sojourn into the heart of a mystery. Deprived of water and stripped, like Bob and his companions, of everything that gives comfort and hope, those called into the desert come face-to-face with the elements, hunger and the most frightening mystery of all: themselves.

The desert acts as a purifying agent, a fiery furnace that cleanses, strengthens and transforms even the worst of humanity into new beings with a new purpose. Here, it is to become servant and guardian of God's most helpless creature: a newborn infant. Religious allegory and symbols abound but, unlike the stultifying tableaux of *The Fugitive*, the spiritual symbolizing of *3 Godfathers* has the easy and gentle lope of a dun horse. Religious imagery not only abounds but forms the substrate upon which the whole narrative rests. The flight into the desert, encountering the Mother and Child, the star that guides, the life-giving and salvific nature of water (baptism that makes the new man), the dead called upon to assist the living (the communion of saints) and the new man presenting the child in New Jerusalem on Christmas Eve, the list goes on and on. There is, in fact, enough allegory to choke the Jordan River but it is never forced, never rammed down the audience's throats in an attempt to proselytize. The emotions, like Ford's compositions of the lost figures struggling blindly through sandstorms and across burning, arid desert, are organic and move in cadence with the surrounding landscape. *3 Godfathers* is Ford at his sentimental and mystical best, but he is smart enough not to get cute with the sentiment or play it with the tongue anywhere near the cheek. On the contrary, he plays the sentiment to the rafters. Toward the end, when Bob is finally beaten into the dust, he throws the baby's bible away after reading the passage from St. Matthew about Jesus commanding the disciples to find and bring him a donkey and colt. He looks up and sees a stray donkey and her foal in the desert, from their packs obviously the property of a local prospector. Bob lays the baby on the donkey's back and his strength is renewed so that he can finish his journey to New Jerusalem. It is a moment for groans and guffaws but the viewer, like Bob and even Ford, are not exactly sure of how it happened but everyone is weary enough from the journey to give God the benefit of the doubt.

<hr />

3 Godfathers was filmed in Death Valley, and the vast, barren stretches of sand and salt flat make for an interesting contrast to the awesome, primal grandeur of Monument Valley. Temperatures during the day soared to an average of 97 degrees and memos from Argosy recommended that everyone on location bring "light weight wool shirts, broad-brimmed hats or sun helmets, light weight boots or high shoes, wind breaker or sweater." The cast and crew were housed at the Furnace Creek Ranch in Death Valley, where they found relief in the resort's swimming pool. Other records show that Ford, Duke Wayne and Ward Bond drove to the location together, and one can only imagine the conversations that transpired between the three to and from the shooting site.[6]

With no John Agar to kick any more and Duke Wayne getting too big to wallop, Ford needed to find a new punching bag to publicly knock around his set. He found it in the twenty-seven year-old son of Ford's good friend and erstwhile collaborator Harry Carey. Harry Carey, Jr., called "Dobe" (short for adobe because of his brick-colored mop of hair) had known Ford since he was a child, and having been terrified of the director as a boy he now trebled his fear quotient as a young man. Dobe had served in the navy in World War II and, after the death of his father in 1947 (Harry Sr.'s body lay in state in the Field Photo Chapel) he became an actor and after a few minor roles made his formal debut in *3 Godfathers*. An extremely genial and kind-hearted fellow, Dobe would become one of the key members of the Ford stock company until 1964 and after regularly appeared in the films of his good friend Duke Wayne. He would also be a firm favorite in dozens of Westerns and television shows as well as an author and raconteur who gave amusing and insightful interviews about his work with Wayne and Ford. Ford promised young Dobe after signing him for the part of the Kid that Dobe would hate him before the end of the production. As Dobe would later say, the director was being much too generous with his time frame: he actually hated Ford after the first day.[7]

As he had with Duke on *Stagecoach* ten years earlier, Ford mercilessly destroyed Carey, sometimes verbally but even at times physically. He would yell, "Cut," and in front of the entire cast and crew berate Carey's performance and bemoan the fact that he did not give the part to Audie Murphy, the highly decorated veteran who had recently gone into acting. Once, when Dobe repeatedly flubbed his movements in the scene where the outlaws lose their horses in the desert, an enraged Ford picked up a rock and hurled it at the actor's head. Fortunately, Dobe ducked but the projectile unceremoniously caught Pedro Armendariz instead.[8]

Whether his behavior was intentionally malicious to exact the performance he wanted or unintentional to mask the affection he felt for the boy and dispel any suspicion of favoritism, the motivation was lost forever in the inscrutable depths of Ford's quirky mind. With Ford, however, sentiment, regardless of how well it was concealed, always trumped brutality. A legal tablet in the Ford Archives at the University of Indiana bears a hastily scribbled notation reading, "In memory of Harry Carey...star in the early western sky, tall in the saddle."[9] At the end of the shoot, Ford had Harry Carey, Sr.'s horse brought over to a soundstage at M-G-M and, unbeknownst to Dobe, had stuntman Cliff Lyons filmed on it sitting on a mound against the backdrop of a sunset sky. The scene turned out to be a tribute that ran after the title credit of the film with the newly modified words: "To the memory of Harry Carey—Bright star of the early western sky." It was a poignant touch meant for Dobe and Ollie (Harry's widow) as much as it was for Ford, who was probably waiting for the younger Carey's entrance in films just so he could visually manifest his love and affection for their father and husband. To Dobe, this unlocked something of the mystery of this profoundly sensitive and loving man who wasted so much time and energy on crafting such a harsh and cynical facade. The communion of saints, the eternal bond of love so strong that it links the living with the dead was not merely a sentimental thread that ran through the finest of Ford's films. It ran through his life as well. Seeing Ford driving around the studio lot after the picture's wrap, Carey stopped Ford's car for a chat. He leaned in the car and said he was very wrong about his "Uncle Jack" and did not hate him, as Ford said he would. On the contrary, Dobe averred, he loved him. According to Carey, Ford offhandedly mumbled something and then drove away.[10]

In 1949, as the decade closed, Ford and Cooper released another picture through RKO, a Western destined to be the second, and texturally richest, of their cavalry trilogy. *War Party* was another James Warner Bellah story that ran in the *Saturday Evening Post* in June of 1948; it tells the story of a retiring captain in the cavalry who is called out of retirement to put down one last Cheyenne uprising. The script, based on Bellah's story, was by Nugent and Laurence Stallings, who also helped script *3 Godfathers* and would later do the same for Ford's *The Sun Shines Bright*. Stallings was yet another war hero (he lost a leg in the fighting at Belleau Wood in World War I) whose literary skills and war-scarred masculinity perfectly meshed with the personality and work of Captain Ford. After alternate titles were bandied about, including *Buffalo Hunt, Forward, War Dance, Buffalo Dance, Ghost Dance* and *Yellow Scarf*, a crayon scribble on the back of a page listing all these possibilities (presumably in Ford's own hand) boldly proclaims the final choice: *She Wore a Yellow Ribbon.*[11]

Once again, Monument Valley would be the location for his production and Goulding's Lodge the base camp. While Ford reveled in the rustic and primitive nature of shooting and living in the valley, far away from wives and studio officials, he had to come to terms with the slowly but increasingly tectonic shift in his relationship with Duke Wayne. By the late 1940s, Wayne's star was steadily rising and his diligence, careful nurturing of his image and nonstop work on one popular film after another paid off. By 1949, he was on the top ten male star list, a position he would hold through the next decade and even as late as 1971. Duke loved the Coach, respected him and did his best work with him but by 1949 it was clear that he did not need him the way he once had. He was now a top Hollywood star standing on his own two feet and proved that he could even turn in great performances without Ford's direction.

In 1948, Duke made *Red River* for Howard Hawks, arguably his best performance in a non-Ford film. In *Red River* he played Tom Dunson, an aging cattleman who relentlessly drives his herd and his men (to the point of mutiny) in a dangerous and desperate gamble to save his failing ranch. It was a remarkable performance, and Wayne not only played a complex, nuanced martinet against type, but he also believably pulled off the whole *gestalt* of a tired, angry old man. The following year he would be directed by Allan Dwan in *The Sands of Iwo Jima*, in one of his most memorable performance as the leather-necked but emotionally wounded drill instructor Sergeant Stryker. His performance for Dwan would garner him his first Academy Award nomination for Best Actor in 1950. Although he would never tell the big lug to his face, Ford was stunned by Wayne's turn in *Red River* and most likely feeling Hawks violated his copyright on Duke's character, decided to reclaim his property.

Captain Nathan Brittles (Wayne), posted at Fort Starke in the southwest territory, is an army lifer whose service in the military stretches back to the Civil War and before then to the Mexican-American War. His life is regulated by tradition and discipline, down to beginning his day by having the bibulous Sgt. Major Quincannon (Victor McLaglen) giving him the time, weather and post gossip. "The army never changes," he tells Quincannon, and it is in the rhythm of this unchanging flow of ritual that Brittles and the men of Fort Starke find the purpose of their lives. Brittles is set to retire within the week, a prospect that leaves him adrift and feeling devoid of said purpose. He just can't see himself sitting on a porch back in Indiana on the banks of the Wabash River.

Wayne's Nathan Brittles is not as deep and complex as his Tom Dunson or Fonda's Owen Thursday, but Ford's intent here is not to trump Howard Hawks or explore the mind of an angry and megalomaniacal officer. Brittles, like Ford, is the center of an almost exclusively male and closed society run on the lines of tradition and obedience. Like Ford, Brittles is surrounded by men who not only look to him with awed respect and devotion but rely on him to lead, guide and care for them. Brittles's main enemy is not the Cheyenne but time. The calendar and the new silver watch the troop give him at a retirement ceremony (one of Wayne's most moving moments in a Ford film) edges Brittles closer to retirement and the end of a world he knows is rapidly disappearing. Brittles, in effect, is becoming a dinosaur in the culture he helped form and defend, and it is only by an eleventh hour skin-of-the-teeth reprieve by the top brass that he is able to continue in his chosen vocation. It is a theme of startling similarity to Ford's own life, one that will appear more and more in his future work.

She Wore a Yellow Ribbon is rife with fewer grace notes and more themes that underlie Ford's emotional and even political state at this particular time in American history. The emotional highlight, along with Brittles's retirement ceremony, is the old man's visit to his wife's grave on the post. Shot on a soundstage in simple composition and backed by Richard Hageman's sweetly melancholy score, the scenes of Brittles talking about the latest news of all their friends (he tells her about the Custer soldiers being wiped out at the Big Horn) continues Ford's leitmotif of the living communicating with the dead who are not actually departed.

He also puts great stress on Brittles's attempts to quell the hotheads in both cavalry blue and Cheyenne buckskin who are eager for a fight. Like his Kirby York in *Fort Apache*, Brittles is a balanced man of bravery yet prudence who knows the only trajectory of war's glory is death.

A magnificent scene toward the end is when Brittles rides into the camp of the hostiles to speak with his old friend Chief Pony-That-Walks (Chief John Big Tree), himself an old warrior rendered impotent by the young braves itching for scalps and honor. Both realize the futility of war and, as Brittles says, it is the duty of old men to prevent war. Never would Ford ever make such an eloquent statement that warned against the growing sense of ill-advised saber rattling and naked militarism rumbling in the America of the late 1940s. Like Kennedy and Khrushchev thirteen years later, Brittles and Pony-That-Walks stand alone among their respective warriors, working toward a peaceful and mutually respectful solution and trying to keep their subordinates' fingers off the button before it is too late. Although the theme resonates through almost all Ford's Westerns and war pictures, in *Yellow Ribbon* he honors the men and the traditions of the military but is careful to delineate them from a sense of mindless militarism.

Yellow Ribbon was shot by Winton Hoch, a former chemist and physicist with the Technicolor Corporation who would shoot four Ford films (*3 Godfathers, Yellow Ribbon, The Searchers* and *The Quiet Man*), all of which would prove to be the most splendid color presentations of Ford's work on screen. Probably due to his past as a laboratory egghead, Hoch had the reputation of being a pedantic and methodical technician; two deadly sins that put him at odds with Ford. Like Michelangelo and Pope Julius II, Ford and Hoch constantly engaged in a battle of artistic and technical wits in order to achieve what both felt to be the best possible set-ups. The result of the clash between these two monumental talents (and egos) was some of the most stunning footage ever exposed on Technicolor stock. The three-color process that saturates primary hues to almost psychedelic levels of intensity is perfectly suited to the theme of the film; it underscores the painterly and heroic dimensions as much as the infrared black-and-white film did for the very different mood of *Fort*

Apache. The pale sky and beige sand populated by troopers in ultramarine greatcoats and braves in shirts of fire-engine red and bright yellow evoke the great western paintings of Frederic Remington, the artist. An easterner like Ford, Remington was a brilliant and bold painter-illustrator-sculptor whose work was heavily influenced by western stories, firsthand experience and the romanticization of the land by artists Albert Bierstadt, George Catlin and the Hudson River Valley School.

Hoch's *piece de resistance* in the film, a truly memorable shot that is still awe inspiring when seen today, is that of the cavalry troop riding across Monument Valley through a thunderstorm. According to legend, Ford and Hoch had a throwdown over shooting the scene, with Ford insisting that the troop actually ride through the storm without rear projection and few studio insert shots. Hoch allegedly refused to shoot the scene out of a fear (and wisely so) that men and horses loaded with metal could act as living lightning rods. Hoch claimed that his hesitations were not so much out of fear of lightning but that shooting into the gathering darkness (Technicolor film needed extreme amounts of light to register properly) simply resulted in a worthless shot. Whatever the reason for the clash of these titans, Hoch shot the scene, under formal protest lodged with the American Society of Cinematographers (ASC), and it became the shot that contributed most to his winning the Academy Award for his work on *She Wore a Yellow Ribbon.*

A more amiable, albeit temporary, relationship was forming between Ford and a young actor who was destined to become yet another integral member of the stock company and one of the most authentic presences in Westerns. Ben Johnson, like Will Rogers, was a real, honest-to-goodness Oklahoma cowboy (and, like Rogers, part Cherokee) who by the time he was a teenager was a nationally recognized rodeo and roping champion. He came to Hollywood as a horse wrangler in the late 1930s and was soon picking up extra work as an extra and stuntman. Johnson doubled for Henry Fonda in some riding scenes for *Fort Apache* and showed up, sans dialogue, as one of Ward Bond's deputies in *3 Godfathers.*

Ford, with his love of heroic and authentic figures as well as his admiration for hard-riding stuntmen, took a liking to Johnson and offered him a lucrative contract as well as expanded roles in subsequent films. In *Yellow Ribbon*, Johnson played the part of Corporal Tyree, the savvy trooper with a mysterious Confederate past (not unlike John Carradine's Hatfield in *Stagecoach*) who knows everything about the Cheyenne despite his protestations that, "It's not my department."

Johnson was not an actor but a real cowboy and his wavy hair and tall build combined with his unaffected drawl gave him a strong, silent and charming persona of innocence and strength. Mostly, however, he was known for his extraordinary riding skills, feats of incomparable grace and artistry that he performed like a Nijinsky on horseback. Every time Johnson hit the saddle, especially in his Ford films, the audience knew that they were in for one or two set pieces of glorious equestrian showmanship. After falling out with Ford on *Rio Grande*, Johnson pursued his own career and resurfaced as Duke Wayne's sidekick in several of Wayne's films in the 1960s and 1970s. A reconciliation with Ford in the 60s led Johnson to be convinced by the director to take the role of the father in Peter Bogdanovich's 1971 film, *The Last Picture Show*. His performance in the film earned him a well-deserved Academy Award for Best Supporting Actor.

She Wore a Yellow Ribbon bears the hallmarks of Ford's finest and most mature work of the 1940s and 1950s; episodic, non-linear but rich in texture, color and values and traditions acted out by lovingly sculpted characters. Ford brought the film in on an estimated budget of $1.6 million and it reaped for RKO a healthy and respectable $2.7 million in domestic rentals. Devoid of the bitter, historically and heroically equivocating of *Fort Apache*, *Yellow Ribbon* remains a splendid, exhilarating exaltation of the western myth and the characters who peopled it. The film also closed the decade of Ford's nearly unbroken string of films that, excepting *Tobacco Road* and *The Fugitive*, were either classics or undisputed masterpieces. The next decade would bring several more triumphs but, on the whole, the coming years would prove a spotty, uneven business and ultimately precipitate the slow and often painful setting of Ford's artistic sun.

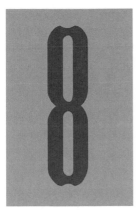

THE 1950S

"Home to Ireland to forget his troubles."

Like any older artist, soldier and celebrity, Ford spent less time collecting awards for present work and accepted them for his reputation and achievements of the past. No doubt the greatest honor, aside from the Oscars conferred upon him by his peers, was that which came in an official letter from the Department of the Navy Bureau of Personnel, dated May 5, 1951. It stated that Ford's request for retirement and to be placed on "the Honorary Retired List of the U.S. Naval Reserve was approved by the Secretary of the Navy, effective 1 May, 1951." It also stated that he was commended by the Head of the Executive Department for "your performance of duty in actual combat" and was being advanced to the grade of rear admiral. The boy from Cape Elizabeth who splashed about Casco Bay and whose hopes of entering Annapolis were never realized was henceforth and forever known as Admiral John Ford.[1]

Even though he was rightfully accorded this esteemed honor by his country, Ford still was not above working strings from behind the curtain to receive the honors with which he professed boredom. In 1948, Ford wrote the American ambassador to Belgium, Admiral Alan G. Kirk, USN, about an upping of his rank in the Order of the Crown bestowed on him by the king of the Belgians. Citing that he previously was awarded the Prix du Roi for his film work, that he was recognized (he said, with all modesty) by Belgians as the leading director of the world and that he directed several OSS drops behind the lines in wartime Belgium, Ford asked if he could be advanced to the rank of officer. He asked, Ford said, not for himself but for his grandchildren for whom "such things are pertinent."[2]

Despite the ease with which Ford slipped into late middle age and the ongoing organic nature of his art, increased rumblings proved all was not well in the body politic of Hollywood and indeed the entire country. The Red Scare, initiated by Woodrow Wilson's Attorney General A. Mitchell Palmer against labor and union agitators since 1919, had by the post-war era morphed into an investigation of all segments of American society. The defeat of Fascism had been accomplished but Soviet Russia was the new enemy and, according to the House Un-American Activities Committee (HUAC), their agents were everywhere. Egged on by J. Edgar Hoover of the FBI, Senator Joseph McCarthy and the Justice Department, HUAC was, with the force of law, intent on ferreting the Reds out from inside the armed forces, schools, universities and almost every institution and home across the heartland of the nation. This included, most especially due to its power and influence, Hollywood.

While writers (intellectuals, whether in Stalin's Russia, Hitler's Germany, Mao's China or 1940s America never fared well) were first in the congressional crosshairs, the web of suspicion netted directors, producers, actors and technicians as well. The lines in Hollywood were soon drawn and by tragic necessity people had to take sides on one or the other. Ten writers and directors, including Albert Maltz, Edward Dmytryk, John Howard Lawson, Ring Lardner, Jr., and Dalton Trumbo, refused to name names and many were cited for contempt and not only blacklisted but imprisoned as well. Some, like Lawson, were indeed hard-core Communists but other blacklist victims like actors Sam Jaffe, Zero Mostel and Anne Revere (a descendant of the American proto-patriot Paul Revere) simply held left-leaning political views and refused to name names out of personal and religious convictions rather than to protect Comintern comrades.

On the other side of the barricade stood the awesomely named Motion Picture Alliance for the Preservation of American Ideals, commonly called the MPA. A bastion of conservative Republicans (more prevalent in Hollywood then than now), the MPA was comprised of powerful, hard-core players like Cecil B. DeMille, Ronald Reagan, Walt Disney and columnist Hedda Hopper, as well as sincere patriots like John Wayne, Irene Dunne, Clark Gable, Leo McCarey and Adolph Menjou who feared foreign subversion of America's most popular art form. Their cause was not helped by the fact the president of the alliance was none other than the lovable but blustery, bull-headed and singularly intolerant Ward Bond.

When the anti-Communist witchhunt swept the nation, Ford was filled with a sense of disgust. When it hit close to home in his backyard, it turned to outrage. Ford always preferred to work behind the scenes when it came to politics, such as his work with the directors' guild to oppose the firing of his fellow directors in 1933. According to Tag Gallagher, Ford offered to hire suspected Communists when they were fired from the studios and in 1947 he helped draft an open letter from a Republican and Democratic Joint Committee of Hollywood for the Preservation of Civil Liberties, and the Defense of the People of the Motion Picture Industry. The letter, in short, did not deny that there were Communists in Hollywood or question the right of Congress to investigate them. What they protested, they said, was the manner in which "political capital and headlines which are to be secured from the seemingly easy target of Hollywood and its people."[3]

In the same month, a special committee of the Screen Directors' Guild drafted another letter, a telegram bearing the names of committee members George Stevens, John Ford, Merian C. Cooper, John Huston, George Sidney and William Wyler. This letter was more of a broadside than the last and made a firmer declaration of patriotism as well as due process of law. "Every signatory of this telegram is an American citizen, opposed to Communism. If there are traitors in Hollywood or anywhere else, let the Federal Bureau of Investigation point them out. Let the Attorney-General bring them before the courts. But as citizens, let them have a fair trial, protected by the guarantees of the Constitution. Such is the Bill of Rights."[4]

In 1950, Ford brought the considerable weight of his name and reputation to bear on a famously combative meeting of the Screen Directors' Guild. That year, the guild (that Ford helped found) was headed by Joseph L. Mankiewicz, a respected and highly talented director whose past credits included *Dragonwyck* and *The Ghost and Mrs. Muir* and would go on to direct *All About Eve*, *Julius Caesar*, *The Barefoot Contessa*, *Guys and Dolls*, *Cleopatra* and *Sleuth*. Even though he was a Republican, Mankiewicz had come under fire from the conservative faction of the Guild (led by the demi-godlike Cecil B. DeMille) for his honorable opposition to compulsory loyalty oaths for its members. At a general meeting in October, the wrangling turned from rancorous to explosive as DeMille attempted to part, as he saw it, the Red Sea of Hollywood and lead the enslaved guild to freedom from Communist infiltration.[5]

At first, DeMille appeared in the light of a penitent conciliator, especially when he saw his strong-arm techniques isolate him from the guild's rank and file. However, when he began to accuse Mankiewicz of Communist guilt through association with known leftists, he completely lost every inch of ground he tenuously held. DeMille sat glumly alone as every director of note, including Willy Wyler, John Huston, John Cromwell, George Stevens and George Seaton (many of whom had served in the war defending the nation they were now accused of selling out) stood up and denounced the venerable DeMille and threw their support to Mankiewicz. While it represented a political victory for the guild president, it still needed an emotional and moral victory to make it a triumph deluxe. Ford, who had sat quietly through the entire proceedings, stood and with his unerring sense of theater and timing delivered the knockout blow. "My name is John Ford," he said, as if he needed to introduce himself, "and I make Westerns." He went on to admonish his fellow members to hold fast together and stand behind Mankiewicz against all the powers attempting to break them and compromise their consciences. He called on the entire board of directors to resign, thus giving Mankiewicz not only a vote of confidence but the power to break DeMille's attempted stranglehold over the guild. He then turned to DeMille and said that while he respected and admired him, he did not like him and what he was attempting to do to their guild. The great man simply sat and icily stared ahead.[6]

Ford's integrity, courage and common sense carried the meeting and delivered a resounding cry of "They shall not pass!" to the forces of reactionary paranoia in his profession. Since his patriotism, heroism and artistic integrity were unassailable, so too was the sense of rationality, balance and proportion he brought to the war against the blacklist hysteria. It was almost as if the industry realized if Ford opposes it, it must be wrong.

Although it was a supremely courageous and noble moment in Ford's professional as well as his personal life, his vocal and public denunciation of such an awesome and even feared icon like Cecil B. DeMille had a curious coda. Shortly after he delivered his vocal thrashing at the guild meeting, Ford wrote DeMille a note and affirmed not only his respect but his affection for the older man. Whether it was out of a generous spirit of *noblesse oblige* toward a titanic talent who had been publicly shown up or out of a Janus-faced desire to ingratiate himself to a powerful man who could be a deadly enemy can only be guessed. On October 23, 1950, a few days after the meltdown meeting, Ford received a letter from DeMille. "Dear John: Thank you for your friendly expression. Attack I am used to, kindness moves me very deeply."[7]

If nothing else, Ford's verbal attack on DeMille followed by his obsequious note was proof perfect that even in his maturity, Ford remained a very complex and extremely enigmatic man.

Despite the political firestorm that raged around him and his courageous stand at one of the most dangerous barricades in the industry, Ford was primarily interested in, as he perennially termed it, "making pictures." His first film of the decade, another Western, would find its own niche outside the Cavalry Trilogy and all his other Westerns and rank as one of his most personal, magical and unusual works. *The Wagon Master* (1950) ostensibly is the tale of a Mormon wagon train emigrating from Nauvoo, Illinois, to the San Juan River in Utah in 1849, through mean desert and mountain country rife with hostile Indians and roving bands of desperadoes. The Mormon party is under the direction of the solemn, pious Adam Perkins (Russell Simpson, who else?) and Elder Wiggs, played by Ward Bond with a verve and "dad blast-it!" earthiness equal to the gambling and fishing Father Lonergan in *The Quiet Man* and the swearing, gun-toting Rev. Captain Samuel Johnson Clayton in *The Searchers*.

The elders, aware of the dangers posed by nature and other human beings, secure the services of two cowpokes, Travis Blue (Ben Johnson) and Sandy Owen (Harry Carey, Jr.) to guide them through the hazards to life, limb and soul that lay ahead. The greatest hazard to the party is not hostile Indians or treacherous terrain but the Cleggs, a murderous clan of mindless robbers ruled by the bearded and rotund Uncle Shiloh (Charles Kemper) whose path Ford makes clear will cross with that of the Mormons.

In a rarity for Ford, the film opens with a prologue that runs before the credits, showing the Cleggs robbing a bank and murdering the clerk behind the counter. Contrarily, as the Mormon train pushes west, their adventure takes on the quality of Homer's *Odyssey* and Chaucer's *The Canterbury Tales* as they meet a strange assortment of good and bad characters who help push the narrative along. Aside from an encounter with Indians that results in a peaceful powwow and invitation to dinner, they also meet the traveling medicine show of Dr. A. Locksley Hall (Allan Mowbray) complete with the drum-banging Mr. Peachtree (Francis Ford) and the two "soiled doves," Fleuretty Phyfe (Ruth Clifford) and Denver (Joanne Dru). Despite the disparate, surreal nature of Mormons, cowpokes, prostitutes and drunken snake oil salesmen thrown together by fate and necessity, the "found community" moves on as one to the promised land beyond the San Juan River.

The violent, pre-credit opening sequence acts as both a prologue but more importantly as an end of sorts. The movie that unfolds after is a new creation with its own feeling, mood and reality that takes the viewer out of a previous reality to an entirely new realm of experience.

The film after the credits beats with such a gentle heart and moves at such a sonorous pace that even flare-ups within the congregation and the encounter with the Cleggs comes across as either innocence or a purification and a cleansing of paradise lost and regained. "I thought you never drew on a man?" asks Elder Wiggs after Travis shoots down Uncle Shiloh. "That's right, sir. Only on snakes." In *The Wagon Master*, as he would again in *The Quiet Man*, Ford magically transcends his traditional realm of myth and history and actually moves into the infinitely more personal and heartfelt land of fable.

The film contains some of the most intimate scenes Ford ever filmed; not so much his famed grace notes as loving compositions that reveal his heart and bare his soul. These scenes include Sandy's easy, liquid movements as he sits at the poker table and later on his horse, completely comfortable in his own skin (in a way Ford never could be) with his leg draped over the table and then on the horn of his saddle. Later, as his romance blossoms with Denver, Ford gives a wonderfully and uncharacteristically erotic charge to the scene where Travis walks his horse to bathe in the stream while his *inamorata* watches from the wagon, draped in nothing but a blanket. The most personally resonant scene is the wonderful nighttime moment showing the dandified Dr. Hall (another of Ford's sagacious and lovable alcoholics) in his bed with his bottle, tears welling up in his sad eyes. The image of the lonely alcoholic, an outsider with a blustery facade drinking alone in the dead of night, is about as dangerously close to an autobiographical moment as Ford ever shot.

The Wagon Master is one of Ford's most vocally musical films, courtesy of the legendary radio and later movie group of western singers, The Sons of the Pioneers. Comprised of several mellifluous tenors and baritones that changed over several decades (that included Roy Rogers and Ford's future son-in-law, actor Ken Curtis), The Sons of the Pioneers provided the director with the musical counterpoints in several of Ford's films; elements as important as script and cinematography that he dearly treasured. Despite the lushness of their sagebrush harmonies, the Sons do not possess the transcendent quality of the arrangements of Alfred Newman or Richard Hageman. On the contrary, they come off a bit like a 1950s LP record of Songs of the Old West for grade-school boys. The exception is the exhilarating *Chuckawalla Swing*, the musical highlight of the film. More than a hoedown, it is a locus of unity and fast-setting glue that bonds previously separated individuals in a celebration of life. This includes Mormons young and old (including Jane Darwell as Sister Ledeyard doing one of the most manic drum-bangings in movie history), cowboys, prostitutes and even Dr. Hall, tapping his foot to the music atop the wagon.

Even though it moves lyrically through its own bucolic reality, *The Wagon Master* is ultimately about pilgrimage. Migration is the physical act of moving from one geographic location to another for any number of social, political, religious or economic reasons. Pilgrimage, on the other hand, is a spiritual movement, couched in the physical, from a previous reality to a new place of transformation, wisdom and openness to the spirit. It is a place of conversion in the sense that the destination of the "Promised Land" is only as rewarding as the profundity of the journey there. Unlike Sean Thornton's pilgrimage from the slag heaps of Pennsylvania's coal mines to the fairy-tale land of Innisfree, or Ethan Edward's journey into and back from a heart of darkness, *The Wagon Master* does not offer closure or resolution but simply a journey. There is no need for redemption at the end of the journey because the pilgrims have achieved it along the way. Their forbearing and loving community, tried in the crucible of violence and sealed in the rhythm of ritual, have already led them to the promised land long before they arrive there.

The Wagon Master may have been a personal triumph for Ford and a work of which he was always and justifiably proud, but in terms of profits it just was not enough. Despite the healthy domestic and international box office business of *Fort Apache, She Wore a Yellow Ribbon* and *3 Godfathers*, Ford and Cooper simply could not drag Argosy out of the massive financial hole where the failure of *The Fugitive* had deposited them. Between the bank notes ready to be called in for loans and the complex distribution deal with RKO (that gave most of the profits to RKO) Argosy was simply hemorrhaging money it did not have. With very few options on the table and desperate to achieve solvency, Cooper and Ford decided to sell Argosy's film library to RKO who would then pay off their debts with the profits the films would (and did) make over time.[8]

When the financial albatross was finally removed more or less from around their neck, Ford and Cooper began to cast around for a new home and base of operations for Argosy. On John Wayne's recommendation, they moved into Republic Studios and signed a new distribution deal with its notorious commander in chief Herbert J. Yates. A former salesman with the American Tobacco Company, Yates had formed Republic Studios in a merger-acquisition of a handful of smaller studios like Mascot and Monogram that became collectively known in the industry as "poverty row." Despite his tailored suits, walking stick and natty homburg hat, Yates was a parsimonious and dictatorial pasha who made no bones about the point and mission of his studio. Republic made little more than cheap serials, profitable but uninspired John Wayne Westerns and the occasional exotic romance starring his wife, the Czech ice skater turned legendarily awful actress named Vera Hruba Ralston. While the other studio moguls began as haberdashers, nickelodeon operators and scrap iron dealers but ended up like Roman emperors and consorted with presidents, politicians and power brokers from around the world, Yates always looked and acted like a tobacco salesman.

Duke Wayne had just about had enough of Yates and over the course of the years engaged in increasingly vitriolic arguments with the studio chief over profits, story quality and artistic freedom. Namely, it was the carrot and stick Yates dangled over Wayne with the promise that he would be able to make his long-cherished dream film about the Alamo. Bringing Ford into the Republic fold was for both men a win-win situation. Duke now had Coach as an ally and the studio acquired a *bona fide* genius whose presence would guarantee a higher cut of quality pictures for the studio in general and for Wayne in particular. For Ford, who had worked with such top shelf players in the industry like Zanuck, Mayer and Goldwyn, the move was a descent of several rungs on the ladder of cinematic prestige. In the director's eyes, however, it was a necessary chunk of humble pie he had to swallow in order to make films, especially his own long-cherished dream of bringing to the screen a short story by Maurice Walsh that he had acquired some twenty years earlier. It was the simple story of a young Irish-American boxer who returns to his native Irish village, falls in love with a local lass and runs afoul of her big bully of a brother. It was called *The Quiet Man*.

Ford was adamant about filming on location in Ireland but his new boss made it clear that he was no Darryl Zanuck and that if the Republic back lot was good enough for in-house directors like Fred C. Bannon and William Witney, it was good enough for John Ford. Yates was a penny-pinching taskmaster when it came to filming Westerns and sci-fi serials in his own studio; shipping a cast and crew across the Atlantic was to Yates the same as shipping them to the dark side of Jupiter. Like a novice director, the five-time Oscar winner Ford had to deliver a money-making picture for Republic before Yates would even consider letting him make his dream project. Once again, Ford turned his eyes west and began preparations on what would become the last, and arguably the weakest, of the Cavalry Trilogy.[9]

Rio Grande, tentatively called *Rio Bravo* during the early stages of production, was another Bellah short story that was adapted for the screen by James Kevin McGuinness. An Irish-born writer, McGuinness wrote screenplays at M-G-M for years, including the first draft of the Marx Brothers' classic, *A Night at the Opera*, as well as Ford's own *The Black Watch* in 1929. McGuinness was also a hard-core right wing anti-Communist and one of the charter members of the ultra-conservative MPA. He was a highly competent and literate wordsmith but between his politics and Bellah's intractable and not so veiled racism, McGuinness delivered for Ford the script of what would prove to be one of his most casually anti-Indian Westerns.

John Wayne reprised the name (but not the character) of his *Fort Apache* Captain and is once again named Kirby Yorke, this time, however, with the rank of Colonel and an "e" loftily tagged on the end of his surname. He is more like Colonel Thursday in *Fort Apache* than Captain Brittles in *She Wore a Yellow Ribbon* in his stern, humorless command of his post and his implacable (though not unhinged) determination to quell Apache uprisings that threaten the region. Yorke's isolation from his men runs to his own depths as Wayne's portrayal shows a man separated from himself, as isolated emotionally from his heart as he is from eastern civilization in the deserts and high chaparrals he patrols. As his estranged wife, Kathleen (Maureen O'Hara) says of him, "He's a lonely man. A very lonely man."

Post routine is interrupted by the arrival of new recruits, chivvied by Sergeant Major Quincannon (Victor McLaglen, reprising his name and his character from *She Wore a Yellow Ribbon*), including Travis Tyree (Ben Johnson, using the first name of his character from *The Wagon Master* and last name of his character from *Yellow Ribbon*) Sandy Boone (Harry Carey, Jr.) and eighteen-year-old Jeff Yorke (Claude Jarman, Jr., the celebrated child actor who had won a miniature Oscar for his moving portrayal as the boy Jody in M-G-M's *The Yearling*). The similarity of Trooper Yorke's name to the post commander does not go unnoticed by the colonel, especially since it turns out the teenager is none other than the son he has not seen in fifteen years. On the heels of the son he doesn't know is his Virginia-born ex-wife Kathleen (O'Hara) who never forgave Yorke for burning down her ancestral plantation during the decimating campaign carried out in the Shenandoah Valley in the Civil War by General Phil Sheridan (J. Carroll Naish).

Rio Grande, like Winnie Hoch's footage of the cavalry company marching through the lightning storm, was filmed under protest and it feels like it. Ford and Wayne undertook the project only as a bargaining chip as well as an insurance policy that allowed them to get Yates's backing on *The Quiet Man*, and their detached and somewhat indifferent attitude both hinders the film as well as giving it a lonely and slightly melancholic edge. We come to discover that Yorke's isolation and sadness stems not only from the rupture in his relationship with his family but also his obsessive attention to his work. Once again, the very best and the very worst of Ford's own character is transmuted onscreen by Wayne into moments of quiet poetry and mythic heroism.

Rio Grande is notable in that it was the first of five onscreen pairings of John Wayne and Maureen O'Hara, three of which would be films for Ford. Their chemical makeup of fire, steel, passion and a certain tender vulnerability made them ideal soul mates and their historic screen coupling remains on par with that of a Garbo and Gilbert, Tracy and Hepburn and Bogart and Bacall. It was also the beginning of a warm, lifelong relationship between the two, who would remain friends with never a hint of scandal but always warm affection and mutual love. In fact, as Duke laying dying from cancer in 1979, it was O'Hara, along with Wayne's other close friend Elizabeth Taylor, who appeared before Congress and successfully lobbied to have Wayne awarded the Congressional Gold Medal for his contributions to film and the spirit of the nation itself.

Yorke's sense of separation from almost everything and Kathleen's deeply-felt sense of loss of the husband she still loves amid the years of bitterness and regret, forms the emotional core of the story. Ford emphasizes this sense of *temps perdu* by giving each a tender and a typically wordless Fordian scene that are the most memorable in the film. When Kathleen looks around Yorke's tent after he leaves on patrol, she finds and opens a music box that plays, "I'll Take You Home Again, Kathleen." Without a word, and strikingly similar to the scene where Ma Joad holds the earrings up to her face in the cracked mirror in *The Grapes of Wrath*, O'Hara's face conveys more memory, thoughts and feelings than two exposited pages of script. The scene then dissolves to an equally wordless candlelight dinner shared by the estranged couple, reminiscent of the dinner scene from *They Were Expendable*, who exchange longing glances before being serenaded by the company musicians outside the tent. The other scene is where Yorke, on patrol in the desert and walking along a riverbank, is stirred into a melancholic reverie by troopers singing Stan Jones' lovely and lonesome campfire tune, "My Gal is Purple."

Walking moodily along the gently flowing bank, Ford closes the scene with a slow zoom on Wayne's face. This, together with the first shot of Ringo in *Stagecoach* and the scene of Ethan in *The Searchers* where he looks hatefully at the Indianized white women in the camp hospital, this shot in *Rio Grande* comprises the second of Ford's three great zooms on Wayne in various stages of age and mood. Unlike the other two, the camera here does not do the zooming work but it is Yorke who walks forward into our space; alone, inscrutable, revealing to us a man who is master of everyone and everything except the existential vacuum deep inside.

Rio Grande, however, is not all loneliness and gloom. There are some spectacular set pieces of military ritual, such as the post women seeing their men off on patrol in a procession of horses, guidons and flags. Later, they wait like Spartan women for the ones who return wounded on their travois or not at all. The raid on the mission church to retrieve the kidnapped children is briskly but not imaginatively staged; it is made up for by several spectacular horse scenes that employ Ben Johnson's majestic riding skills. At the beginning of the film, Quincannon challenges Travis and Sandy to try at "Roman riding" during their training. They accept and each man jumps on the bare backs of two horses and ride them, a foot on each horse, at a breakneck pace around the track and even over a four-rail jump.

Despite Ford throwing Johnson plum moments showcasing his equine elan and dash, the young actor joined the ranks of those ostracized from the director's inner circle during the making of *Rio Grande*. While dining on location Moab, Utah, Ford mistook some conversation he heard between Johnson and Dobe Carey as an insult to his direction. In front of the entire company, Ford demanded that Johnson repeat what he had said, tossing in a few epithets as well. Johnson was no forbearing Duke Wayne or Ward Bond and did not want to hear any, "Oh, Coach didn't mean anything by that" talks. He walked over to Ford and told him *sotto voce* as much and then stormed out. Ford, realizing that once again he had gone too far, sent Carey out to get Johnson and bring him back to the table, the closest thing to an apology he could muster. Johnson finished the film and it appeared that an *entente cordiale* had been reached but, true to Ford's form, he did not employ Johnson again until *Cheyenne Autumn*, some thirteen years later.[10]

The one disturbing element of *Rio Grande*, more so since it is so patently un-Fordian, is the casually denigrating way in which the Apache are portrayed. The fact that the film was shot in Moab and Monument Valley employing the same Navajo men (and now their sons) who can be seen in all his valley films beginning with *Stagecoach*, does nothing to mitigate the harsh way in which the indigenous people are shown. Rather than individuals with names, faces and anger at betrayal by the invading forces, they are shown amorphously as barbaric, bloodthirsty savages in need of suppression. Unlike *Fort Apache* or *She Wore a Yellow Ribbon*, *Rio Grande* does not boast a noble Cochise who has been wronged and lied to or a venerable Pony-That-Walks who longs for an honorable peace. Even though Ford takes pains to show their sacred nighttime rituals while in captivity (even their chanting comes across as creepily dissonant) they are for the most part faceless, even drunken nonentities and Ford nearly succeeds in getting the audience to root for Phil Sheridan when he orders Yorke, like MacArthur in Korea, to pursue and destroy the hostiles even if it means violating another country's borders. An odd and fairly chauvinistic tack for a man whom the Navajo people called, with gratitude and respect, Natani Nez (Tall Soldier).

The Quiet Man was based on a short story by Irish novelist and nationalist Maurice Walsh that first appeared in the *Saturday Evening Post* on February 11, 1933. The story, simplicity itself, is the tale of Shawn Kelvin, a 35-year-old boxer who returns to Ireland from America during the Depression to live in peace on his family's cottage in County Kerry. He falls in love with the fiery and acid-tempered Ellen O'Grady and has a run-in with her brother Big Liam of neighboring Moyvalla, who wants to marry his sister off to the Yank he despises so he himself can marry a propertied widow. When Big Liam's plans fall through he takes his rage out on Shawn and refuses to give Ellen her dowry, although her new husband could not care less about the money. Ellen shames her husband into fighting her brother for the money and when he does it finally brings peace and quiet to their lives and the community.

Ford had dreamed of making *The Quiet Man* since he optioned the rights to the story back in the mid 1930s, and by the time he signed on with Yates at Republic it had become an obsession with him of quixotic proportions. However, if Ford was the moonstruck knight tilting at Celtic windmills and *The Quiet Man* his Dulcinea, Yates was Dr. Carrasco, continually shaking the madman from his dream into the reality of Hollywood financing. Republic had never filmed a picture too far away from Hollywood, let alone outside the country, and Yates was in a state of absolute panic at the thought of the cost of a potential flop. Furthermore, Ford's insistence that the movie be shot in the wildly expensive Technicolor format (Republic had shot only a few films in this process) did nothing to allay Yates' chronic nervous condition. However, a deal was a deal and with *Rio Grande* bringing in the necessary profits, by 1951 the wheels were turning on casting, script and location scouting. Without doubt the leads, and as far as Ford was concerned it could have been carved in the Blarney stone, would be John Wayne and Maureen O'Hara.

Ford expanded on Walsh's rather lean prose and put more substantial meat on the skeletal narrative. His first thought was to "open up" the action to include side stories involving the Troubles, Nationalist sermonizing and the I.R.A. The Ford archives have a memo about how pre-production on the film helped to re-shift the focus of the narrative: "Following our lengthy discussion with Sean Nunan of External Affairs we thought it would be better to show our phase of the Anglo Irish War of Liberation in as briefly and as novel a form as possible."[11]

Ford set Frank Nugent to writing the script, both of them opting to forgo the historical and political in favor of myth, fable and a mystical encounter with the romantic Isle of Innisfree of William Butler Yeats rather than the Ireland of turmoil and Eamon de Valera. Nugent, saddled with an armful of books checked out from the Republic Research Department such as *Irish Names and Surnames*, *1000 Years of Irish Poetry*, *Family and Community in Ireland* and Liam O'Flaherty's *Land*, started work in earnest. In the Ford Archives there is also a page ripped from a magazine called *Information on Ireland* from Autumn

1950. An article, "The Irish Story, " by John Brennan, the pen name of a "well-known Irishwoman," begins with, "Well, then, I'll begin at the beginning." Mr. (or Mrs.) Brennan had unwittingly supplied Ford and Nugent with the opening line of the film spoken by the narrator Fr. Lonergan. It would become one of the most famous and recognizable opening lines in Ford's or any director's films.[12]

The changes in the script personalized the story and not only streamlined the narrative but gave it more of Ford's own Irish and personal DNA, beginning with the names. Shawn Kelvin became Sean Thornton, the change reflecting the Gaelic spelling of Ford's own name, John, and the surname honoring his distant Galway relations, the Thorntons. Ellen O'Grady became Mary Kate Danaher, a loving tribute to the two greatest loves of Ford's life: Mary, his wife, and Kate Hepburn. Big Liam O'Grady became Squire "Red" Will Danaher and was played with a wonderful, almost Kabuki-like exaggerated bluster by Victor McLaglen. Ward Bond, as Fr. Lonergan, did double duty as the parish priest and narrator. True to Ford's Manichean and very Irish sense of devotion to church but a distrust of the clergy, he showed Lonergan as a shepherd of his flock but with a weakness for gambling, fishing, fights and an occasional nip over at Cohan's Public House.

The casting of the immortals of the stock company is merely, to paraphrase Lonergan, the beginning of the beginning of the most nepotistic and cinematically cross-pollinated film in Ford's oeuvre. Aside from the given that Wayne, Bond, O'Hara and McLaglen would anchor the film, it was a character created by Nugent who forms the heart, chorus and funny bone of the film: Michaeleen og Flynn. Barry Fitzgerald, who ought to have won a second Oscar for his performance, plays Innisfree's taxi driver, matchmaker, bookie, gossip and genial town drunk rolled into one absolutely unforgettable performance. Michaeleen has all the best lines and steals every scene he is in, a dangerous feat that Ford not only tolerated but actually encouraged by giving the impish actor unscripted flourishes like gestures, long, unbroken reaction shots and bits of business that are remembered as much as his words. His reaction to Sean and Mary Kate's broken marriage bed the morning after the wedding (unbeknownst to Michaeleen, it is smashed when Sean throws his wife on it in a fit of rage) should be registered as a national treasure.

Instead of importing a handful of players from the Abbey Theatre in Dublin as he did for *The Plough and the Stars* in 1936, Ford merely had them train over, en masse, to his primary shooting location in Cong, County Mayo, on Ireland's west coast. His headquarters were in Ashford Castle near Cong. It was the only hotel large enough to accommodate the huge cast and crew imported from the States, Ireland and the U.K., and Ashford Castle forms the background for the opening sunset credits. Fitzgerald's brother (and another stock company regular) Arthur Shields, played the Anglican vicar, Rev. Mr. Playfair, while Maureen O'Hara's brother, Charles Fitzsimmons, was one of the two squires who lounge about Cohan's smoking, drinking and casually insulting Will Danaher. Other Abbey players and native character actors included Eileen Crowe (Mrs. Playfair), May Craig (the fishwoman with the basket), Eric Gorman (the train engineer) and even John Wayne's makeup man Web Overlander, who played the mustachioed stationmaster, got into the act. The wonderful Irish actor Jack Mac-Gowran played Danaher's weaselly lickspittle named Feeney, a playful take on the director's real last name.

Francis Ford, in one of his most famous and typically non-credited roles, played the old bearded man Dan Tobin, who leaps up from his deathbed as though shot from a cannon when he hears the distant fight between Thornton and Danaher. As was his wont when actor friends were in need of work, Ford put Mildred Natwick in the delightfully stodgy role of the tweedy Widow Tillane and Mae Marsh as the mother of Lonergan's young curate, Fr. Paul. Even Duke Wayne's four children, Michael, Melinda, Toni and Patrick, appear as the young teens watching the horse race with Maureen O'Hara. To insure that no one was left out, Ford's new son-in-law, Ken Curtis (one of the Sons of the Pioneers and increasingly a regular in the stock company), shows up as the accordion-playing Dermot Fahy.

Behind the camera, the nepotism was even more rampant and one wonders if there were any of Ford's friends, cronies or relations who were not on the Republic-Argosy payroll during the summer of 1951. Ford's brother, Eddie O'Fearna, despite their stormy and often physical on-set confrontations, did his usual duty as assistant director, as did Ford's brother-in-law, Wingate Smith. Victor McLaglen's son Andrew, who would go on to a very successful career as a director in film and television, scrambled around Ford as second assistant director. Winnie Hoch, who had endured many standoffs with Ford on *She Wore a Yellow Ribbon*, delivered, along with second unit cameraman Archie Stout, some of the most magical Technicolor footage ever lensed. Despite the dearth of sunshine and the surfeit of rain during the location shooting in June and July, Hoch's photography of the wet, verdant Irish countryside read magically. Far from being a mere "Let's Visit Ireland!" travelogue, the landscape of the west country was rendered so beautifully that it became as great a character as the actors themselves. Ford's daughter, Barbara, acting as the assistant editor on the film, wrote Ford from Hollywood in June 1951. "We're receiving film regularly—it is just beautiful—the prettiest film I've ever seen—your Technicolor camera is not missing one single thing and it's just like being there—everyone is enthused."[13]

One of the criticisms leveled against Ford for the picture is that, like the mining village in *How Green Was My Valley*, the film does not reflect the harsh, socioeconomic realities that existed but was a sentimentalized and roseate imaging of a world that never was. As Ford clearly shows the story of Huw and his valley unfolds in the mind of an adult looking back through the veil of years and not in objective reality, so too does Ford show us that Sean is entering a mystical admixture of fable and memory. Innisfree is a world far removed from war, poverty, political turmoil and, as Old Dan Tobin proves as he rises from his sickbed, death itself. Innisfree, like Huw's valley, is not just a world that was envisioned in Ford's wildly romantic Gaelic imagination but a world that should be and will be. Men sit in pubs, drinking, talking and singing for days on end with no visible source of income, husbands plant roses for their wives instead of potatoes and Catholic men and women stop and tip their hats or curtsy to visiting Protestant bishops. Contrary to what the Widow Tillane says to Sean about Innisfree being "far from heaven," neither Sean nor Ford nor the viewer believes her.

When Sean alights from the train at the beginning, he encounters a group of locals who try to tell him where he is and where he is going. It is pointless from the start and soon the conversation turns into a living, breathing Tower of Babel. It is only when Michaeleen silently emerges into the frame, grabs Sean's valise and walks to the other side of the stationhouse does the mystical journey begin. Sean likewise enters the portals of the station like a stargate or rabbit hole and emerges on the other side into another realm, another world that gives precious little hint of a particular time but only the fullness of place. In fact, the first stop on Sean's pilgrimage home is a stone bridge where he looks across a brook to the "wee, humble cottage" where he was born. He hears in voice-over the sonorous tones of his mother, cooing, "Don't you remember, Seaneen, and how it was?"

Despite the gentle and mystic chords of memory that dominate the film, *The Quiet Man* is without doubt the most erotic film Ford ever made. The sexual tension between Sean and Mary Kate, perhaps manifesting Ford's deep and unfulfilled love for Kate Hepburn, is palpable from Sean's first glimpse of the barefoot Mary Kate as she drives sheep over a distant hill. Their passion, their longing (which remains unconsummated even after their marriage due to Sean's refusal to secure her dowry) gives the narrative an unusually hot tempo and moves it forward on sheer sexual energy. The passion is wordless and conveys through balletic and suggestive movements a sort of libidinous counterpoint to the other grace notes of the film. These include Sean scooping up holy water from the font in his hand, into which Mary Kate dips her fingers to bless herself, followed by Sean catching her cleaning his cottage. In the dark, wind-whipped living room, Sean grabs her arm, kisses her on the mouth and then, releasing her from his silent embrace, dodges the mean right hook she throws in quick succession. Later, during their courtship, Mary Kate leads Sean on a silently smoldering chase across the countryside, pausing and then re-suming the fertility dance like a doe pursued by a buck in heat. The scene culminates in a passionate embrace in a graveyard in which they seek shelter from an approaching thunderstorm, presaging their tu-multuous marriage. Soaked to the skin, with Sean's fine form showing through his wet shirt and Mary Kate's stockings dangling limply in her hands, Wayne and O'Hara clutch in the most sexually suggestive scene since Burt Lancaster and Deborah Kerr rolled in the Hawaiian surf in *From Here to Eternity*.

Another criticism leveled at Ford, especially during the militantly revisionist period after the 1960s, is the supposedly rank misogyny of the film manifested by the director through Wayne's character. The lack of a dowry (tying Mary Kate to the old life of women-as-chattel) followed by Sean's dragging his wife through the mud and fields back to her brother as returned merchandise is still a turnoff to many, espe-cially women. What is patently overlooked, however, is that O'Hara's character is in fact one of the first truly liberated women in American film. Not only is Mary Kate the owner of her property (350 pounds, furniture and household goods) but more importantly she is in full possession of her own body. Adamant about what physically belongs to her, she then refuses Sean the sexual consummation that he believes is his right (but manfully refuses to take by force) until she gets it. Mary Kate is a woman in complete possession of every facet of her existence and allows no man, neither her husband nor her bully of a brother, to take it from her.

The Quiet Man ends on the same note of fairy-tale fable with which it commenced. The climactic fight scene between Sean and Red Will has turned them into brothers-in-law, neighbors and friends and peace once more comes to Innisfree. In order to keep the Protestant minister and his wife in their Catholic community, Fr. Lonergan covers up his Roman collar and leads the entire village in cheering the visiting Angli-can bishop, thus making it look like Mr. Playfair has a larger congrega-tion than the one or two he actually has. In Fordian communities, be it in the Old West, on a PT boat or in a poor Welsh mining village, people dwell in forbearance, unity and equality not known in the out-side world. The villagers take their bows to the camera like characters in a play while Sean and Mary Kate wave their farewells as well. Now free to consummate to their heart's content, Mary Kate whispers a sug-gestion into Sean's ear and, momentarily shocked, he then turns and once more bounds after her into their pretty little cottage. The look of shock on Wayne's face was genuine, as Ford told O'Hara beforehand what to whisper, unbeknownst to Duke, into his ear. What she said was a secret that all three agreed to take to their graves.

The Quiet Man opened in August of 1952 to glowing reviews and a box office bonanza that must have made Yates feel, albeit for a short time, like L. B. Mayer and Samuel Goldwyn. Lines queued around theaters all over the country and by 1953 the initial outlay of $1.7 mil-lion had returned over $3 million, making it not only Republic's top grosser but one of the highest earners of the year.

The film's prestige continued to soar when it was nominated for seven Academy Awards, including Best Picture, Best Director, Cin-ematography, Adapted Screenplay and McLaglen in Best Supporting Actor category. Obviously absent was the score by the great Victor Young, whose lush soundtrack, employing tunes ranging from "The Isle of Innisfree" and "The Wild Colonial Boy" to the 7th Cavalry's jaunty march, "Garryowen," helped give the film as much heart and soul as Hoch's brilliant camerawork. In the end, Ford and Hoch right-fully took home the Oscars, and Ford also took home the knowledge that he fulfilled a nearly twenty-year dream and created one of the few films left in his canon that would unequivocally be called a clas-sic. This was probably best underscored by a letter he received from Lindsay Anderson, his young British friend, the future director and a devoted disciple. Anderson, who had received a cool reception from his erstwhile mentor after giving an unvarnished and unwelcome cri-tique of *The Fugitive*, found himself back in Ford's good graces as a sort of bellwether of European reaction to his work. Anderson wrote Ford in April of 1952 about his reaction to *The Quiet Man* after its European release. He could have been speaking for almost everyone who saw the film then and since. "A friend said as we came out 'It's like lying in a warm bath...Or rather, it's like being splashed over with nice things.'"[14]

As he said was his pattern, Ford followed the runaway success of *The Quiet Man* with one of those numerous time-killing films he could breeze through on autopilot in his own way and in his own time. *What Price Glory?* was based on a play by Maxwell Anderson and Laurence Stallings, a serio-comedy set in World War I, that had been made as a silent film in 1926 by Raoul Walsh starring Victor McLaglen and Edmund Lowe. Since Fox owned the property, Zanuck talked Ford into coming back to the studio to remake it with sound, Technicolor and broad comedy. Zanuck even toyed with the idea of turning it into a musical but, as the director made quite clear to his old chief, John Ford did not do musicals.

Captain Flagg and Top Sergeant Quirt are nail-tough Marines who have had a lifelong animosity and rivalry with each other that does not improve when Quirt is assigned to Flagg's unit in France. Even though Quirt whips Flagg's green recruits into fighting leathernecks, he re-ignites his commander's ire when he begins courting the local inn keeper's daughter, Charmaine. The only problem is that Flagg fancies her as well.

James Cagney, who had long since ceased his reign at Warner Brothers as one of their top stars, filled the role of Flagg to snarling, combustive perfection while the amiable and dependable song-and-dance man Dan Dailey parried and thrust back as Quirt. Fox's French import Corinne Calvet, one of the alliteratively named beauties who dazzled American audiences in the 1950s and 1960s (Brigitte Bardot, Claudia Cardinale) played Charmaine. The studio's newest heartthrob, twenty-one-year-old Robert Wagner, rounded out the leads as Lewisohn, the juvenile love interest.

Cagney, like Ford, was a respected Hollywood A-lister who was always associated with his Irishness and tough, pugnacious persona. He was a well-seasoned old bird and an Oscar-winning legend who did not need Ford, or the film, to make or break his still successful career.

Unlike Ford, Cagney's two-fisted persona (as a young man he was a good street fighter and had done some serious boxing) was mainly for the screen and in life was a hard-working yet fun-loving and easygoing guy both on the set and off. He was not a member of the stock company and saw neither the charm in Ford's crusty persona nor the rationale in excusing and justifying his behavior as was the wont of many of his company friends. To Cagney, Ford was a mean-spirited, bullying brute and Cagney realized the best thing to do was to avoid eye contact, keep silent and simply get the job finished as quickly as possible. Cagney, who had done battle over contracts and money with Jack Warner and was no pushover, sized up Ford with the dead-on accuracy only another member of the tribe could possess. Ford's Irishness, Cagney said, could be described in one word: malice.[15]

What Price Glory? works best as a comedy, and the broader it was played the better it worked. The scenes where Flagg and Quirt immediately get to a fist fight the minute they meet again and another scene where a drunken Flagg is being beaten about the head with wet towels are standouts. However, when the comedy veers back into war drama, the whole endeavor simply goes AWOL. No one did barrack room humor better than Ford, from the snapping irascibility of officers and the hapless ineptitude of young recruits to the stylized rituals and roughhousing of military life. The film, however, plays the broad and farcical too strongly against the reality of war, which is death and destruction. Aside from the pro-forma scenes of white crosses, the horrors of trench warfare and the dying soldier asking, "Why?" there is little sense of either war or the men who wage it; both known intimately by Ford. The artificiality of emotion is made worse by the obvious use of soundstages for the battle scenes. There is none of the expressionistic claustrophobia of the soundstage battle scenes Ford shot for *Four Sons*; on the contrary they simply look phony.

Joe MacDonald's camera work, veering between deep chiaroscuro and saturated primary colors, is superb and on the whole the picture is lovely and, at times, gorgeous to look at. The principals all acquit themselves with honor and of course Cagney could not give a bad

performance if he wanted. However, with the nation once again coming out of a shooting war (this time in Korea) and young Americans
once again being shipped home in coffins because of a police action no
one understood or wanted, *What Price Glory?* should have said something more substantial and less cavalier and jocular about that price.

The Sun Shines Bright (1953) marked Ford's last film for Yates and
Republic, ending a relationship that began on the rocks and went down
from there. Like Wayne, Ford had had enough of haggling with Yates
over profits and saw just a fraction of the massive monies made by *The
Quiet Man* due to the studio's dubious accounting methodology. In
a more aesthetic sense, the film would close Ford's period of mature,
lyrical storytelling that began four years earlier with *3 Godfathers*. Generally lost in the shuffle of the numerous films Ford continued to make
during these busy years, *The Sun Shines Bright* is an overlooked jewel
as well as a fitting coda to this magical period in the director's career.

The story itself, a conflation of three Irvin S. Cobb short stories
("The Sun Shines Bright," "The Mob from Massag" and "The Lord
Provides"), is a revival of Ford's own 1934 Judge Priest and the ghost of
Will Rogers' sagacious, homespun jurist who attempts to bring sanity,
humanity and tolerance to an unjust world. The setting is the same,
1905 Kentucky, but this time around Billy Priest is played by the white-
haired and avuncular Charles Winninger, his only lead role in an otherwise busy character acting career. Judge "Bugler" Billy Priest, a diminutive veteran of the Confederate cavalry, is now the Solomon of Fairfield,
dispensing wisdom and trading barbs with his friend, majordomo,
housekeeper and supplier of his barrel-aged "medicine," Jeff Poindexter
(an older Stepin Fetchit reprising his role from the 1934 film).

The Sun Shine Bright, like all Ford's best work, continues the tradition of loose narrative and gentle pacing and the film actually juggles
several storylines within the confines of its 90-minute running time.
They all, however, converge upon a core foundation of injustice and
intolerance. The soul of the film centers on the false accusation of rape

leveled against the banjo-playing Black man, Ulysses S. Grant, Wofford, and Billy's successful stand against the mob that storms the jail with the intent of lynching him (a highly inflammable scene deleted from the original film). Like Abe Lincoln in Ford's 1939 film, Billy employs a solitary form of courage to cow the mindless mass, and his white linen suit makes him stand out even more as a shining symbol of justice and virtue. Unlike Lincoln, however, old Billy Priest does it with a kind word and a gun that he draws and he threatens to shoot the first man who tries to enter the jail. He not only values common sense and talk but economy of effort, and even his tolerance extends only so far.

Similarly, the heart of the film centers on the true parentage of the pretty young schoolmarm, Lucy Lee (Arlene Wheelan), and the return of a dying prostitute (Dorothy Jordan), who threatens to reveal a secret everyone in the town knows or suspects but never reveal. The film's culmination is the funeral of the prostitute, without doubt one of the most stunningly powerful moments in all of Ford's work.

Running the risk of losing his re-election bid, Billy organizes and leads the solemn, silent procession to the church; he transforms a shameful and unseemly event into a locus of unity and forbearance. The nearly ten-minute sequence (it avoids monotony through crisp editing and a deft balance of long shots and close-ups) is almost completely silent, except for the sound of the wheels of the white hearse and the clop of horses and footsteps in the gravel. The liturgical procession (a parade and march of a different sort) brings together Yankees and Rebels, bluestockings and backwoodsmen in a communion of love and conversion.

In the church, Billy literally is transformed into priest, giving a eulogy based upon Christ's forgiveness and the woman taken in adultery. When he speaks the words, "He that is without sin among you be the first to cast a stone," a singular moment of repentance by the guilty party occurs and all present find themselves confirmed and strengthened in their own beliefs. In the space of a few extraordinary moments, Ford manifests the efficacy of almost all seven sacraments in their ineffably transformative and symbolic glory. There is baptism (rebirth), communion (unity), marriage (rightful recognition of a spouse), confirmation (strengthening of individual faith), holy orders (Billy transformed into minister), confession (repentance) and extreme unction (the Pre-Vatican II name for the anointing for the dying).

The Sun Shines Bright, despite its wince-inducing racial stereotyping and the horrendous way in which all Blacks, regardless of their age, are referred to as "boy," is one of Ford's most underappreciated masterpieces. In many ways it is a better and less precious film than *The Quiet Man*; tighter in construction and more profound in its message. Ford and Yates, however, were pretty much finished with each other and Republic simply put the film on the back burner of a cold stove. Yates did not know what to do with the film nor did he much care, as long as the profits from *The Quiet Man* kept ka-chinging in his coffers. Largely ignored by the critics, given a limited release and having suffered the final indignity of extensive cuts, *The Sun Shines Bright* quickly slipped into oblivion and with it Argosy's distribution deal. Contemporary scholars, however, now rank it with Ford's greatest classics and the director himself, who would change the list of his personal favorites from day to day, always declared *The Sun Shines Bright* as his favorite and finest achievement.

The House Un-American Committee (HUAC), blacklisting and politics aside, there were other rumbles on the horizon that proved all was not well in post-war Tinseltown. The slow demise of the studio system and the rise of independent production was exacerbated by an even greater villain in the deceptively simple guise of a wooden box and glass screen. By the end of 1946 there were only around 50,000 television sets in American homes. A mere four years later there were nearly twelve million and by 1953 almost half of American homes boasted a television set.[16]

Television was making about as rapid an inroad into the motion picture business as movies had done to vaudeville fifty years earlier, and the studios scrambled to find ways to lure people away from Lucy, Milton Berle and Sid Caesar and back into the theaters. To make matters worse for the studios, in 1948 the Supreme Court issued the landmark decision of *United States v. Paramount Pictures*, forcing the major studios to give up the chains of movie theaters that showed only their films. Stripped of their monopolized rule over the movie-going public, what they needed and what they gave the people was the oldest and most brilliant trick in the book: something ever old but ever new.

M-G-M's new studio head, Dore Schary, was a young, liberal writer who became head of production at the studio in 1948. When Louis B. Mayer was ousted in a 1951 coup, Schary took over as head of the entire studio and, although he favored smaller, intellectual "message" pictures, he still green-lighted big potboilers such as *Quo Vadis?*, *King Solomon's Mines*, *Scaramouche* and even old products like *The Prisoner of Zenda* and *Red Dust*. In 1953, *Red Dust*, a sizzling jungle romance that helped propel Clark Gable to stardom at the studio, was slated to be remade by Ford with the same plot and lead star but a different name and locale.

Mogambo, like *Red Dust*, told the tale of a torrid love triangle between a great white hunter, a playgirl and the proper young wife of an even more proper British anthropologist in Africa. Whereas the original was set in the jungles of Malaysia, *Mogambo* followed in the footsteps of *King Solomon's Mines* and transferred the action to the African Serengeti. Of the original female leads, the platinum bombshell Jean Harlow was dead and Mary Astor's career was on the wane due to age, chronic alcoholism and emotional instability. Clark Gable, however, was very much alive and well and although a bit doughier and grayer at the temples, at fifty-two he was still the king and a box office draw with great appeal for both ladies and men.

Gable plays Vic Marswell, career big-game hunter who runs safaris for wealthy tourists and dignitaries from around the world. He takes in the stranded "Honey Bear" Kelly (Ava Gardner), a maharajah-chasing party girl who has not only been around the block but a couple of continents as well. As things heat up between Marswell and Honey Bear, anthropologist Donald Nordley (Donald Sinden) arrives with his young bride Linda (Grace Kelly) to make a documentary about gorillas. Emotional levels quickly escalate from torrid to incinerating as the young but beautiful Linda begins to fall for Marswell as well.

In *Mogambo*, Ford presses deep into the Victor Fleming-Howard Hawks world of the sexpot and he apparently mightily enjoyed the journey. Ava Gardner was at the peak of her reign as the quintessential, raven-haired Hollywood sex symbol and her tempestuous marriage with Frank Sinatra was making weekly headlines. In fact, Sinatra visited Gardner on location in Africa and Ford enjoyed the ribald and naughty interplay between the two, who would divorce four years later. Grace Kelly, quite contrarily, was the model of beauty and decorum one would expect from Her Future Highness, Princess Grace of Monaco. Kelly, the daughter of Philadelphia millionaire and politician Jack Kelly, had gone into acting as a teen and scored a big hit as Gary Cooper's beautiful but passive Quaker wife in *High Noon* (1952). Ford saw a screen test of Kelly and rightly judged that a mother lode of class and quality lay beneath the pretty window dressing, and he was right. One would think that Ford would have made mincemeat out of the wealthy, finishing-school ingenue, but he knew the genuine article when he saw it and was able to coax a loose, organic performance out of Kelly that she rarely gave once she was transformed into a Dior-wearing, sculpted goddess. *Mogambo* not only garnered Kelly a Golden Globe but her first Academy Award Nomination as Best Supporting Actress and paved the way for her wildly successful collaboration with Alfred Hitchcock (*Dial M for Murder, Rear Window, To Catch a Thief*) as well as other films like *The Country Girl, The Bridges at Toko-Ri, The Swan* and *High Society*.

Ford's relationship with Gable was cordial but by no stretch of anyone's imagination did they become friends. Gable, despite the fact he was a pleasant, consummate professional who never took his title of "king" too seriously, tended to be a cool, aloof man who shunned intimacy and preferred the solitude of his dressing room when not working. Like Ford, Gable was a decorated war veteran and had flown dangerous B-17 bomber missions over Germany and when not making pictures enjoyed fishing, poker and imbibing copious amounts of liquid restoratives. The two men, however, could not establish an emotional bridgehead with the other and despite some minor frictions maintained a mutually respectful but distant relationship. Perhaps this was due in no small part to the fact that the film was a very expensive location shoot and, working on M-G-M's dime and not Argosy's, Ford did not have the time to poke, prod and spar (as he had with George O'Brien, Victor McLaglen, Hank Fonda and Duke Wayne) in order to mark out his he-bull territory.

Mogambo was shot in Technicolor by Robert Surtees, M-G-M's epic cameraman-in-residence, who had shot *Quo Vadis?* in Rome and would do similarly honorable work on the studio's future epics *Ben-Hur* and the remake of *Mutiny on the Bounty*. He was assisted in his endeavors by Freddie Young, who was a decade away from his own epic collaboration with David Lean on *Lawrence of Arabia, Dr. Zhivago* and *Ryan's Daughter*. The film was produced by the genial, gentlemanly Sam Zimbalist, the quiet but legendarily competent prime mover behind *Quo Vadis?, King Solomon's Mines, Beau Brummel* and the studio's gargantuan *Ben-Hur*, on whose set in Rome he would suffer a fatal heart attack in 1958. Locations for the film were vast and included sites in Kenya, Uganda, the Congo and Tanganyika. Since no gorillas are to be found in Kenya, stuntman Yakima Canutt was flown over as the second unit director and given the ticklish assignment of locating and filming charging gorillas in the equatorial regions farther to the south.

Ford enjoyed the experience and the location shoot with such fine actors but always saw *Mogambo* as a mere pleasantry and little more. As he told Peter Bogdanovich, "I liked the script and the story, I liked the set-up and I'd never been to that part of Africa—so I just did it."[17]

No one must have been more surprised than the director when *Mogambo* turned out to be an international hit, returning more than $5 million at the U.S. box office alone. This pleasantry turned out to be the biggest money-making hit of Ford's career. Although *How The West Was Won* made ten times that much in the next decade, it was the work of three directors and not a Ford project alone. Monies aside, the film's success, both domestically and abroad, must have been gratifying to Ford in that it proved (especially after the humiliating treatment he received at the hands of Yates at Republic) he was still a world-class director who could deliver a money-making hit for a prestige studio.

1953 may have been a good year for Ford in terms of his career and his bank account but personally it was utterly dismal. Ford's older brother, Frank, whose last screen appearance was as the buck-skinned backwoodsman Feeney in *The Sun Shines Bright*, died at the age of 72 in September 1953. Frank had been in failing health for some time, his condition exacerbated by alcohol and the anxiety caused by the prospect of unemployment and penury. Even though Ford helped Frank out by giving him small roles in many of his films, his elder brother never seemed to be able to pull his increasingly obscure life together. In April 1952, Frank's second wife, Mary, wrote to Ford, "I am terribly worried about Frank. He hasn't worked for over a year... he walks the floor constantly. We try so hard to make ends meet on his pension...if there is anything you can do to help us we would appreciate it a million times."[18]

Francis Ford, the dashing, innovative silent film director who strode with such confidence and swagger from one lucrative project to the next while his kid brother languished in his shadow, had been reduced to a forgotten, floor-pacing old man barely existing on a pension. Ford never resolved his complex emotions for his older brother and to the end of his days they remained a mixture of love, respect and resentment. Without Frank, who blazed the family trail into film and inspired his awestruck brother with his bold cinematic visions and a love for history, there would not have been a John Ford. It was a strange and ironic twist of fate that without John Ford, there probably would not have been a Francis Ford after his career tanked in the post-sound era. Despite the animosities, resentments and the ignominy of the small and wordless parts he was thrown by Jack, family was still family and as Frank had taken care of his wet-eared kid brother so did Jack take care of the down-and-out older Frank. The parts Frank was given in his later years, regardless of how small and seemingly insignificant, were eccentric and colorfully memorable, such as drunken bartenders, cackling backwoodsmen and death-defying old Irishmen. They gave him a cinematic immortality of sorts he otherwise would not have had and, to an old ham actor like Frank, that was about the greatest legacy for which he could have asked.

The other hit Ford took in 1953 was right in the eyes. His lifelong abysmal eyesight was progressively worsening and for an artist of Ford's caliber where everything depended on light, depth and composition, it was a potential professional death sentence. While shooting interiors for *Mogambo* at M-G-M's British studios outside London, Ford became painfully intolerant of light and spent most of his non-working time in dark rooms. He was diagnosed with cataracts, which necessitated surgery when he returned to California that same year. Recovery was slow and while healing in his Odin Street house he was unable to do much, even read books, his favorite solitary past time.

Most men are traditionally bad patients but for a man like Ford, who hated to be caged, infirm and deprived of the work that gave his life meaning, the time was particularly excruciating. Although the pain eventually abated, Ford was now permanently robbed of a great percentage of his sight, a deficit that Joseph McBride pointed out placed him in good company with similarly visually challenged artists in history such as Claude Monet. When Monet became almost completely blind he did not give up painting; on the contrary he simply intensified his palette on a bigger and bolder scale. Not a bad bit of advice that Ford would eventually cop from the impressionist's playbook.[19]

Ford had been making pictures for forty years and his instinct for composition would not be too severely hampered by his compromised depth perception. The fact that after 1954 he would move, relatively effortlessly, into wide screen formats such as Cinemascope, VistaVision, Super Panavision 70 and perhaps the most problematic one of them all, Cinerama, is proof perfect that Ford was neither hamstrung by nor afraid of the precarious state of his visual senses. One of the few signs of his compromised eyesight was that in order to read he now had to hold things up a few inches away from his eyes. The other was that, to protect his light-sensitive orbs, he also took to wearing a black eye patch over his left eye. As awful as it was for Ford, it did help complete his iconic look and along with his fedora, dark glasses and rumpled flannels created, for once and for all, the look of the John Ford of myth and legend.

Another sign of the encroachment of time, progress and the unforgiving cycle of life's seasons that even his stubborn bellicosity could not turn back, was the loss of his own modest castle. His Odin Street house, where he and Mary had lived for nearly thirty-five years, was slated by the city of Los Angeles for demolition in order to make way for the Hollywood Bowl's expanded parking. In his films Ford could wax poetic on the themes of loss of home and community and the sacred nature of pilgrimage, but in real time things tended to get a bit more sticky and problematic. The Fords were given sixty days to vacate their home and, with no bargaining chips or legal recourse, they bought a new house on Copa de Oro Road in the fashionable Bel Air district. Geographically and financially, the move was an upgrade from Odin Street with perks for both: Ford now had more room to read, brood and stockpile his mementos while Mary now had the prestige of a Bel Air address. Emotionally, however, there was a cold, strange artificiality to the house and despite all the trappings and prestige it never quite felt like the home that the "little gray house on the hill" had been.[20]

The Long Gray Line (1955) was a celebration of two sacred institutions that Ford considered the backbone of America: the military and the immigrant experience. Preferably, Irish for the latter. The film was based on *Bringing Up the Brass,* the book by Master Sergeant Martin Maher, who for nearly half a century was the beloved athletic instructor at West Point on the Hudson. Maher (1876-1961) was an immigrant from County Tipperary in Ireland who came to the Point as a waiter before enlisting in the army in 1898. He became the swimming instructor and, until his retirement in 1946, some of the greatest names in the nation's military roster swam through his natatorium.

The Long Gray Line was notable (but, alas, not too memorable) mainly for its technical aspects. It was the first film Ford shot in the wide-screen process known as Cinemascope. Even though 70mm wide-screen features had been toyed with since the 1920's, Cinema-scope was formally launched by Fox in 1953 for its biblical epic *The Robe*. The process employed an anamorphic lens (created by Bausch & Lomb) to create images of a 2.66.1 ratio, almost doubling the previous industry standard of 1.37.1. Visually, the square, boxy images projected on the screen now became nearly three times as wide as they were high and directors, failing eyesight or not, had to recalibrate their entire sense of lighting, balance and composition. Ford, to no one's surprise, hated it. He told Peter Bogdanovich, "You've never seen a painter use that kind of composition—even in the great murals, it still wasn't this huge tennis court. Your eyes pop back and forth and it's very difficult to get a close up."[21]

For a man of Ford's intensely painterly style, especially his belief that the eyes held the mystery of a character's soul, the wide-screen format was an impediment to his artistic vision. However, as he had with sound and Technicolor, Ford adjusted and fearlessly got in line with the march of progress in his profession. While emotionally Ford's films were tinged with memory and celebrated the myths and traditions of the past, technologically he was no shrinking violet stuck in the Victorian horse-and-buggy era. At the age of sixty, he not only embraced innovations in the industry but, as his future films proved, he mastered them as well.

Ford's choice of actor to play Marty Maher was an original one, although ultimately probably not the best. Tyrone Power, like Gable, was a reigning star at his studio (Fox) in the 1930s and 1940s and had served with distinction in World War II. Sold by Fox primarily as a pretty boy, the handsome "Black Irish" Power eventually transcended the glamor parts meted out by the studio and proved himself adept in epics (*Marie Antoinette*), swashbucklers (*The Mark of Zorro*), Westerns (*Jesse James*), drama (*The Razor's Edge*) and any number of musicals made with Alice Faye and Don Ameche. Released from his contract with Fox and now independent, Power wisely began casting about for opportunities to stretch his artistic legs on stage as well as in daring, atypical screen work in films like *Nightmare Alley* and *Witness For the Prosecution*.

Despite his noble intentions, Power is completely miscast here and comes across like a vaudevillian with an annoyingly bogus brogue telling "Paht and Moik" jokes. Although Ford needed Power's name and wattage to sell the film, it is interesting to wonder what could have come of the project had he made a "smaller" picture using one of his Abbey Theatre Irish alums like Jack McGowran, Charles Fitzsimmons or Sean McGlory. Power is simply much too old to convincingly pull off a green, twenty-something immigrant and too young to look like a seventy-six-year-old army pensioner. It doesn't help matters that he is also saddled with the phoniest succession of mustaches since Groucho Marx and his greasepaint.

Maureen O'Hara fares much better as Mary, his immigrant lass wife. Her silent, wide-eyed and mouth-agape scenes during their courtship play nicely against Marty's ebullient and boisterous blarney. After their marriage, Mary becomes a dutiful and quintessentially Fordian heroine in that she is resolute, strong in the face of death and loss and subordinates everything to her husband and the military.

The Long Gray Line was intended as a militarized version of *Goodbye, Mr. Chips*; a loving tribute to the institutional icon with the seemingly unimportant role who actually influences several generations of the nation's leaders. In the line of graduates of the class of 1915 march fresh-faced and newly minted officers like Omar N. Bradley and Dwight D. Eisenhower (played by Dobe Carey in a cameo no doubt appreciated by the sitting president). Soldiers come, grow up, move on, marry, have children, go off to war and die. Marty, however, never leaves and simply instructs one swimming class after another, and yet when he retires the entire Point turns out in full dress to honor a living and beloved legend. As Robert Francis says to Betsy Palmer, "It's been a great day for Marty." "It's been a great life for Marty," Palmer responds.

Despite its flaws, the film is wonderfully antithetical to the usual Fordian theme of the outsider, the loner longing for the community of which he knows he could never be a part. The Fordian community is generally found on the fly, where and when it can. Ford usually shows the hero as dynamic and the community as static but here it is just the opposite. The hero, Marty, is rooted in the embrace of the community, and it is the community that constantly passes by in time and space under the guise of parade and military tradition.

Ford enjoyed making the film on location at West Point and no doubt reveled in the opportunity to be Admiral Ford in a sea of Army brass. It also allowed him the opportunity to showcase the talents of sixteen-year-old Patrick Wayne, John Wayne's son and Ford's godson. Ford first used Pat as an eleven-year-old child extra in *Rio Grande* and gave him increasingly larger speaking roles. Pat had his father's striking good looks and charm and after appearing in several films for Ford (*The Searchers, Cheyenne Autumn*) and his father (*The Alamo, McClintock!, Big Jake*), struck out on his own career in films and television.

From whatever angle one stood, Ford's next project, continuing with the military theme of *The Long Gray Line*, was a triumph deluxe just waiting to happen. What should have been a hit that could not miss resulted in one of the most embarrassing and disappointing messes in his career. *Mister Roberts* (1955) was based on the hit 1948 play, produced by Leland Hayward and directed by Joshua Logan, that ran on Broadway for six years and over 1,000 performances before moving on to London. Henry Fonda, who had taken an eight-year absence from the screen to pursue a stage career, played the lead role of Lt. Doug Roberts, the easygoing, benevolent executive officer of the cargo ship *Reluctant* during World War II. Bored to tears with delivering fresh fruit and vegetables to real soldiers in the Pacific, Roberts longs to see action but is mindful of his duties and his men who suffer from the draconian rule of the captain, Lt. Cmdr. Morton. The crew is a motley assemblage of odd, lovable swab jockeys who want nothing more than liberty and the "goils" on shore, both of which Roberts will do anything to give them. The comic relief is supplied by Ensign Frank Thurlowe Pulver, a pussycat in khaki who dreams up elaborate schemes to get dates and booze and roars defiantly at the captain in the privacy of his bunk when the captain is nowhere to be found.

Fonda won a Tony for the role that, like Yul Brynner's King of Siam and Rex Harrison's Professor Higgins, became inextricably linked with his real persona. For the rest of his life, Fonda was invariably associated with the affable, perennial nice guy Doug Roberts and people were often disappointed when they discovered that he was not. Fonda not only acted the role for years but inhabited it like gas; he knew every twist, every turn, every subtle nuance of not only Robert's character but every character in the play. To Fonda, the script was like holy writ and any deviation or change would be as blasphemous as deciding to write a fifth gospel and tacking it on the end of St. John's.

When it went to the screen, Fonda believed, it had to be done right and faithful to the work he and Logan had so lovingly and painstakingly created. By bringing Ford in to direct with those type of caveats, the project was already doomed from the start.

Fonda, surprisingly, was not Warner Brothers' first choice for the role of Doug Roberts. At forty-nine, he was considered too old to play the lead and Jack Warner felt contemporary audiences would prefer a younger face like William Holden or Marlon Brando. Fonda had simply been away from the screen too long and was now suited for more fatherly, middle-aged roles than young naval lieutenants but Ford was adamant. His caveat was that he would direct on the condition that Hank Fonda was to take the lead.

In the eight years Fonda had been away from Hollywood much had happened, as well Ford knew, that shifted the balance of power away from the studios to the independent stars and producers. With the breakup of the studio system and the releasing of stars from long-term contracts, actors ceased to be factotums of corporate giants and legally obliged to take whatever roles were meted out to them. They now often headed their own production companies and came to the table with greater leverage and control over their pictures. *Mister Roberts* was, in effect, a Fonda vehicle but while Ford could take guff from a Darryl Zanuck or Sam Goldwyn, he was damned if he would have policy dictated to him by one of his own actors. Especially if it was a member of his stock company whom he had fought to bring into the project.

Next, Fonda knew the play as intimately as he did the nooks and crannies of his own house. He understood the stress points and the soft spots, the interplay of characters and the necessity of subordinating the comedy to the drama. What Fonda wanted, basically, was for Ford to film the stage play, intact and with no innovations or changes that he believed would cause the center to drop out of the narrative. Ford, however, was not brought in to make a play but a movie, which entailed opening up the action and broadening every element in the play in order to make it read better on the screen.

Last, the supporting roles of the sailors and non-coms were played on Broadway by capable and dependable actors like Murray Hamilton, Harvey Lembeck and Lee Van Cleef, all of whom would go on to successful character- actor careers in film and television. Instead of importing actors who, like Fonda, thoroughly understood the play and the rhythm of their parts, Ford replaced them with members of his own stock company. Ford always felt safer when he worked surrounded by loyal friends and thus Ward Bond, Harry Carey, Jr., Ken Curtis and even young Pat Wayne were signed on as the disgruntled sailors of the *Reluctant*. It was with a light heart and a sense of familial bonhomie not known since he filmed *The Quiet Man*, that Ford sailed the *Araner* to Hawaii and then pressed on to Midway to begin principal shooting on *Mister Roberts*.

What began as a prospective pleasure cruise with old friends on familiar territory, turned into a cinematic gale of horrendous proportions soon after filming began. The *Araner* was moored in Hawaii and the cast went to Midway Island for exterior shooting aboard the U.S.S. *Hewell* standing in for the *Reluctant*. Also on board were James Cagney as the tyrannical captain and the unflappable Hollywood great, William Powell, who had been coaxed out of retirement to play the avuncular Doc. Making his first major splash was a young Jack Lemmon, whose first film of note was the year before in the Judy Holliday comedy *It Should Happen to You*. Lemmon, who had gone to Phillips Academy and then Harvard and was on his way to becoming one of the great actors of the second half of the century, was signed to play the timidly scheming Ensign Pulver

Lemmon, despite his blue blood pedigree, possessed a suave and urbane persona combined with a quirky comic mania that immediately endeared him to Ford; sort of a William Holden scripted by George S. Kaufman. The combination gave him an American Everyman quality that allowed him to do great comedy work for Billy Wilder, Blake Edwards and Neil Simon as well as solid drama in films like *Days of Wine and Roses, Save the Tiger, Missing* and *The China Syndrome*. Lemmon's Pulver (for which he would win an Oscar for Best Supporting Actor) was played like a Michaeleen Flynn put to sea. Ford recognized Lemmon's inherent comic genius and threw him unscripted bits of comic business that not only expanded and intensified his role but also slightly shifted the focus on him and away from Fonda's laconic, staid and contemplative Roberts.

To Fonda's chagrin, Ford began adding touches of comedy across the entire deck, adding scenes and touches of broad slapstick comedy that made *Mister Roberts* look more like *South Pacific*. The old pros like Cagney and Powell, smart enough to see the hurricane that was brewing, wisely opted to keep quiet, stay out of the line of fire and simply do the job for which they were hired. It was just a matter of time before things came to a head between Ford and Fonda, and that they finally did while still on location in the Pacific. There are several accounts of what exactly happened but the results were unfortunately and unerringly the same. While bunking in the BOQ (Bachelor Officers Quarters) on Midway, Fonda and Ford had a late night conversation and it was not about fishing, poker or Ward Bond. What began as a discussion about the progress of the film became a progressively heated exchange and soon voices were raised in a shouting match. In an interview Dobe Carey gave to Lindsay Anderson in 1978, Carey claimed that Ford jumped out of his chair and punched Fonda in the face.[22]

Lemmon, who was awoken by the exchange and had scrept down the hall to silently witness what was going on, remembered it as a shouting and shoving match, seeing Ford swinging wildly at Fonda who threw Ford back on the bed. Regardless of who did what to whom, Ford's control over *Mister Roberts* as well as his sixteen-year friendship with Henry Fonda was essentially finished. Unlike Harry Carey, Sr., George O'Brien or even John Wayne, Fonda (who finished the film and went on to the second phase of a highly successful screen career) did not maunder about waiting for Pappy to call and welcome him back into the fold. Fonda and Ford would exchange, "How's it going?" calls over the years and Fonda would raise hosannas to Ford in several documentaries made before the director's death in 1973 (even appearing together walking around the old Fox lot), but professionally it was over for good.[23]

Ford was, literally, out to sea and with the *Araner* moored back in Hawaii he had no avenue of escape from the project that he had helped to spin out of control. He then did what he did whenever things started to go south for him: he started drinking. For all his legions of faults and weaknesses, beginning with alcohol, Ford almost always and admirably maintained a sober professionalism whenever he was working. He was an alcoholic but despite the disease his primary narcotic was not alcohol but picture-making. Alcohol was merely the recessive gene that became dominant when he needed to stave off the crippling effects of boredom, melancholia and personal turmoil. His last serious working-hour bender was twenty years before when he went off on a binge instead of finishing *Arrowsmith* for Sam Goldwyn.

The drinking continued when the unit returned to Hollywood to shoot interiors at Warner Brothers. Things actually became so bad that Ford's gall bladder gave out and he was taken to the hospital for surgery. Ford's hospitalization no doubt gave Leland Hayward, Josh Logan, Fonda and even Ford himself the convenient cover to gracefully ease the director off the picture. Veteran director-producer Mervyn LeRoy was brought in to finish the film and despite his noble declamation that he was finishing a John Ford film and not making his own, the hodgepodge pastiche of scenes shot by two men (including a handful shot by Logan) made for a very jumbled and uneven film. Ford's crisp and vibrant location exteriors were artlessly intercut with LeRoy's flat, inorganic medium and close-up shots on studio sets against obviously painted backdrops. Pacing and rhythm start and stop and the long unbroken shots taken during soliloquies attest to the fact that with LeRoy now at the helm, Fonda got exactly what he wanted: a filmed stage play.[24]

Cut and scored, *Mister Roberts* was released on July 30, 1955, and despite the tempestuous nature of its production and all the hands that held the wheel, it met with good reviews and a return of over $8 million at the box office. While *Mister Roberts* is a good movie, it is really not a John Ford film due to the dearth of his footage that ended up in the final cut. Even if it did not all go sour after principal location commenced, in hindsight, something about the project made it less than the perfect marriage of man and material it originally seemed. The ever-insightful, ever-observant Dobe Carey (who admitted that he himself was miscast as the beefy sailor Stefanowski) summed it up once and for all in an interview he gave Lindsay Anderson when he said that Ford should never have directed the picture in the first place.[25]

The success of *The Quiet Man* and *Mogambo* aside, the decade (now half spent) had not been abundantly good to Ford. He had made personal and rewarding films like *The Wagon Master, The Sun Shines Bright* and *The Long Gray Line* that were received indifferently. He also made time-killers for a paycheck, like *When Willie Comes Marching Home* and *What Price Glory?* The *Mister Roberts* debacle, however, which arose from his combativeness with Fonda and resulting alcoholic binge, put him on a particularly slippery professional slope. If Ford was to regain his good name and reputation, he needed to make a film that was not only critically and commercially successful but the work of the genius who was John Ford. What he made in the following year was more than that. In fact it was a film that, even today, is considered one of the greatest in the history of twentieth-century film.

More has been written about *The Searchers* than any other Ford film, including *Stagecoach* and his Oscar-winning masterpieces from his early 1940s apogee. The film warrants not just essays and chapters of biographies but to be the focus of a book itself and in recent years it has duly received that. *The Searchers* is Ford's magnum opus and his own *Don Giovanni*; a dark, disturbed and disturbing epic journey into murder, madness, racism, sex, revenge and redemption.

The *Searchers* was based on a book by Alan LeMay, an Indiana-born writer of Westerns whose books included *Along Came Jones* (made into a classic Western starring Gary Cooper) and *The Unforgiven*, another tale of miscegenation and revenge made by John Huston in 1960 with Audrey Hepburn and Burt Lancaster. LeMay also wrote the screenplays for the Cecil B. DeMille epics *Northwest Mounted Police* and *Reap the Wild Wind*. The book, *The Searchers,* is the tale of the Edwards family, who work a hard-scrabble homestead in post-Civil War Texas, fighting both the elements and hostile Comanche Indians who rightfully claim the same land as their own. When most of the family is killed in a Comanche raid, the dead man's brother and black sheep of the family, Amos Edwards, takes his adopted nephew Martin Pawley (who he despises due to his quarter Cherokee blood) on a five-year search for his two captive nieces.

The basis for the story is the actual kidnapping of Cynthia Ann Parker, a nine-year-old girl who was taken by Comanche warriors during a raid on her grandfather's fort in east Texas in 1836. For nearly twenty-five years Cynthia was first a captive and then a bride of the Comanche warrior Peta Nocona, for whom she bore three children including the last great Comanche leader Quannah Parker. In 1860 Cynthia was recaptured by Texas Rangers during a raid on her Co-manche village and returned to her family and "civilization." However, separated from the only husband, children and culture she had ever known and loved, Cynthia fell into a deep depression and, refusing to eat following the death of her daughter, died in 1870. Even though her rescue was trumpeted throughout the country as a God-ordained triumph of white civilization over the brutal, heathen Indian ways, Cynthia was white in skin only. In her heart and soul, she was Comanche.

The financing for *The Searchers* would come from a bit more of a reliable source with deeper pockets than Argosy, which would be liquidated after the film was released in 1956. Cornelius Vanderbilt Whitney (known professionally as C.V. and personally as Sonny) was the rich-as-Croesus progeny of Harry Payne Whitney and Gertrude Vanderbilt (yes, *those* Vanderbilts), two of the most wealthy and prominent social register families on the East Coast. Despite being the issue of two gilded age eagles, C.V. proved to be a shrewd (some would say heartless) businessman in his own right and made fortunes in finance, mining and horse-breeding as well as helping Juan Trippe launch Pan-American Airlines. Unlike his gentlemanly, philanthropic cousin, John Hay "Jock" Whitney, who had scored big by financing David O. Selznick in the production of *Gone With the Wind*, C.V. was more of a rawboned, sunburned buckaroo and investing in a gritty Ford Western seemed just to fit his pistol.

Frank Nugent used LeMay's book as the catalytic agent for what became the finest script of his career, changing names, adding characters, and as he did with *The Quiet Man*, shifting around the political and historical so as to make the search more of an inward and personal journey. Amos Edwards became Ethan and the search for Debbie (young Lana Wood, who would be replaced by her older sister Natalie as the teenaged Debbie) and Lucy (Pippa Scott) was intensified from a simple retrieval mission to an eviscerating and daring meditation on race hatred, solitude, community and the schizophrenic nature of a warm loving heart beating in the compromised and corrupted flesh of fallen humanity.

If Henry Fonda had not fallen out with Ford the year before, it is possible that he would have made a profoundly chilling impression as Ethan Edwards. His tendency toward detached coolness and emotional unavailability would have perfectly suited him to play the angry and distant searcher. That is why John Wayne inhabits the role with such monumental grandeur and epic fury: he was fundamentally cast against type. Under Ford's direction, Wayne revealed a new and dark dimension of his persona that he never did before and would not do in the future. In *Stagecoach* Duke admitted that he was basically playing Ford and in *Red River, The Sands of Iwo Jima, True Grit* and almost all roles in between he played John Wayne. *The Searchers* was Wayne's One Time Only performance, an atypical foray into a disturbing shadowland that was new and unexplored territory for both men. Grasping the utter novelty of where these men went to create both the character of Ethan and the cinematic tapestry into which he was woven is merely one piece of the puzzle of greatness of *The Searchers*.

Ethan returns to the family homestead in 1868, emerging out of the sun, desert and rocks draped in a mystery as heavy as his Confederate greatcoat and the wide-brimmed black hat that shadows his eyes. His brother, Aaron (Walter Coy), welcomes him home as does his sister-in-law, Martha (Dorothy Jordan), and it is apparent through Ethan and Martha's protracted glances and gestures that between them there exists a deep and passionate love. What Ethan was doing since the end of the Civil War is, like everything about him, a mystery. The medal he gives young Debbie, as Ford told Bogdanovich, suggests that he likely served with many ex-Confederates who went to Mexico after the surrender at Appomattox and joined Maximilian's Imperial Army.[26]

The only person who sniffs around Ethan and tries to connect the dots is Captain The Reverend Samuel Johnson Clayton (Ward Bond) who, when he isn't commanding the company of Texas Rangers, is ministering to the homesteaders' spiritual needs. Bond's Capt. Rev. Clayton both looks and acts like the John Brown of John Steuart Curry's *Bleeding Kansas* mural in the state's capitol. Gun in one hand, bible in the other, Sam Clayton roars gigantically and defiantly at all comers, ready to use both instruments in subduing Christian and heathen alike for the greater glory of the Lord. Like his Sheriff Buck Sweet in *3 Godfathers*, Sam Clayton suspects that Ethan's activities since the surrender have not been legal or peaceful. "You fit a lot of descriptions," he says while eyeing the prodigal brother suspiciously. What is made clear is Ethan's pathological hatred for Indians, regardless of their tribe or breeding. His racism is not that of the homesteaders, who simply want the Comanche off the land they have stolen fair and square. To Ethan, there is an *untermenschen*, bacterial element to the indigenous people that calls for their extermination from not only the human race but human memory as well.

After Aaron, Martha and their son are slaughtered (Martha raped before being killed) and the two girls kidnapped, Ethan sets out on a vengeful search to bring them back. At first he is joined by Clayton, the Rangers, Martin and Lucy's beau Brad Jorgensen (Harry Carey, Jr.) and then after being ambushed by the Comanche, with Martin and Brad alone. Brad is killed after he attacks the Comanche single-handedly when Ethan reveals that he found Lucy's violated dead body; the two discover Debbie is in the hands of a fierce chief named Scar (Henry Brandon). Scar catches on to what is unfolding and for five years leads the two on a cat-and-mouse search from Canada to New Mexico. The search itself, unlike the sacred pilgrimages of Ford's wagon trains or the procession of the community in military marches or parades, is unholy and obsessive. Ethan is motivated throughout the film by one overarching emotion: hatred. The first part of the film he is driven by hatred of Scar for kidnapping his pure, virginal white kin. The second part of the film, when Ethan finds Debbie has grown into womanhood and is not only sexualized as one of Scar's wives but completely Indianized, it turns into an obsessive mission to kill her for her betrayal. Raw, naked hatred compounded by twisted sexual fury detonates in Ethan like an emotional atomic bomb.

Ford alludes to, but does not telegraph, the probability that the tender love between Ethan and Martha could have resulted in an adulterous liaison that produced Debbie. While it is not clear, it is entirely probable that Ethan's psychosexual rage and obsession to rescue, and then later to kill, Debbie is due to the fact that she may be his daughter. This is amazingly underscored in a scene between Ethan, Martha and Sam Clayton just before they set out on the patrol that allows Scar to move in and slaughter the family. After Martha gently caresses Ethan's greatcoat and hands it to him, Ethan softly kisses her forehead while Clayton discreetly but knowingly averts his eyes and drinks his coffee. Like a priest vowed to silence in the confessional, Clayton sees all and knows all without seeing or knowing anything; he simply puts on his hat and walks out the door.

The Searchers was filmed in Monument Valley with second units going to Colorado and Alberta, Canada, for the snowbound and 7th

Cavalry fort scenes. Winnie Hoch was back as cameraman shooting in the high fidelity VistaVision format, and his compositions outdo even those he created for *Yellow Ribbon*. The studio mockups of the Edwards cabin, campfires and even a misty river crossing look like typical 1950s Western sets used for *Bonanza* and *Gunsmoke*. The exteriors, however, possess a primal magnificence and every inch of space, positive and negative, is saturated with extraordinary shades of primaries and pastels. Here, Ford and Hoch are no longer emulating the economic, high-contrast arrangements of Frederic Remington but the full-bodied, dramatic western theater of Charlies Russell and Schreyvogel.

Typical of Ford, his shooting in Monument Valley brought a small fortune to the struggling Navajo populace, and in the cast can be spotted familiar faces from previous Westerns shot there such as Bob Many Mules, Harry Black Horse and Jack Tin Horn. Ford was unstintingly generous to his friends, especially those in need, and when he helped the Navajo it was with great affection, respect and none of the psychological strings he usually pulled with his Anglo friends. In the early 1950s, the valley was hit by severe blizzards that obliterated livestock and other necessities the people needed to work, eat and live. With little fanfare, Ford used his military connections to have foodstuffs and supplies airlifted into the valley, thus insuring survival for the people whom he had so much love and genuine respect.(27)

The Searchers is an ensemble piece for the stock company, and includes Ken Curtis, Pat Wayne, Ollie Carey, John Qualen, Frank Borzage and his accordion and Ford's beloved stuntmen Chuck Hayward and Chuck Roberson (a dead ringer for Wayne, whom he doubled for well into the 1970s). A newcomer was the lovely Vera Miles, a Maureen O'Hara type who tomboys her way through the role of Laurie Jorgensen, Martin's love interest, with a strong combination of toughness and kittenish vulnerability.

The picture, however, belongs to Wayne. There are the recurring Fordian motifs such as the doorway as portal; it is through the opening door (opening shot) we first see Ethan arrive and through the closing door that we see him depart in the last frame. The community is symbolized by hierarchy such as fathers, ministers and rangers as well as strong earth mothers such as Martha and the redoubtable Mrs. Jorgensen, who waxes poetic about the need for bleached bones in the soil before Texas can become a fit place for families. There is also the ritual component, symbolized by everything from noisy, disorganized breakfast tables and courting protocols to funerals and weddings. Ethan does not partake of any of the rituals (in fact, he interrupts his family's funeral, telling Sam, "Put an 'Amen' to it...there's no more time for praying! Amen!") but always observes as an outsider from the sidelines. Ethan's world is the organic, violent expanse of the desert where rituals are for survival and hierarchy is determined by the alpha male who can kill fastest.

The only Fordian theme missing is the one that is usually the most dominant in his films: the communion of the saints and the connection of the living with the dead. In the past, Ford's characters would feel some kind of mystical bond with their dead loved ones and through words, gestures and even music (the "Ann Rutledge theme" from *Young Mr. Lincoln*) feel their genuine and living presence. Here, when Ethan's great love is raped and savagely murdered, he feels no connection to her, nor does Ford allude to any. In *The Searchers,* the dead, for the first time, are truly dead and truly gone.

Despite the typical rituals of a Ford production in Monument Valley, *The Searchers* was not business as usual. There was an eerie, tangible sense of loneliness and isolation about Wayne and Ford that fed the performances in the final film. Dobe Carey told Lindsay Anderson that, unlike previous Ford productions, there was little of the playfulness and easy-going bumming around that usually marked Wayne's persona. He kept mostly to himself or spent time huddling quietly with Ford deep in conversation. Usually, Wayne expressed his innocence, charm or surprise through raised eyebrows and his anger through a near-sighted squint. His Ethan Edwards had an icy, hard and utterly terrifying look in his eyes; an almost animal-like signal that warned people not to tangle with him or even get close. It was a look he never had prior to *The Searchers* and one that would never appear again.[28]

Ethan, who is a stranger to the family he loves and defends, is actually more at one with the Indians he hates and kills. He knows the way of the Comanche, he reads the earth for signs, understands their way with horses, women, warfare. He carries his rifle, not in a saddle scabbard like the Rangers, but in a beaded leather one like the Indians. He knows, as the Rangers obviously do not, Comanche spirituality and theology of the body. This is demonstrated when he shoots the eyes out of the dead Indian declaring that without eyes he can never enter the spirit world and has to wander "forever between the winds." When he finally meets Scar, Ethan understands the Comanche language and, earning the grudging respect of the chief, enters his tent saying that he "Don't stand talking in the wind."

Theoretically, it could be that Ethan's hatred of all Indians is not merely racism but actually a self-loathing, a hatred of the Indian he himself has become and necessitates the killing of Debbie to spare her the same riven and unsettled existential condition. When Ethan and Martin encounter a buffalo herd on the Canadian plains, an enraged and almost demented Ethan begins to fire wildly at them, his unhinged rationale being that dead buffalo mean dead Indians. Later, at the 7th Cavalry post they look over a group of white women recaptured from Indian camps, their identities as white human beings crushed in a compost of madness and a childlike stupidity by their ordeal. At the sound of a woman's lunatic whimpers, Ethan turns to look at her and the shot culminates in the last great Fordian zoom in on Wayne. It is a universe away from the first zoom in *Stagecoach* announcing the arrival of a young, heroic god and the second from *Rio Grande* showing the loneliness of a duty-bound man longing for wife, child and home. *The Searchers* zoom takes us directly into the volcanic phrenology of Wayne's face; his stubbly jaw hard and his eyes revealing his heart of darkness. It is a supremely terrifying moment in which the viewer becomes voyeur on a face that is almost too awful to behold. "Hard to believe they're white," the medical officer says to Ethan. "They ain't white...anymore," Ethan responds, "they're Comanche."

Ethan, like Debbie and the female captives at the fort, are neither fully white nor fully Comanche but hover between two worlds, wandering between the winds. When Ethan shoots the eyes out of the dead Indian, kills the buffalo and then attempts to kill Debbie (until one of Scar's braves puts an arrow through his shoulder) it is not so much murder but a form of suicide. He attempts to kill that which he is not; his struggle is titanic as he strives to become who he truly and essentially is: human. Earlier in the film, when Ethan secretly discovers the brutally violated body of Lucy on the trail (but does not tell Brad and Martin), he executes a small and seemingly insignificant grace note that is one of the boldest and brilliant ever done in a Ford film. Almost falling out of his saddle in shock and horror, Ethan pulls out his knife and begins absentmindedly to stab at the sand with his knife. His motivation is unclear but it could be that he is either miming the horrific act of violation or is simply punishing the mother earth from which he came for allowing him to be born and witness such an unspeakably awful scene.

The original script had Ethan pursuing Debbie into the cave and advancing on her with his hand on his pistol before relenting, reholstering his piece and saying, "You sure favor your mother." It is poignant and resuscitates, at the conclusion of the film, the theme of the communion of the saints (Ethan sees the face of the dead Martha in Debbie). However, a greater theophany is revealed with more pith and less exposition.[29]

When Ethan corners Debbie and lifts her up in the air like a priest before the sacrifice, he repeats the same gesture he made when he first saw her as a little girl at the beginning. However, like Abraham on Mt. Moriah with Isaac, his hand is stayed from murder by the hand of God. Had Ford followed the original script, Ethan would have refrained from killing Debbie due to the fact that he sees the shadow of the dead Martha in her eyes. The motives there would have been selfish and self-serving and not from any grasp of Debbie's true essence as human *and* other. The emotional payoff that is rendered in full and overflowing measure results from the fact that Ethan does recognize Debbie's intrinsic and individual humanity, proving St. Thomas Aquinas' dictum that defines love as "willing the good of the other *as* other." Thus, love in its true and unsentimental meaning becomes the catalytic agent for recovering not only Debbie but Ethan's own deeply-felt humanity.

As Ethan cradles Debbie in his arms he says softly, "Let's go home, Debbie." If Ethan is the loner and the ambiguous outsider with no home, what does he mean? The interpretation here suggests that Ethan recognizes his bond with Debbie and recovers his own identity as a member of a humanity larger than the temporal one back on the homestead. He has not saved Debbie from a terrible fate with a violent and primitive people, he has simply helped recover her rightful place in the cosmic order and in so doing has recovered his own.

Accepting that, how does one interpret the famous closing scene of the film? Ethan returns Debbie to the Jorgensens who, in a sustained shot taken from inside the dark doorway of the house, take her inside and are followed by Martin and Laurie. Ethan stands alone outside (grabbing his arm like Harry Carey, Sr., which made the normally implacable Ollie Carey start to cry out of camera range) before turning and slowly walking away as the door closes and fades the screen into darkness.

The accepted interpretation is that Ethan, the eternal loner, is shut out from the community, from family and home and doomed to forever wander between the winds. But is he? Ford shows the family entering into a dark void that we cannot see but assume to be the comfort and security of a home. Ethan, contrarily, stands illluminated in the vast, breathtaking expanse of the desert, the sand, the wind, the sky, the universe. At the beginning of the film, the door opens to a man truly alone, sundered by hate and filled, as it were, with emptiness. Purged and cleansed by the desert and transformed by love, Ethan returns Debbie to her home and must now return to his. He does not wander between the winds, he belongs to the wind and is part of the fiber of the vast infinity beyond the dark confines of the limiting void of "bed and board." Ethan is, as God promised He would do for Israel, settled on his land.

The Searchers, contrary to the same urban myths that surround *It's A Wonderful Life*, was considered neither a flop nor just another Western when it was released in the winter of 1956. It made nearly $5 million in North America alone the first year of its release and Bosley Crowther of the *New York Times* recognized the depth of the film despite the episodic nature of the plot. The film's dark, brooding gestalt and themes of race, injustice, miscegenation and genocide appealed to filmmakers in succeeding decades, and such noted directors like Steven Spielberg, Martin Scorsese, George Lucas, John Milius and Walter Hill would cite its influence on their work and cinematic psyche. Across the Atlantic, French New Wave director Jean-Luc Godard thought it one of the most influential films of the age and famously declared that he hated John Wayne for supporting Goldwater and yet loved him tenderly when he took Natalie Wood in his arms.

Ford was doggedly devoted to his friends but to those who served in wartime and suffered for it, there was a certain reverence that, like the Field Photo Farm, he felt duty-bound to render. Such was the driving force behind his interesting and often overlooked *The Wings of Eagles* (1957) a heartfelt tribute to his friend Spig Wead, the navy pilot turned screenwriter who had written *Air Mail* and *They Were Expendable* for Ford as well as the Oscar-nominated scripts for *Test Pilot* and *The Citadel*.

Before he was paralyzed in a freak domestic accident in 1926, Wead was a pioneer in naval aviation, whose air races and record-setting speed competitions (namely with the dreaded rival, the U.S. Army) convinced Washington of the need for advancing naval air technology. After a writing stint in Hollywood, where he became friendly with Ford, Spig, despite needing leg braces and canes, returned to active duty in World War II and served aboard the U.S.S. *Yorktown* and the U.S.S. *Essex*. For Ford, Spig was not only a patriot but a courageous visionary who overcame great personal, marital and physical hurdles while never losing sight of the bigger historical picture and his part in painting it. The 1950s were the years of the biopic; the fluffy, saccharine lionizing of cultural icons that resulted in pretty but pretty inaccurate films like *The Glenn Miller Story*, *The Great Caruso*, *The Buster Keaton Story*, *The Stratton Story*, *The Jolson Story* and, lest anyone forget just how perfect and lofty the lives of the famous can be, *Jolson Sings Again.* Ford loved sentiment like no one else but he could not stomach schmaltz. What he wanted and what he made was an honest, warts-and-all tribute to a genuine hero as well as a genuinely flawed man.

John Wayne was paired with Maureen O'Hara for the third and last time in a Ford film as Spig and his long-suffering wife, Min. Ford and Wayne created Spig as a devil-may-care hellion who flies his biplane into the admiral's swimming pool during high tea and busts up the Army Air Corp's dinner with a donnybrook that lands Army-Navy first into the swimming pool and then the brig. After being promoted to commander, Spig tumbles down the stairs at home and is paralyzed. He falls into a deep depression but is pulled out of it by his best mate, "Jughead" Carson (Dan Dailey, in his third outing with Ford), who pushes Spig into a punishing rehab that allows him to walk with braces. He then sets out on a second career as a screenwriter in Hollywood.

Wayne gives a nuanced, ultimately thoughtful and reflective performance as the heroic but flawed Spig, going so far as to portray the old soldier without his toupee, by now a constant companion since his hair began thinning in the late '40s. The most robust character, however, is the gruff director in Hollywood who befriends Spig and furthers his career. Ward Bond plays the director, who wears rumpled flannels, dark glasses and smokes a pipe in an office cluttered with movie and cowboy memorabilia. If anyone did not catch on to the fact that Bond was playing Ford's cinematic *doppelganger*, the director's name in the film is that of another American car: John Dodge.

Despite Bond's exuberant, tongue-in-cheek portrayal of Ford, in many respects it is Spig who truly seems to be the autobiographical character in *The Wings of Eagles.* Spig is a devoted husband and father who conforms to the duties imposed by marriage and parenting. However, he flourishes most in the all-male hothouse of the navy, where relationships are gloriously uncomplicated and where intimacy is sealed in the warrior-class rituals of drinking, brawling and battle. When Spig is paralyzed, his accident becomes a metaphor for a deeper emotional wound. As Spig's paralysis symbolizes his intrinsic unavailability to everyone except a handful of loyal navy friends, so Ford's alcoholism and personal demons rendered him a solitary and basically unhappy man.

The accident ruptures his relationship with Min and it is Jughead who effectively steps into the role of wife, nursing Spig, pushing him on the road to recovery and keeping the fires of hope burning bright. Spig recovers his sense of identity and purpose, not in the comforts of home and family, but in the manic pressure-cooker world of the military and movie-making. It all plays a little too close to the bone and despite his heroism and sense of duty, Spig is ultimately a very lonely and unfulfilled man. At the end of the film, after having resumed his duties in World War II, Spig is transferred from a carrier to a destroyer in a breeches buoy in the middle of the Pacific. Even though the ship's company turns out to salute him for his service (including Spig's old nemesis, an Army Air Corps officer) Spig ends as a man at home neither on water nor land but tenuously suspended in the air between. Unlike Ethan Edwards, who belongs to the wind, it appears that it is Spig who is condemned to wander forever between the winds.

Like many Hollywood players of the 1950s, Ford was lured by the siren song of overseas production. Producers and directors, weary of fighting the studio front office, labor unions and the government and attracted by foreign government subsidies, cheaper labor and production costs, found it increasingly profitable to make their large and small-scale productions overseas with American stars and European technicians. Following in the wake of former Studio System titans like Darryl Zanuck and David O. Selznick came directors like Stanley Kramer, John Huston and Otto Preminger. Actors also signed on board for joint American-European production and ranged from A-listers like Kirk Douglas, Burt Lancaster and Anthony Quinn to Tarzan and Hercules he-men like Lex Barker and Steve Reeves. Ford, however, had no desire to lounge languidly about in the heat of the south of France or sweat it out in Rome's Cinecitta Studios. He naturally wanted to go farther north where it was colder, wetter and decidedly more green.

Ford's on-ramp into Irish film production was Michael Morris, an Irish-Catholic journalist, author, soldier and businessman who, although he was born in London, had distant familial ties to the Feeney clan of Spiddal in Galway. It did not hurt matters that Morris was also the third Baron Killanin, a peer of the realm and future President of the International Olympic Committee. Ford and Lord Killanin, even though they were kin, had a warm and lifelong friendship and it was through his noble Irish cousin that Ford cleared many an obstacle to making *The Quiet Man* in the West Country in 1952. Encouraged by the success of the earlier film, Killanin lobbied hard with Ford to join him in building up the film industry in Ireland and envisioned a flourishing output to equal that of the Korda, Pressburger and Powell, Carol Reed, David Lean and Ealing Studio classics emanating from England during the same time. Along with Ford and the noted Irish film director, Brian Desmond Hurst (another lifelong friend of Ford), Killanin formed Four Provinces Productions based in Ireland. Hurst, who as a young soldier had survived the horrors of Gallipoli in World War I, went on to work in Hollywood where as a young man he stood next to a young John Wayne when both played extras in Ford's *Hangman's House*. Hurst would go on to a prolific film career in England, two of his greatest hits being *The Malta Story* with Alec Guinness and *A Christmas Carol* with Alastair Sim, considered to be the classic telling of the Dickens classic. Hurst was openly and unabashedly homosexual (even though that practice was still punishable in the United Kingdom with prison time), and lived in his Belgravia town home with a charming flamboyance that earned him the moniker "The Empress of Ireland." Ford always prided himself on his studied alpha-male machismo and the fact that he had such affection and respect for Hurst shows how genuinely non-judgmental he was of a person's sexuality and how he valued talent and friendship above one's private life.[30]

Ford's contribution to the Four Provinces canon was a 1957 trilogy of Irish short stories from some of the leading lights of the Irish literary revival of the early and mid-twentieth century. It was called *The Rising of the Moon* and was based upon "The Majesty of the Law," by Frank

O'Connor, "A Minute's Wait," by Martin McHugh and "1921" (taken from the play, "The Rising of the Moon") by Lady Augusta Gregory.

"The Majesty of the Law" has Inspector Dillon (Cyril Cusack) going off to arrest Dan O'Flaherty (Noel Purcell) for assault, only to encounter a maker of *poitin* (an Irish grain and potato alcohol slightly weaker than napalm and long outlawed in the island) along the way. Guilt, innocence, the drink and a willingness to serve prison time are themes bandied about in a typically inimitable Gaelic way.

"A Minute's Wait," set in the Dunfaill train depot, plays like the wonderfully eccentric opening scene of *The Quiet Man* extended into a single-act play. While waiting for the delayed train, a madly disparate group of passengers crowd into the station canteen for tea. Couples court, old housewives gossip about the bishop's approaching jubilee and marriages are arranged, all to the utter bewilderment of an elderly British couple (Anita Sharp and the legendarily mustached Michael Trubshawe), who end up sharing their compartment with a goat and a crate full of lobsters. It is a bizarre and surreal gathering of people and events that, like the dear denizens of Innisfree, no one finds bizarre or surreal.

"1921," the last installment, is the finest of the trilogy. Sean Curran (Donal Donnelly), is about to be hung by the British for his I.R.B. activities during the Troubles. He is visited in prison by two young "nuns," one in high heels and the other claiming to be his sister. They turn out to be actresses and spirit the condemned patriot out disguised in their habits. When the manhunt ensues, Constable O'Hara (Denis O'Dea) is assigned to watch the waterfront and he daydreams about the £500 reward with his stridently nationalist wife (Eileen Crowe, who played Mrs. Playfair in *The Quiet Man*). When Curran tries to escape in a boat dressed as a ballad-singing tinker, O'Hara asks him to do a rendition of "The Rising of the Moon." His terrible crooning, however, tips the constable off to the ruse. Curran makes his escape on the boat and as O'Hara raises his hand to sound the alarm, he slowly relents and walks off singing "The Rising of the Moon."

The film in many respects is another of the extraordinarily personal films that marked Ford's later years. He was back on familiar and deeply emotional territory and seemed to be making the film for personal fulfillment rather than for mass appeal. The themes of country justice, broad Irish humor and the nationalist struggle are the only ones Ford appears to be exploring in the film. No sweep of history, the processional pilgrimage of a people through time and the bonding of the living with the dead. Very little about myth, community, family and the destructive effects of time on them all. Here Ford is at his most bard-like which means at his most Irish; like his silent films he is not interested so much in themes and motifs as the art of pure storytelling for its own sake.

The Rising of the Moon allowed Ford the joy of making a film in Ireland at his own pace and surrounding himself with the superbly talented members of the Abbey Theatre. In order to give the film an appeal to Americans, Ford also enlisted the aid of Tyrone Power to "introduce" the film at the beginning but it did not help. *The Rising of the Moon* may have run from Ford's depths but it certainly did not garner oceans of viewers or praise and, like its namesake, it quickly waxed and then waned.

Ford's next project, like his last, put him on well trod turf but instead of the Old Sod it was the smoky back rooms of New England Irish politics. *The Last Hurrah* was based on Edwin O'Connor's multiple-prize winning novel about the final and hardest fight of an incumbent mayor trying to hold to power that is quickly slipping away.

Ford had not worked with Spencer Tracy since they made *Up the River* twenty-eight years before. Since then Tracy had gone on to win two consecutive Oscars (for *Captains Courageous* in 1937 and *Boys Town* in 1938) and establish himself as one of Hollywood's most bankable and likeable stars. Despite the kudos from old legends like George M. Cohan, peers like Gable, Bogart and Cagney and even later method actors he inspired with his natural, organic innovations he brought to his profession, Tracy was a frightfully fractured and unhappy man. His alcoholic binges and depression (his symptoms suggest that he suffered from a bipolar disorder), his guilt over his deaf son, his infidelity and perceived failure as a Catholic left an angry, raw hole in the center of his being that nothing could fill or cauterize. Regardless of his anger, alcohol and insecurities, Tracy remained a consummate pro who continued to turn in extraordinary performances until his death in 1967. Ford not only identified with Tracy through their common bond of Irish-Catholicism, alcoholism and Kate Hepburn (who would remain Tracy's devout but discreet partner from 1941 until his death), but Tracy was also one of the few actors Ford genuinely respected.

The cast included Tracy, old cronies and stock alums like Pat O'Brien, Donald Crisp, Basil Rathbone, Jimmy Gleason, Edward Brophy, Edmund Lowe and Jane Darwell. There were also newer members like Jeffrey Hunter, Ken Curtis, Carleton Young and Willis Bouchey; the last two became regular faces in Ford's later films. The script was by Frank Nugent and Columbia gave Ford the adequate (but not prodigal) budget of $2.3 million. With everything so right there was no way he could go wrong.

———

Frank Skeffington (Tracy) is mayor of a "New England city" that sure n' begorrah is Boston just as "John Dodge" was "John Ford" in *The Wings of Eagles*. Frank is an old-school politico, a four-term boss who rose from the streets to control the city with a well-oiled machine run by cronies, hacks and cigar-chomping ward enforcers. The city works but does so by the graft, kickbacks and favoritism, overseen by Skeffington, that could make it any American city from Bangor to Seattle.

Skeffington is challenged in his bid for a fifth term by another native son, Kevin McCluskey, a young, inexperienced war veteran who runs on a platform of ending the corruption that has infected the city via the old mayor's reign. The church, press and business interests, tired of the old Skeffington shenanigans, have no choice but to throw their weight behind McCluskey. Skeffington's nephew, sports writer Adam Caulfield (Jeffrey Hunter) comes along for the ride as an observer of his Uncle Frank's last great political donnybrook.

Skeffington is a dinosaur whose enemy is not only time but also technology. Frank only knows back alley fighting, cronyism, the gentle, personal touch and buckets of Irish charm as the way to getting and staying elected. McCluskey (not unlike a young John F. Kennedy) has in his arsenal the strongest weapons of all: youth, money and the media. Times are changing and Skeffington does not realize that despite his chops and devotion to the people of the city, elections are no longer won by kissing babies, attending wakes and delivering food when the old man is out of work but by who sounds best on radio and looks best on television.

What should have been a landslide victory for Skeffington becomes a crushing defeat. Although he talks about a possible gubernatorial run, Frank is finished and he knows it. He suffers a heart attack and dies soon after.

Ford's political, like his spiritual and artistic sensibilities, were formed when he was a child growing up in Portland, Maine. If he learned his prayers and catechism at his mother's knee, he learned the art of power and politics in his father's saloon. Daddo, like Skeffington, was an old political pro who knew that in politics people come first and everything else comes second. Both men found jobs for the unemployed, delivered food to the poor and widows, consoled the grieving at funerals and had a quick smile and kind word for all. They did this not only out of common decency and Christian charity but because both men knew that the more turkeys delivered in December guaranteed more votes the following November. Bismarck famously said that politics is "the art of the possible," and in the 1960 movie, *Spartacus*, Gracchus (Charles Laughton) reminds a young Julius Caesar (John Gavin) that "politics is a practical profession." Somewhere between these two maxims lay the secret of Daddo's and Skeffington's Irish ward politics; the art of gently feeding someone their daily bread while holding on to them by the scruff of the neck.

This may have been Daddo's and Skeffington's *modus operandi* but it was essentially Ford's *modus vivendi*. In attempting to navigate Ford's labyrinthine and contradictory personality, one comes closest to success when they understand Ford basically ran his life and career along the lines of Portland waterfront politics. As opposed to his brother Frank, whose zenith in film was marked by flamboyance, innovation and a healthy respect for the rewards of fame, Ford cared little for money and celebrity status and instead based his power model on that of the Portland political boss. As generous as Ford was to his friends, he had to be, as was said about Theodore Roosevelt, the bride at every wedding and the corpse at every funeral and thus crafted the Ford Stock Company as his very own political machine. Within the confines of Ford's inner circle, one was protected in a family- like womb of love, friendship and security. Ford was the boss who could either giveth or taketh away, and while unemployed or underemployed actors, extras, stuntmen and technicians would be taken care of, the only thing Ford asked in return was complete and unqualified loyalty, obedience and respect. When it was given, the dividends were paid and the generosity boundless. However, as it has been seen with Harry Carey, Sr., George O'Brien, John Wayne, Ben Johnson and Henry Fonda, when one did not render to Caesar what was Caesar's, the resulting banishment was swift and heartless.

What Ford craved most was intimacy, not sexual, but the warm, comforting bath of being able to reveal one's self to another or a group without fear of condemnation or rejection. In order to retain the power and control that made him John Ford, he had to maintain the crusty, terrifying façade *of* John Ford and to let his guard down for a moment was running the risk of having the whole enterprise crumble and fall. The greatest tragedy and hurt in Ford's life, as Dobe Carey said, was that Ford wanted simply to be one of the guys but knew that he could not because that which gave his life meaning was being "Pappy," "Coach" and now "The Admiral" who could preside but never participate.[31]

Like Frank Skeffington's world, however, the safe, medieval cosmology and order of the universe was changing and giving way to a newer and younger generation whose leaders had to be young and handsome and whose opinions would now be shaped by television. When Skeffington loses the election, he shrugs it off with a laugh and tells his cronies to go home for the night. That's life, Ford appears to be speaking through Skeffington, and there is nothing anybody can do about it. Like all Irishmen, though, both Skeffington and Ford accept the fact that the world has once again broken their hearts and yet that is the price they pay for the dignity and honor of their heritage. This sense of loss and isolation is underscored by Skeffington's solitary walk home through the park after his defeat. The march of progress, the procession of the community toward its destiny, is symbolized by McCluskey's jubilant supporters as they wend their way down the street with a torchlight parade. Interestingly, for the first time Ford juxtaposes the movement forward, which in the years past was a point of exuberance and hope, with the image of the lone hero walking *back* as the community moves forward. Solitary, pensive, bereft of everything except the now hollow memories of former triumphs, the great man thoughtfully but resignedly moves back into the night of the past.

The last hurrah, indeed.

In 1958, Ford made another curio that came and went without people noticing it even passing by. *Gideon's Day* was based on a popular series of *Gideon of Scotland Yard* novels by J. J. Marric (the *nom de plume* of British author John Creasey), chronicling the detailed, day-to-day police work of Detective Chief Inspector George Gideon.

The film Lord Killanin produced for Columbia was shot in color on location in and around London by the great Freddie Young. The role of Gideon was played by Jack Hawkins, the square-jawed, wavy-haired British stalwart who, since the death of C. Aubrey Smith, had emerged in post-war cinema as the very model of a modern major general. Even though he is best remembered for his spit and polish military roles in films like *Bridge on the River Kwai*, *Ben-Hur* and *Lawrence of Arabia*, Hawkins was in reality a liberal man who constantly tried to stretch his acting legs with daring and challenging parts that would counter-weigh his militarily macho persona. The role of Gideon may not have been the stretch Hawkins was looking for, but all the same he fills the role with ease, class and the strength of his impressive presence.

The film basically follows Gideon through the frantic twenty-four hours of an ordinary day in the detective chief inspector's life, beginning with the deadly early morning battle he must wage with his children for bathroom time. His day gets off to a tense start when he is ticketed for running a red light by a young constable (Andrew Ray), who is less impressed with the august chief inspector and more impressed with his pretty, ballet-student daughter (Anna Massey, daughter of actor Raymond Massey, who was making her film debut). Through the course of the day Gideon must deal with a member of his department suspected of being on the take, a demented murderer and a gang of bold robbers whose daylight heists Gideon connects to the work of a solitary and improbable kingpin. Through all the travails and dastardly doings of London's criminal world, Gideon must also remember to get the salmon needed for the dinner being hosted that evening by his dutiful and patient wife (Anna Lee).

Critics and biographers have traditionally dismissed *Gideon's Day* as an oddity, an unwanted cinematic stepchild that carries little of Ford's DNA. There is, however, a wide and substantial difference between the time-killing, paycheck-motivated nonsense that Ford made for Fox in the 1920s and the relaxed, pure storytelling period that marks Ford's best work in the 1950s. *Gideon's Day* is Ford simply enjoying himself with a harmless, charming little tale that flies purposely under the critical radar. The theme of a man obsessed with his work to the borderline neglect of his home life is certainly a key Fordian theme, almost a *mea culpa*, during this period and there is some splendid photography by Young. The shot of the mental patient, slowly ascending the stairs to commit his murder, ranks with some of Hitchcock's and Welles' best camera work and the hip, swinging-London studio of Peter the Painter has an unusually contemporary and "with it" feel for a Ford film.

Ford enjoyed shooting in London and it also gave him the opportunity to reconnect with Lindsay Anderson, who was moving from criticism and experimental documentaries into the features that would make him one of the great *auteurs* of British social realism with films like *This Sporting Life*, *If...* and *O, Lucky Man*. Anderson enjoyed the time he was able to spend with his celebrated pen pal and mentor. He found Ford in exceptionally good humor, even to the point of asking Ford to come and view one of his latest documentaries; the cinematic equivalent of the novice lion tamer sticking his head into the biggest and meanest cat's mouth. He did, as he noted in his book *About John Ford,* find that the director looked old and weary and seemed a bit unsteady on his feet. Ford dutifully gave interviews (Anderson found him equally grouchy toward British journalists as he was toward the Yanks) and made the obligatory rounds of lunches and fêtes in his honor. Through a friend Anderson learned that at one dinner given by a group of British admirers, just a few drinks soon had Ford three sheets to the wind. It was a condition that would not improve with time.[32]

It had been three years since Ford made an outdoor action picture and even though he dearly loved the tang of the peat and smell of the moss in Ireland, it was time to return to the quintessentially American fragrance of gunpowder and saddle leather. While not technically a Western, *The Horse Soldiers* was set in the American Civil War, for Ford the next best historical setting and one he had not visited in *toto* since he made *The Prisoner of Shark Island* in 1936.

The movie was based on a novel by Harold Sinclair, which in turn drew from the 1863 Grierson Raid led by Union Colonel Benjamin Grierson as a diversion from Ulysses S. Grant's ultimately successful Vicksburg campaign. Grierson was an Indiana-born cavalry commander who, despite a fear of horses after being kicked by one as a child on his father's farm, led 1,700 Illinois and Iowa troopers on a daring 1,700-mile raid from LaGrange, Tennessee, to Baton Rouge, Louisiana. The raid through the heart of the Confederacy destroyed railroad and supply lines along the way and was considered by General William Tecumseh Sherman the most brilliant of the war.

Colonel John Marlowe (John Wayne playing the Grierson character) is ordered by Grant (Stan Jones, the balladeer who composed and performed much of the music in *The Wagon Master*) to undertake the raid even though it means death or imprisonment in Andersonville Prison if captured. Hoping to travel light and fast, Marlowe is incensed to be saddled with a surgeon, Major Henry Kendall (William Holden) who immediately becomes the focus of Marlowe's wrath.

At the Greenbrier Plantation, the Yankees encounter its young mistress, Hanna Hunter (the lovely, Grace Kelly look-alike Constance Towers), and her slave-friend, Lukey (Olympic Gold Medalist Althea Gibson) who, although they feign charm and innocence, actually spy on the soldiers to learn their plans. Marlowe is forced to take them both along on the raid when he discovers their espionage, which only increases Hannah's hatred for the colonel and all dirty Yankees. The Confederate cavalry is on their heels but the raiders press on deeper into enemy territory, with snipers and regulars increasingly dogging them at every turn. Sensing warmth and vulnerability beneath Marlowe's gruff exterior, Hannah's antagonism slowly evolves into a tender affection and then love for the Union colonel. During a drunken rampage, Marlowe reveals to Hannah that his hatred for Kendall and the medical profession stems from a botched operation that took the life of his young bride. After a battle against schoolboys from a local military academy, the Yankees make it to a final river crossing. Forced to leave Kendall behind to tend the wounded and Hannah to assist him, Marlowe makes a promise to find her again after the war and rides off over a bridge moments before it explodes. He heads toward Baton Rouge with the Confederates in pursuit.

Like *The Last Hurrah*, *The Horse Soldiers* had all the ingredients of a slam-dunk blockbuster. With John Wayne and William Holden starring in a thundering cavalry picture directed by John Ford, it was almost a guaranteed classic. From the start, however, too many things happened along the way that simply refused to let the project come together.

Both Wayne and Holden were at the peak of their screen dominance (although Holden's career would wane in the early 1960s until it was resuscitated by Sam Peckinpah for his gritty Western, *The Wild Bunch*, in 1969) and the expectations for the film set perhaps too high a bar for the director and cast to clear. *The Horse Soldiers* is a rip-roaring historical action film that Ford could have directed in his sleep, and the problem is that is exactly where it feels that he directed it. The action is first rate, as is William Clothier's camerawork, but the tempo is non-existent and it feels as though Ford was dragging himself out of bed and through the working day to finish it. Holden, with his Brylcreemed pompadour and urbane charm seems completely out of place in a period piece and since he and Ford did not get on from the start, it looks as though he simply showed up and read his lines.

By this time, John Wayne was deep in the massive pre-production logistics of his long-cherished project of making *The Alamo* and his head and heart were simply focused elsewhere. The script by John Lee Mahin and Martin Rackin (who would go on to head Paramount Pictures in the mid-1960s) did not have the polish, depth or force to move the narrative forward and sustain a sense of energy as well as character development. Particularly awkward is John Wayne's long, stilted soliloquy about his hatred of doctors and the death of his wife. What Ford would usually convey with an economy of words and artfully silent gestures and glances, he was now expositing with several pages of flowery dialogue that telegraph emotions instead of conveying them. Compare this with the zoom of John Wayne in *The Searchers*, the wordless glances between Ringo and Dallas in *Stagecoach* or Wayne's beautifully modulated and emotional soliloquy when he finds the pregnant mother in *3 Godfathers*, and *The Horse Soldiers* looks and sounds like a TV Western. This "more is less" approach is a new and tired note in Ford's films; a sort of laziness in reverse that unfortunately dogs this and many of his later films.

What truly derailed Ford during the production was the death of Fred Kennedy, a stuntman who had worked on Ford's films for over a decade. The short, stocky Kennedy was performing what should have been a simple (if there is such a thing) horsefall during the film's climactic battle. It was something Kennedy had done a hundred times but, he landed wrong, and when Ford yelled cut and the crew rushed over they found Kennedy dead on the ground with a broken neck. Ford was completely devastated by the Kennedy's death, more so since as a director or commander Ford felt a deep responsibility for the lives of the men who served under him. The death on the set plunged Ford into a deep depression and the plans to end the movie with a celebratory arrival in Baton Rouge were summarily abandoned. Ford simply lost interest in the film, ended it with Marlowe's farewell to Hannah at the bridge and went home to half-heartedly finish shooting interiors back in the studio.[33]

Because of Wayne's and Holden's exorbitant salaries, percentages and the complex participation of so many production companies, *The Horse Soldiers* would have had to have been another *Gone With the Wind* to pay out any money. Unfortunately, the returns on the film were too meager for anyone to have made a profit. The audience and critical response to the film was lackluster; not so much because it was a bad movie as it did not have the look or feel of films Ford was making ten years earlier, let alone twenty. It was neither a pleasant nor a heartening way to close the decade, and yet Ford pressed on into the next one with less energy but still the resolve to keep doing the only thing he knew how to do: make pictures.

THE 1960S

"Print the Legend."

By the 1960s, the Zen-like reversal of destinies in the master, John Ford and the disciple, John Wayne, was complete. As the new decade dawned, John Wayne was one of the most popular and powerful movie stars, not only in Hollywood but in the world and Ford was becoming a cinematic equivalent of Frank Skeffington: a quaint relic of another age fast slipping away.

The name John Wayne on the marquee meant money in cash boxes all over the world. Being the age of the mega-deal, it meant that Wayne could go to literally any studio or top producer and cut a lucrative, multipicture deal for his production company, Batjac. Ford, on the other hand, had to go hat in hand and beg and barter in order to get funding for just one picture a year. Tyrone Power and Bogart were gone, Gable and Cooper would be dead within a few years of the new decade and Fonda and Stewart were content with smaller screen projects and occasional returns to Broadway. Among the screen titans, Duke not only held his own with newer class of anti-heroes like Paul Newman, Steve McQueen, Marlon Brando and Richard Burton (soon to include Al Pacino and Dustin Hoffman), he continued to tower over them.

In 1959, the eyes of Hollywood were on the small, dusty Texas

town of Bracketville, which even though it was forty miles from nowhere was the location where Wayne was finally mounting his $12
million epic, *The Alamo*. Technically, the 180 brave defenders of the
mission-fortress were neither Democrats nor Republicans, but Wayne
saw the 1836 battle that led to the liberation of Texas from the control
of the Mexican dictator, General Miguel Lopez de Santa Ana, as a
metaphor for a greater worldwide struggle. America, Wayne felt, was
getting soft on the Communists who he and his conservative Republicans felt were making strident gains on the world stage and threatening
the very bastion of freedom and democracy. From Stettin in the Baltic
to Trieste in the Adriatic, Winston Churchill declared, an iron curtain had descended upon the European continent. Not only in Europe
but across Asia and Africa, Communist ideology was taking root and
threatening the stability of pro-Western governments that were often
as brutal and dictatorial as Marxist states. Worse still, the Caribbean
had become a hotbed of Communist insurgency and even threatened
a foothold in Cuba, ninety dangerously close miles from the United
States. Liberty, democracy and the American way were on the defensive, and sincere patriots like Wayne were scared and felt it was time to
recover some of the red-blooded, freedom-loving Spirit of '76 or, in the
case of the Alamo, '36. The year 1960 was an election year and Wayne,
along with strong conservative blocs in the nation, felt that the U.S.
government was playing it too light and soft with the Reds. Instead
of modern-day Neville Chamberlains kowtowing and giving in to the
Commies, Wayne wanted to see Americans make a stand and defend
liberty and freedom like the Alamo defenders did; smooth-bore rifle in
hand and, if need be, to the death. The October release date of the film
was no accident and, being one month before the presidential election,
would help America see *The Alamo* not so much as a movie but as a
referendum on which direction the nation wanted to go: strength and
resolve or weakness and decline.

The production of *The Alamo*, pre-, post- and the actual shoot itself,
was mammoth and, up to that time, one of the most expensive films
made on the North American continent. Ford had never made a film

even remotely reaching the epic proportions of *The Alamo*, and the pressure on Wayne as producer, director and star was on a level Ford had never experienced even in his worst independent years. Wayne's first mistake was asking Ford's advice in the casting of the film. This set a dangerous precedent and opened a Pandora's box that Wayne would not only come to regret but also find impossible to close. It was a line in the Texas sand that, out of a combination of affection, respect and intimidation, Wayne could not bring himself to cross.

Wayne's chagrin (to put it the most politely) can therefore only be imagined when Ford showed up on the set in Bracketville two weeks into the production, uninvited and unannounced, and plopped himself down in the director's chair. Chagrin rapidly morphed into horror when Ford saw the way Wayne was playing a scene and growled at him that he was doing it wrong and to try it again. This was no simple back-lot production but a monumental location-shoot that was being run almost like a military operation to the tune of tens of thousands of dollars a day. Wayne had neither the time nor the inclination to sit back and play second banana to Ford as he took the helm of his decades-long dream project. The problem was that he also did not have the heart to put Ford in a corner or bundle him back to Los Angeles on the next puddle jumper out of Bracketville.

A solution of sorts was suggested by the film's cinematographer, William Clothier, who had first worked with Ford on *Fort Apache* as a second unit cameraman and went on to shoot *The Horse Soldiers*. Clothier was a leather-tough old bird, a World War II veteran who wasn't intimidated by Ford and knew the best way to handle the Old Man. He suggested that Wayne give Ford a camera (the film was being shot in the impressive but wildly expensive Todd-AO wide-screen format) and send him off to do second-unit photography work. This, Clothier said, would not only make Ford feel wanted and important but would keep him out of Wayne's hair and away from the principal actors and the straight acting that Wayne jealously guarded as his personal domain. At a cost of several hundred thousand dollars, Ford's second-unit foray proved to be the most expensive baby-sitting operation in film history but it not only preserved Duke's relationship with the Coach but provided him with some very good second unit footage. Ironically, for scenes shot as a diversionary tactic, including scenes of the Mexican artillery crossing the river, vistas of Santa Ana's vast army (trained by Ford's long-time extra and military crony Jack Pennick) approaching the mission and a spectacular backflip horse fall by stuntman Chuck Hayward before the final assault are among the most crisp, exciting and memorable in the film. Ford, even when he was an unwanted afterthought, showed himself head and shoulders above all comers.[1]

As the decade began, Ford showed the same sparks of daring innovation and poetic vision that marked his best films of the early 1940s and early 1950s, and *Sergeant Rutledge* is without doubt one of his most interesting films that never quite found its audience. The year before, in 1959, Otto Preminger's *Anatomy of a Murder* was a groundbreaking examination of the horrors of rape and both shocked and fascinated audiences with its graphic details and language. *Sergeant Rutledge* tackles the same subject but with the additional powder keg of racism thrown into the bargain.

Braxton Rutledge (Woody Strode) is a 1st sergeant serving with the all-Black 9th Cavalry (known as the Buffalo Soldiers) at a southwest fort during the Indian Wars. Rutledge is court-martialed for the alleged rape and murder of the post commander's white teenage daughter. Rutledge's story is told through a series of flashbacks during the trial, prompted by questions from his defense counsel, Lt. Tom Cantrell (Jeffrey Hunter), as well as by the abrasive cross-examination of the prosecutor, Captain Shattuck (Carleton Young).

Despite circumstantial evidence that weighs heavily against him, Rutledge's honorable record, courage under fire and spirited defense on the witness stand brings about the eventual unmasking of the true culprit and Rutledge's complete exoneration. On hand are Constance Towers as Cantrell's love interest and Rutledge's champion, as well as other stock company players, new and old, like Willis Bouchey, Chuck

Hayward, Jack Pennick and Hank Worden. The venerable ladies of the post are ably represented by Ford favorite Mae Marsh as well as the always delightful Billie Burke (Good Witch Glenda from *The Wizard of Oz*), who absentmindedly chirps her way through the role of the court president's wife, Mrs. Fosgate. *Rutledge* was shot in Monument Valley in WarnerColor by Bert Glennon. Glennon, who had photographed *Young Mr. Lincoln*, *Drums Along the Mohawk* and *Stagecoach* for Ford, knew every peak and crag between Goulding's Lodge and Kayenta and how to shoot them as well as Ford did. The outdoor vistas are finely composed and shot, with the beige buttes and blue sky contrasting with the cool, dark, constricting confines of the courtroom.

Although Hunter is stolidly at the fore in terms of credits and star power, the towering sentinel who becomes the emotional heart and moral center of the story is Woody Strode as Braxton Rutledge. Woodrow Wilson Strode, who at 6'4" seemed more sculpted than made of flesh, was an extraordinary mountain of a man who began his career as a celebrated and barrier-breaking athlete. After achieving fame as a decathlon champion who set world records in the shot put and high jump, Strode went on to play football at UCLA with Kenny Washington and Jackie Robinson; the first Black athletes to do so. Strode later played pro football with the Los Angeles Rams before moving on to glory in professional wrestling and martial arts. Had Strode lived in ancient Hellas, he would have been crowned with the laurel wreath of a god; in mid-twentieth century America, he was denied use of hotels, restaurants and even bathrooms in many parts of the country.

When Strode made the transition to films, his natural athletic prowess and height pigeonholed him into the standard exotic warrior and jungle chieftain roles in rent-payers like *Jungle Man-Eaters*, *Son of Sinbad* and *Tarzan's Fight for Life*. However, his intelligence and education, combined with the awesome dignity of his presence trumped the racial stereotypes of the day. Slowly, he started getting roles of more complexity and depth like the cowardly soldier in *Pork Chop Hill* and the humane gladiator who dies so that he does not have to kill Kirk Douglas for sport in *Spartacus*. Strode, who would remain devoted to

Ford and was one of the few people present at his death, was the director's beau ideal of the perfect man and, in the seminal cinematic age of Sidney Poitier and Harry Belafonte, Ford hoped to do for Strode what he had done for John Wayne.

The climax of the film comes on the witness stand when in a paroxysm of rage and agony Rutledge declares not only his innocence but his paramount dignity as a man over his racial category of a man of color. It is a heart-breaking, soul-searing moment of sheer beauty that Ford stripped of any superfluous patronizing or sentimental idealization.

In order to get the convincing combination of emotion and anger that Strode required to give the witness-stand climax its punch, Ford employed one of his oldest, nastiest and therefore most effective tricks. Ford told Strode that he needed to take some time off and, as his presence would not be required for a few days, to go celebrate with a monumental bender (just as he did with Victor McLaglen right before filming *his* big scene in *The Informer*). It was a big mistake but Strode innocently and joyfully complied with Ford's suggestion and went off on a well-deserved toot on the town. The next morning Ford suddenly and purposely called Strode to the studio to shoot his courtroom soliloquy. Suffering the pains of a hangover hell in his head and enraged by Ford's screaming and brutal needling, Strode exploded with the most powerful and moving performance of his career and completed the scene in one take. After Ford yelled cut, the exhausted and humiliated actor, unsure as to what just happened, broke down in tears. Everyone on the set, not knowing what to do, remained frozen until Ford went over to Strode, quietly put his hand on his shoulder and gently talked him down. It was a magnificent and awesome moment; a one-time-only mystical breakthrough that Strode remembered for the rest of his life.[2]

Sadly, Ford followed the bold, heartfelt *Sergeant Rutledge* with the cold and singularly uninspired *Two Rode Together* (1961). It is not surprising (but painfully obvious) that Ford took on the project for the paycheck and little else. Technically, it was meant to be *The Searchers redux*, a dark and grim tale of an obsessive search by two unlikely partners for white captives of a fierce Comanche chief (Henry Brandon, reprising the role he played as Scar in 1956).

The bright spot of the otherwise dismal experience was that it allowed Ford the opportunity to work with two stars who, despite their wariness toward the legendarily mercurial director, became two of his favorite leading men. James Stewart had just come through a decade populated with evolutionary, and for him, revolutionary, acting when directors like Alfred Hitchcock and Anthony Mann explored the dark underbelly of his amiable personality in thrillers like *Rear Window, The Man Who Knew Too Much, Vertigo* and brooding Westerns like *Winchester 73, The Man From Laramie* and *The Naked Spur*. Stewart was not only a star on equal footing with John Wayne (his Hitchcock films put him back on the top of the popularity lists) but in the hands of a solid director he could go deep into foreign territory and create complex and even disturbing characters.

Adding to Stewart's portfolio was the fact that he was a war hero and one of the most decorated American soldiers of World War II. He flew bombing missions over Germany with the 8th Air Force and, having won the Distinguished Service Medal, Distinguished Flying Cross and the French Croix de Guerre (with palm), was promoted to full colonel. A few years before they worked together Stewart was then promoted to the rank of brigadier general. John Ford the director knew how to cut his big boys down to size but Admiral Ford knew the genuine article when he saw one and wisely backed off from pushing General Stewart too hard.

Richard Widmark was another star with whom Ford could identify, but in a different way. Widmark was a hardy Mid-westerner of Swedish and Scottish stock who cemented his tough guy reputation playing the psycho-thug Tommy Udo in Henry Hathaway's 1947 noir classic *The Kiss of Death*. The talented but slightly thorny Widmark was comfortable in urban thrillers or Western sagas but, when pushed by hardcase directors, he knew how to push back. Ford first met Widmark on the set of *The Alamo* where, playing Jim Bowie, he went toe-to-toe with Duke Wayne and proved the most problematic and combative of his otherwise affable and compliant cast. Ford loved a good territory-marking fight but knew with Dick Widmark he had a blonde and square-jawed tiger by the ears and handled him accordingly.

In *Two Rode Together*, Marshal Guthrie "Guth" McCabe (Stewart) pairs with army lieutenant Jim Gary (Widmark) to find captives held by Quannah Parker, the great, half-white Comanche chief. Unlike Ethan Edwards, both Guth and Jim have love interests (Shirley Jones and Linda Cristal) and once again the themes of miscegenation and revenge are explored but nothing ever pops. Even with a script by Frank Nugent and appearances by stock company regulars and irregulars, the film drags along with nothing to animate or move the lifeless narrative. Ford turned Guth into an unscrupulous and morally ambiguous character, hoping to push Stewart (a la Wayne as Ethan) into daring moves against type. With his cynical, backslapping and double-dealing airs, however, Stewart comes across more like a suburban used-car salesman than a demon-ridden, good-bad man. One of Ford's other tricks on the set was to divide and conquer: put his stars at odds with each other with him in between feeding hearsay and gossip back and forth like a small-town operator. Both Stewart and Widmark were hard of hearing (which explained much of Widmark's aloofness on the set of *The Alamo*) and Ford would purposely mumble or speak into their bad ears to throw them off and keep them in a state of professional imbalance.

This was made clear when he filmed probably the only interesting scene in the entire movie, a five-minute unbroken shot of Guth and Jim discussing money, women and morality (or lack of it) at the edge of a river. Ford shot it from the middle of the stream, barking orders from above the sound of the water, knowing they would not hear and would be forced to try and one-up each other as though they were playing a game of cinematic five card stud.

Ford lost both his interest and his energy halfway through *Two Rode Together* and finished it with even less brio than he did *The Horse Soldiers* and with more disgust. He had been on the set of *The Alamo* and watched Duke Wayne stride the set like a divisional commander while

Ford was bundled off into the desert with a camera like an unwanted mother-in-law. His first two Westerns of the decade were either unnoticed, like *Sergeant Rutledge*, or unwatchable, like *Two Rode Together*. To protect himself after a failure, Ford would always profess, in hindsight, boredom with the project or claim that he did it for money or to kill time. While most of the time it was true, it was increasingly becoming a way to cover his tracks or excuse his declining energy, vision and artistry. In the case of *Two Rode Together*, Ford claimed that he did it as a make-good for Harry Cohn, president of Columbia Pictures, who had died in 1958. True or not, it was at least safe and rested on the reality that dead men tell no tales.[3]

As he did when he was bored with the studio confines and rote pictures in the late 1930s, as he did after the debacles of *The Fugitive* and *Mr. Roberts*, as he did whenever the hole in the center began to get deeper and darker: Ford went west with his mind, soul and body and did something extraordinary. It was a cinematic hat trick that never failed him in the past and had resulted in *Stagecoach*, the Cavalry Trilogy and *The Searchers*. He was, however, much older now and, running out of both time and hats, Ford knew that whatever he did, he had to make it good.

Understanding, or even just having a basic appreciation, for *The Man Who Shot Liberty Valance* (1962), is impossible if it is not contextualized properly in the artistic, emotional and spiritual arc that spans Ford's life and work. Decontextualized, *Liberty Valance* is like the head of a statue severed from its body in an impersonal museum: incomplete, jagged and curiously detached from an artistic totality. Contextualized, it becomes a coda, a culmination as well as summation of an old poet in the winter of his art.

The plot, based on a short story by Dorothy Johnson and scripted by old Ford hands James Warner Bellah and Willis Goldbeck (who also produced), takes the director out of the realm of simple storytelling and once again into the tangled depths of narrative and plot development. Like a Mahler symphony, it is complex, dark edged and pulsating with a deep angst that strikes the viscera in a way one cannot quite understand or resolve.

Senator Ransom Stoddard (James Stewart) returns to the western town of Shinbone with his wife Hallie (Vera Miles) some time after the turn of the century for the pauper's funeral of Tom Doniphon (John Wayne), a former rancher turned forgotten town drunk. Stoddard is a pompous, self-important old politico who basks in the adulation he expects and instead of conversation drops patronizing platitudes on everyone as though they are undecided voters. Ranse and Hallie are horrified at the sight of Tom's wooden coffin, the presence of only his devoted Black ranch hand, Pompey (Woody Strode), and the fact that the dead man has no boots, spurs or pistol.

Meanwhile, Hallie and the former marshal, Link Appleyard (Andy Devine) drive out to Doniphon's burnt-out and abandoned ranch house in the desert, an empty shell surrounded by the cactus flowers she dearly loves. As the "Ann Rutledge" theme from *Young Mr. Lincoln* comes up (symbolizing, as it did in the earlier film, the sad longing for a lost love), it becomes clear that Hallie was and is still in love with Tom and that this was to have been their home. Hallie and Link say little to each other and hardly exchange looks, almost as if the pain is too great; back around Tom's coffin, the small group appears to be the ones who are dead—distant, isolated and haunted like "graveyard ghosts."

The press, led by the *Shinbone Star* editor, Maxwell Scott (Carleton Young), want to know why a senator, two-term governor, former ambassador to the Court of St. James and potential Vice-Presidential candidate, have come from Washington for the funeral of a forgotten derelict and demand the story.

Pressed by the editor, Ranse gives in and in flashback tells the story of his arrival in Shinbone as a young, idealistic lawyer intent on bringing law and justice to the violent, gun-toting territory. On its way into town, the stage is held up by a gang led by a vicious brute named Liberty Valance (Lee Marvin), an enforcer for the greedy cattlemen intent on keeping the territory an open range rather than becoming a state. When Ranse attempts to defend the honor of a woman abused by Valance during the hold up, Ranse is savagely beaten by Valance with his silver-tipped bullwhip (similar to Old Man Clanton's in *My Darling Clementine*).

Ranse is found and brought into town by Tom Doniphon to be tended by the Swedish couple who run the town restaurant (John Qualen and Jeannette Nolan) and Hallie, the young girl who works for them. Tom, who is engaged to Hallie, is amused with Ranse more than anything else and yet he admires his pluck and tenacity, especially in his aim to put the wild polecat Valance on trial and behind bars.

Less amusing to Tom is the sway that Ranse begins to have on Hallie. She sees Ranse endeavor to teach the locals reading, American history and the basic precepts of law that he sees as the foundation of a civilized society and Ranse starts to loom large in her eyes. Ranse, backed by the perpetually intoxicated but valiant founder-editor-floor sweeper of the *Shinbone Star*, Dutton Peabody (Edmond O'Brien, playing the last and one of the finest in the long line of Ford's noble, silly, Shakespeare-quoting lovable drunks) leads the call for statehood and is elected the conventional delegate.

Valance, infuriated by the upstart Stoddard challenging both his rule and the power of the cattle barons, calls the lawyer out for a gunfight but, to everyone's surprise, it is Valance who goes down with a bullet through his heart. Riding the crest of grateful popularity for his brave deed, Ranse not only gets the nomination and the fame but he also gets Hallie. Tom, desolate and inconsolable, burns down the house he built for his former love and becomes a town drunk but not before revealing the truth to Ranse, who is on the verge of a career that will take him to the heights of American politics. It was not Ranse who shot Liberty Valance, but Tom, hiding in the shadows across the street, who drilled the thug not only to protect the lawyer he has come to care for but also to save him for a future and fortune with Hallie that Tom could never give her.

Back in present time, Ranse is now released from his vow of silence by Tom's death and makes a full confession of the truth to the editor.

When Ranse asks the editor if he is going to print the true story of who shot Liberty Valance, Scott crumples up the interview and utters the most famous quote in a John Ford film. "This is the West, sir. When the legend becomes fact, print the legend." They then take leave of Doniphon's coffin, which has a single solitary cactus flower planted on top.

On the train back to Washington, Ranse breaks the grim silence between him and Hallie who, like her and Link, do not look at each other but stare off into a distant void. When Ranse discovers that it was Hallie who placed the cactus flower on top of Tom's coffin, he reveals to her his desire to move back to Shinbone and open up a law office in the now booming town that he helped create. Ranse recovers his bluffness and bluster when thanking the conductor for all the courtesies extended him and Hallie and the conductor jauntily replies, "Nothing's too good for the man who shot Liberty Valance."

The wilderness may have become a garden, but it is Ranse and Hallie who are now desolate, empty and consigned to the artificial confines of the train that symbolizes the progress and prosperity Ranse helped to create. In *Stagecoach*, Doc Boone and Curley send Ringo and Dallas across the border in their buckboard to spare them "the blessings of civilization." Twenty years later, the older Ford shows an older couple who are now doomed and damned by it.

The Man Who Shot Liberty Valance has been described primarily as Ford's brooding meditation on myth, history and the necessity of eventually revealing the lies behind them both. Ford's idea of myth was classically American in that he saw the cowboy and the tales of the West as pieces of the American soul that defined who they are as a people in the greater compost of history. More than mere Manifest Destiny, Ford saw in Western lore the means by which the American odyssey could take its place on the world's literary stage alongside *Gilgamesh, Beowulf, the Mahabharata*, Norse mythology and *Le Morte D'Arthur*.

Yet in *Liberty Valance,* Ford has been compared to an old wizard who, nearer the end than the beginning, opens the box, pulls back the curtain and shows the magic to be nothing more than smoke and mirrors. The look and feel of the film substantiate this interpretation. Much has been said about the cheap, tacky, television western look of the sets and exterior locations. Many have seen this as Ford's intentional desire to de-glamorize the film and purposely make it look as though his beloved legends can collapse as easily as the walls of the Shinbone barroom and train depot. When Peter Bogdanovich asked Ford if this was so, if *Liberty Valance* represented his increasingly funereal feelings toward the West as a celebration of the American spirit, he responded "Possibly—I don't know—I'm not a psychologist. Maybe I'm getting older."[4]

Depending on who one asks (or reads), Paramount wanted the film to be a handsome, high and wide epic in Technicolor and Cinemascope, but Ford insisted on a lean, stripped-down style commensurate with the dark and claustrophobic atmosphere of the story. In reality, Paramount exec A. C. Lyles (who favored stark, economic black and white Westerns) pushed the budget-cutting line of the studio and had Ford shoot without color on the back lot with the allotted budget.

Also telling are the simple yet chromatically symbolic costumes designed by the studio's legendary *costumier,* Edith Head, and the following year, *Liberty Valance* became one of the few Westerns to be nominated for an Oscar in that category. For a film labeled as Ford's most anti-Western Western, the costumes proved to be some of the most iconic and indelibly associated rigs of the genre. Still photographs of John Wayne in his jet black shirt with the double row of buttons and the white ten-gallon hat that looks like it could easily hold twenty are among his most widely reproduced and instantly recognized. The juxtaposition of dark black and bright white are, despite Ford's denials, highly Freudian and speak volumes about Tom's noble, straightforward and unequivocally virtuous character.

Liberty, with his black hat, embroidered black vest and black leather whip, conveys a sort of sexual, sadomasochistic quality to his brutality, and the viewer is not only seduced but fascinated by his evil. James Stewart's Ranse Stoddard is, in flashback at least, dressed in a drab gray, evoking a sort of Everyman correlative with his ambiguous courage and idealism which, after it is debunked, devolves into bloviating, self-righteous egoism. Only at the end, as an old man disposed toward revelation and contrition, does Ranse's garb become the black and white of the truly noble, truly heroic, but dead and forgotten Tom.

Another interpretation of the film's meaning that bears examination, is that *Liberty Valance* is not about Ford destroying the myths he himself honored and celebrated through his work. Not only would Ford never have undermined that which formed the substrate of his artistic soul, but he himself shows us both the legend and the fact without lies or artistic sleight of hand. Like Wayne's Captain York, who defends the arrogant stupidity of Colonel Thursday's charge at the end of *Fort Apache*, Ford honors the courage behind the legend without hiding the ugly facts behind the curtain of myth.

Ford always projected his persona through the Promethean person of John Wayne, from the classical heroism of the Ringo Kid to the mature, wise vigor of the Cavalry Trilogy to the dark and violent corners of Ethan Edwards. In Tom Doniphon, Ford appears to manifest himself for the final time, not so much to kill the myth of the West but to say farewell. Despite Tom's power, strength and presence, he is, oddly enough, passive to the point of impotence and while he can kill the evil Liberty Valance, he loses everything to the gentle pacifist, Ranse Stoddard, and everything he represents. The themes of myths, legends and lies do not predominate in *Liberty Valance*, it is the inevitable march of time, progress, civilization and the awful persistence of loss that culminates in death. Time is up for Tom and his West and there is nothing he can do about it but burn down his house, mourn the things and people he has lost and drink.

Fourteen years later, John Wayne would eerily play out his farewells in the roman a clef movie, *The Shootist*, in which he plays a gunfighter dying of cancer in the waning days of the West who prefers to go out in a blaze of glory rather than suffer the undignified death of a bedridden invalid. Even though Wayne professed interest in other projects, it is probable he knew this would be his magnum opus because on the set he began experiencing the symptoms of the cancer that would kill him three years later. Similarly, even though Ford had several more films left in his canon, *The Man Who Shot Liberty Valance* would be the last film of his that would be called great. Accepting the interpretation that this was his last will and testament, it arguably can be called his greatest, albeit most heartbreaking, masterpiece.

The *Liberty Valance* shoot, like its mood and theme, was not pleasant. Poor Duke Wayne could simply not get out of the doghouse and had to take it on the chin as the coach dished it out. Between Woody Strode, who Ford called "the real athlete" (Wayne gave up his football career at USC after a shoulder injury) and Stewart, who Ford held up as an authentic war hero, Wayne was getting more flak than a 55-year-old superstar, father and grandfather was obliged to take.

Stewart had dodged the Ford bullets for a second time in working with the director and, to the irritation of Duke Wayne, was getting a little smug about his unprecedented achievement. Out of nowhere, Ford one day asked Stewart what he thought of Woody Strode's overalls and work-shirt costume. Stewart harmlessly (he thought) declared it to be a little "Uncle Remus-y". Ford suddenly called a halt to the production and gathered the entire cast and crew around them. He repeated Stewart's comment to the assembly and, saying that he was not sure if it reflected some kind of prejudice or racism on Stewart's part, dismissed everyone and told them to go back to work. Stewart said he wanted to crawl into a mousehole. A beaming Duke Wayne told Stewart (who was a gracious gentleman to everyone and far from being a racist), "Welcome to the club. I'm glad you made it. I really am."[5]

The most serious clash, fomented by Ford himself, was between Wayne and Strode. Sharing a common bond of imposing presences, quiet strength and athletic prowess, both men seemed perfectly suited to become fast friends and future collaborators. Ford's old schoolgirl jealousy no doubt was piqued and he did all in his power to pit the two men against each other, especially in the way he lauded Strode's football and military records. In the scene where Wayne drives the two of them back to his ranch in a mad, drunken rage, Wayne appeared to lose control of the wagon. Strode tried to take the reins and when Wayne slapped his hands away, both men jumped out of the wagon, red hot and ready to rip each other to shreds. Ford, knowing that Strode was younger and in better shape than Wayne, quickly defused what could have been a thermonuclear explosion. Wayne, ever the professional and, despite his temper, unable to hold a grudge for long, called a truce with Strode but the two men never worked together again.[6]

Lee Marvin (1924–1987), cast as the chilling psycho-killer Liberty Valance, was coming out of a decade of journeyman support work in films (*The Wild One, Bad Day at Black Rock* and *The Caine Mutiny*) as well as TV (*The M Squad*) and in the '60s and '70s would be propelled into the ranks of hardboiled, he-men superstars such as Clint Eastwood, Charles Bronson and Burt Reynolds. He would win an Oscar for his dual role as Kid Shelleen/Tim Strawn in the 1965 comic Western *Cat Ballou*. The prematurely silver-haired Marvin (who never truly recovered from the wounds he sustained as a young Marine in the horrendously bloody Battle of Saipan) was pretty much the hard-drinking, hard-smoking, skiing and hunting macho-man off screen that his characters came to embody onscreen. Personality wise, Marvin was an affable, gentlemanly and eminently capable professional who had the good cinematic fortune to simply look like a tough guy the same way friends said Warren G. Harding looked like a president.

Unlike Old Man Clanton in *My Darling Clementine* or Uncle Shiloh Clegg in *The Wagon Master*, whose unmotivated evil stems from some unnamed, organic disturbance deep in the human condition called Original Sin, Marvin's Valance possesses a more dangerous and interesting edge since his evil has a purpose. He is a button man and enforcer for the cattle interests. As Ethan Edwards saw dead buffaloes meaning dead Indians, so Liberty Valance translates the dead letter of law and justice into a Miltonian hell, an existential vacuum in which the rule of evil will become the dominant and objective reality. Thus, like Fonda's Wyatt Earp and Ben Johnson's Travis Blue, Stewart's Ransom Stoddard begins by simply defending himself and his community but slowly emerges as an avenging angel, driving rattlesnakes from a West they see as a potential Paradise Regained.

Ford's 1962 was an unusually busy year. Aside from *Liberty Valance*, he ventured again into the brave new world of television. *Flashing Spikes*, made for Alcoa Premiere, reunited Ford, Stewart and (in a cameo as an umpire) John Wayne in a tale of bribery and lost innocence in the often dubious world of professional baseball. Ford's first foray into the ether was in 1955 with *Rookie of the Year* (another tale of crooked sports with Wayne in a cameo as a sports writer) followed by *The Colter Craven Story*, done as an episode for pal Ward Bond's hit series *Wagon Train* in 1960. The small screen suited Ford well and the tight confines of the limited budget and time constraints made for interesting and relatively stress-free exercises that were reminiscent of his silent-era work at Fox.

Ford's other 1962 project, diametrically opposed to the black-and-white teledramas, was to direct the Civil War segment of the M-G-M and Cinerama monumental epic, *How the West Was Won*. Despite Cinerama's original novelty in the 1950s, moviegoers soon tired of rollercoaster rides, flights over the Grand Canyon and Lowell Thomas travelogues using a three-lens camera that, when projected on a massive, 146° curved screen, approximated the human field of vision.

Along with the largely forgotten *Wonderful World of the Brothers Grimm* released in the same year, *How the West Was Won* represented the first narrative use of the widest of wide-screen processes. Boasting "24 major stars!" and a symphonic masterpiece of a score by Alfred Newman, the film surpassed the confines of its gimmickry and turned out to be a highly entertaining, well-scripted and acted epic that proved one of most profitable films of the decade. The film tells the tales and travails of several generations of the Prescott family (patriarched and matriarched by, respectively, Karl Malden and Agnes Moorehead) as they move from the Ohio Valley in the 1830s to the lawless Arizona frontier in the 1880s. The drama is built around several spectacular action pieces (wildly overstaged and shot by veteran second unit director/stuntman Richard Talmadge in order to maximize the Cinerama effect) such as a white- water rapids shoot, a Comanche attack on a wagon train at full gallop, a 2,000-buffalo stampede through a railroad camp and a blazing gunfight aboard a runaway train.

How the West Was Won was an even larger endeavor than *The Alamo* and was filmed across several states and required the services of three credited directors, four cinematographers, M-G-M's top technicians and some of the biggest stars of the day including Gregory Peck, Debbie Reynolds, Henry Fonda, James Stewart, Robert Preston, Carroll Baker, Karl Malden, Richard Widmark, George Peppard, Eli Wallach and John Wayne. Ford was assigned the *Civil War*, George Marshall took the helm on *The Railroad* while Henry Hathaway shouldered the bulk of the heavy lifting with *The Rivers, The Plains* and *The Outlaws*.

Like *Gideon's Day, How the West Was Won* is written off by many critics as a mere pleasantry; a paycheck-grabbing diversion that in this case represents Ford's lucrative contribution to the epic fever that swept the industry in the late 1950s and early 1960s. On the contrary, Ford's work on the film may not represent a high-water mark in his 1960s canon but, like most of the film's drama and romance, it is a surprisingly tender and intimate *contrapunto* to the broad and noisy action pieces. Zeb Rawlings (George Peppard in a strong performance that carries the entire second half of the film) wants to get off his Ohio farm and join his father (Stewart) in the Union army following the shelling of Fort Sumter. The only thing holding him back is the love of his strong-willed mother Eve (Carroll Baker), who eventually relents and sends him off down the road to war.

At the bloody Battle of Shiloh in 1862 (after which, narrator Spencer Tracy says, "the South never smiled,"), Zeb unknowingly befriends an AWOL Reb soldier (Russ Tamblyn) and eavesdrops on a conversation between General William Tecumseh Sherman (John Wayne) and a downcast Ulysses S. Grant (Harry Morgan). The scene is short but well-crafted and in a few scenes Ford is able to convey the poetry, tragedy and unutterable horror of the conflict: the apple blossoms blooming over the rows of dead Union boys (mouths agape and composed like a Matthew Brady photograph) and the doctor in the makeshift hospital throwing a bucket of bloody water over the table before another wounded man is placed upon it. There is also the water of the stream, pink from the blood of the day's dead, that Zeb and the Reb splash through like Israelites passing through the Red Sea.

Not surprisingly, Ford hated the Cinerama process. The field of the camera's scope was massive (making compositions even more complex), close-up shots were impossible due to the lens distortion closer than a few feet and the cameras themselves were about the size of a Volkswagen. To complicate matters further, actors had to look feet away from each other's faces and stand at awkward angles; odd compensations for the three-lensed camera that would aright themselves when the image was projected on the curved screen.

Regardless of these bizarre technical demands that rendered normal emoting nearly impossible, Ford managed to craft a delicate and moving sequence between Zeb and Eve, his mother. The compositions are simple, the framing is geometric (to hide the lines joining the three projected screen panels) but not forced, conveying the noble, sparse dignity of the last farewell between a mother and her son. The dearth of dialogue, mostly about inconsequentials like clean shirts and underwear for the journey, suggests oceans of unspoken emotion between the two that is too painfully deep for words.

When Zeb goes off to war, the communion of saints once again and for one of the last times in a Ford film, becomes a locus of unity between the living and the dead. Eve, tearfully dropping to her knees at the grave of her father, asks for guidance and understanding at the departure of her husband and now her son. "You gotta help me pray, Pa. You gotta help me pray." Her long kerchief (like Doc Holliday's after being mortally wounded in *My Darling Clementine*) flutters in the wind as if to say she has already given up her spirit.

The shoot, both on location in Kentucky with Peppard, Baker and Andy Devine and then back at M-G-M with Duke Wayne was pleasant and relatively stress free. Ford fortunately did not have to shoot the Battle of Shiloh scenes—they were pinched from the studio's 1957 antebellum epic *Raintree County* and would be used again three years after the Cinerama epic in the opening scenes of Andrew McLaglen's Civil War melodrama, *Shenandoah.*

Ford was hired to give a sense of prestige to *How the West Was Won* above and beyond the usual beige fare paraded as monumental movie-making and the investment paid off. The film's initial and continued success must have given Ford no little sense of accomplishment and the fact that the New York office could still sign off on him meant that given the right material, cast and budget, the old wizard could still dazzle the front row.

Donovan's Reef (1963) paired Ford and John Wayne in a feature film for the last time. It was a fun, broadly played slapstick romp that married the exotic, easygoing buddy atmosphere of the Hope and Crosby movies (Dorothy Lamour even managed to turn up in a sarong!) with the screwball comedies of Leo McCarey and Frank Capra. And, for good measure for measure, there were comic buffos and passionate lovers, mistaken identities and rapid-fire repartee to give it a South Seas Shakespearean feel.

Mike "Guns" Donovan (Wayne) is the proprietor of Donovan's Reef, a Tiki-tacky bar on the French Polynesian island of Haleakahola. The primal bliss of the island is shattered by the arrival of two people. The first is Tom "Boats" Gilhooley (Lee Marvin in a more decidedly affable and playful mood than he was in his last Ford picture), an old war buddy of Donovan's who jumps a freighter and comes ashore to perpetuate their twenty-one-year tradition of duking it out on their birthdays.

The other is Amelia Dedham (Elizabeth Allen) a beautiful but starched bluestocking from Boston who is the heir to the shipping company running rum out of the island. She is also the daughter of Doc Dedham (Jack Warden), a fact that is kept from her along with the fact that Doc was married to a Polynesian woman and fathered two Hapa children, though Donovan pretends they are his. Unlike *Liberty Valance, Donovan's Reef* is populated by mythic types who are content not only in their South Sea paradise but in their mythology. Everyone is settled on their land and, like Ms. Dedham, if they are not, the magic and charm of the island will win them over. Unlike other exotic films made around the time of *Donovan's Reef* like *Mutiny on the Bounty* or *Hawaii*, Anglo-Saxons do not bring syphilis, smallpox and colonial tyranny to the "Territory of Heaven"; they merely show up as Boston Brahmins who simply put an end to the boys' boozing and brawling.

Having avoided red-button topics like racism and prejudice in the post-war years, Ford began to touch on it, directly or obliquely, in films like *The Sun Shines Bright*, *Sergeant Rutledge*, *Donovan's Reef* and soon after with *Cheyenne Autumn*. Here, the prejudice directed against Dedham's mixed-race children by his own daughter (and their sister) is not shown to be morally wrong or unjust. On the contrary, it is simply made to look ridiculously insignificant against the primal infinity of the South Pacific. Like the aforementioned films, *Donovan's Reef* at best can be seen as taking a leisurely stroll on the outskirts of the race issue and touching on it with a twenty-foot palm branch. At worst, like *The Searchers*, it can be mistakenly seen that Ford is perpetuating racist stereotypes instead of destroying them; the work of a racist man and not the work of a man making a film about racist bigotry. Ford was not Stanley Kramer and could not make *The Defiant Ones* or *Guess Who's Coming to Dinner* any more than Kramer could have made *The Quiet Man* or *The Searchers*. He made his films from the emotions he felt and the principles he held and his films that touched on race and racism may not have been daring and angry but since they came from who the man was they were honest.

Donovan's Reef is as careless as it is carefree and if nothing else reflects the fact that Ford was older and not as careful with details as he once was. The *Araner* showed up as a character in the film (giving him a chance to polish her up for her auspicious debut) and the location shoot in Hawaii surrounded by his diminishing members of the stock company had the feel of a family getaway reminiscent of *The Quiet Man* and the Monument Valley shoots.

It was symbolic that Ford and Wayne's professional pairing would end on a light, upbeat note and not the dark grand guignol of *Liberty Valance*. Duke still had great love and affection for Coach and maintained an affectionate relationship with him until his death, despite the treatment he continued to suffer during productions. The fact was that, for Wayne, it was finally time to move on. In order to recover the financial solvency he lost by putting everything he owned into *The Alamo*, Wayne threw himself into a non-stop, breakneck schedule of two, sometimes three films a year. Almost all were location shoots, the Westerns generally taking him to Durango, Mexico, or Tucson, Arizona, while bigger and more involved productions like *Hatari!*, *The Longest Day* and *Circus World* took him to, respectively, Tanganyika, France and Spain. He was wearing himself out and was plagued by a persistent, hacking cough that seemed to get worse as the months went by.

Wayne was not an ingrate. Ford had not only made him a star but an actor and with his philosophy of myth and history had given Wayne an existential context in which he could frame his persona. Conversely, Wayne had lent his name and talents to Ford's films in the sure-fire guarantee of audiences and profits. In Wayne's eyes, the debt had been repaid and he did not want to spend the rest of his life fearing that when the phone rang it was Ford telling him it was time to make another picture.

Then again, it was time to cut ties and say goodbye to many people. Grant Withers, Ford and Wayne's close friend who had supporting roles in several of their films, committed suicide in 1959. Depressed by failing health, lack of work and a string of divorces (including his first, to actress Loretta Young) Withers swallowed a handful of pills washed down with vodka and quickly ended his pain. In 1960, Ward Bond, the third in their legendary triumvirate, died after suffering a massive coronary while in Dallas attending a football game. Bond finally achieved the celebrity and stardom he knew all along was rightfully his as the star of the hit TV series, *Wagon Train*. His smoking, diet and manic workload, however, took its toll and by the end of the decade's first year he too was gone. In death, Bond achieved the grandeur that Ford and Wayne refused to confer upon him and invariably when the two remaining friends got together the conversation culminated in Bond and how much they loved and missed him.

Pedro Armendariz, the handsome, Mexican-American friend of both Ford's and Wayne's who had lent such solid support to three of Coach's films, was also gone before the new decade was even half finished. While filming the 1963 James Bond thriller *From Russia, With Love* (playing Bond's Turkish intelligence counterpart, Kerim Bey) on location in Istanbul, Armendariz began suffering the painful effects of kidney cancer which quickly metastasized. It was suspected—but never proven—that Armendariz's cancer was the result of filming Duke's ill-fated and ridiculous 1956 Genghis Khan horse opera *The Conqueror* in Nevada downwind of a government nuclear test site. Out of the two hundred cast members who filmed in and around the highly radioactive desert location, nearly half, including Armendariz, Susan Hayward, Agnes Moorehead, director Dick Powell and even Wayne himself, contracted some form of cancer in the following decades. Regardless of how he contracted the disease, Armendariz did not want to suffer a slow and painful decline into death and in 1963, oddly, like his character in *3 Godfathers* did, he shot himself through the heart with a borrowed gun.

Ford's somber, fatalistic mood about the times and how they were a- changin' was patently reflected in his next film, *Cheyenne Autumn* (1964). Intended as an epic *mea culpa* to the Native Americans for the monumental injustices they suffered at the hands of the government, *Cheyenne Autumn* ended as Ford's longest, most expensive and ambitious projects. If it was not doomed from the start, it quickly passed the point of no return soon after production began. It was envisioned as an epic along the lines of *How the West Was Won* and reunited Ford with its writer, James R. Webb, and producer, Bernard Smith, a former editor at Knopf turned movie executive with whom Ford would form his last production company.

The film was based upon the book of the same name by Mari Sandoz, a Nebraska-born daughter of Swiss homesteaders whose historical novels and biographies of Plains Indians and pioneers were far ahead of their time in their carefully researched details and sympathy toward the Indians. Sandoz's book, faithfully adapted by Webb, told the true story of the Northern Cheyenne exodus of 1878-79 from the agency at Fort Robinson in the Oklahoma Territory to their ancestral hunting ground in Wyoming. Led by Dull Knife (Gilbert Roland) and Little Wolf (Ricardo Montalban), the Cheyenne are pursued by Captain Thomas Archer (Richard Widmark), a sympathetic soldier determined to stop the exodus with no bloodshed or war. On his side are the equally sympathetic Secretary of the Interior, Carl Schurz (Edward G. Robinson) and a Quaker schoolteacher (Carroll Baker) with whom Archer falls in love. In support are Sal Mineo as the hot-headed young brave Red Shirt, the bigoted Prussian Captain Oscar Wessels (Karl Malden) and the beautiful Dolores Del Rio as the Spanish woman. James Stewart made a short but memorably humorous cameo as a shady, double-dealing Wyatt Earp with Arthur Kennedy as Doc Holliday.

The film is honestly grim and, more than *Liberty Valance*, turns the Fordian sense of the community and medieval order in the universe upside down and inside out. The people who populate *Cheyenne Autumn* (aside from the Cheyenne), unlike his Trilogy outposts, World War II units and small communities, are not microcosms of the coming kingdom where all dwell in harmony and love. Ford shows, as he did in *She Wore a Yellow Ribbon* and *They Were Expendable*, people from all cultures coming together to form one hierarchical institution, one community, one country. There is the WASP Captain Archer, Irishmen like Sean McClory's Doc O'Carberry, Poles like Mike Mazurki's Sergeant Wichowsky and Malden's "I was only following orders" Prussian Captain Wessels. However, there is no longer any unity or synthesis of common goals or ideals. Just men on either side of an increasingly blurred moral line.

Some nice, Fordian touches in the film that, aside from the grand sweep and cinematography, chromatically nail the soul of Monument Valley and show that the Old Master was down but not completely out.

Carroll Baker had lost most of the cinematic baby fat of her Baby Doll days and was growing into a mature actress; having survived both Henry Hathaway and Ford on *How the West Was Won,* she proved herself Ford's kind of actress. Had Ford continued making films, no doubt she would have made a worthy heir to Anna Lee, Millie Natwick, Joanne Dru and herself, Maureen O'Hara. One of the most poignant scenes, a heartfelt moment pregnant with Ford's DNA, is a solitary communication between Secretary of the Interior Schurz (Edward G. Robinson) and an Alexander Gardner daguerreotype of Abraham Lincoln on the wall. Torn about the path to take in resolving the Cheyenne situation without bloodshed, Schurz, reflected in the glass of the photograph, sadly asks, "Old friend, what would you do?" For the final time, Ford clearly shows the link between the quick and the dead to be a living reality and a bond of love so strong that it is not one's memory that aids those on earth but their very life force.

Widmark, as always, is a forceful actor with great style and technique. He does not, however, have either the presence or the moral authority of Wayne's Captain Brittles. Like Brittles, he is sympathetic toward the Indians and wants to avoid a slaughter. Unfortunately, he is more of a policeman in a Vietnam-like police action and while he can act according to his conscience, he does not have the authority to stop a war. Like Tom Doniphon in *Liberty Valance*, Captain Archer is a man of courage and integrity but is ultimately impotent in the face of greater and more irresistible enemies: progress and change.

Cheyenne Autumn was, at $4 million, a very expensive and logistically complex project to lay on the shoulders of a man who was almost seventy years old. By the early 1960s, movie production was again sinking and giving way to the world of television. The allure of the widescreen and the cachet built up by in-house blockbusters like *Ben-Hur* began to wane as quickly as it had waxed. By the mid-1960s, the major studios began to produce and distribute television programs as much as movies, and soon they had to sell off back lots for operating capital and lease their soundstages to independent production companies. Warner Brothers, the studio producing and releasing *Cheyenne*

Autumn, had paid a record $5.5 million for the rights to Lerner and Loewe's Broadway smash *My Fair Lady* and placed great hopes on both it and *Cheyenne Autumn* as blockbuster roadshows. Roadshows were exclusive, limited engagement performances in major cities with extended versions of the film including overtures, entr'actes and exit music that approximated the highbrow experience of the theater or opera. *My Fair Lady* went on to bring in over $70 million in a few years, while *Cheyenne* did not even make back its initial $4 million investment.

The major problem with *Cheyenne Autumn* was similar to the fate suffered by George Stevens' legendarily turgid biblical epic, *The Greatest Story Ever Told*, the following year. Both films were so well intentioned, so novel in their interpretations (the Ford film looking at the plight of the Indians from their perspective and the Stevens film an anti-spectacle, "thinking person's" take on the gospels) and so lofty in their mood and *so* long in their telling that audiences were bored, if they remained awake at all, by the time the intermission rolled around. The film was shot in Super Panavision 70 in Monument Valley by William Clothier and, despite contrails obvious in several scenes, neither the valley nor the Technicolor in a Ford film ever looked so magnificent and luscious. However, as George Stevens did in his telling of the life of Christ, Ford created not so much a narrative and flesh and blood humans as he did groups of static, statuesque compositions so noble, so dignified and so cold that they look as though they just stepped off a pedestal. In his heartfelt and sincere attempt to right the wrongs of American history and Manifest Destiny, Ford turned the Cheyenne into marble men and women and takes things so far in the other direction that the film becomes demeaning and dehumanizing in the opposite direction.

Composition, not only of landscape but of groupings of people, is what always gave Ford's best work a certain *frisson*, a crisp organic nature that used space and form to wordlessly convey a person's relationship to other people or to the earth. Take, for instance, the dinner table groupings of *Stagecoach, The Grapes of Wrath* and *How Green Was My Valley*, the symbolic symmetry of troopers in the Cavalry Trilogy, the controlled chaos of the Edwards' breakfast in *The Searchers* or the lonely, disconnected distance between Link and Hallie and Hallie and Ranse in *Liberty Valance*. In *Cheyenne Autumn*, all the organic and symbolic beauty flies and instead everyone is arranged beautifully but in an operatic manner, as though they are mounting a Native American Oberammergau Passion Play.

Ford must have sensed the trail of tears down which his film was getting lost and once again he rapidly began to lose interest. Compounding the angst of the production was the news that hit the cast and crew on Friday, November 22, 1963. Word of the assassination of President Kennedy in Dallas thoroughly depressed Ford and after wrapping on location, he went back to Hollywood to shoot interiors at the Warner's Burbank studios. The steam, however, had run out long before then. Even on location in Monument Valley, Ford's perennially mystical playground and summer camp, he was depressed and detached. He said to his old chum, George O'Brien, playing a final cameo in the director's final Western, "It's just not fun anymore."[7]

Like the Cheyenne, Ford pressed on in the hopes of finding better and happier hunting grounds but 1964 did not bring any better news for him. Duke finally gave in to his wife Pilar's badgering and had a checkup to investigate his persistent, hacking cough, which was now bringing up blood as well. For decades, Wayne had smoked an average of six packs of cigarettes a day (even more when he was filming *The Alamo*) and it had finally caught up with him. A checkup at the Scripps Clinic in La Jolla revealed a tumor on his left lung slightly smaller than a tennis ball. The surgery in September 1964 was successful but was a physical and emotional nightmare for Wayne and his family. During the operation, Ford sat with Pilar in the Good Samaritan Hospital and did his best to comfort and assure her that all would be well. However, it was Ford who needed the support and catharsis since the prospect of losing the man he considered a son so soon after losing Bond was too crushing to contemplate. If nothing else, it emphasized his own decline and mortality and forced him to own, as Frank's death did ten years earlier, the shabby treatment he meted out to those closest and dearest to him. "I love that damn Republican," Ford said to Pilar, the greatest compliment and expression of love the old liberal Democrat could extend to anyone.[8]

A mere four months after the surgery, Wayne, grouchy, irritable and eager to reclaim his image of heroic indestructability in the eyes of the world, returned to work on *The Sons of Katie Elder* (1965). The director, Henry Hathaway, was known for treating his leading ladies slightly better than the horses and stuntmen and his leading men even worse, and he knew that what Duke needed was work and not coddling. Hathaway, literally, let Wayne have it. The *Katie Elder* shoot was in Durango, Mexico, and Wayne did as many stunts as he could, including fistfights, gun battles, horse riding and a wagon jump into the icy Chama River. Interiors were later filmed in the gasp-inducing heights of Mexico City's Churubusco Studios and, although Duke put on a good act for cast, crew and *Life* magazine, he was in agony the entire time. On all future location shoots he would keep an oxygen tank handy and need a crate to mount his horse, facts discreetly kept from Duke's fans by the media. Although *Life* proclaimed that Duke had "Licked the Big C," and Wayne bravely became one of the first stars to admit cancer and publicly encourage people to have yearly checkups, the experience radically changed him. After 1965, Wayne's inner circle saw, despite his return to a normal work schedule, a new Duke who was older, wearier, slightly angrier and possessed of an intractable intolerance that would rapidly extend to his politics. The old, carefree, ebullient Duke was gone and it seemed that Michelangelo's magnificent David, like the Master who sculpted him, was slowly cracking from age and the brutally unforgiving winds of time.

Sean O'Casey (1880-1964) was born John Cassidy in Dublin and like Ford was a tough, Irish bird and a dark, brilliant, tortured terror to everyone he met. Like Ford, he was a product of the working class and deeply committed to the cause of Irish nationalism (he joined James Connolly's Irish Citizen Army in 1914) as well as Irish literature. Their only divergence was doctrinal: O'Casey was a lapsed member of the Church of Ireland, the Emerald Isle's Protestant church, in communion with Canterbury instead of Rome. O'Casey was a hard-core socialist and his plays and writings were seen through a political lens and manifested in the effects of war, upheaval and poverty on the working class. His two most notable plays, mounted at the Abbey Theatre, were *Juno and the Paycock* (made as a film by Alfred Hitchcock in 1930) and *The Plough and the Stars* (dispiritedly made by Ford in 1936).

In 1965, a film on O'Casey's life and work, based upon six autobiographical volumes he produced between 1939-1956, was mounted by producers Robert Emmett Ginna and Robert D. Graff for M-G-M. The film was titled *Young Cassidy* and was written for the screen by John Whiting as a conflation of all six volumes of O'Casey's autobiographies.

Following the massive, worldwide success of M-G-M's *Ben-Hur* in 1959, the studio dusted off other silent hits from their vault and hoped to update them with Cinemascope and Technicolor and achieve the same gold-dust results. However, the public's taste for rehashed epics did not go much further than chariot racing and the failure of the studio's string of very expensive remakes like *Cimarron* (1960), *Four Horsemen of the Apocalypse* (1962), *King of Kings* (1961) and *Mutiny on the Bounty* (1962) quickly strangled the lion's once-mighty roar. Metro President Sol C. Siegel was cashiered and Hollywood businessman Robert O'Brien took over at the studio with the intent of trimming the fat and concentrating on smaller, manageable crowd pleasers like *Flipper* (1963), *The V.I.P.s* (1963) *The Unsinkable Molly Brown* (1964) *The Cincinnati Kid* (1965) and a seemingly interminable string of Elvis films. A 1965 promotional film for the studio's upcoming releases placed great stock in *Young Cassidy*, putting special emphasis on the fact it would be directed by the great and legendary John Ford. Like Warner Brothers' hopes for *Cheyenne Autumn*, it was a tall order and mythic buildup to lay on the thin shoulders of an aging giant.

Sean Connery, hot off his string of highly successful James Bond films, was first approached for the part of Cassidy. When he proved unavailable and went off to make *Thunderball*, the part was then given to the handsome, broad-shouldered Australian actor Rod Taylor. Taylor was one of the last M-G-M contract players and was groomed by the studio as a sort of Cary Grant with muscles. After supporting parts in films like *Giant* (1956), *Raintree County* (1957) and *Separate Tables* (1958) Taylor moved on to starring roles in hits like *The Time Machine* *(1960)*, *The Birds* (1963) and opposite Doris Day in *The Glass Bottom Boat* (1966).

Taylor would prove to be the last of the Fordian he-men with whom the director would bond as in the days long gone, and he was an affable, respectful and brawny successor to George O'Brien, Henry Fonda and John Wayne. Taylor and Ford became good friends and as all Ford's former drinking buddies were either dead, grown up or simply unequal to the task of benders any more, the older man attempted to prove his endurance with a man half his age. The results were both horrific and pathetic. With Wayne, Bond, Fonda or any of the *Araner* gang, a toot with Ford was like drinking with an older brother but in 1965 it was like bar-hopping with one's alcoholic grandfather. When Ford was not tying one on with Taylor in the pubs of London, he was sleeping off his hangovers and holding meetings in bed, his pajamas covered with cigar ash while he struggled to find the heart of a story that, as Captain Ahab said, should have been familiar as the veins in his arms.

Taylor was in awe of Ford and his reputation, as were most of the cast and crew, including Maggie Smith, Michael Redgrave, Dame Edith Evans and David Lean's legendary editor, Anne V. Coates. Less generous was Taylor's co-star, the ravishing young blonde Julie Christie, who was on her way to international stardom as Lara in *Dr. Zhivago* and an Academy Award for her role as an unhappily swinging party girl in *Darling*. According to Scott Eyman, who interviewed Taylor, Christie was deep into her "Cockney phase," and with London in full swing and the action centered around the Beatles, Mary Quant, Carnaby Street and Twiggy, could not be bothered with an old, drunken American director who was legally blind. Regardless of her youthful indifference to an old master, Christie smote Ford and her natural, spontaneous acting abilities impressed him so much that he personally recommended her to David Lean, in the midst of preproduction on *Zhivago*, for the part of Lara.[9]

In a sense, *Young Cassidy* struggled to be what *Zhivago* ultimately became; a tale of a brilliant young writer, consumed by the flames of his art and passion for a beautiful girl, set against the tumult and upheaval of historical events. Even with such great material and first-rate actors and technicians, *Young Cassidy* taxis around the runway but never gets enough thrust and lift to take off. The scenes between Taylor and Christie are erotically tender and Taylor brings a macho yet tender vulnerability to his scenes, especially the one where he weeps as he watches his mother's funeral from afar. Michael Redgrave (W. B. Yeats) and Edith Evans (Lady Augusta Gregory) could not throw a performance if the future of the empire depended on it and Maggie Smith likewise has several good scenes. There is a static, forced quality to the entire patina of the film, and the barroom brawls and Easter Uprising riots might as well have been unused footage from *The Plough and the Stars*.

As he did while making *Mister Roberts* ten years earlier, Ford began to drink and soon had buckets of stout with him on the set. He was, however, ten years older and unable to drink the way he used to, let alone drink and function as the director of a large, overseas production. After three weeks work on the film, Ford went home and the studio, as Warners did for *Mister Roberts*, cited the "illness" of the director, who was replaced with Jack Cardiff, the great cinematographer. Like Robert Parrish, Cardiff made an easy transition from cameraman to director and did a noble job to bring *Young Cassidy* to a satisfactory but far from brilliant close. As a concession to the old director and hopefully to generate some name-association interest in the film, it was released in April 1965 and billed by M-G-M as "A John Ford Production—Directed by Jack Cardiff."[10]

Ford's association with producer Bernard Smith was genial but nothing close to that which he enjoyed with Merian Cooper, and if *Cheyenne Autumn* was a bellwether of the risks now involved in making films with the director in such a diminished capacity, it was obvious they needed to tread with caution. *7 Women* (1966) was based on *Chinese Finale*, a book by Norah Lofts. It told the tense tale of female missionaries in 1935 China caught in a rampage by a brutal warlord, Tunga Khan. The mission is led by the matronly, sexually repressed Agatha Andrews (Margaret Leighton) assisted by Miss Argent (Mildred Dunnock) and a beautiful, impressionable young blonde, Emma Clark (Sue Lyon, who had recently played the nymphette in Stanley Kubrick's *Lolita*) to whom Agatha has an obvious sexual attraction. Also on hand is the screeching, middle-aged pregnant wacko, Florrie (Betty Field), and her gray, weakling husband, Charles (Eddie Albert).

When another local mission is burnt out by Khan's men after the regular Chinese army flees in fear, Agatha reluctantly takes in its staff, including Miss Binns (Flora Robson), Mrs. Russell (Anna Lee) and Miss Ling (Jane Chang). Into this frustrated, heavy starch atmosphere steps Dr. D. R. Cartwright (Anne Bancroft), a leather-jacketed, whiskey-chugging, chain-smoking atheist who upsets the moral tone of the place with her secular ways but passionate attention to the sick, the dying and the pregnant stuck in the mission. She also arouses Agatha's ire by becoming the object of young Emma's respect and fascination, thus robbing Agatha of the young woman's affections.

When Tunga Khan (Mike Mazurki) brutally invades the mission and kills several of the workers, assisted by his lieutenant, the Lean Warrior (Woody Strode), Cartwright sees the only way for the inhabitants to escape is to appeal to his sense of tribal justice. She offers herself to the warlord in exchange for the lives of the residents. Donning the robes of a courtesan, she pours two drinks for herself and Khan—laced with poison—and after he keels over dead she sneers, "So long, ya bastard!" and downs the second cup.

If *Young Cassidy* represented a film that should have been like one that was to be released in the future (*Dr. Zhivago*), *7 Women* is astounding in that it looks, sounds and feels like a film that could have been made thirty years before. The year 1966 was the year of films like *A Man For All Seasons*, *Who's Afraid of Virginia Woolf?*, *Georgy*

Girl, Alfie, A Man and A Woman, Harper and *The Russians Are Coming, The Russians Are Coming!* The sexual revolution was beginning to go into full swing, mores and values in Hollywood were rapidly changing and a film featuring a main character with obvious lesbian tendencies, atheism, suicide and sexual concubinage would have fit right in and gained an eager audience. However, there is an odd feeling about the film that makes it look like a Victorian carriage in a parking lot full of 1965 Mustangs.

Ford originally sought Kate Hepburn for the lead of Agatha Andrews and Jennifer Jones as Dr. Cartwright. Smith shot down the idea of Hepburn but they did agree on Patricia Neal but after a few days work on the film she suffered the massive stroke that nearly killed her and from which it took several years for her to recover. Anne Bancroft, the Italian, Brooklyn-born actress had won an Academy Award for her performance as Annie Sullivan in *The Miracle Worker* and was nominated for another in *The Pumpkin Eater* and seemed to have the right combination of grit, backbone and beauty to pull off the part of Cartwright. Like Ford, Cartwright's cynicism and sardonic wit hides a deeply sensitive compassionate soul, so much so that unlike the morally upright Christian women who disdain her, she is willing to lay down her life for the sake of others. Agatha Andrews is not just a pharisee, she is a nutty one. Ford despised pharisaic behavior, among his friends, in his church and, as his brave stand at the Screen Directors Guild meeting proved, his country. Having been the subject of scurrilous gossip himself, Ford took great pains to show the Pandora's box of gossipy demons as prune-faced old biddies. There is, for instance, the hypocritical Ladies of the Law and Order League in *Stagecoach*, the old harridans listening to the gossip about Angharad in *How Green Was My Valley* and the canny locals who endeavor to know everything about Sean and Mary Kate's marital woes in *The Quiet Man*. Cartwright and Ford both were not the ideal visions of Christian charity and piety but their honesty was their integrity and in that sense they had more in common with the Beatitudes than all the pious posing of the churchgoing phonies around them.

Ford must have still harbored the illusions of working with Katie Hepburn because his attitude toward Bancroft was cool and, in the absence of the writers on the set, he simply put his head down and plowed through the production. Bancroft was no shrinking Brooklyn violet and with her career firmly on the fast track, made it through the shoot and the following year went on to permanent fame as the college-boy seducing Mrs. Robinson in Mike Nichols' *The Graduate*. The idea of using Western actors from central casting for the role of exotics was quickly becoming a thing of the past, and audiences demanded a bit more authenticity and one wonders what Ford was thinking in his casting for *7 Women*. Mike Mazurki and Woody Strode, with latex skin wigs, Fu Manchu mustaches and slit eyes border on the ridiculous and undermines the whole endeavor from their first appearances. The film was shot entirely on the soundstages of M-G-M and, like *Liberty Valance*, it has a claustrophobic, artificial atmosphere that gives it a stagy, melodramatic look as though it were a filmed stage play. "I think it was a good story," Ford said about the finished film to Peter Bogdanovich. "And it was a good switch for me, to turn around and make a picture all about women. It didn't do well here, but it was a sensation in Europe. I thought it was a hell of a good picture."[11]

In hindsight, there is some merit to what Ford said, and in the following decades *7 Women* made three lists: the "Most Misappreciated American Films of All Time" list, Sight and Sound's 360 Films Classic List and Syndicat Francais de la Critique de Cinema Favorite Films List. Andre Bazin's venerated French film critique magazine *Cahiers du Cinema* rated it the 6th Best Film of 1966.

Audiences, however, were totally oblivious to the encomiums and hosannas raised by overseas intellectuals and stayed away in droves. The film received a limited release and went unnoticed by mainstream American critics and ticket buyers. While no one was looking, John Ford quietly struck the set, shut down the lights and for the last time walked away from a feature film project. His career of fifty years as a filmmaker was, for all intents and purposes, over.

The simple, unavoidable fact was that Ford was tired. Tired of fighting producers and the studio, tired of raising money, tired of the long, arduous shoots and unable to shoulder the burden of directing and the myriad details it entailed. Directing, like war, is a young man's game and while Ford had the inclination and the desire, he no longer had the energy.

Although most of his peers were dead or retired, some still had a few more films in them that would prove to be a mixed bag of the good and bad. George Stevens never recovered from the monumental failure of his biblical epic, *The Greatest Story Ever Told,* and made one more film (another expensive flop), *The Only Game in Town* (1970) before calling it quits for good. Willy Wyler continued to make films, including the smash hit musical, *Funny Girl* (1968), which made a star out of Barbra Streisand. After that, he had one more in him, *The Liberation of L. B. Jones,* and that was that. Billy Wilder was probably the most prolific and, although just ten years younger than Ford, made some good, bad and middling films through the 1970s and 80s.

Unlike most other directors, stars and especially the producers, Ford could not sit back, enjoy retirement and manage a multimillion-dollar stock portfolio. Unlike Gene Autry and Fred MacMurray, Ford did not invest in ocean-front real estate, oil wells in Bakersfield or sports teams, and in the absence of work he and Mary had to adjust to living on a fixed income. Duke Wayne was busier than ever and back on a non-stop schedule of two films a year and would end the decade with an ebullient, stylized, self-parodying performance as the drunken, eye-patched Marshal Rooster Cogburn in Henry Hathaway's *True Grit* (1969). In the following year, Wayne would win his first, only and well-deserved Academy Award. In his speech he would gratefully acknowledge not Pappy or Coach but "Admiral John Ford."

By the late 1960s, the Field Photo Farm was becoming increasingly run-down and superfluous; not so much a viable and thriving community as an empty shell haunted by the ghosts of memories and the echo of raucous laughter, Christmas carols and the beer calls of old friends long gone. In 1969, the Farm was destroyed by a fire and with no need or desire to rebuild, the corporation sold the land to the Motion Picture and Television Relief Fund. Like donated organs, the Farm may have died but it continued to serve its mission in being of service to comrades in the industry who would be in need of assistance in the future.[12]

The deepest cut, and one that severed Ford from all that was and the sign that it could never be again was the selling of his beloved ketch. The *Araner* and Ford grew old together and neither weathered the winds of time well. The yacht was increasingly expensive to maintain and, in any event, neither he nor Mary (who was exhibiting the first signs of the Parkinson's disease that would take her life in 1979) were up to cruises to Catalina Island let alone across the Pacific to Hawaii. What was one of the most famous yachts in Hollywood history was sold for a paltry $25,000 and some shares in a Hawaiian resort. As with everything else that was lost and gone forever, Ford shrugged and looked ahead to another project in the future. He had kept the façade of the crusty old admiral for so long he could not let on now that it all must have been ripping his heart to pieces.[13]

In 1966, Ford entered into talks with Samuel Goldwyn, Jr., about the possibilities of bringing Howard Fast's 1961 novel *April Morning* to the wide screen. The story of the Battle of Lexington and Concord, in which the "shot heard around the world" started the American Revolution, was one close to Ford's heart. As the nation devolved into chaos with race riots, anti-Vietnam protests and a loss of faith in government following the assassinations of John F. Kennedy, Martin Luther King, Jr., and Robert F. Kennedy, Ford became more depressed at what was happening to the America he knew. It was a story that the country needed to hear again and Goldwyn knew that only Ford would be the man to tell it. The talks progressed and John Wayne was even approached for the starring role of Moses Cooper, the reluctant father who tries to keep his son Adam out of the revolutionary struggle. It would be an epic along the lines of *Cheyenne Autumn* but epics along those lines were now being made in Europe, not America, and the few that were, like *The Hallelujah Trail, The Greatest Story Ever Told* and

The Great Race were either financial or critical flops. In any event, a 60-year-old John Wayne in buckled shoes and pigtailed wig was not the best of ideas and the talks soon fizzled out.[14]

In 1968, the United States Information Agency approached Ford to make a documentary about the conflict in Vietnam, doing in a *cinema verite* style what Wayne did at the same time in a naively patriotic way in his film *The Green Berets*. Ford may not have supported the war in its morality and motivations but the idea of the U.S. government being maligned and vilified by its own people rankled him and he agreed to do it. To make *Vietnam! Vietnam!* (one wonders the reason for the jubilant exclamation points) Ford traveled to Vietnam and observed the conflict firsthand, including "atrocities" supposedly committed by the Viet Cong. The journey also gave him the chance to reconnect with his grandson Dan, who was serving with forward units in the jungle; a source of great pride for the old soldier. The project was largely the work of producer Bruce Herschensohn, and Ford did little more than supervise the scripting and editing but was not involved in any camera work. Charlton Heston was engaged to narrate but by the time the film was officially released in 1972, the American public had become disgusted with the war and any flag-waving attempts to put a good face on one of history's most hated and unjust conflicts.[15]

Ford's last project, another flag-waving, drum-thumping tribute to a parade that had gone by, was a documentary on the life of Lt. General Lewis "Chesty" Puller, USMC. Puller was a highly decorated, extraordinarily brave soldier and legend of the Corps who was a personal friend of both Ford and Wayne. Military men, especially generals, were being shown in an increasingly horrific light, either as power-lusty egomaniacs like George S. Patton in *Patton*, screw-loosed cuckoos like Jack D. Ripper and Buck Turgidson in *Dr. Strangelove* or addle-brained nincompoops like Henry Blake in M*A*S*H. With Wayne narrating, Ford endeavored to show a true American hero, a humble, patriotic leatherneck whose love for America and all she stands for was the foundation of his noble heroism. *Chesty* is a moving tribute to a true American hero and scenes of actual battle and archival footage are juxtaposed with Puller, in mufti, walking around his cottage and growling in interviews about the battles he has seen and then pausing at the grave of General Robert E. Lee at Washington and Lee College. A few scenes show Ford—shot from behind but obviously him from the wispy, bald head, cigar, eye patch and Maine *ahc*-cent—putting a few questions to Chesty personally.

In 1950 or possibly even 1960, *Chesty* would have been received with great respect and reverence. In 1970 America, anyone over thirty was not trusted, while anyone over thirty in uniform was considered the enemy. In watching the documentary today, it is notable primarily as it is the last work to which the Master put his hand. Aside from that, it feels like a recruiting film urging the 18- year-old boys of 1970 America to cut their hair, stop smoking dope and head down to the nearest recruiting depot like good patriots.

It was all over. With no projects or the energy to undertake them, Ford did what old directors do: answer the questions he was asked and talk about films. The industry may have been finished with him but fate was not. In the late 1960s and early 1970s, a rediscovery of Ford's darker films, like *The Grapes of Wrath*, *The Long Voyage Home* and most especially *The Searchers* and *The Man Who Shot Liberty Valance* were rediscovered by a younger generation of film critics and *auteurs* from both sides of the Atlantic. Ford began giving a series of extended and highly insightful interviews to young journalists and, despite his feigned irritation and crotchety crust, he appeared to enjoy them immensely. Here and there, he revealed the feelings, thoughts and emotions that he either avoided or did not have the answers for thirty years earlier. Ford traveled to France or would be visited in his home by importuning young journalists and filmmakers and in the late 1960s gave extensive interviews to Eric Leguebe (1965), Jean Narboni and Andre Labarthe (1965), Axel Madsen (1966) and perhaps the most insightful of all, a long and fascinating discussion about films with Bertrand Tavernier. A left-wing French critic who wrote extensively on the works of Ford and Jean Renoir, Tavernier went on to become a celebrated filmmaker himself. His 1986 film about Black Jazz musicians in Paris, *Round Midnight*, has become one of the great cult classics of the decade.

Ford, like most short-fused curmudgeons, did not know that the angrier he got the funnier things he said. Time and age may have robbed Ford of work, friends and vigor but he retained his wonderfully wicked and pungent sense of humor. Most of the time, Ford simply toyed with the interviewers, grandly dropping French phrases or asking questions about French art and history on completely unrelated topics. Ford seemed genuinely fond of the younger generation and appreciated their serious, intellectual and enthusiastic study of his work and in a sense they became the conduits to insure that his art would carry on into the next generations.

One time, however, the anger was not feigned but genuine and almost spelled the abrupt end of the interview. British journalist Philip Jenkinson, interviewing Ford in his home in 1968, casually asked Ford if he saw the "systematic destruction of the Red Indian" as a blot on American history. Ford, who prided himself on his sympathetic view of the Native Americans and his personal love and respect for their culture, saw red. Jenkinson had pushed the wrong button on the wrong sailor. "My sympathy is all with the Indians," Ford shot back. "Do you consider the invasion of the Black and Tans in Ireland a blot on English history? Being Irish, it's my prerogative to answer a question with a question. Do you consider that a blot on English history?" Jenkinson stammered something about not knowing enough about the subject to make a judgment call but Ford would not let him go. It was one of those occasions where Ford's ire was not a smokescreen but real, and when the film is viewed today, his icy, completely justified rage still comes across like an electric jolt.[16]

What Jenkinson discovered, to his peril, is that while the old lion may have been molting, he was by no means toothless and that his growl was just as bad as his bite. The extensive and in-depth interviews that Ford now deigned to give his young admirers also proved that, as the decade ended, Ford also had more time to talk about films than actually to go out and make them.

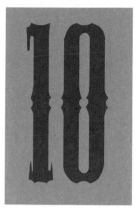

THE FINAL YEARS

"Lest we forget."

Ford was not happy with but now resigned to the fact that he would not nor could not work again. There was simply no way he would be able to get the insurance to cover him for the rigors of an overseas or back-lot shoot. To fill up time, of which he now paradoxically had too much but also a limited amount, he read, smoked, devoured chocolate bars throughout the night and slept during the day.

He would drive and visit friends (often sick or dying), go to mass, pray the rosary and chat with Mary about household chores that needed to be done. When people asked what he was up to, he would give the inevitable answer of the old director who has nothing to do: "Oh, I've got a few projects in discussion right now." As Scott Eyman said, however, despite the Homeric sense of greatness passed and the harsh, dreadful facts of age and infirmity, Ford never looked back, but always forward, always to the future. Perhaps it was due to the fact that he truly believed, somewhere in a warm, moist corner of his heart, that one fine day he would get the call, find the funding and begin work on yet another picture. Or perhaps it was because he was too Irish and that looking back on dearly departed days and people, like an immigrant mooning over Mother Machree and the Old Sod for too long, would simply tear and tug at the heart until it became unbearable.[1]

The Ford house on Copa de Oro in Bel Air had simply become too much, size-wise and economically, for the aging couple to handle and they began to scout out a new home on a smaller scale. Since both Mary and Jack could not handle the big staircase and the upkeep, they sought out a ranch style home to facilitate mobility and through friends found a nice home in Palm Desert, outside Los Angeles. For Ford, the move added a poetic, dramatic touch to a man who lived by poetry and drama his entire life. Somehow the smog, noise and tony artificiality of Bel Air did not seem the suitable place for the greatest artist in the history of American film to end his days. Like Ranse Stoddard, after a life of glory and stratospheric celebrity built around a well-crafted persona, Ford was returning to the simplicity, honesty and purity of the desert.

It was a prescient move that saw the curtain movingly begin to close on his final act. In 1971, Ford experienced severe abdominal pains and went to see his doctor and the diagnosis was cancer. Terminal. Almost as if his family, friends and admirers were fighting a clock, documentaries, retrospectives and tributes began to go into motion one after the other. *The American West of John Ford* was aired in late 1971. It was produced by Ford's grandson, Dan, and ran on CBS. It reunited Ford and Wayne for the last time as they shot a mock horse fall in the desert with Chuck Roberson doubling for Duke and Brick Marquard, an old FPB associate, on the camera. James Stewart waxed poetically and humorously about his experiences working with Ford and Henry Fonda shows up on the old back lot of Twentieth Century-Fox to reminisce about their old shooting locations.

Next came *Directed by John Ford*, an extraordinary documentary written and directed by Peter Bogdanovich. The young man, a great admirer of Ford, had first met him on the set of *Cheyenne Autumn*. Bogdanovich had written several magazine articles about Ford and was probably the greatest catalytic agent for the resurgence of interest in Ford in the 1970s. Bogdanovich was doing nearly single-handed in America what the young French *cineastes* were doing *en masse*: bringing the works of the Old Masters to the younger generation of the New Hollywood. Bogdanovich had made critical reappraisals of Orson Welles and Howard Hawks and began an intensely profound and deeply respectful relationship with Ford that started with conversations and culminated in an exhaustively comprehensive chronicle of Ford's work.

The documentary was released in 1971 and gathered Stewart, Fonda and Wayne together for more extensive conversations about Ford's work, interspersed with scenes narrated by Orson Welles from Ford's major films. The film also includes an amazingly yet truly Fordian interview with the old director, who was plunked moodily in a director's chair in Monument Valley and ready to effortlessly cut his young friend into fish bait. Los Angeles Dodgers cap pulled down over his eyes, lighting cigar after cigar and doing the best impersonation of John Ford to date, Ford laconically answers Bogdanovich's questions with all the irritation and grouchiness expected of him. When Bogdanovich asks Ford how he shot the elaborate land rush in *3 Bad Men*, Ford casually replies, "With a camera." Cut. When asked if it was true that *The Sun Shines Bright* was a little picture he made for himself, Ford expands with even more depth and insight by responding "Yep. Uh-huh." Cut. Then asked if Ford is aware of the darkening mood of his Westerns over the years, comparing *The Wagon Master* with *The Man Who Shot Liberty Valance*, Ford simply says, "No. I don't know what you're talking about." Cut. So far, so good. When Bogdanovich asks what it is about the Western that appeals to him, Ford continues on this transparent and helpful path, responding, "I wouldn't know." Cut. Then, to really get an insight into the nature of his art and films, Bogdanovich asks if the point of *Fort Apache* was that the traditions of the military took precedence over one individual, Ford summed it up by saying, "Cut!" Cut.[2]

The American Film Institute (AFI), at that time presided over by Charlton Heston, gathered their top brass together to see about presenting a Life Achievement Award to a member of the film industry who exemplified the very finest standards of excellence in the industry. Without hesitation, they all agreed "John Ford." Ford was about to receive the first ever AFI Life Achievement Award, an honor that has been regularly bestowed upon a single individual ever since.

On March 31, 1973, Admiral John Ford was wheeled into the Beverly Hilton for a banquet honoring him for his fifty years of greatness in the field of film. Danny Kaye hosted and John Wayne and dozens of celebrities were on hand for the first-ever presentation, including members of the government like Henry Kissinger. Dovetailed with the honor would be the awarding of the United States Presidential Medal of Freedom—the highest civilian award the republic can grant to its citizens—to be presented by President Richard M. Nixon.

Ford by now was hardly recognizable, the cancer had wasted him away in bulk and in height. Despite being ravaged and wizened by the disease, Ford managed to stand and salute during the national anthem and to stand at the podium, leaning over it for support, in order to receive the Medal of Freedom and the Life Achievement Award. He even managed to exchange a few appropriate bon mots with Nixon, who as a young lieutenant commander in the Pacific, certainly knew how to bandy naval quips with Admiral Ford. "I don't have the admiral's cap with me" Nixon can be heard saying to Ford as the old man smiled impishly and stood at the podium.

Darting his tongue out repeatedly like an old iguana, due to a combination of emotion and his medication, Ford turned the moment into an opportunity to deflect praise from him and his career and instead honor veterans recently returning from Vietnam. He quoted Captain Jeremiah Denton, the naval officer and POW recently released after spending eight years in the "Hanoi Hilton," talked about "praying his beads," and blubbering like a baby when he saw the veterans arriving home. In closing, he ended with "a simple prayer" that probably made F.D.R. spin in his grave and Ward Bond beam in his: "God bless Richard Nixon."

As the cancer continued to eat away at Ford, friends began to arrive at the Palm Desert house, ostensibly for a visit but in reality to say goodbye. The leitmotif among all of them was that they hardly recognized Ford, who was down to around a hundred pounds. The talk was always about the future, the next project and how damned miserable it was to be old and sick. The conversation was bright and cheery, the bonhomie and "remember whens" flowing like ambrosia but many knew this was the last farewell. Duke Wayne was a regular visitor and each time Jack would allude to a final parting, Duke would say "Hell, Jack, you'll bury us all." Always, they talked about Ward Bond and how much they missed the big dope.[3]

Lindsay Anderson, in Los Angeles to promote his latest film, *O Lucky Man*, stopped by the house to make his *au revoirs* to the friend and mentor with whom he had maintained such a close relationship even though they had met face-to-face only a handful of times. Inevitably, the talk turned to "pictures," what Anderson was working on and what project was next. When Anderson made his goodbyes, he asked Ford if he needed anything. "Only your friendship," Ford replied. "You have that," Anderson averred. Before leaving he took Ford's thin, waxy hands in his and kissed them.[4]

Perhaps the most poignant farewell was when Kate Hepburn stopped by with Ford's grandson Dan for a visit. Their conversation was taped for Dan to use in his planned biography on his grandfather but when he left the room and accidentally left the recorder going, he inadvertently gave posterity a remarkable and powerfully moving moment of *transparence* that Ford had never shown in public. Believing they were alone and out of earshot, Ford, his voice heavy with emotion and pain, tells Hepburn of his true and undying feelings for her. While she fusses about his cigar ash and speaks in the briskly cheerful voice of a nurse fluffing the pillows of a dying patient, Ford finally revealed his heart. "You're dropping ash all over the place," Hepburn says. "Is anyone listening?" Ford responds. When Hepburn says no, Ford simply says, "I love you. Thank you. You have a woman's intuition, don't you?" At the end of his life, with no more need for a façade or the bluster or rage with which he both defined and protected himself, Ford showed what everyone had known all along. His life, his heart and his soul were neither about myth nor history nor the art that brings them to life in the epic westward story of American Civilization. It was about love and the people in his life who made that love both possible and real.[5]

John Ford died in the evening of August 31, 1973. Present at his death was his son Pat, his sister and Woody Strode. After Ford breathed his last, they draped his body with an American flag and drank a toast with brandy. In order that the sentiments would be eternal and not compromised in any way, much like the work of the man would prove to be, they smashed the glasses to bits on the floor.[6]

On September 5, after a mass at Blessed Sacrament Church, Ford was buried nearby in the consecrated ground of Holy Cross Cemetery in Culver City. In attendance were John Wayne, Henry Fonda, James Stewart, Charlton Heston, Dobe Carey, Anna Lee and many surviving members of the Ford Stock Company. Fellow directors Frank Capra, George Cukor, William Wyler and William Wellman paid silent tribute by their presence. The Irish were ably represented by legends such as Pat O'Brien and George Murphy while Gilbert Roland, Ricardo Montalban and Cesar Romero represented the Latin contingent of friends and co-workers. Naval officers in dress blues mingled with the civilians and an honor guard folded the flag, which was presented to Mary as she sat there in a black dress and mantilla. Like the funeral of England's King Edward VII in 1910, it was one of the last great gathering of royalty come together to salute a fellow monarch.

Mary joined her husband in death six years later and lies beside him, not far from his brother Frank. Duke Wayne, after fighting a heroic battle against cancer that won him the plaudits of the industry and the heart of the world, died in 1979 after being received into the Roman Catholic Church on his deathbed by the Archbishop of Panamá, Marcos McGrath. Ford no doubt would have been immensely proud of Duke for rejecting his beige, noncommittal Christianity in favor of the ancient, full-blooded richness of Roman Catholicism. His joy, no doubt, would have been made complete knowing that the prelate who received him, although Hispanic, was possessed of a good old-fashioned Irish name.

In Graham Greene's 1982 book, *Monsignor Quixote*, the author does a modern take on Cervantes' tale by making his hero a simple but holy priest in modern Spain who is a direct descendant of the legendarily mad knight. This "Fool for God" journeys on the highways of Spain with his atheist friend, the ex-Communist mayor of El Toboso, Sancho Panza, and encounters as many adventures as did his fabled forbear but in modern correlations.

The sweetly pious man, who has never been outside his remote corner of the world and therefore has never had his faith challenged, begins to have a recurring nightmare that fills him with an unspeakable dread and horror. He dreams that no sooner had Christ been nailed to his Cross that he climbed down off of the offending instrument, "triumphant and acclaimed," and stood in power and glory before all the people. The Roman centurions stopped mocking, the people of Jerusalem stopped jeering, the disciples took heart and the Blessed Mother suddenly stopped weeping and rejoiced as everyone fell down in awe, worship and belief. The horror aroused in Monsignor Quixote is that the salvation of the world was achieved with no suffering, humiliation, doubt, death or any of the terrors of the night that ultimately lead three days later to the early morning and the empty tomb.

If John Ford had stopped making films after *How Green Was My Valley*, if he had come home from the war and decided to retire or just produce films or even if he never came back at all, the works that he created between 1917-1941 would still stand the test of time and be discovered, rediscovered, assessed and reassessed time and time again. Conversely, if he continued to make films of the caliber of *The Grapes of Wrath*, *The Long Voyage Home*, *She Wore a Yellow Ribbon*, *The Quiet Man* and *The Searchers* up to his official retirement, he would have left the studio for the last time, "triumphant and acclaimed," instead of the old, tired, nearly forgotten man that in reality he became. He also would have undermined and negated the key strands that formed the fabric of his art, his life and his heart.

In Ford's greatest, least and middling films, one does not have to watch too long before beginning to pick up on the simple but recurring theme that God is eternal and everything else is not. Families, communities, nations, friendship, memory, myths and even art and movies blaze through time afire with the glow of the divine spark, but are ultimately destined to one day pass away. If the works of John Ford, every film, every documentary, every book, every interview and sign that he ever lived and created great and beautiful works of art were to pass away from the memory of this and succeeding generations, Ford would be the first one to growl, "What was I telling you for fifty years?"

John Ford had to decline, his art had to weaken and begin to wither around the edges in films like *Two Rode Together*, *Donovan's Reef*, *Cheyenne Autumn*, *Young Cassidy* and *7 Women* because that is the mystical reality his art proclaimed for fifty years. Like Tom Joad in *The Grapes of Wrath*, Ford reckoned that his art, like the soul, was not an individual's solitary possession but is absorbed, through struggle and pain, into a bigger story and a bigger soul resting in the incalculable immensity of God. Ford could show the manifestation of that soul through the forces of time, history and family but how he did it he could only say, "*Secretum meum mihi,*" "My secret is my own."

So then, what remains? To answer that question one would need to return to the 30,000 acres of the former ocean that is now a desert stretching from northern Arizona into southern Utah. It is populated by towering rock sentinels with names like The Mittens, The Twin Sisters, The King on His Throne and The Totem Pole. Tens of millions of years ago, it was the domain of giant, carnivorous monsters both in the vast sea as well as creeping along the shore. For slightly less than two thousand years, Monument Valley has been the sacred land of the great and proud Navajo people. However, another presence is there, just as strong and powerful. It is the eternal one alluded to by Captain York (John Wayne) at the end of *Fort Apache*. When the reporter says that all the recently massacred troopers are now dead and forgotten Captain York corrects him and says, "You're wrong there. They aren't forgotten because they haven't died. They're living. Right out there." Even though the troopers passing by York in the next scene are reflections that were tricked up as process shots back in the studio, York believes it because Ford believes it, and we believe it because Ford does. It is not the fact that so many people believe it that makes it true but the love behind the sentiments that gives it an objective reality.

To affirm if the aforementioned statement is true or not, one simply needs to go out to Monument Valley, near John Ford Point, preferably on a day when the valley is not overrun with tourists, off-road vehicles and weekend cowboys riding in single file on horses rented by the hour. Between the winds, one might be able to discern sounds drifting on the edges of the howling, eternal breezes that prove unequivocally that, indeed, "They're living. Right out there." Coach, Duke, Hank Fonda, Ward Bond, Dobe Carey, Ben Johnson, the stuntmen, the old and doggedly loyal cameramen, gaffers, sound men, the old soldiers and sailors who stood next to the Old Man in war and peace. They're there, making pictures, yelling, "Cut," trying it again, executing horse falls, riding through desert storms, playing cards, drinking and making jokes about Ward Bond. They're there, sitting around the campfire, telling stories and singing songs while Danny Borzage plays "Gather at the River" and in the distance a lone bugler plays "Taps." They're there, tucking in for the night in their tents, sleeping the sweet slumber that comes after a hard day's work and waiting for the first glorious burst of the dawn of the new day.

NOTES

Chapter 1 – Beginnings: *The Boy Who Would be Pappy.*

1. Hardiman, James, *History of The Town & County of Galway* (Dublin: W. Folds & Sons, 1820), p. 5.

2. McBride, Joseph, *Searching for John Ford* (New York: St. Martin's Press, 2001), p. 20.

3. Morris, James, *Heaven's Command* (San Diego: Harvest/HBJ Books, 1973), pp. 152-155.

4. McBride, p. 22.

5. Ibid., p. 22.

6. Ford, Dan, *Pappy: The Life of John Ford* (New York: Da Capo Press, 1998), pp. 2-3.

7. Eyman, Scott, *Print the Legend: The Life and Times of John Ford* (Baltimore: Johns Hopkins University Press, 1999), p. 29.

8. Stoehr, Ken L., et al, ed., *John Ford in Focus: Essays on the Filmmaker's Life and Work* (Jefferson, N.C.: Macfarland & Company, 2008), pp. 86-88.

9. Ibid., p. 36.

10. John Ford Archives, Lilly Library, University of Indiana (Bloomington).

11. Eyman, p. 35.

12. Ford, Dan, *Pappy*, p. 8.

13. Eyman, p. 37.

14. Ibid., p. 40.

Chapter 2 – Hollywood: *"Any relation to Francis Ford?"*

1. Eyman, Scott, *Print the Legend: The Life and Times of John Ford* (Baltimore: Johns Hopkins University Press, 1999), pp. 40-44.

2. Griffith, Richard, & Mayer, Arthur, *The Movies* (New York: Simon and Schuster, 1970), p. 20.

3. Everson, William K., *A Pictorial History of Western Film* (Secaucus, NJ: Citadel Press, 1971), pp. 24-25.

4. Ibid., pp. 28-32.

5. McBride, pp. 71-72.

6. Gallagher, Tag, *John Ford: The Man and His Films* (Berkeley: University of California Press, 1986), pp. 13-15.

7. Peary, Gerald, ed., *John Ford Interviews* (Jackson, MS: University of Mississippi Press, 2001), p. 89.

8. Gallagher, p. 16.

9. Ibid., p. 16.

10. Eyman, pp. 49-50.

11. Mayer/Griffith, pp. 87.

12. Ibid., pp. 92-93.

13. Eyman, pp. 56-57.

14. Ibid., pp. 66-67.

Chapter 3 – The Fox Years–1: *"Just a job of work."*

1. Thomas, Tony, & Solomon, Aubrey, *The Films of 20thCentury Fox* (Secaucus, NJ: The Citadel Press, 1979), pp. 15-18.

2. Eyman, Scott, *Print the Legend: The Life and Times of John Ford* (Baltimore: Johns Hopkins University Press, 1999), p.74.

3. McBride, pp. 122-123.

4. John Ford Archives, Lilly Library, University of Indiana (Bloomington).

5. Gallagher, p. 25.

6. Eyman, pp. 67.

7. McBride, pp. 120.

8. John Ford Archives.

9. McBride, pp. 120-121.

10. Ibid,, pp. 138-139.

11. Eyman, pp. 126-127.

12. McBride, pp. 140-141.

13. Peary, p. 78.

14. Eyman, pp. 126-127.

15. Gallagher, p. 32.

16. Ibid., pp. 41-45.

17. Ibid., pp. 40-41.

18. Bogdanovich, Peter, *John Ford* (Berkeley, CA: University of California Press, 1978), pp. 47-48.

19. John Ford Archives.

20. Eyman, p. 98.

21. Ibid., pp. 109-110.

Chapter 4 – The Fox Years–2: *A Portrait of the Young Director as an Artist*

1. Peary, p. 73.

2. Anderson, Lindsay, *About John Ford* (London: Plexus, 1999), p. 193.

3. Eyman, Scott, *Print the Legend: The Life and Times of John Ford* (Baltimore: Johns Hopkins University Press, 1999), p. 106.

4. John Ford Archives, Lilly Library, University of Indiana (Bloomington).

5. Ibid.

6. Eyman, p. 356,

7. Gallagher, p. 519.

8. Adamson, Joe, *Groucho, Harpo, Chico and Sometimes Zeppo: A Celebration of the Marx Brothers* (New York: Touchstone Books, 1973). p. 245.

9. Eyman, p. 21.

10. Ibid., pp. 305-307.

11. McBride, pp. 201-202

12. Ibid., p. 188.

13. Peary, p. 106.

14. Ibid., p. 63.

15. McBride, pp. 173-174.

16. Peary, p. 9.

17. Gallagher, p. 121.

18. Eyman, p. 151-153.

19. Peary, p. 79.

20. John Ford Archives.

21. Ibid.

22. Ibid.

23. Eyman, p. 173.

24. Ibid., p. 172.

25. Ibid., p. 182.

Chapter 5 – Apogee: 1939-1941 *"Bound for Lordsburg!"*

1. Gallagher, pp. 145-146.

2. Eyman, Scott, *Print the Legend: The Life and Times of John Ford* (Baltimore: Johns Hopkins University Press, 1999), p. 201.

3. Ibid., p. 195-197.

4. Bogdanovich, Peter, *John Ford* (Berkeley, CA: University of California Press, 1978), p. 72.

5. John Ford Archives.

6. Gallagher, p. 164.

7. John Ford Archives.

8. Ibid.

9. Ibid.

10. Fonda, Henry, *My Life* (New York: Dutton Adult, 1981), p. 25.

11. John Ford Archives.

12. Anderson, p. 219.

13. Eyman, Scott, *Print the Legend: The Life and Times of John Ford* (Baltimore: Johns Hopkins University Press, 1999), p. 224.

14. Ibid., p. 227.

15. Crowther, Bosley, "The Long Voyage Home: Magnificent Drama of The Sea," *New York Times,* Oct. 9, 1940.

16. John Ford Archives.

17. Gallagher, p. 184-185.

18. Eyman, p. 240.

19. Ibid., p. 326.

20. Ford Archives.

Chapter 6 – Word War II *The War According to John Ford.*

1. Gallagher, p. 202.

2. John Ford Archives, Lilly Library, University of Indiana (Bloomington).

3. Ibid.

4. Eyman, Scott, *Print the Legend: The Life and Times of John Ford* (Baltimore: Johns Hopkins University Press, 1999), pp. 264-265.

5. John Ford Archives.

6. Ibid.

7. Ibid.

8. Ibid.

9. Ibid.

10. Eyman, p. 259.

11. John Ford Archives.

12. Ibid.

13. Gallagher, pp. 207-208.

14. Ibid., p. 214.

15. Peary, p. 139.

16. John Ford Archives.

17. Ibid.

18. Gallagher, p. 213.

19. Ibid., p. 217.

20. John Ford Archives.

21. Ibid.

22. Ibid.

23. Gallagher, p. 217.

24. Ibid., p. 217.

25. Bogdanovich, Peter, *John Ford* (Berkeley, CA: University of California Press, 1978), p. 83.

26. Eyman, p. 277.

27. Anderson, pp. 226-227.

28. Gallagher, p. 224.

Chapter 7 – Independence: *"Been thinkin' I'd maybe push on west."*

1. Gallagher, p. 218.

2. Capra, Frank, *The Name Above the Title* (New York: Da Capo Press, 1997), p. 372.

3. Eyman, Scott, *Print the Legend: The Life and Times of John Ford* (Baltimore: Johns Hopkins University Press, 1999), p. 328.

4. Ibid., p. 336.

5. Ibid., p. 328.

6. John Ford Archives, Lilly Library, University of Indiana (Bloomington).

7. *American Masters: John Ford/John Wayne: The Filmmaker and the Legend,* Directed by Samuel Pollard (2006: PBS Home Video, 2006), DVD.

8. Eyman, p. 347.

9. John Ford Archives.

10. Ford, Dan, *Pappy: The Life of John Ford* (New York: Da Capo Press, 1998), p. 223.

11. John Ford Archives.

Chapter 8 – The 1950s: *"Home to Ireland to forget his troubles."*

1. John Ford Archives, Lilly Library, University of Indiana (Bloomington).

2. Ibid.

3. Ibid.

4. Ibid.

5. Gallagher, pp. 339 -340.

6. Eyman, Scott, *Print the Legend: The Life and Times of John Ford* (Baltimore: Johns Hopkins University Press, 1999), pp. 384-385.

7. John Ford Archives.

8. Eyman, pp. 372-373.

9. Ford, Dan, *Pappy: The Life of John Ford* (New York: Da Capo Press, 1998), p. 232.

10. McBride, pp. 499–500.

11. John Ford Archives.

12. Ibid.

13. Ibid.

14. Ibid.

15. Eyman, p. 413.

16. Radio Electronics Television Manufacturers Association (RETMA) 1953 Statistics.

17. Bogdanovich, Peter, *John Ford* (Berkeley, CA: University of California Press, 1978), p. 141.

18. John Ford Archives.

19. McBride, pp. 534-535.

20. Ibid., pp. 536

21. Bogdanovich, Peter, *John Ford* (Berkeley, CA: University of California Press, 1978), p. 92.

22. Anderson, p. 215.

23. Eyman, p. 440.

24. Ibid., p. 439.

25. Anderson, p. 215.

26. Bogdanovich, Peter, *John Ford* (Berkeley, CA: University of California Press, 1978), pp. 92–93.

27. Gallagher, p. 341.

28. Davis, Ronald L., *Duke: The Life and Image of John Wayne*, (Norman, OK: University of Oklahoma Press, 1998), p. 204.

29. John Ford Archives.

30. Eyman, pp. 300-301.

31. Gallagher, p. 380.

32. Anderson, pp. 137-140.

33. Eyman, pp. 470-471.

Chapter 9 – The 1960s: *"Print the legend."*

1. Clark, Donald, & Anderson, Christopher, *John Wayne's The Alamo: The Making of an Epic Film* (New York: Carol Publishing Group, 1994), pp. 81-82.

2. Eyman, Scott, *Print the Legend: The Life and Times of John Ford* (Baltimore: Johns Hopkins University Press, 1999), pp. 476-477.

3. Bogdanovich, Peter, *John Ford* (Berkeley, CA: University of California Press, 1978), pp. 97-98.

4. Ibid., p. 100.

5. *Directed By John Ford*, directed by Peter Bogdanovich (2009; Los Angeles: Warner Home Video, 2009), DVD.

6. Davis, p. 241.

7. Anderson, p. 173.

8. Davis, pp. 258-259.

9. Eyman, p. 515.

10. Ibid., p. 517.

11. Bogdanovich, Peter, *John Ford* (Berkeley, CA: University of California Press, 1978), p. 107.

12. Gallagher, p. 453.

13. Ibid., p. 454.

14. Eyman, pp. 529-531.

15. Ibid., p. 534.

16. Peary, p. 139.

Chapter 10 – The Final Years: *"Lest we forget."*

1. Eyman, Scott, *Print the Legend: The Life and Times of John Ford* (Baltimore: Johns Hopkins University Press, 1999), pp. 550-551.

2. *Directed By John Ford*, directed by Peter Bogdanovich (2009; Los Angeles: Warner Home Video, 2009), DVD.

3. Eyman, p. 557.

4. *Directed By John Ford*, directed by Peter Bogdanovich (2009; Los Angeles: Warner Home Video, 2009), DVD.

6. Eyman, p. 557.

BIBLIOGRAPHY

Adamson, Joe, *Groucho, Harpo, Chico and Sometimes Zeppo: A Celebration of the Marx Brothers*. New York: Touchstone Books, 1973.

Anderson, Christopher & Clark, Donald, *John Wayne's The Alamo: The Making of an Epic Film*. New York: Carol Publishing Group, 1994.

Anderson, Lindsay, *About John Ford*. London: Plexus, 1999.

Bogdanovich, Peter, *John Ford*. Berkeley, CA: University of California Press, 1978.

Capra, Frank, *The Name Above the Title*. New York: Da Capo Press, 1997.

Crowther, Bosley, *"The Long Voyage Home: Magnificent Drama of The Sea"* New York Times, Oct. 9, 1940.

Davis, Ronald L., *Duke: The Life and Image of John Wayne*. Norman, OK: University of Oklahoma Press, 1998.

Directed by John Ford. DVD. Directed by Peter Bogdanovich. 1971; Los Angeles: Warner Brothers, 2006.

Everson, William K., *A Pictorial History of Western Film*. Secaucus, NJ: Citadel Press, 1971.

Eyman, Scott, *Print the Legend: The Life and Times of John Ford*. Baltimore: Johns Hopkins University Press, 1999.

Fonda, Henry, *My Life*. New York: Dutton Adult, 1981.

Ford, Dan, *Pappy: The Life of John Ford*. New York: Da Capo Press, 1998.

Gallagher, Tag, *John Ford: The Man and His Films*. Berkeley: University of California Press, 1986.

Griffith, Richard & Mayer, Arthur, *The Movies*. New York: Simon and Schuster, 1970.

Hardiman, James, *History of The Town & County of Galway*. Dublin: W. Folds & Sons, 1820.

John Ford Archives, Lilly Library, University of Indiana, Bloomington, IN.

John Ford/John Wayne: The Filmmaker and the Legend, American Masters. DVD. Directed by Samuel Pollard. 2006; New York: PBS Home Video, 2006.

McBride, Joseph, *Searching for John Ford*. New York: St. Martin's Press, 2001.

Morris, James, Heaven's *Command*. San Diego: Harvest/HBJ Books, 1973.

Peary, Gerald, editor, *John Ford Interviews*. Jackson, MS: University of Mississippi Press, 2001.

Stoehr, Kevin L., et al., *John Ford in Focus: Essays on the Filmmaker's Life and Work*. Jefferson, N.C.: Macfarland & Company, 2008.

Thomas, Tony & Solomon, Aubrey, The *Films of 20th Century-Fox*. Secaucus, NJ: The Citadel Press, 1979.

INDEX

3 Bad Men 48, 49, 307
3 Godfathers 6, 48, 135, 191, 192, 195, 198, 199, 208, 224, 243, 263
    making of 193, 194
7 Women 146, 296, 298, 312

A

Abbey Theatre 88, 126, 143, 217, 234, 255, 293
Aga, John 189
Agar, John 186, 188, 193
Air Mail 68, 250
Alamo, The 235, 263, 266, 267, 271, 272, 282, 286, 291
Anderson, "Broncho Billy" 24
Anderson, Lindsay xi, xvi, 221, 238, 240, 246, 260, 261, 309, 317–323
April Morning 300
Araner xii, 76–79, 86, 95, 120, 154, 163, 174, 237, 239, 285, 294, 300
Argosy Pictures 119, 148, 154, 175, 184, 188, 189, 191, 193, 208, 209, 218, 226, 229, 241
Armendariz, Pedro 135, 183, 186, 191, 194, 287
Arrowsmith 66, 67, 89, 239
Astor, Mary 90, 227

B

Baker, Carroll 282, 283, 288, 289
Bancroft, Anne 146, 296, 297, 298
Bancroft, George 96
Battle of Midway xix, 156, 157, 159, 160, 162
Battle of Midway, The 157, 160–162, 164
Baxter, Warner 83
Bellah, James Warner 185, 195, 210, 273

Berman, Pandro 29
Black Watch, The 61, 62, 90, 210
Bogdanovich, Peter xvi, 167, 200, 233, 306, 307, 317–323
    relationship with Ford 48, 229, 243, 277, 298
Bond, Ward xvi, 78, 80, 111, 199, 203, 213, 238, 281, 286, 287, 294, 308, 313
    relationship with Ford 63, 64, 77, 101, 152, 153, 193, 237, 287, 291, 309
    roles of 6, 46, 63, 120, 123, 169, 177, 183, 186, 191, 206, 216, 243, 251
Brando, Marlon 175, 188, 236, 265
Brandon, Henry 244, 271
Brennan, Walter 123, 178

C

Cagney, James 65, 82, 152, 222, 223, 237, 238, 255
Cameo Kirby 40, 41, 93
Canutt, "Yakima" 94, 103, 229
Carey, Harry 23, 25–28, 31, 34–36, 40, 43, 46, 51, 56, 59, 92, 95, 135, 176, 191, 194, 195, 239, 249, 258
Carey, Harry, Jr. "Dobe" 46, 101, 135, 191, 194, 195, 206, 211, 213, 234, 237, 238, 240, 244, 246, 258, 310, 313
Carey, Olive 36, 45, 195, 245, 249
Carradine, John 46, 90, 96, 111, 115, 200
Cheyenne Autumn xvii, 42, 104, 145, 213, 235, 285, 287–291, 293, 295, 300, 306. 312

325

Christie, Julie 294, 295
Clothier, William 263, 267, 290
Cohn, Harry 29, 81, 273
Colbert, Claudette 109
Connolly, James 37, 292
Connolly, Michael 5
Cooper, Gary 35, 36, 92, 151, 152, 228, 241, 265
Cooper, Merian C. 72, 73, 119, 148, 154, 175, 184, 189, 195, 203, 208, 209, 295
Crisp, Donald 126, 129, 132, 159, 256
Crossman, Henrietta 69
Crowther, Bosley 122, 181, 250, 318, 323
Cunard, Grace 19, 22
Curtis, Ken 207, 217, 237, 245, 256

D

Dailey, Dan 222, 251
Darwell, Jane 4, 46, 110, 114, 118, 159, 177, 208, 256
December 7th 160, 162
Del Rio, Dolores 183, 288
DeMille, Cecil B 19, 67, 87, 203, 204, 205, 241
Devine, Andy 96, 174, 274, 283
Doctor Bull 70
Donovan's Reef 284, 285, 312
Donovan, William Joseph "Wild Bill" 148, 149, 156, 157, 160, 162, 164
Dru, Joanne 206, 289
Drums Along the Mohawk xvii, 15, 108, 109, 114, 269
Dunne, Irene 203
Dunne, Phillip 77, 125, 126, 129, 169

E

Eyman, Scott xi, 4, 34, 50, 85, 130, 131, 185, 294, 305, 315–323

F

Feeney, Barbara "Abby" 4, 7, 8, 10, 13, 23, 33, 37, 71, 129
Feeney, John Augustine "Daddo" 4–8, 13, 23, 33, 37, 66, 71, 129, 257

Fetchit, Stepin 42, 46, 70, 224
Field Photo Farm 173, 174, 250, 299
Field Photographic Branch (FPB) 149, 159, 162, 166, 173, 177, 189, 306
Fighting Heart, The 47, 59
Figuerora, Gabriel 184
Fitzgerald, Barry 42, 46, 88, 120, 139, 216, 217
Fonda, Henry 23, 36, 43, 80, 105, 109, 151, 174, 179, 181, 199, 235–240, 265, 282, 294, 306, 307, 310, 313, 318, 323
  relationship with Ford 77, 101, 105, 140, 164, 188, 229, 236, 238–240, 242, 258, 294
  roles of 46, 105–107, 114, 118, 159, 177, 179, 182, 183, 186, 187, 197, 235, 236, 238
Ford, Barbara 34, 76, 77, 153, 165, 218
Ford, Dan xi, 34, 77, 301, 306, 309, 315, 320, 323
Ford, Francis "Frank" 13, 15–23, 26, 31, 35, 50, 58, 104, 111, 163, 230, 258, 291, 310
Ford, Mary McBryde Smith 32–34, 36, 38, 43, 44, 45, 76, 77, 85, 147, 150–153, 157, 163, 216, 232, 299, 300, 305, 306, 310
Ford, Patrick 33, 34, 76, 100, 150, 310
Foster, Preston 77, 87, 133
Four Men and A Prayer 90
Four Provinces Films 253
Fox Pictures 20, 30–32, 34, 40, 41, 44, 48, 52, 53, 57, 58, 60–63, 68, 70, 77, 82, 84, 88–90, 93, 105, 112, 123–127, 147, 152, 162, 164, 165, 175, 177, 178, 181, 185, 222, 233, 239, 260, 281, 306, 316, 324
Fox, William 28, 29, 30, 31, 44
Fugitive, The xvii, 182–184, 190, 192, 200, 208, 221, 273

G

Gable, Clark 35, 93, 151, 183, 203, 227, 228, 233, 255, 265
Gardner, Ava 227, 228
Gideon's Day 259, 260, 282
Glennon, Bert 99, 110, 269
Goldwyn, Samuel 29, 66–68, 81, 89, 125, 126, 209, 221, 236, 239
Goldwyn, Samuel, Jr. 300
Goulding, Harry 102
Grapes of Wrath, The xvii, 4, 83, 112, 120, 123–125, 159, 170, 172, 190, 212, 290, 302, 311, 312
Greene, Graham 181–183, 311
Gregory, Lady Augusta 39, 254, 295
Griffith, D. W. 21, 23, 32

H

Hangman's House 58, 253
Hart, William S. 25, 26, 35, 92
Harte, Bret 40, 48, 95
Hathaway, Henry 271, 282, 289, 292, 299
Hawkins, Jack 259
Hayward, Leland 235, 239
Hepburn, Katharine 84–87, 127, 154, 212, 216, 219, 256, 297, 298, 309
Heston, Charlton 125, 183, 301, 307, 310
Hoch, Winton 198, 199, 211, 218, 221, 245
Holden, William 236, 238, 262–264
Horse Soldiers, The 261–264, 267, 272
House Un-American Activities Committee (HUAC) 125, 187, 188, 202, 226
How Green Was My Valley xvii, 4, 9, 46, 67, 88, 124, 127–132, 154, 159, 161, 169, 218, 290, 297, 311
How the West Was Won 42, 104, 229, 281, 282, 284, 287, 289
Hurricane, The xvii, 64, 74, 89, 90
Hurst, Brian Desmond 253
Huston, John 35, 65, 152, 154, 161, 203, 204, 241, 252
Huston, Walter 161

I

Ince, Thomas 17, 18, 19, 21, 25, 91
Informer, The xvii, 4, 73–75, 87, 121, 133, 190, 270
Irish Civil War xx, 37–39, 73, 87, 133, 295
Irish Republican Brotherhood (IRB) xx, 37–39
Iron Horse, The xvii, 41–44, 48, 49, 84, 102, 104

J

Jarman, Claude, Jr. 211
Jenkinson, Philip 162, 303
Johnson, Ben 46, 101, 199, 200, 206, 211, 213, 258, 313
Johnson, Nunnally 83, 113, 114
Jones, Buck 31
Jones, Stan 212, 261
Jordan, Dorothy 225, 243
Judge Priest 21, 70, 74, 224
Just Pals 31

K

Kelly, Grace 227, 228, 262
Kentucky Pride 47

L

Labarthe, Andre 40, 78, 302
Laemmle, Carl 18, 19, 22, 23, 26, 29, 81
Last Hurrah, The 255, 262
Lean, David 229, 253, 294
Lee, Anna 46, 126, 260, 289, 296, 310
Leguebe, Eric 55, 302
Leighton, Margaret 296
LeMay, Allan 241, 242
Lemmon, Jack 237, 238
LeRoy, Mervyn 239
Lightnin' 47
Lincoln, Abraham 2, 42, 70, 83, 84, 104–109, 112, 114, 117, 145, 225, 289
Logan, Joshua 235, 236, 239
Long Gray Line, The 232–235, 240

Long Voyage Home, The 74, 115, 119, 120, 122, 190, 302, 311
Lost Patrol, The 72, 73

M

Madsen, Axel 21, 302
Maher, Martin 232, 233
Malden, Karl 281, 282, 288
Mankiewicz, Joseph L. 204
Man Who Shot Liberty Valance, The xvii, 129, 144, 188, 273–279, 281, 284, 286, 288, 289, 291, 298, 302, 307
Marvin, Lee 274, 280, 284
Mary of Scotland xvii, 84, 85, 87, 101
Mascot Studios 92, 93, 209
Mature, Victor 177, 178
Mayer, Louis B. 29, 81, 82, 173, 209, 221, 227
Mazurki, Mike 288, 296, 298
McBride, Joseph xi, 2, 34, 36, 231, 315–317, 321, 324
McDowall, Roddy 126
McLaglen, Andrew 284
McLaglen, Victor xvi, 36, 46, 58, 59, 60–62, 72, 75, 186, 197, 211, 216, 218, 221, 222, 229, 270
Men Without Women 64, 72, 74
Miles, Vera 46, 144, 245, 274
Miller, Arthur 127, 128, 132
Mister Roberts xvii, 140, 235–238, 240, 295
Mitchell, Thomas 90, 97, 101, 103, 120
Mogambo xvii, 227–231, 240
Monogram Studios 25, 92, 93, 100, 101, 209
Montgomery, Robert 151, 168, 170, 171, 172
Monument Valley xiii, xiv, 97, 99, 101–103, 127, 141, 180, 193, 196, 199, 214, 244–246, 269, 285, 288, 290, 291, 307, 312, 313
Mother Machree 51, 58
Mowbray, Allan 180, 206
Murnau, F.W. 43, 51, 55–58, 73, 90, 184
My Darling Clementine xvii, 15, 160, 177–181, 275, 280, 283

N

Naish, J. Carroll 183, 211
Napoleon's Barber 60, 61
Narboni, Jean 40, 302
Newman, Alfred 9, 67, 82, 111, 158, 207, 281
Nichols, Dudley 74, 77, 84, 92, 95, 96, 104, 119, 122, 183
Nixon, Richard M. 308
Nugent, Frank 77, 103, 185, 186, 191, 195, 215, 216, 242, 256, 272

O

O'Brien, George 23, 36, 41, 43, 44, 46–48, 51, 57, 59, 63, 72, 148, 189, 229, 239, 258, 291, 294
O'Brien, Pat 65, 256, 310
O'Casey, Sean 39, 87, 133, 292, 293
O'Flaherty, Liam 4, 39, 73, 74, 77, 215
O'Hara, Maureen 46, 68, 110, 126–128, 139, 211, 212, 215–217, 220, 221, 234, 245, 251, 289
Oliver, Edna May 110
O'Neill, Eugene 119, 121, 123
Outcasts of Poker Flat, The 40, 95

P

Pascal, Ernest 89, 125
Pegg, Vester 27, 46
Pilgrimage 69
Plough and the Stars, The 87, 133, 217, 293, 295
Potato Famine 3, 37
Power, Tyrone 22, 125, 151, 233, 234, 255, 265
Prisoner of Shark Island, The 42, 83, 89, 90, 104, 113, 261
Puller, "Chesty" 301

Q

Quiet Man, The xvii, 129, 139, 206, 207, 210, 211, 214, 219–222, 224, 226, 237, 240, 242, 285, 297, 311
actors in 15, 88, 254
making of 198, 215, 253

R

Reed, Donna 169
Republic Studios 152, 209, 210, 215,
    218, 221, 224, 226, 230
Rio Grande xvii, 138, 200, 210–215,
    235, 247
Rising of the Moon, The 143, 253, 255
RKO Studios xvii, 29, 72, 73, 84, 87, 88,
    115, 126, 195, 200, 208, 209
Rogers, Will 21, 46, 69, 70, 74, 83, 199,
    224
Roosevelt, Franklin D. (F.D.R.) 73, 79,
    147–149, 160, 162, 308

S

Salute 62, 64
Searchers, The xvii, 46, 73, 78, 120, 141,
    142, 212, 240, 243, 246–249,
    270, 273, 285, 291, 302, 311
    actors in 28, 63, 206, 235, 242, 245,
        263
    making of 198, 241, 244, 246
Sergeant Rutledge 268–270, 273, 285
Shamrock Handicap, The 47
Sheehan, Winfield "Winnie" 30, 31, 44,
    49, 50, 53, 58, 68
She Wore a Yellow Ribbon xvii, 129, 136,
    197, 198, 208, 210, 214, 245,
    288, 311
    actors in 88, 109, 200, 211, 218
    making of 196, 198–200
Shields, Arthur 46, 88, 111, 120, 217
Simpson, Russell 46, 111, 115, 169, 170,
    177, 206
Smith, Bernard 146, 287, 295, 297
Smith, C. Aubrey 90, 259
Sons of the Pioneers, The 207, 217
Soul Herder, The 27
Spiddal (County Galway) 1–4, 7, 38, 253
Stagecoach xvii, 46, 48, 74, 92, 95, 96,
    103, 115, 172, 178, 180, 194,
    214, 240, 263, 276, 297
    actors in 15, 95, 98, 100, 200, 242
    making of 99, 119, 212, 247, 269,
        273, 290

Stallings, Laurence 195, 222
Stanwyck, Barbara 87
Steamboat Round the Bend 70, 74, 83
Steinbeck, John 112, 113, 115
Stevens, George 60, 150, 152, 157, 175,
    203, 204, 290, 299
Stewart, James 105, 144, 151, 174, 265,
    271, 272, 274, 277, 279, 281,
    282, 288, 306, 307, 310
Stout, Archie 166, 189, 218
Stout, Junius 166, 167, 189
Straight Shooting 27
Strode, Woody 268–270, 274, 279, 280,
    296, 298, 310
Stuart, Gloria 83
Submarine Patrol 64, 90
Sun Shines Bright, The 78, 195, 224, 226,
    230, 240, 285, 307

T

Tavernier, Bertrand 71, 302
Taylor, Rod 294, 295
Temple, Shirley 46, 84, 88, 89, 186, 188
They Were Expendable xvii, 68, 165,
    167–169, 171–173, 212, 250,
    288
Tobacco Road xvii, 123, 124, 200
Toland, Gregg 115, 117, 122, 127, 147,
    160, 162, 184
Tornado, The 22
Towers, Constance 262, 268
Tracy, Spencer 65, 66, 85, 86, 93, 151,
    152, 212, 255, 256, 282
Trevor, Claire 97, 99
Trotti, Lamar 106, 108
Two Rode Together 270, 272, 273, 312

V

Vietnam! Vietnam! 301

W

Wagon Master, The 137, 205, 207, 208, 211, 240, 261, 280, 307
Wanger, Walter 92, 102, 104, 119, 123
Warner Brothers 29, 60, 65, 73, 81–83, 93, 105, 112, 175, 222, 223, 236, 239, 289, 291, 293, 295
Wayne, John "Duke" xvi, 36, 43, 53, 56, 64, 80, 85, 94, 99–101, 103, 104, 152, 153, 171, 174, 175, 183, 200, 203, 209, 211–213, 217, 224, 235, 242, 250, 262–267, 270–272, 277, 278, 280, 283, 286, 287, 291, 292, 300, 301, 306–308, 310
  relationship with Ford 63, 64, 77, 78, 95, 100, 101, 127, 138, 151, 153, 164, 171, 178, 188, 193, 194, 196, 229, 239, 258, 267, 279, 286, 292, 294, 299, 309
  roles of xvii, 23, 28, 46, 58, 63, 68, 93, 95, 97, 99, 120, 135, 136, 139, 141, 142, 144, 147, 168, 176, 178, 186–188, 191, 196, 197, 209–213, 215, 216, 220, 221, 242, 245–247, 251, 253, 261, 263, 264, 272, 274, 278, 279, 282, 284, 286, 289, 312
Wayne, Patrick 46, 235, 237, 245
Wead, Frank "Spig" 68, 72, 165–167, 171, 250
Webb, James R. 287
Wee Willie Winkie 88–90, 125
Welles, Orson xvi, 115, 122, 183, 260, 307
What Price Glory? 222–224, 240
Whitney, C.V. 241, 242
Widmark, Richard 271, 272, 282, 288, 289
Wings of Eagles, The 68, 250, 251, 256
Winninger, Charles 224
Withers, Grant 177, 186, 286
Wurtzel, Harry 30, 154, 165
Wurtzel, Sol 30, 41, 44, 49, 50
Wyler, William 50, 125, 126, 152, 175, 191, 203, 204, 299, 310

Y

Yamamoto, Isoruku 155, 156
Yates, Herbert J. 152, 209–211, 215, 221, 224, 226, 230
Young, Carleton 256, 268, 274
Young Cassidy 293, 295, 296, 312
Young, Freddie 229, 259, 260
Young Mr. Lincoln xvii, 15, 56, 78, 104, 106, 108, 109, 132, 172, 179, 246, 269, 274
Young, Victor 221

Z

Zanuck, Darryl F. 81–83, 88, 89, 104–106, 108, 109, 112–114, 123–126, 132, 152, 162, 164, 175, 177, 178, 181, 185, 209, 210, 222, 236, 252
Zimbalist, Sam 229

ABOUT THE AUTHOR

Joseph Malham is an iconographer, writer and speaker who studied art in Rome through Loyola University's Rome Center. He graduated from Loyola with a BA in History. Since 1999 Malham has been artist-in-residence at St. Gregory the Great Church in Chicago. His panels and icon banners have been acquired by churches and individuals around the country. Malham has lectured frequently—at the Art Institute of Chicago and  various religious institutions—on the topics of iconography and religious art. His first book, *By Fire into Light: Four Catholic Martyrs of the Nazi Camps* (Peeters-Leuven 2002), tells the stories of four heroic figures who transcended the horrors of the death camps through their experiences of faith.